Pedagogical Theater

Pedagogical Theater

Dramaturgy and Performance Practice for the Lower, Middle, and High School

Arthur M. Pittis

Published by
Waldorf Publications
Research Institute for Waldorf Education (RIWE)
38 Main Street
Chatham, NY 12037

ISBN: 978-1-943582-00-6

An earlier version of this book was originally
published by AWSNA Publications in 1996.
The present work has been revised and expanded
to include original plays and
pedagogical indications for the high school.

Contents

Part III: Producing the Play

Preface

Twenty years ago when this work was written originally as a master's degree graduate project in dramaturgy for Johns Hopkins University, the pedagogical foundations for theatrical work had been little explored within the context of Waldorf education, even though class plays occupied then, as they do now, a prominent place in the cultural life of every Waldorf school. This deficit was surprising given the amount of attention that had been given to the appropriateness of the way every other subject is introduced and taught depending on the children's stage of physical, emotional, intellectual, social, and spiritual development. A similar situation existed in the mainstream literature. There were, however, a great deal of orally transmitted thinking on this subject, as well as some short, popular articles, offering general remarks on how class plays support academic, artistic, and social work with a class; but no formal pedagogical research had been done in the English speaking world on the topic, even though many collections of plays by class teachers existed.

This omission seems to reach deeply back to the origins of Waldorf Education. Karl Stockmeyer's *Curriculum for Waldorf Schools*, which catalogs all Rudolf Steiner's pedagogical indications, makes no mention of theater, as distinct from the literary study of drama; and the same is the case with Caroline von Heydebrand's *Curriculum of the First Waldorf Schoo*l, including the supplemental section by Eileen Hutchins on working with English as the mother tongue. Secondary books on Waldorf education, such as Marjorie Spock's *Teaching as a Lively Art*, say nothing; and A.C. Harwood's masterpiece *The Recovery of Man in Childhood* makes only passing reference to the delight children experience in acting in plays and drama within the context of literary studies. Nor did Rudolf Steiner in his lecture cycle to actors, entitled *Speech and Drama*, give any indications for specifically working with young people in a pedagogical setting.

At that time it was clear that work needed to be done. In the interim much as changed, not just within the Waldorf literature, but also within the mainstream as well. Eric Mueller's insightful personal account of his work with adolescents within the context of Waldorf Education became available, followed by David Sloan's excellent curricular guide and pedagogical reflections, *Stages of Imagination*, and most recently Roswitha Spence's beautiful *Clothing the Play*. Each of these works is a valuable resource not just for the teacher but also for the researcher interested in the role of theatrical productions in Waldorf, specifically, and for education in general.

This deficit had not been limited to Waldorf Education. The only thoughtful mainstream literature available for those working artistically and pedagogically in English with non-conservatory students were Viola Spolin's works, the most popular and valuable being *Theater Games*; and the British educator Gavin Bolton's theoretical essays on drama in education. Bolton's works present many provocative ideas regarding how a theater teacher can work dynamically with students, focusing on the exploratory, situational potential of plays, and not just their presentation of story, character, and idea. Unfortunately, almost everything else available in English (and especially in the United States) was of the "Let's do a play!" genre and did not penetrate the meaning of theatrical arts much deeper than "kids really like dressing up!" Sad to say, one could find hundreds of titles of this ilk. Fortunately, the situation is improving. An invaluable contribution to the field was made recently—once again from Great Britain—with Mike Fleming's thoughtful *Starting Drama Teaching*. Fleming is a professor of education at Durham University in Great Britain; he not only explores the practical role of drama and theater in education, but also penetrates into the deeper pedagogical reasons for having the theatrical arts play a key role in education. Similarly, other serious books on drama and theater in education are becoming available, and the reader can find an excellent list of these on the website TheatreBooks.com from Toronto. For the thoughtful practitioner of pedagogical theater the drought is ending, as more and more teacher/writers begin to publish their thoughts on this subject.

The observations and suggestions in this book serve, therefore, as a continuation to this work and a practical and pedagogical reflection of my more than thirty years work in pedagogical theater with students of all ages. It is primarily designed for teachers, especially those new to theater; and focuses on the writing and producing of class plays in light of Waldorf pedagogical principles. This book strives to be an exploration and examination of fundamental principles of theater and Waldorf Education, and how each individual teacher can develop his or her own theater curriculum, as one would do with any other discipline. To this end, the book provides the basic information needed to write and produce plays with classes of all ages in Waldorf schools.

As such, it is laid out in four parts: the first part presents an overview of the origins of pedagogical theater from an anthroposophic perspective of child and adolescent development; the second examines the dramaturgical elements that are the foundation of the art of playwriting; the third focuses on producing a play; and the fourth presents a set of plays illustrative of the previous three parts. While the book is primarily aimed toward the reader who knows Waldorf Education but not theater, it will hopefully be interesting both to readers who know theater but not Waldorf Education, and readers who are familiar with neither. It is further hoped that the book will provide a picture of how the fundamental arts of theater and Waldorf Education—as generally practiced in North America for the past half century—can work together.

This work contains footnotes and endnotes. The footnotes provide immediately useful information and are designated with small case Roman numerals. The endnotes provide extended information and are designated with Arabic numerals.

Pasadena, California
December 2014

Part I:
Origins of Pedagogical Theater

Chapter 1
The Transformation of Imaginative Play

Theater[1] provides us with reflections of what it means to be human. In its most basic form, theater requires nothing more than a performer, an audience, and a space where the two can share an enacted, imaginative experience. Building on these foundations and classic Aristotelian theory, theater needs only the elements of story, characterization, idea, language, tone and rhythm, and spectacle to be realized. Out of these elements humanity has built the grand cultural edifice of theater, whose roots reach back through all its myriad cultural manifestations to two, most fundamental human activities—exploring and explaining the suffering and sacrifice of what is divine in the human soul and spirit, and the imitative, creative play of children.[2]

Theater, as a living performance art, is by its nature ephemeral. Unlike recorded arts, such as literature and cinema or painting and sculpture, theater exists only during the moments of its performance and then evaporates into memory. When it is most vital, it strives for those brief moments when performer and audience, enactor and beholder, are lifted into a state of shared imaginative consciousness, which may be called theatrical moments, moments that are luminous and dynamic thresholds where performer, audience, and play meet in communion, and something transcendent is enabled to spiral into life out of the constellation of creative forces that are combining to realize it. These are moments when we, individually and collectively, can recognize ourselves as becoming human beings.

Theater is therefore, by its immediate, experiential nature, first and foremost a social art, one that assists in bringing into dynamic balance the social polarities of individual and community. While the most obvious manifestation of this phenomenon exists between performers and audience, it also exists within the cast of enactors themselves and between the individual members of audience. The theatrical moment exists when there is a simultaneous convergence of these three relationships. Then true theater comes into existence.

Pedagogical theater is true theater. And as such, its practice should forever strive to create theatrical moments that are age-appropriate, entertaining, and thoughtful for performers—(the students)—and the audience—(the school community). It is the purpose of pedagogical theater to consciously work with all the qualities and practices of the theatrical arts in a way that guides each individual student, teacher, and class toward a healthy understanding of what it means, individually and socially, to be a human being in the most universal meaning of that phrase.

Although pedagogical theater works with the conventions of adult theater, just as dance, choral and orchestral music, drawing, painting and sculpture, (or basketball, for that matter) work with the form of their respective arts, pedagogical theater requires a translation of adult practices and forms through the informed, creative synthesis of conscious pedagogy and dramaturgy[3] and theatrical practices into age-appropriate forms. It is therefore a vehicle for the inner and outer development of the human being, and not a technique for theatrical training, as one would find in a conservatory or acting class setting, or simply for entertainment, as theater exists mostly in the wider world. The intention of pedagogical theater, then, is to help bring the soul faculties of thinking, feeling, and willing into an ever more balanced relationship; faculties that are essential for young people's coming to a more complete understanding of themselves socially and individually.

Understanding pedagogical of theater requires reflecting on how children creatively play and what they learn through their creative play. Play is essentially an imitative/creative process of building up and tearing down, a microcosmic imitation of a macrocosmic processes of nature. Play is an outer representation of the organic and spiritual processes that are taking place in the child's inner life as the forces of thinking, feeling and willing encounter the world and then support and guide the process of incarnation. When children play, they are utilizing these forces of creation and destruction, just as metabolism, emotions, and thoughts create and destroy the inner and outer worlds that comprise our human existence. As such, children are internalizing and externalizing the very processes that inform all natural and artistic activity. When children imitate people, animals, and things through their play, they take these things, through imitative observation, into themselves, make them their own, and then play-act them as imaginatively imbued actions, thereby developing out of play-consciousness a living imagination of the inner and outer world.

From standing upright and walking, to the blooming of puberty, and finally to the full realization of egoic self, play is one of the fundamental activities of the human being; and it undergoes an evolution in which its imitative nature is metamorphosed into the creative capacity to make something new out of one's inner resources.[4] The imitative nature of play is the foundation of all pedagogical and artistic activities, imitation being the process by which we imaginatively take hold of something that exists outside of ourselves and, through the formative, sculptural powers of will, make that thing inwardly our own before reproducing it in a slightly different, outward form. Creativity is therefore metamorphosed imitation. In art, the powers of thinking, inspired and practiced by the sympathies and antipathies of feeling, take hold of what is known initially by imitation and put it into a form that can be communicated to an audience wider than oneself, this narrowness being the situation of a young child's play. As such, creativity, although intimately based, is emancipated imitation. Understanding where children and adolescents stand on this evolutionary continuum is at the root of any pedagogical artistic work.

The type of playacting that has theatrical potential begins whenever two or more children gather to cooperatively and creatively imitate and reenact some human activity they have previously observed. Pedagogical theater begins when a teacher starts to guide this play by working out of a conscious insight into what the play calls forth from the children's past, what it addresses in their present, and what it seeds for their futures.[5] When one watches a group of children, regardless of their age, playacting a story, several fundamental characteristics become apparent. First, the story is self-absorbed and inwardly directed; and second, it is cooperative and takes place in the round; that is, with the children facing inward and playing across the common space between them. In short, it is social and contains all the elements of theater in embryonic form. This orientation to the round is of utmost importance in that it allows the children to be simultaneously the participants in and observers of the play. They can step forward, engage themselves, enact the story, and then step back to once again become a participant-observer. Every child-player can act, see, and hear equally well; and the circle of players, facing inward, gives to each individual and the group a nurturing feeling of security and community. This playacting always involves a story and characters, an idea, and some type of special language; a tonal and rhythmic presentation, and some type of extraordinary appearance, no matter how simple. Such playacting is a theatrical event, but it lacks one of the most significant conventions of western theatrical practice—the mutual alienation of performer and audience from each other that is created by both groups self-consciously facing each other across a performance space.

Pedagogical theater in its most primal form arises out of a teacher's watching a class playacting a story from the curriculum and sensing whether a theatrical play lives in the children's relationship to the story, its characters, and its themes. The teacher's pedagogical task then becomes finding the right constellation of theatrical imaginations that will make the birth of the theatrical play possible. This midwifing of play into theater is largely a transformative process by which the teacher slowly directs the elements of the children's imaginative playacting into a theatrical play.

Chapter 2
Curricular Foundations of Pedagogical Theater

Theater is enacted story; and as such, it is one of the many paths available for experiencing the great archetypal tales of human experience, whether fairy tales, legends, mythologies, literature, history, or daily events. Within the context of pedagogical theater as it can be practiced in Waldorf Education, the story used for a class play will have originated either in the language arts or history curriculum in the lower school; and in the high school the material is from the dramatic literature canon.[6] The types of stories that comprise these curricula were indicated by Rudolf Steiner and developed by the cumulative pedagogical research of Waldorf teachers over the past century for their appropriateness for the different stages of human development. Therefore, story selection for pedagogical theater performance is markedly different from how plays are selected for conventional theater. Instead of focusing on the current theatrical fashions, which is often the case in children's theater groups, Waldorf Education places the developmental needs of the class and its individual students at the heart of the selection. Because of the richness of the Waldorf school curriculum the range of subjects for pedagogically appropriate plays is vast.

The Lower School

In first grade (six/seven-year-olds), fairy and folk tales that present archetypal pictures—imaginations—of the soul's passage through earthly life are used as the basis for the teaching of writing and reading, and thereby can provide the material for class plays. These stories range from the most serious (such as the German "Brother and Sister") to delightfully humorous (as the English "Three Sillies"). Their plots are linearly episodic, and the main character can be immediately identified as a representative of what is universally human in the soul. The secondary characters are themselves archetypal images of the forces that support or hinder the soul's spiritual progress through life and thereby provide episodic focus for the story.

In the Waldorf language arts curriculum for second grade, two types of stories are employed from a variety of spiritual and cultural traditions—saint legends and animal fables. The saint legends present images of human striving to live as kindly, piously, and beneficently as possible in the service of the highest spiritual ideal, listening to the voice of the higher self, while the fables present images of the instinctual life of impulse, desire, and self-serving activity as portrayed through representatives of the animal kingdom—essentially the moral conflict of lower versus higher self. As the children at this age are beginning to be faced with choices in their lives, such stories provide an ethical framework for their nascent judgment. Episodes from the life of Saint Francis or Rabbi Akiva, as well as Aesop or animal fables from West Africa, provide good material for class plays.

In third grade the child is going through a profound change in his/her soul life, called "the nine-year change" in Waldorf Education. This change is characterized by the first existential questions of life: "Who am I, really?"; "Why is there evil in the world?"; "Does God truly exist?"; "Who are my brothers and sisters?" and "Who really are my parents?" This time can be challenging in the soul life of children in that the inner harmony and security of childhood is quickly passing into shadowy uncertainty.

The mytho-historic stories of the spiritual/social evolution of the Hebrew people in their relationship to the divine and the secular, as chronicled in the Old Testament, provide the children with a wealth of tales that address these questions. The stories of Cain and Abel, Noah and the Flood, Joseph and his brothers, Moses, Saul, and David, King Solomon, Daniel, and Queen Esther, to name a few, can all be turned into wonderful plays for nine-year-old children. Each of these stories speaks eloquently to the crisis of individual, social, and spiritual identity the children are feeling at this time. The task facing the teacher wishing to work theatrically is identifying which stories speak most appropriately to his or her specific class.

In fourth grade, Norse mythology serves as the foundational material for the language arts curriculum. From this mythology we receive some of the finest comic, tragic, and epic stories ever recorded. The Norse mythologies provide poignant instances of suffering and sorrow that must be transformed through the courage and sacrifice of the hero. They are among the finest mythic descriptions of the evolution of the human soul and its struggles with the physical forces that serve as obstacles to its development, and their pedagogical value lies in the reassurance and inspiration they bring to the children who hear them.

Wonderful instances of comedy and tragedy exist also in this mythology. The hilarious story of the thunder god Thor's visit—(dressed as a blushing bride)—to the land of the Frost Giants is a perennial favorite. On the tragic side, there are few stories more moving than the "Death of Baldur," the sun god, who is unwittingly struck down by the hand of his blind brother Hodur, the representative of the darkness of material existence. These stories speak eloquently and profoundly to the children, regardless of ethnic, cultural, gender, or racial orientation, and they rejoice in having their own inner struggles reflected through these myths.

In the fifth grade as the children are moving away from childhood and toward preadolescence, the language arts curriculum makes a sweeping, westward-moving survey of western mythological proto-history from ancient India, through Persia, Mesopotamia, and Egypt, to ancient Greece. This curriculum is too elaborate to list in detail, but one of its general thematic intents is to follow the evolving perspectives human beings have experienced over the millennia about our individual and social relations to spiritual and earthly existence. The class teacher can choose from a vast number of stories for a theatrical vehicle.

Episodes from the *Ramayana* and the *Mahabharata* are possibilities from the Indian culture, and there are any number of themes in each of these stories with which a teacher can work. From ancient Persia the life of Zarathustra and his teaching human beings how to relish living in the material world is studied. From ancient Mesopotamia the story of Gilgamesh provides a wonderful opportunity to artistically explore the deepest aspects of friendship and the dread of death. From ancient Egypt the story of the murder and dismemberment of Osiris and the devotion of Isis to make him whole again speaks eloquently to the need for loyalty and dedication to those one loves on a secular level while; on a spiritual level it tells of the soul-spirit's eternal transit from life to life. And finally the mythologies and mythic histories of ancient Greece can be extensively explored.

The fifth grade language arts curriculum, if handled well, seamlessly passes from myth to history in the study of ancient Greece. The mytho-historic characters of the pre-archaic period of Greek culture give way to the historical personalities and events of classical Greece. This transition from legend to biography gives the students their first imaginations of actual, instead of mythic or legendary, human beings in real life historical situations.

The Middle School

In sixth grade historical biographies are used as the first symptomatic pictures of a given historical period. The primary thematic intent is to explore the conflicts that exist between individuals, between different social groups, and between the outstanding individual and his/her society. These stories are preparing the class for the historical emergence of the individuality of conscience that will be explored biographically in the middle school and then as symptomatic representations of historical phenomenon in the high school.

The study of ancient Rome and medieval Europe[7] provides the sixth grade class teacher with the historical/cultural material. Roman history is one great stream of conflict—peoples versus peoples, class versus class, individual versus individual, state versus individual, belief versus belief, and so on. During the study of medieval Europe the theme of conflict begun with Rome is continued, but the emphasis shifts to the emerging trials of conscience that arise out of the struggles between secular and religious authorities, as well as the knightly struggle to live according to Christian ideals in a society that was essentially violent and unjust. Stories such as the struggles between Thomas à Becket and Henry II of England, and Henry with his wife, Eleanor of Aquitaine, are marvelous vehicles for such explorations.

The history curricula of the seventh and eighth grades brings the students up to modern times, using the Renaissance and European cultural expansion, and the ages of industrial/technological and political revolutions, respectively, as the source materials for widening and deepening the students' understanding of what it has meant to be a human being in ages past. At this time the class teacher works with the biographies of those men and women whose lives, for good or ill, have come to stand as representative pictures of actual human struggles in a particular time. For a play's subject the teacher often and naturally turns to the great biographies and stories we as a civilization have chosen to remember.

The High School

In the Waldorf high school a major shift takes place in the relationship between pedagogical theater and the other curricular subjects. Whereas the lower school theater program reflected the content of the language arts and history curricula, a high school theater program works directly with drama and theater as disciplines in their own right, still working, of course, with the fundamental principle of the age-appropriateness of material. Drama is studied as a branch of literature, just as lyric poetry or the novel, and theatrical productions are developed in much the same way one would produce any of the other performing arts. To this end, most plays produced in high school come from the established dramatic canon; but sometimes original plays are presented, especially if there is a playwright on the faculty who can write at an aesthetically appropriate level for high school students. Similarly, but more rarely, if a student or team of students are artistically capable of writing for their class, their work could be staged.

While a direct topical connection to that year's curriculum is significant in high school pedagogical theater, it is essential, nevertheless, to establish a pedagogical connection that works in support of the developmental stage of the students. In the lower and middle schools the Waldorf teacher's focus is on nurturing the health of the already-born physical and etheric bodies, and nourishing the "pre-natal" astral body and ego.[8] The high school teacher's focus is, first, on nurturing the newly born astral body and using its emancipated forces for educational purposes; and, second, on nourishing the still embryonic ego. In this light, the curriculum and its teaching methodology uses the emancipated astral forces to support the moral development of the feelings and the conceptual maturation of thinking, both of which are absolutely necessary for the healthy birth of ego. To this end, theater is well suited as an "art of human-being."

Most schools have as part of their core-curriculum a ninth grade main lesson block that focuses on the archetypal polarities of tragedy and comedy, and uses dramatic literature for their examination. While some speech and even scene work might be done in this block, it is not a theater but a literature block. The best use of theater in ninth grade as a performing art is within the context of a comprehensive theater skills class and not a full-scale production. This perspective arises from several factors, some simply practical, others a result of observing how ninth graders, individually and as a class unit, experience the powerful forces recently released with the birth of their astral bodies.

Practically, there is usually stiff competition in a Waldorf school for rehearsal and performance space, given that each grade not only does a play, but that there is a full calendar of chorus, orchestra, and eurythmy performances. The schedule is simply so full that whatever can be done to relieve it is good for the social life of the school. A second practical consideration is that the high school humanities faculty usually carries the high school theater program in addition to their main lesson and skill teaching responsibilities, so adding a third full-scale show might send them blithering into the nether zones.

Even if time, space, and personnel were available, from a pedagogical perspective it is good for the students to step back from a class play in ninth grade. Ninth graders, for the most part, are enthusiastic for meeting ideas and developing new skills, especially those that have practical application. As a result, they need to establish and settle into new academic habits and routines, something, which, quite frankly, a full-scale play production interrupts. But more importantly, the students need time to mature somewhat into their young astrality. In light of these considerations, a new orientation to theater as an art is appropriate, one built on foundations different from their middle school experiences, no matter how fine those have been.

Therefore, the ideal ninth grade theater program should have three components: speech formation, stage movement, and technical theater. Developing a conscious aesthetic relationship to their voices and bodies, and the consequent working through the self-consciousness thus stimulated, is important for taking hold of the sometimes thoughtless explosion of vocal and physical expression that is an adolescent liability. Similarly, learning to properly operate light and sound boards and developing a basic understanding of light and sound design is a good practical skill and one which makes sense within the performance culture of Waldorf schools. Such a two-part program gives each student the opportunity to focus attention in subsequent years on an area of genuine interest instead of winding up in one area or the other by default or assignment. The technical training is also invaluable to give a school community a well-trained team of high school students who can operate the light and sound equipment properly, and who can support not just lower and high school productions but community events as needed.

In tenth grade, full-scale productions are generally staged. As with other areas of the tenth grade high school curriculum, the thematic focus is on working with and understanding a start-to-finish process. In literature classes, for instance, attention will be paid to how a work such as the *Odyssey* is structured as a series of stories within stories, all coming together in a logical and aesthetically satisfying whole. Similarly, in a physiology block, the focus will be on the integrated, health supporting or undermining processes that result from the interaction of our bodily organ systems and how we live in the world. The key pedagogical goal of a tenth grade play is the process of experiencing a productive artistic and social process from start to finish, building it up from its component parts, and taking ownership for one's individual role in the process.

Tenth graders should be intimately involved in every aspect of the production and should be given responsibilities equal to the type of responsibilities they are developing in their other schoolwork. Taking responsibility and feeling pride in one's accomplishment is important for any adolescent, but it is an especially important focus for tenth graders. The opportunity to play a significant, even indispensable role in a productive social and artistic activity, such as a class play, is a powerful antidote to the existential powerlessness that plagues youth in our society and drives them into socially and self-destructive behaviors. Artistic work of this type clearly says, "Yes, I matter."

While the subject of a tenth grade play is not prescribed by the curriculum as it often would be in the Waldorf grade school, it is a good practice to alternate between ancient and modern classics, melodramas, and light comedies, depending on the disposition of the class. From the ancient works *Antigone* is good for tragedy, and *The Braggart Warrior* or *The Twins* for comedy. Aristophanes is tricky to produce because the text must be reworked substantially; but whatever you do, if your text is faithful to even a fraction of the original it will stimulate indignation and outrage in some factions in the school community. So beware of Aristophanes; he made trouble in ancient Athens, and he will make trouble in the modern Waldorf World. Doing Shakespeare in tenth grade is far more appropriate than in eighth grade, and a romantic comedy such as *A Midsummer's Night Dream* or *Twelfth Night,* as well as accessible tragedies such as *Julius Caesar* or *Romeo and Juliet* make a fine choice. For more modern comedies the plays of Goldoni or Moliére are good (if editorial discretion is exercised). For an even more closely modern option, *Our Town* always works well. And, of course, Dickens or Hugo provide excellent source material for large scale melodramas if the class has many students.

The most important pedagogical reason for having a play in tenth grade is the social cohesiveness it brings to a class. The transition to high school is often difficult for a class. The students who transition from eighth grade, even though many of them have been together for years, feel a legitimate need to redefine their interpersonal relationships now that they are in high school. Compounding this challenge is that some students have left the class, new students have joined, and the class teacher is no longer present. Social relationships, by simple circumstance, must be re-established. While by the end of ninth grade a new class identity and social cohesiveness have been established, a tenth grade play, with all the working together and mutual support it entails, completes the process.

In eleventh grade, practices vary greatly. Some schools do small-production scene work or have the students compose and perform their own one act plays. For example, at the Austin Waldorf School, where we had an exceptionally strong high school language program and a language teacher with extensive theatrical experience, we presented children's-theater plays in German and Spanish to the whole student body from first through twelfth grades. Such plays are an excellent way for the eleventh grade students to use the languages they are studying in a practical and demanding artistic context. They also showcase the language program to the school community, which is extremely valuable given the low importance many Americans place on working in a second language. Most importantly, the plays provide the eleventh graders with the opportunity to perform in a way that takes into deepest consideration the soul life of those younger children who are their audience, and the social and moral responsibility for supporting it.

It is a common practice that twelfth grades present a full-scale production as their closing core curriculum activity just before their senior trip and graduation activities. A twelfth grade should do the finest piece of theater possible. After all, this is the year they may have studied Goethe's *Faust*, along with masterworks of Russian and American literature. Trivial theatrical junk food such as adaptations of popular movies should not be the closing pedagogical activity of a secondary student's school life! In the same vein, they should not be doing edgy social commentary plays; let that wait for college. A twelfth grade should do a great play: Brecht's *Caucasian Chalk Circle* or *The Good Person of Szechuan*; Calderón's *Life is a Dream*; Synge's *Playboy of the Western World*; Gogol's *The Inspector General;* Shakespeare's T*he Tempest* or *The Winter's Tale;* Sheridan's *School for Scandal*; Schiller's *Mary Stuart*; Beaumarchais' *The Barber of Seville;* Ibsen's *Peer Gynt*; Wilde's *The Importance of Being Earnest* (a very hard play to do well); Miller's *The Crucible*; Wilder's *The Skin of Our Teeth*; or Friel's *Dancing at Lughnasa.*

There is a practice described in Rawson's and Richter's *The Educational Tasks and Contents of the Steiner Waldorf Curriculum*: having seniors write, produce, and direct their own play. While I have only heard vague rumors of this being done in North America, it is an intriguing, even tempting idea, but the rigors of the American college admissions process would probably make it too difficult to realize effectively. The pedagogical value of such a practice is immense, however, in that it provides a perfect final artistic class opportunity for integrating individual and social responsibility into an aesthetic and practical activity.

Conclusion

Theater, as a performance art, is the most human of the arts, requiring the whole of the human being—body, soul, and spirit—as the instrument of its aesthetic presentation. With the exception of dance, no other artistic medium, not even singing, is so absolutely dependent on the physical and emotional beingness of the artist as the expressive vehicle. Every other art is removed by one degree or more by an instrument, a brush, pen or pencil, chisel or a mallet, a needle or a loom; or, in our modern arts, a camera, synthesizer, or computer.

When working in pedagogical theater, the teacher should periodically recall the twin origins of theater as an art; one arising from the deep historical past when the disciples of the sun-god Apollo revealed, through enactment and in homage of Dionysius, the mystery of suffering and death; and the other arising millions of times every day in every culture on the earth from the play-acting of children as they explore through creative play what it means to be a becoming human being.

Part II:
Composing the Class Play

Chapter 1
Dramatic Genres

There are three archetypal genres of literature: tragedy, comedy, and melodrama. Tragedy and comedy are polarities, and melodrama holds a middle ground between them, leaning generally toward tragedy while having comic characteristics. Within these three genres, there are the two subcategories of epic and historical stories that are often used in pedagogical playwrighting; these subcategories may treat their subject matter either comically, tragically, or melodramatically. In a grade school setting historical and epic melodrama will be the most commonly used forms. In high school comedy, melodrama (historical or epic), and tragedy will be used, generally in that order.

Tragedy

Tragedy, deferring to Aristotle, presents a story of serious import, involving a protagonist worthy of respect, even admiration, but who suffers from a serious character flaw to which s/he, the protagonist, is blind. This tragic flaw ultimately dooms the protagonist to a catastrophic reversal of fortune and the consequent downfall. The tragic protagonist, although driven by an antagonist, is always responsible for the crisis that brings about the downfall, and the character always recognizes and accepts the consequences of his or her deeds, acting nobly in the face of crisis and doom. The audience feels inferior to the protagonist; and the true tragedies always end in death, even if not literal, thereby eliciting deeply reflective feelings of pity and dread from its audience.[9] The consequences for the antagonist, on the other hand, have changed from ancient to modern times. The Greek antagonists generally succeeded against their protagonists, only to meet their own tragedy somewhere down the line of their myth. In the modern theater as developed by Shakespeare, the tragic antagonist comes to a well-deserved bad end.[10]

Comedy

Comedy, on the other hand, presents a story of light import, involving a personage not worthy of respect and, in extreme cases, worthy of scorn. The comic protagonist suffers from a serious character flaw that ultimately dooms the character to a catastrophic reversal of fortune and subsequent downfall, but the downfall does not usually result in catastrophe… unless the play is by Gogol. Comic protagonists are always responsible for their crisis, and instead of embracing the crisis as the tragic hero does, the comic protagonist flees it and accepts the consequences only when expediency demands; comic protagonists will most certainly continue to act in the same way once the conflict is over and danger is past. The audience feels superior to comic characters, especially the protagonist, and leaves the theater laughing at what has been enacted.[11] Comedy generally ends well for the ancient antagonist, usually in marriage. In modern comedy, if things do not end well, they at least end neutrally for the antagonists.

Melodrama

Melodrama[12] is the most popular genre in our time, slightly ahead of comedy. It is an eclectic form. It tells a serious story, contains light moments, and always resolves its action positively, despite its sad and even dangerous incidents. It appeals primarily to our feelings and usually focuses on a struggle between good and evil. Its characters are stock, but the principals are afforded a generous amount of depth to keep them interesting. Mood is key to melodrama, and therefore special effects and incidental music are common, each being used to heighten the emotional effect. Melodrama exaggerates by nature. Our movie theaters are full of all sorts of melodrama, from big budget action films to small scale indies. The Hollywood classic *Casablanca* is a nearly perfect example of the genre.

History

History plays can be comic, tragic, or melodramatic, and they explore some aspect of the character of a historical personage. They may be serious or light, comic, tragic, or melodramatic. They are best limited to a discrete event or set of events in the figure's life. The narrative danger posed by them is that they easily ramble, so they require the imposition of strong dramatic form, especially regarding plot and supporting characters. If doing a historical drama about Lee's surrender to Grant at Appomattox, it would good to limit the background story since one runs the risk of having to deal with the whole Confederate and Union armies, their governments, and the people of the United States. Besides, ten eighth graders in blue and grey uniforms with wooden guns representing Grant and Lee's armies could be a tad comical.

Epic

Epic plays are similar to historical, except they tend to deal with legendary subjects. They are often episodic adventure stories, such as the legend of Gilgamesh, or the adventures of Robin Hood; and, as such, are inherently more entertaining than history. This type of story is very popular with grades five through eight. In high school, a production of Hugo's *Les Misérables* or Dickens' *A Tale of Two Cities* would classify as epic, as would Brecht's masterpiece *Caucasian Chalk Circle.*

Some stories incline more naturally to one genre than another. A historical play about George Washington Carver is best suited for melodrama and not comedy, as would be Elizabeth Cady Stanton's organizing the Seneca Falls Conference. Historical subjects are usually poorly suited for comedy, unless being satirized, which is a subgenre that a pedagogical playwright should flee from for his or her life. A story about mistaken identity and romance is usually well suited for comedy; whereas the stories of Joan of Arc or Galileo are appropriate for tragic handling. The genre used will depend on the story chosen.

Chapter 2
The Dramatic Elements

Aristotelian dramatic theory describes six elements: plot, character, theme, diction (the type of language used), music (the "heard" onstage) and spectacle (the "seen" onstage). The first four elements are literary and the last two concern performance. These elements are archetypes and, as such, inform all theatrical events and have survived even the most brilliant attempts to dislodge them.

Plot

Plot is the representation of a series of essential unified actions. The structural components of plot are exposition, development, and resolution. Or put another way, the order of a piece of dramatic literature is from an inception of action that triggers a rising of tension that results in a crisis and climax, followed by falling action, a releasing of tension and ultimate resolution The nineteenth century drama critic Gustav Freytag articulated the dynamic relationship of these archetypal components with his famous "pyramid." Most plays, regardless of genre, follow this formulation, and it is essential for anyone who wishes to compose a play to understand its placement.

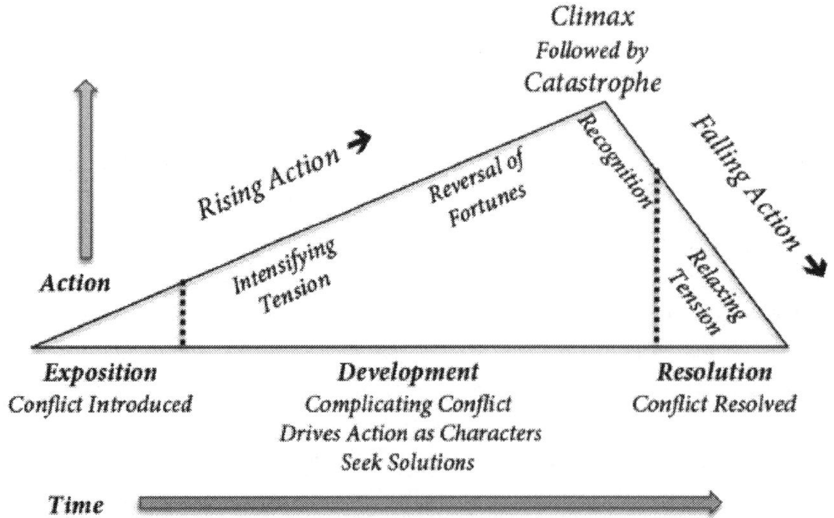

Variations in structure, of course, occur, especially regarding the placement of exposition. In its simplest form and as practiced up until modern times, exposition comes first; but starting in the late nineteenth century, playwrights began to present the exposition in a subtler manner by distributing it throughout the play. Naturally, the development of the intensifying conflict and the complications that thereby arise are central motivating forces of a play, and must precede the climax. The climax can occur earlier or later in the play's timeline, depending on whether the playwright wishes to give more attention to the complications that give rise to the climax or that arise from it.[13] There can also be multiple false climaxes or secondary climaxes in a play. Whether comedy or tragedy, the climax is followed by a catastrophe. Tragedy tends to place the climax closer to the middle than the end since such placement allows for an in-depth examination of consequences. Melodrama tends to place the climax closer to the end; and since this genre avoids catastrophe for the protagonist, its resolution usually involves some surprise twist to the plot.[14] In comedy, the climax happens as close to the end of the play as possible, ideally within its final moments, and the catastrophe proves to be not as dangerous as supposed but simply embarrassing. Once the climax has been reached, the play relaxes and moves toward resolution.

Exposition

Exposition is the first subcomponent of plot. Every play needs clear exposition, since without appropriate background information the audience will not be able to understand why the action of the play is unfolding as it does. There are various ways of presenting exposition. The oldest and simplest was to have a prologue explain what happened in the story prior to the play's action. In classical Greek theater this information was handled by the Chorus in its opening speech. In Roman comic theater a one-person Chorus directly told the audience what it needed to know, as well as apologizing beforehand for the offenses committed in the play. In Renaissance drama, the exposition became part of the opening action. The classic example of this technique is the first act of *Hamlet* during which we learn everything we need to know about why "There's something rotten in Denmark." In the modern theater of Ibsen, Chekhov, and O'Neill, the exposition is distributed in a naturalistic manner throughout the development as the characters incrementally reveal why they are in conflict. And in the "who done it" play, the final key to the exposition is withheld until the moment of climax.

Pedagogically, the ancient method of directly explaining to the audience what they need to know to understand about the background story is a highly effective expositional technique until fifth grade, and is illustrated below in this opening choral speech from a first grade play called *The Three Sillies.*

> Each evening as the sun dipped low
> To a farmer's house a squire rode.
> Yet tasty as his meal would be,
> Only the daughter he wished to see—
> Red were her cheeks, rosy and round,
> The fairest maid for miles around.
> One evening when the meal was done,
> And after many songs were sung,

The cider jug—empty stood.
The squire frowned...†

The next example, from an adaptation of Hugo's *Les Misérables* written for adolescents, uses the opening scene's dialogue to present everything that the audience needs to know about the conflict between the protagonist and antagonist that will drive the ever increasing complication of the plot.

(Curtain opens on convicts struggling to move a great rock. Jean Valjean pushes others aside, raises it effortlessly. A Guard summons Valjean. Walking bowed, with a noticeable limp, he follows into office of Inspector Javert, at desk, in full uniform, writing.)

GUARD: *(Saluting)*
Captain Javert; 42601.

JAVERT: *(Reading from papers)*
"42601: Jean Valjean. Crime: theft. Sentence: nineteen years. Completion: October 11, 1815." Today. *(Stamps paper.)* "Condition of parole: to remain in the district of Dijon; leaving said district will result in being returned to prison for twice the original term." *(Stamps papers & hands them to Valjean.)* Understand?

VALJEAN: *(Mumbling)*
Uhmm.

JAVERT:
Speak up, 42601, when addressing an officer. *(Looking up.)* I recognize you; you're the Hercules, Jean-the-Jack; you saved that man who was being crushed. You risked your life. Why? *(No answer.)* Speak. Answer when questioned by an officer.

VALJEAN: *(Mumbling)*
He was suffering.

JAVERT:
He broke the Law. He was convicted. He suffers. It's the Law. *(Holds out stamped papers.)* Your parole. *(Valjean takes papers.)* What did you steal, 42601?

VALJEAN: *(Mumbling)*
Bread.

JAVERT:
Speak up, I said.

VALJEAN: *(Strongly)*
Bread.

JAVERT:
Bread! You're all the same: belly aches . . .

VALJEAN: *(Stronger)*
. . . The children starved.

† Unless otherwise designated the plays and excerpts of plays in this book are by the author.

JAVERT:

Don't interrupt an officer, 42601! I know your kind: your cunning, your excuses, your disobedience before the Law. *(Slaps sack on the table.)* Your pay: one hundred ninety francs: ten francs per year. Dismissed. *(Valjean takes sack as Javert sorts papers.)*

Development

Development is the second subcomponent of plot and the longest in terms of stage time. It serves as the vehicle for the rising tension and complications that are fundamental to dramatic presentation. Open any play after the first few pages and read for a while and you will experience rising complication and tension. If you cannot find them you are probably reading a weak play. Since the complication develops over such a long period, only a single theatrical beat[†] within the development is given by way of example. The passage that follows is from a fifth grade treatment of the *Gilgamesh* epic, *He Who Saw the Deep*. The following scene happens just before the play's mid-point. Gilgamesh and Enkidu have just returned from slaying the forest demon Humbaba and are met at the city's gate by the goddess Ishtar.

(ENTER ISHTAR)

ISHTAR: *(Blocking their way)*

O Gilgamesh, Ishtar greets thee!
O king most mighty,
Be my husband.

ENKIDU: *(Blocking her)*

O brother, ignore this goddess;
Push right past her. All men know
She only will betray you.
She'll treat you like a toy.
And once she's done, she'll
Cast you right aside.

ISHTAR:

O puny beast-man, shut your mouth!
Great King, most handsome.
Behold my beauty.

GILGAMESH: *(Imperious)*

Be gone, foolish goddess.
I care nothing for your wiles.

(EXIT GILGAMESH & ENKIDU, pushing past her triumphantly)

ISHTAR: *(Outraged)*

O careless mortal! Dare to mock me!

---

† Beat is the term for the smallest division of action in a play's plot.

Floods! Plagues! Drought! Fleas! These
I shall release!

The above passage has all the micro-elements of plot: a beginning, middle and end. It also reaches a micro-climax in its action. Since it happens during the development section of the play, it seeds the escalating tension and complication of the play.

Climax, Relaxing Tension, and Resolution

Climax, relaxing tension, and resolution are the final subcomponents of plot. As described earlier, placement of the climax and the subsequent relaxation of tension and ultimate resolution of the conflict can happen anywhere in the final part of the play's action. The scene that follows places these sub-elements at the very end of the play and is from an adaptation of Gogol's *The Inspector General*, set in near contemporary times.†

But first, some exposition. Immediately before this scene, the Mayor has been triumphantly lording over his fawning minions with the news that his daughter is going to marry the man everyone—except the audience—believes is a mighty Inspector General from Washington. He is suddenly interrupted by the postmistress who rushes in with a letter written by the imposter. This letter, which is read aloud to the horror of all, exposes everyone for what they really are—groveling fools of the most venial sort. The audience thinks the letter is the climax, but Gogol has a surprise up his sleeve as he condenses the reversal, climax, recognition, and resolution into a single catastrophic moment.

MAYOR: *(Tearing up the letter)*
He's slit our throats, slit them from ear to ear. I'm done for, completely done for. *(Waves his hand.)* Catch him, bring him back here and I'll skin him alive!

CHARLIE:
Catch him! How, boss? You gave him your new Cadillac police car!

THELMA:
That was smart.

CHARLIE:
I could call all the surrounding counties and have them chase him down.

MAYOR:
No, we'd never live it down!

AMOS:
But you have to catch him; he borrowed three hundred dollars from me.

MADGE: And me.

DOLLY: *(Sighing)*
And from me, too.

† *The Inspector General* is strange genre-wise. Consisting of a series of humorous episodes characteristic of comedy, it ends with catastrophe that makes one feel ashamed of having laughed at the characters. It is essentially a tragedy masquerading as a comedy. I transposed the setting to Nixon-era Oklahoma, thereby overcoming the problems of period references and dated humor.

BOBSIE:
I gave him a quarter.

DOBSIE:
Oh, no you didn't, it was only a dime.

BOBSIE:
No, a quarter.

THELMA: *(Throwing up her hands in perplexity)*
How's this possible? How could you have been so off guard?

MAYOR: *(Beating his forehead)*
How could I, how could I? Thirty years of public service and I fall for a swindling impostor . . . like any schoolboy. Thirty years! And not one merchant, not one contractor; not one insurance adjuster has ever been able to put it over on me. I've got the best of them all — IRS inspectors, state police, Texas Rangers; I've beat them all, and now some puny no account . . .

ANNA:
This isn't possible, J.R.; he's engaged to Mary Jane.

MAYOR: *(In a rage)*
Engaged! Engaged!? We're lucky that's the least she is with him! *(In a frenzy.)* He's made idiots of us all. *(Shakes his fist at himself.)* Oh, you stupid idiot; you mistake that little turd for someone of importance! *(To audience.)* What are you laughing at? You think this is funny? You're laughing at yourselves! *(Stamps his feet.)* What I wouldn't give to have that bottom feeder and anyone who laughs at what he's done; I'd smash them to a pulp and . . . *(Shakes his fist and stamps his feet on the floor. After a brief silence.)* Get a hold of yourself, J.R. How, how did this happen? All of a sudden everybody is calling him an Inspector General. Who? Who said it first? WHO!!!???

THELMA: *(Throwing up her hands)*
You could torture me and I couldn't remember. We were so frightened and confused.

AMOS:
I'll tell you who. *(Pointing to DOBSIE and BOBSIE)*

BOBSIE:
So help me God, it wasn't me!

DOBSIE:
I never said a thing, I swear to God!

THELMA:
Of course!

LUBBY:
Yes, you did; you came running in here chattering, "He's a big shot from Washington, DC."

AMOS: *(Pointing at BOBSIE)*
I remember it all! You said "Aha!"

[All crowd around them.]

BOBSIE: *(Pointing at DOBSIE)*
No! She said, "Aha!"

DOBSIE:
But it was you who said he was an Inspector General.

BOBSIE:
Official, maybe, but not an Inspector General.

MAYOR: *(Approaching BOBSIE & DOBSIE)*
I ought to take you for a ride.

(ENTER FEDERAL MARSHAL with warrant in hand. MERCHANTS & WOMEN huddling in behind him.)

CHARLIE:
Boss; there's someone here.

TROOPER: *(Presenting warrant)*
Your attention, please. You all are summoned to appear immediately before the Inspector General; room #2 at the EZ On EZ Off Motel.

All are struck as by a thunderbolt. A cry of amazement bursts from ANNA and MARY JANE simultaneously. The whole group suddenly shifts positions into characteristic accusatory poses. They remain standing so as if petrified, ideally for a full-minute tableau, before the curtain slowly closes.

The Challenge of Narration

The challenge inevitably arises of what one does with all the back, side, and bridging episodes when dramatizing a story. One simply cannot represent everything. The simple solution is to have a chorus or narrator tell those parts of the story that are not enacted. In the primary grades this solution is fine, pedagogically and aesthetically, since direct choral narration is an excellent way to present a story. There follows a short example of direct, choral narration, again from The Three Sillies.

Squire:
Two sillies that will be.
Now only one more must I see.

Chorus:
But on he rode for a long, long time,
And no more sillies did he find
Until one night when the moon was high
Around a pond a crowd he spied.

The Squire comes upon a crowd that is beating a pond with sticks.

After fourth grade, however, this direct technique is neither pedagogically or aesthetically appropriate (except as light parody). This, however, is not to imply that direct narration should be scorned, as post-Shakespearean and pre-Brechtean dramatic theory has insisted. Several narrative techniques are available to the pedagogical playwright, who is, after all, working with children.

If working in a quasi-classical style of playwriting, one can simply use a Greek chorus to not just tell but comment on action. There follows the opening, expositional choral speech from *Ariadne at Naxos*, a eurythmy play for fifth graders. The reader will see that at least one whole play's worth of story has been condensed into these twenty-four lines.

Strophe: Athenian Youths

We were the pride of Athens' race;
Our youth in games and song was spent.
The joy of life shone from our face
Until we learned that we'd be sent

To Crete across the wide, dark sea –
Our fate decided by the draw.
Our parents wailed most piteously
When it was clear there was no more

That they could do to save our lives.
We were like goats beneath the knife –
Strong, without flaw, but sad of eye –
Beauty offered up as sacrifice.

Then Theseus, our prince, stepped forward,
Proclaimed that he would share our fate.
"To stay behind," he cried, "is fit for cowards
Who earn men's scorn and lasting hate.

"Come my friends! Our glory beckons!
For Crete we sail with hearts so full
Of strength and courage that all will reckon
Greatness 'gainst our deeds against the bull."

He brought great Minos to his knees;
The Minotaur he stalked and slew,
And thus he backed his words with deeds
And with his strength our hearts imbued.

One can also introduce a narrator who frames the play in a story-within-a-story style. Brecht uses this device most effectively in *The Caucasian Chalk Circle*. In the popular movie *A Christmas Story*, a narrator, who is the protagonist Ralphie's adult self, nostalgically introduces and wryly comments on the film's episodes. Similarly the actors themselves can narrate bridges in the story as done by the Royal Shakespeare Company in its 1980 production of *The Life and Adventures of Nicholas Nickleby*.

Hopefully these examples of the components of plot will be able to serve as models for how the they function in a dramatic text. It is strongly recommended that one of the first things done when writing a play is to reduce the story to this three-part plot structure. If this cannot be done easily then the story is probably too unwieldy for the stage. Imagine reducing *The Odyssey* and you will see that it would be much better to focus on just one episode, for instance, the cyclops's den. The key thing to remember is that a good plot has an easy-to-understand dramatic arc, one that moves logically from exposition through developing complications and resolves in way that an audience can understand and appreciate.

There is a pedagogical aspect of plot that warrants notice. The ability to follow and ultimately construct a plot is one of the primary vehicles by which a child awakens and develops the capacity for logical, sequential thinking. Waldorf education is particularly rich in this regard, thanks to the powerful role played by storytelling in its curriculum and methods. When listening to a story, especially descriptions of actions and personalities, the child's imagination actively makes inwardly held mental pictures. The child then connects these mental pictures into the logical wholeness of the story. This type of active, imaginative combining and repetition guides and strengthens the development of thinking.

Comprehending a plot and its characters and themes through reading and rehearsing a piece of dramatic literature is more challenging than listening to or reading a story. A told or read story provides far more information for the imagination than is available in a dramatic text. The wide range of repetitive activities involved in the cumulative process of rehearsing a play, however, provides a splendid opportunity for thinking to develop out of the child's discovery of the sequences of and motivations behind the actions represented, thereby strengthening the ability to think in a logical manner.

Character

When Aristotle writes of character in his *Poetics* he is referring primarily to the moral nature of the individual being represented. We, of course, have multiple overlapping meanings: the ethical quality of a person's behavior; or an individual personage in a story; or an exceptional and noteworthy personality. From a pedagogical theater perspective, the term will be used according to its first two meanings—the ethical qualities of personality and the individual roles in a play.

Basically, a play is a series of conflicted interactions between characters whose natures fall somewhere between the poles of ethicality. The primary conflict is between a protagonist, who drives the action, and an antagonist, who counters the protagonist's action. They are called the principals. Naturally, a class play is going to need more than just principals; in fact, it will require a whole constellation of secondary and tertiary characters. These characters are known as the supporting roles. The principals carry the ethical meaning of the play; and as such, are key to a play's pedagogical appropriateness and success. The supporting roles add greater dimensionality to the drama, and their character will fall somewhere between the two ethical poles.

In the grade school the ethical character of the principal roles—how they behave and the consequences of their deeds—should have an edifying effect on the class performing the play and the audience watching it. The more serious the import of the play the more edifying the experience should be. Students and audience alike should feel admiration for the protagonist, even if the story ends badly. With lighter, comedic plays, edification is not the goal unless one wants to be preachy. Poking fun at human foibles and ridiculousness is the objective. Comedy should entertain. A grade school comedic play should not generate cynicism, however, which is why satire is an inappropriate subgenre for this age. The audience of a grade school should delight in the performance, not feel uncomfortable or smug.

In high school the type of theatrical characters that are appropriate expands. As in the literature curriculum, the characters should be a vehicle for critical thinking, not pre-digested, didactic conclusions. When studying and developing the characters in a play, the students should feel challenged, and not just in the sense that building a character is hard work. They need to wrestle with great questions of human existence, which working creatively with a demanding theatrical characterization can certainly provide. While the ethical conflicts faced by the protagonist must remain central, the protagonist's behavior does not necessarily have to be ethical or edifying. Take Goethe's *Faust* for instance, which is often taught in twelfth grade. The protagonist Faust is about as far from being an edifying example of a human being as possible. He makes a bargain with the devil, lusts after and seduces an innocent young woman, provokes her into unwittingly killing her mother, gets her pregnant, kills her brother, then abandons her, and completely gets away with his crimes. Not edifying. The play, however, is thought-provoking, and it is beautiful; but it does not leave us with a didactic moral resolution. Rather, it challenges us to struggle with its ambiguity and reach our own resolution within our individual conscience.[15]

Pedagogical Role of Characterization

In the primary grades, characters are of the simplest types: a king and queen, their sons and daughters, and some type of nemesis; a saint, disciples, and some type of seeker or sinner; a set of animals; or Old Testament figures such as Abraham and Sarah or Joseph and his brothers. The characters are all archetypal; they stand as representatives of deeper ideas. Who they are in themselves is of little interest, as would be the case in a post-Shakespearean drama. Archetypal characters have, by their nature, no psychological depth; and they experience little character development, as Hamlet does, other than coming to wisdom over the course of the plot. In fourth and fifth grades, theatrical characters assume more personality and the children begin to actually perform them, masking themselves with the voice and gestures of the character. Then in fifth grade, one begins to see the first inklings of the art of acting with some of the children. At this point it is pedagogically important that the teacher understands that a theatrical character is no more than a costume for the ideas the playacting is exploring.

Characterization prior to middle school depends on two things: what was stated in the text and the temperament[16] and physical build of the child assigned a role. Although a role in a class play may be written for a particular child, the teacher-playwright should write for temperament. A character written for a choleric child, for instance, can be personalized for any number of individual children who share that temperament; this can easily be done by adding an idiosyncratic phrase or two that the child will recognize as belonging to him or her. This method of working has two practical advantages: it gives children the opportunity to be themselves, and it allows a play to be easily adapted for and performed by various groups of children.

Starting in sixth grade, it becomes pedagogically appropriate to begin working with theatrical characterization. It is a time when the students know and think about the world by how they feel about it; and theater provides the opportunity to give expressive form to this life of feeling by allowing them to play, to try on the voice, gestures, and attitudes of another self, albeit an imaginative and therefore a comfortably removed one. Naturally, one should begin modestly; there is no need for psychological analysis of character or probing for deep motivations. Simplicity is the key, which is why melodrama or situational comedy with their stock characters and their clear thematic struggles are excellent genres with which to start this work.

One should never underestimate, however, the importance an individual middle school student can attach to the character s/he plays in a class play. Few activities are more fun and generate more enthusiasm for a middle school student than playing a bombastic role. In *Oliver Twist* there is a beadle named Mr. Bumble. He is a petty, blustering, cruel, and stupid man. Fortunately, few classes have any student fitting this description. However, in my first class there was a boy who was the very opposite: a thin, tall, loosely jointed sanguine-melancholic of great intelligence who had experienced difficulty feeling recognized and treated fairly by his classmates. While being kind hearted, by eighth grade he had become fascinated with the grotesqueness and violence of punk subculture. In addition, he was the kind of student who is easily overlooked in a class. This description does not imply that he was a weak boy; on the contrary, he was a very hard worker and had overcome obstacles that would have defeated other children. Simply put, he was naturally slow in coming to a sense of his own strength and being able to express it.

When I gave out the texts, he declared that he wanted to be Mr. Bumble, having watched the David Lean film with his father as soon as the play was announced. Everything about Bumble fascinated and delighted him. In rehearsals he bellowed at the orphans, fawned obsequiously before his social betters, and whimpered self-pityingly when dominated by Mrs. Corney. Years later in Catholic high school when he was asked to write an essay about what had been the most important event for him in elementary school, he wrote about playing Mr. Bumble. Until his mother sent me a copy of that essay, I had naively thought that he had simply done a good job, but after reading his paper I realized that the role had served as a way for him to exorcise his feelings about how he had been treated by some of his classmates when very young; and by playing the type of person he would never want to become in life, he had been connecting with his own inner strength and experiencing the transformative power of pedagogical theatre.

One example from high school will conclude this examination of the creative, moral power of pedagogical characterization. Several years back as I reviewed plays for a twelfth grade, I was primarily concerned with finding one that had a strong female lead that an extraordinarily gifted student actor could play. I was inclined toward Schiller's *Mary Stuart* because it is one of the greatest female roles in the theater and felt that the grandeur of Mary's character would be a perfect opportunity for this young artist. Then one day in the class the twelfth graders asked me what play they were doing and I mentioned Schiller. How they moaned and begged to do a comedy. So, on the spot I said, "What about Wilder's *The Skin of Our Teeth*?"Oh, that's a great play!" someone responded.

Now, I had seen *The Skin of Our Teeth* multiple times over the preceding thirty years: two professional productions, one college conservatory program, one tenth grade production, and two recordings of professional stage productions, one from Great Britain in the 1960s and another from Los Angeles in the late 1990s. In all the productions Mrs. Antrobus was little more than a foil for Mr. Antrobus and the seductress Sabina, and I was a bit disappointed that this young actress could not have a better role than Mrs. Antrobus (she was no Sabina) for her final show at school. But the play has a lot of good supporting roles (solving the perennial problem of employing everybody in the class productively) and some interesting set and soundscape challenges; so I went with it.

The true genius of a role is its potential, and I wonder whether Wilder knew that Mrs. Antrobus could be the most important role in the play. I certainly didn't until rehearsals. The young woman came to the first rehearsal completely off book; she was ready to make theater. It was also obvious by the way she spoke her lines that she was thinking deeply about the character of Mrs. Antrobus, and it became more and more clear with each subsequent rehearsal that her Mrs. Antrobus was going to be the true center of this production. Mr. Antrobus and Sabina, the technical protagonist and antagonist, would support the Mrs. Antrobus' character.

One instance of the depth of moral character that she developed for Mrs. Antrobus deserves attention. In the second act Mr. Antrobus tells his wife that he is leaving her for Sabina. The scene is deeply ironic in that all his plans are being made against the cataclysmic end of the world, and nobody will be leaving anybody as the characters realize that their only hope for survival is to cling together and strive forward. When reading the following excerpt, imagine the complexity of feelings and thoughts that the actor playing Mrs. Antrobus must convey.

ANTROBUS:

You're a fine woman, Maggie, but...but a man has his own life to lead in the world.

MRS. ANTROBUS:

Well, after living with you for five thousand years I guess I have a right to a word or two, haven't I?

MR. ANTROBUS: *(To SABINA)*

What can I answer to that?

FEMALE REPORTER:

Mr. Antrobus, the hurricane signal's gone up. We could begin right now.

MRS. ANTROBUS: *(Calmly, almost dreamily)*

I didn't marry because you were perfect. I didn't even marry you because I loved you. I married you because you gave me a promise.

(She takes off her ring and looks at it.)

That promise made up for your faults. And the promise I gave you made up for mine. Two imperfect people got married and it was the promise that made the marriage.

MR. ANTROBUS:

Maggie, . . . I was only nineteen.

(She puts her ring back on her finger.)

MRS. ANTROBUS:

And when our children were growing up, it wasn't a house that protected them; and it wasn't our love, that protected them —it was that promise.

The scene is then interrupted by their flirtatious daughter, and Mrs. Antrobus needs to step out of her deeply personal role as an indignant wronged woman and shift suddenly into her other role as a boundary-setting mother. But then she catches herself and realizes that she must send a message to the future about not just who she is, but who all women are. So clutching the daughter's arm she momentarily suspends her wife-mother identity, and directly address the audience:

MRS. ANTROBUS: *(Claps her hands peremptorily)*

. . . Before I go I have a letter . . . I have a message to throw into the ocean.

(Fumbling in handbag.) Where is the plagued thing? Here it is.

(She flings a bottle over the audience into aisle.)

It's a bottle. And in the bottle's a letter. And in the letter is written all the things that a woman knows.

It's never been told to any man and it's never been told to any woman, and if it finds its destination, a new time will come.

We're not what books and plays say we are. We're not what advertisements say we are. We're not what you hear on the radio or see in the movies [or on television or the Internet], for that matter.

We're not what you're all told and what you think we are:

We're ourselves. And if any man can find one of us he'll learn why the whole universe was set in motion. And if any man harm anyone of us, his soul—the only soul he's got—had better be at the bottom of that ocean,—and that's the only way to put it.

Gladys, come here. We're going back to the hotel.

This scene is profoundly demanding of the actor, requiring not only technical skill in the stage business (extracting a bottle from a purse while holding a squirming teenager, delivering a monologue, and then throwing the bottle properly over the audience) but also the expressive virtuosity to shift suddenly between the different roles her character plays in life. Now add to those demands the fact that the actor needs to focus and communicate the whole moral vision of the play clearly and powerfully in these lines. Fortunately, the young woman's performance was so magnificently realized that she not only achieved these objectives but was also able to inspire the type of cohesive ensemble work that gives rise to that profoundest of artistic events, a theatrical moment, when audience, performers, and play are one. Only the realization of character, in its widest sense of the word, can do that.

Idea

Every pedagogical story, whether it is told, read, or performed must have an intentional, ethical meaning that its teller wishes the listener to hear; otherwise it is not true but counterfeit art.[17] Just as the ethical qualities of a play's characters are revealed through their actions, so the theme of a play reveals the ethical lesson the playwright wishes to examine with an audience. For the pedagogical playwright, there is an additional purpose: what the students will examine, experience, and learn by rehearsing and performing the play.

The theme of a play, therefore, has a profound effect on the student performers. Consider how much time a class spends working with a play and thereby actively engaged with its ideas in their thinking, feeling, and willing, and one will immediately appreciate why the play's ideas should have pedagogical significance. The tricky part here, of course, is presenting ideas that are intellectually and emotionally inspiring for the students and audience alike.

Since in the elementary school, especially before sixth grade, most plays will be adaptations from the language arts curriculum, the theme will be established already, so little needs to be done beyond adapting it to the basic requirement of theatrical storytelling—being easily followed and understood by the children and their audience. If, however, the teacher writes an original play then careful consideration needs to be given to the thematic element, since plot and character will not be sufficient if one wants to have a play with aesthetic integrity.

In middle school, and then especially in high school, theme is of the utmost pedagogical importance. The teacher-writer-director can never lose sight of the fact that education is not only about developing skills, whether academic or aesthetic, but about the moral quality of the ideas to which the students are introduced and with which they work and thereby transform into life-guiding experiences of consciousness. A play that lacks ideas or celebrates debased ideas is unworthy of pedagogical theater. Then, on the other hand, didacticism and preachiness, while very satisfying for some elements of an audience, make for banal artistic work and are prone to suffer righteous rejection by the class, the older it gets.

A word about edgy ideas is appropriate. Adolescents delight in the feeling that if they could only do something that would push the boundaries and shake things up, they would have made some important statement about their independence and identity that the community needs to hear. Unfortunately, thinking beyond this impulse and understanding its consequences is not their strong suit. One will frequently encounter this feeling masquerading as an idea in rehearsals, particularly in some of the suggestions they offer. Simply receive this stuff with humor and explain as neutrally as possible why it would not fit. If however, the teacher-playwright-director works with the students in a way that they can imagine how their play will be experienced by its audience, and the type of experience they really want to feel at the play's end, this impulse will correct itself, and the substantive ideas of the play will become manifest.

Everything that happens on a stage, the way a play sounds and looks, is communicating its idea.

Language

After clarifying the plot, characters, and themes of a play, the pedagogical playwright's final preparatory task before the actual writing of the text will be to decide what type of language will be used, verse or prose; how this language will affect the students by their speaking it; how it will sound onstage; and how it will be experienced by the audience.

Class plays for the first through fourth grades are traditionally written in verse that is both vivid and musical. The rhythmic quality of the verse is of the utmost importance. Rhythmic verse, like a repeated healthy physical activity, nourishes the etheric body, develops habit, and strengthens the will when used properly. This repetitive, will-strengthening quality of verse, however, is also its greatest liability. Just as repetition easily becomes lodged in the physical body as a habit, so can strongly rhythmic verse, if mishandled, easily degenerate into a relentless beat that overwhelms the meaning and tone of the words and literally has the children shaking in unison onstage.

Experience has shown that the best verse form for young children is one that is naturalistically rhythmic, approximately tetra metric, and rhymed either alternately (ABABCDCDEFEF or ABCB) or in couplets, (AA BB CC). Good and regular internal rhymes are also a nice enhancement. Nursery rhymes and good children's poetry provide excellent models for the type of verse that speaks directly to the ear of children, resulting in ease of memorization and the ability to carry its speakers merrily along on its fluidity.

> Little Bo-Peep has lost her sheep,
> And can't tell where to find them;
> Leave them alone, and they'll come home,
> Wagging their tales behind them.

Short stanzas are better than long; and if possible, they should be constructed so their delivery can be distributed between several different groups of speakers, especially during choral narration or dialogue. This practice has several advantages. It breaks the potential monotony of the speech and helps greatly in creating the theatrical illusion of a variety of characters actively interacting with each other. It also requires the children to be more conscious of what they are speaking and how they are speaking it; and the practice directs attention through its slight tonal shifts to the meaning of the words while supporting the action being enacted onstage. Rhyme also imparts similar effects.

It is always important for the versifier to remember that beat enslaves; it is powerful but mindless, and draws its speakers and listeners down into unconsciousness. Rhythm, on the other hand, enlivens; it has strength and derives its authority from its subtle irregularities; it permeates sound with consciousness and intentionality. The beat is the pure will of a line, while rhythm is will infused with emotional and intellectual consciousness. Verse can be easily kept from sounding artificial and deadening by holding it to the natural syntactic rhythms of everyday speech. And of course, the writer should eschew doggerel; this time-dishonored device is best reserved for comedy where it will sound like wit, especially when put into the mouth of a fool.

That said, the teacher must guard against overwhelming the storytelling with the rhythm and rhyme of the lines. End rhyme—finishing a sentence and a line on the rhyme,—is problematic but cannot be easily avoided given the shortness of the stanzaic speeches in a class play, usually about four lines. As a consequence, the playwright has to work consciously against the overwhelming feeling of conclusiveness it naturally imparts. It is also good to break the impelling nature of the rhyme scheme by inserting a blank verse stanza, as the following example from *The Three Sillies* shows.

CHORUS:
. . . The cider jug—empty stood.
The squire frowned.

SQUIRE:
This isn't good.

FARMER:
Daughter—quickly fetch some more!

WIFE:
The squire thirsts; his throat is sore!

CHORUS:
While drawing cider she chanced look up –
Above a beam a mallet was tucked –
With dust and webs it was all covered,
So on a bench she sat and blubbered.

DAUGHTER:
Supposing he did marry me
And a handsome son we had
And once while drawing cider
That horrid, horrid mallet

Fell off that beam
And killed the poor boy dead.

As the children grow older, a wider variety of verse forms can be employed. In the fourth grade the Norse myths provide the opportunity to work with unrhymed alliteration. Alliteration is particularly good for fourth graders in that its strong consonantal emphasis strengthens the firmness with which they must stand upon the earth as they emerge from the nine-year change.[18]

The following example of simple alliterative verse is from *The Lay of Baldur's Doom*, a choral play for fourth grade.

CHORUS OF AESIR:

Odin, All-Father, weary world wanderer,
Hear our heart-heavings, master magician.
Sorrow-songs sing we; loud our lamenting.
Sheathed all in dread stand our fair mead halls.
Baldur the Beautiful battles dark dream-dread,
The cries of the Bright One shatter our sleep.

An equally effective poetic scheme from fourth grade on is a combination of metric and rhyme schemes that differ according to the character speaking. This device is pedagogically appropriate because it emphasizes individualization and thereby directs the student's consciousness aesthetically toward the child's developing self-identity. The use of a variable scheme is also theatrically effective in that its wide variety of tonal and rhythmic colors, in the musical sense, makes it easy for the audience to differentiate between the characters, in the Aristotelean sense of the word.

This technique of giving each individual character his or her own idiosyncratic verse form can be called polychromatic[†] verse. Just as characters each have their own distinctive psychological, physical, and tonal aspects, so the language that they use should possess a variety of distinctive musical colors and characteristics. In the classical Greek theater, the poets used a wide range of metric and tonal patterns depending on the type of verse being spoken, who was speaking, or the placement of the verse in the action of the play. In Shakespeare's dramaturgy, he used a similarly wide set of verse forms, ranging from the noble patterns of blank iambic pentameter through the classic Italian and French forms of prosody to prose. (There is a commonly repeated error that Shakespeare used prose only for his vulgar commoners and clowns; this misunderstanding is put to rest by Hamlet's eloquent prose reflection "What a piece of work is a man!") In the golden age of Spanish playwriting during the seventeenth century, this polychromatic technique was also used, depending on the character speaking and the speech's context. Therefore, one should consider this form an essential tool of playwriting.

The next two examples from *The Lay of Baldur's Doom* demonstrate polychromatic verse for the Norse goddess Frigga, then the shape-changer Loki. Frigga's verse has an

† This term was apparently coined by one of my dramaturgy professors in graduate school, since I have never found it elsewhere. The same idea appears in the less colorful term polyrhythmic verse.

alliterative gesture, but it is essentially a descending eleven beat, rhymed line. While the whole play could have been composed in this form, its use in conjunction with the more highly alliterative lines of the Chorus and then the disturbingly short, irregularly rhymed pattern given to Loki shows the type of variation possible.

FRIGGA:
Forgetfulness would I weave 'cross our bright brows
And cloak all our sorrows with dread-shrouding clouds.
Terrible the time that my son's dream foresaw;
That vision of darkness brings Doom to our door.

Loki's lines are distinctly different and are meant to make the audience uncomfortable.

LOKI:
Sport they make
With their pet.
No fun is here
If no harm is met.
No danger's near,
And no death-blow counts.
None feel fear,
So soon I pounce.

Starting in fifth grade, blank or rhythmic free verse can be used. By this time, the students are beginning to insist that they are no longer little children and should be given more independence. Rhyme and the metric patterns so effective in the lower grades feel old-fashioned and restrictive, and the students want to feel freed from such imposition, imposing instead their own wills on their experience. Blank and free verse require that the speaker work hard in bringing individual initiative and thoughtfulness to both what is being said and how it is being said, more than was previously needed. The verse line can also become longer and assume a naturalistic iambic meter, as can be felt in this dialogue from a play for fifth graders entitled *Ariadne at Naxos.*

THESEUS:
Stay, guard her from herself.
I'll soon defeat these Amazons.

PHAEDRA:
You think that they are Amazons?
They are the Maenads of the youngest god,
Dionysus, who takes Ariadne for his bride,
And weds her with a crown of stars.
Challenge him, and be destroyed.

A little later, in sixth grade, and as appropriate for the subject matter, prose can be introduced. The introduction of prose works well when coordinated with the student's first work in creating characterizations. With prose the teacher/playwright needs to be careful about how the rhythmic qualities of syntax are employed. If the speeches lack a natural rhythm and begin to sound like formal, written language, the dialogue will lose all life. Similarly, if the prose sounds like thinly disguised free verse, either because of the injudicious use of figurative language or rhythm, the language will be equally disturbing to the ear. The same criterion must be applied to prose as to verse: does its sound fit the story?

The first of the following prose examples is from a sixth grade play about Thomas à Becket, *The Holy Blissful Martyr,* and is in a formal, deliberately rhythmic, and elevated style.

NOBLEMAN:

This is no deacon, despite his humble robes, but a prince of the Church whose greatness seeks to equal even a king's. It is he whose exile, these seven years, has caused our King such equal measures of joy and woe.

ELEANOR:

It's Becket then of whom you speak.

How calm this field seemed until this report. Not even the cries of battle sound greater alarms! From wind-swept northern heaths to fragrant southern groves, we've subdued all who have raised their banners against our throne. But now a single soul, without the force of arms, rises up before us like a mighty host, armed not with martial steel but iron will.

Blast this honeyed-tongued, ambitious, prideful merchant's son who seeks to split asunder all we've made and grind it into dust. May the devil take his soul!

The next two prose examples are from adaptations of Dickens' *Oliver Twist.* One of the advantages of adapting Dickens for the stage is that dialogue can be lifted directly from the novels and needs only minimal editing to make it suitable for the contemporary ear.

SOWERBERRY:

We were just passing by and thought we would inquire about a boy.

BUMBLE:

A boy?

SOWERBERRY:

Yes, a boy, a sad, melancholic boy, for a mute. Noah has become too large. I need a pale boy for the grief-stricken to pity—a boy to accompany the hearse at children's funerals.

CORNEY:

Mr. Sowerberry, I have just the boy for you.

SOWERBERRY: *(Examining Oliver)*

Melancholy expression; thin in the wrist; pale enough, but a bit too plump.

BUMBLE:

A diet of the thinnest gruel is what he needs, not the rich food the parish provides.

Writing for Eurythmy

The art of eurythmy[19] is one of the great advantages Waldorf schools have over any other place where pedagogical theater is practiced. Through the integrated use of eurythmy in a play, the choreographic potentials of groups can be so enhanced that a whole new and much deeper level of communication is possible between performers and audience. The gestures and choreography of eurythmy are not abstract but actual visualization of the tones, dynamics of speech, and their meaning. By writing verses that can be accompanied by eurythmy, the playwright gains access to multiple aesthetic and practical devices, not least of which are solving the problem of imparting life to choral narration; representing abstractions; and solving the perennial modern dilemma of how to deal with the choral dances and odes in Greek tragedy.

While one does not need to be a eurythmist to write for eurythmy, one does need to know enough about the eurythmic speech gestures to write lines that a eurythmist can effectively choreograph. The following classical-style choral ode from a fifth grade Gilgamesh play entitled *He Who Saw the Deep* was written deliberately for eurythmy.

MAGI: *(Spoken to eurythmy)*
What cannot kings do for glory,
For immortality bestowed by words,
To live forever through a story
That by the countless generation's heard!

HIGH PRIESTESS: *(Spoken to eurythmy)*
Are not such stories like the wind?
Rush loudly past, then silent fall,
As lasting as a passing whim,
Glorious for a moment, then no more?

The final eurythmy example, from the same play, is in polychromatic verse and uses a long, descending, driving, blank verse line and presents the slaying of the forest demon Humbaba. Notice the use of strong assonance and consonance, as well as gesturally descriptive phrasing that can be elongated in time, thereby allowing for descriptive action to accompany the speech. The words and their phrasing were deliberately picked for how they would work narratively and dynamically with two major components of eurythmy: tonal gestures and choreographic forms. The lines also can be distributed between various speakers, thereby increasing the auditory action of the speech.

MAGI & HIGH PRIESTESS: *(Alternating choral & solo narration)*
Vast the forest spread around them, towering high above their heads;
Dark the shadows that engulfed them, silence stretching mile on mile.
Suddenly they heard Humbaba, thundering through the fearful dark,
Crashing through the trees and bracken, rushing closer, closer, closer,
Till the forest heaved and shuddered, great trees falling, crashing round them.

Then Humbaba loomed above them, laughing loudly, laughing cruelly,
Contemptuous of the puny mortals. "Tremble now you little insects!

Humbaba is my dreadful name. Only gods may look upon me, only gods
May enter here, only gods live to leave here, only gods escape
My wrath. Wretched death I'll pile upon you."

Writing Lyrics

When writing lyrics it is helpful but not absolutely necessary to know whether they will be sung *a cappella* or accompanied. If accompaniment is desired, it is good to have a sense for what instrumental voice will work best. It is equally important to realize that although meter is important, rhyme is more so, since the composer will probably alter meter for dynamic effect. Only in the case of chants will the original meter remain mostly unchanged.

The following short lyric is from a tenth grade production of Sophocles' *Antigone*. This particular tenth grade was capable of working in a wide range of musical forms, from choral songs and individual arias to full-scale incidental music and soundscapes. This aria takes place just before Antigone is led off to her death. Although the composition was short, the students in charge of the show's sound design composed a powerfully slow and somber arrangement for cello, violin, celeste, and percussion.

ANTIGONE:
O Theban land,
O city of my fathers,
O altars of my gods
Behold my execution
For defying a tyrant and
Fulfilling Zeus' highest obligation.

It is important to understand that songs and lyrics explore character and theme but do not advance plot, since plot is integrally connected to advancing action. While it can be done, using song to provide narrative exposition can easily overwhelm the audience's interest and attention. One effective and entertaining way to get around this limitation in a non-musical play is to have a character sing a ballad that presents expositional material. In classic American musical theater, the opening numbers of the show, combined with the introductory dialogue, usually provide the basic expositional information. Nevertheless, the playwright should never forget that telling about an action is far less effective than doing it.

Writing for Musical Theater

Raw lyrics are the conceptual skeleton upon which the composer creates the living flesh of a musical number. A few years back I had the privilege of working with the composer Peter Stopschinski on a full-scale musical theater version of Dickens' *A Tale of Two Cities*. The text that follows, called "Cake," is the second production number in the show, taking place at an aristocratic party shortly after the audience has been introduced to the wretched, seething-with-hatred Parisian slums. This scene and its lyric were reworked multiple times as the musical framework and content were developed.

(Curtain opens on a grand gathering of aristocrats.)

FEMALE ARISTOCRAT 1:
Mon dieu! NO! Oh, Marquis, you jest! *(Hiding behind her fan in great enjoyment, then peeking out.)* Tell us more!

FEMALE ARISTOCRAT. 2:
But really, my dear; you can't be surprised?!

FEMALE ARISTOCRAT 3:
But I didn't think she had the wit.

FEMALE ARISTOCRAT 4:
Oh, Contessa! Have you heard? *(Drawing CONTESSA to her.)* Please Marquis, tell us again. You tell it so well!

(A clutch of aristocrats are drawn into the conversation.)

EVRÉMONDE: *(In a conspiratorial tone)*
. . . so when the Farmer-General reported to his Majesty that the people were without bread, the queen said (or so Monseigneur Le Blanc says; I heard it from him) "Let them eat cake."

CONTESSSA:
The child!

FEMALE ARISTOCRATS: *(A medley of delight)*
Mon dieu! Sacre bleu! How delightful! Oh my! No!

(Orchestral introduction, they swirl about dancing & singing, alternating lines.)

MALE & FEMALE CHORUS OF ARISTOCRATS:
Let them eat cake?
As much as they like! Yes.
Let them eat cake
That's creamy and light;
It's truly delightful!
Yes, let them eat cake;
It's simply so sweet
The mis'rable wretches need something to eat;
Something to eat;
They need something to eat!
Ah! Ah!

FEMALE ARISTOCRAT 1 & EVRÉMONDE:
Let them eat cake;
As much as they like, yes!
Let them eat cake
That's creamy and light;
It's truly delightful!

FEMALE ARISTOCRAT 2 & EVRÉMONDE:
Let them eat cake
It's simply so sweet,
And the wretches need something to eat—
Something to eat;
They need something to eat.

MALE & FEMALE CHORUS OF ARISTOCRATS:
Ah! Ah!

EVRÉMONDE:
Let them eat cake!
It's better than meat
It makes any luncheon divinely complete!

CONTESSA:
Let them eat cake!
It's simply so sweet
But when watching your figure,
It's not such a treat.

FEMALE ARISTOCRAT CHORUS:
It's simply so sweet!
But when watching your figure,
It's not a good treat.

MALE & FEMALE CHORUS OF ARISTOCRATS:
Cake! Cake! Cake!
But then it's simply so sweet! *(repeat)*
Better than sweet! Better than meat! *(repeat)*
Cake! Cake! Cake!
But when watching your figure,
It's not a good treat.
Let them eat cake; *(repeat)*
How charming, how nice!
So let them eat cake,

(ALL, led by EVRÉMONDE & CONTESSA, grotesquely mock a begging mob, pleading: "Food, wine, bread, shelter!")

But only one slice.

(EXEUNT dancing & laughing.)

Music

The writing of lyrics leads us naturally into the penultimate Aristotelean element—music, an element far more comprehensive than its most immediate definition conveys. Music encompasses everything that is heard in the performance space, including, of course, instrumental and vocal music, the tone and rhythm of the speech, the sound effects and soundscape, but also including the unheard tempo of the performance, especially its deliberate silences. Unlike the previous four elements that are literary, music, in classical theory, is considered an enhancement, a secondary element, because the elements of plot, character, idea, and language are sufficient to understand the drama. From a purely literary perspective (the reading of a play) this position is begrudgingly true, but from a theatrical perspective, this position collapses; and music, along with the last element, spectacle, is essential.

The most obvious form of this element is instrumental and vocal music. While it is generally a good practice to have music in plays, its inclusion should support and deepen the presentation of the story, not decorate it.[20] The best type of music is that which the students perform themselves, and the very best is what they compose. By using the instruments with which the students have facility (in the lower grades the pentatonic flutes or recorders, simple percussion instruments and, if available, kinder harps [lyres]; and in the middle and high school, the full range of orchestral, band, and even "found" instruments) the play will be greatly enhanced.

Speech

Speech is the primary thing heard onstage and is therefore the most important aspect of a play's musicality. It is also the primary vehicle by which all the preceding four elements are made manifest in a dramatic performance. Since people are generally unaware of how their voices sound to their listeners, it is also one of the hardest things to get right in a production. Although more will be written about how to work with speech in the later section on rehearsals, a paragraph about consciously writing words that can be spoken onstage is important.

When writing a text for performance it is of utmost importance that the playwright hear the text when composing, audibly, and not just in imagination. Actively hearing and feeling how the individual words and phrases are articulated is essential, especially in discerning whether they are easy or difficult to speak; whether they are immediately clear in their sound/meaning function; and whether their tone and rhythm are appropriate to the character speaking them and to their meaning. Therefore when composing lines, the playwright should always speak the words aloud, as the character would speak them onstage. If they ring true, go with them, but if they feel in the least degree false, rework them until they sound right.

Soundscape

The final component of music is the soundscape, which includes everything from incidental music to sound effects. The intensive use of a soundscape arose in the nineteenth century melodrama through the extravagant production values of popular theater in the great cities of the world. With the addition of recorded sound to the movies in the early 1930s the presence of soundscapes, not only as incidental music or individual sound effects, but as an actual expressive component, started to work its way into popular imagination and the serious, "legitimate" theater. After a century of this practice, most of us hear some type of soundscape in our minds when we imagine a performance. It is with the use of sound design that modern dramaturgical theory and practice challenges the fundamental Aristotelean supposition that the element of music in its broadest sense is simply an enhancement of a play's meaning. Modern musical-sound practise, especially what has developed out of nineteenth century opera and the cinema, shows that this element can be integral in carrying and deepening the meaning of a play. As a result, soundscaping has become more than an enhancing art in service of the creation of theater.

Live musical soundscaping is a fine way to engage the musically inclined members of a class who would prefer not to be actors. Since live soundscaping is part of the performance, the sound designers and performers need to rehearse and then perform with the actors. In a tenth grade production of Sophocles's *Antigone* I had a crew of half a dozen musicians develop a live performance soundscape that accompanied long sections of the performance. The only condition I set was that none of the sounds could be prerecorded; everything, whether acoustic or electronic, needed to be performed live so there would be a living interaction between their performance and that of the actors onstage.

The musical team studied the text along with the actors, and they watched some of the key scenes before I discussed with them the mood needed. They then went off to work on their own and with the school's composer-in-residence, Peter Stopschinski, who had worked with most of them the previous year on *A Tale of Two Cities*. The team played among themselves with a variety of musical ideas; they had a combination of percussion, string, wind, and keyboard skills. Once they had some sketches, they rejoined the actors and began to work together building up the scene under my direction, each group commenting on how the other group's work could be best coordinated with their own. They then worked on writing into notation with Peter what they had developed. It was a marvelous instance of creative collaboration since there was no formal musical score that preceded the social, artistic process.

Some scenes, however, absolutely require prerecorded soundscapes. In *Les Misérables* Valjean escapes with the severely wounded Marius on his back from the slaughterous street fighting into the sewers of Paris. There is no way to present this episode onstage except through a narrated light- and soundscape. Orson Welles' 1937 radio theater adaptation provides a brilliant starting point for such a treatment. In the Austin Waldorf School production, we basically did a sound and light show. The sound mixing consisted of prerecorded narration and multiple sound effects: dripping and flowing water, footsteps, splashing, and strange unidentifiable distant noises, all of which were downloaded from the website SoundDogs. Using Garage Band, each individual track was enhanced with echo and reverb filters and then mixed together with the prerecorded narration to produce the sound-scene, which was played during the performances while the tech crew generated the light effects.

Similarly, in *The Skin of Our Teeth* there needs to be a hurricane that escalates over the course of the final quarter of the second act. This storm needs to build so cataclysmically that the actors have to shout to be heard. This scene was trickier than the *Les Misérables* scene in that the prerecorded sound elements needed to be played live, especially the thunderclaps, which had to be precisely timed to the dialogue. We built up a two-part soundscape, one part of which was the prerecorded, escalating wind, rain, and waves. We played this track in the background, varying the volume as needed but not being too concerned with exact timing. Because we had a pretty good sense of the scene's running time we could simply play this track in the background, allowing the actors, in rehearsal, to time their delivery to it. We had a second set of thunder clap recordings that we manually cued at the exact moment needed. For these we varied the volume as needed. Much rehearsal was, of course, needed to make everything work together.

Pedagogically, sound design, such as incidental music and sound effects, can enter productions in fourth grade. Then in middle school, the students can begin to work with true, modern soundscaping on a simple level; and by high school, it can become an actual element, one that not only enhances the plot but conveys a play's ideas.

Spectacle

Spectacle is the what is seen onstage, and as such entails the appearance of the performance: the costumes, the actor's tableaus and movements, the set, the props, and the lighting. In short, the whole visual presentation of the play. Most aspects of spectacle, however, are only enhancements since all that is really needed are the expressions and gestures of the actor.

Costuming

Costuming is the primary component of spectacle and, while clearly an enhancement, serves two key purposes and cannot be ignored in pedagogical theater. The first and most obvious is that it helps the audience suspend disbelief that a ten-year-old is the mighty Gilgamesh. Secondly, and most importantly, it helps the student performers feel more imaginatively engaged with their characters.[†] Remembering back to the play-acting of the young child and the importance of the simple playcloth or found object for making a character, one can easily see the value of costume as a passageway into theatrical characterization.

In the continental European theatrical tradition, costume is not just the clothing worn by a character but also the make-up and assumed vocal and gestural mannerisms. In the psychologically safe and emotionally hygienic acting method developed by Michael Chekhov, the actor dons the total costume of the character being played, imaginatively as well as physically. This is a method profoundly different from the emotionally and psychologically dangerous Stanislavski method in which the actor lives the character and expresses through this being the character in performance.

† A great artist can simply use inflection of voice to create the total imagination of a character. The great late-nineteenth century French actress Sarah Bernhardt could conjure up the character of Judas Iscariot, despite being seventy years old, one legged, overweight, and declaiming in French to English speaking audiences.

The key difference of pedagogical importance between these two methods is that in the Stanislavski method the performer *becomes* the character, whereas the Chekhov actor wears the character. The former encourages and allows the characterization to fill the performer's inner soul being, something completely inappropriate for the young child, and appallingly unsavory and dangerous because the adolescent lacks the ego forces needed to exert mastery over the type of unsettling astrality that is an inherent danger of the theater. In the Chekhov approach, the inner self is kept safe, and the costume—the character—is worn and then discarded, such as a garment or face paint, resulting in a firm boundary that protects the young astral body. One might say that costume, in pedagogical theater, is a shield, and like the shield it establishes a protective boundary between inner world of soul and the outer world of performance.

The students' involvement with costuming a production undergoes a significant change from lower school to high school. In the lower school, the costuming is traditionally done by parents. By middle school the students should be doing as much as possible on their own; and in high school, they should be completely responsible for the costuming, with adult support and supervision as needed. The teacher-director is truly fortunate when s/he has some superb parent and/or student wardrobe mistresses[†] who can collaborate with the school's handwork teachers in developing a show's costume design. Fortunately, in high school, there are always students who have talent in the area of costume design; and when these students are supported by a skilled seamstress, whether a fellow teacher or parent, a wonderful artistic, educational, and mentoring experience arises.

It is a general rule of the theater that body type plays a commanding part in determining what roles an actor can play. It would be unimaginable to cast a diminutive and extremely portly older man as Marc Anthony in a play about Cleopatra. Similarly, an audience would have a great deal of trouble believing that a towering Valkyrie with a huge voice and penetrating gaze was Fantine in *Les Misérables*, particularly when, coughing and pleading, she is ridiculed and pushed into the gutter by wimpy fops. This kind of casting is the stuff of satire or the theater of the ridiculous. So when writing or choosing a play for a class, one needs be considerate of this convention. The physical body is, after all, the instrument of the actor and thereby the foundation of spectacle.

Tableau and Movement

Spectacle also entails the physical arrangement and movement of the performers onstage and should be considered from the very start when creating or staging a text. Most plays will not be served well by being static, or overly busy for that matter. Similarly, if the performers are too close together or too far apart, if they stand in meaningless straight lines, move from one position to another in straight lines, or if they upstage[21] each other or themselves for no meaningful reason, the performance will be visually dull or difficult to watch. A play is a representation of an action, so an audience expects to experience the outer movement on the stage stimulating inner movement in

† A professional theater term that is gender neutral.

themselves. A static stage makes an audience feel uncomfortable, which is exactly why it is used in the plays of Samuel Beckett or Harold Pinter, not that either of these men's works would be appropriate even for high school.

Set

Set is the next component of spectacle, immediately informing the audience where the play is happening. But set does not represent only the outer, geographic setting of a play; it also represents the thematic and psychological setting. Sets can vary between minimalistic or realistic, fully detailed, and operational representations of rooms to abstract visual gestures representative of the play's theme. Therefore, one of the first things a teacher-director has to decide when designing a show is what type of set will be used.

In the classical Greek theater the set was little more than a painted backdrop designed to indicate place. Most of the spectacle was carried by costuming, and for the vast majority of theater history, this remained the case. In the nineteenth century, however, the obsessive materialism of that age pushed theatrical sets to stupendous heights of illusionary realism. There were theaters in New York and Europe that put rivers, waterfalls, and lakes onstage, and even had real horses or desperate characters plunge into the water. So obsessed with realism, they reproduced seemingly real buildings, from around the block, across the seas, or in a far-off Rocky Mountain mining town. These productions supported acres of suburban greenhouses dedicated to producing real grass, flowers, and trees needed for this level of realism, as well as employing hundreds of people responsible for the technical requirements of such realism.

Sets in school productions are limited, of course, to much more humble conditions, generally using simple, open stages or the simplest sets, a couple of chairs, some steps and screens and platforms (all easily shifted by the actors) and a few outline indicators of buildings. The merit of these sets is that the students can play a large role in their construction, dressing, and manipulation, something that becomes especially important starting in fourth or fifth grade. True, some schools can support the building of full scale exterior and interior sets, some whimsical and others very realistic; but grand, lovely, or highly expressive sets, as with costumes, are not worth much if the show is a turkey.

Lighting

The final component of spectacle is lighting.[22] The lighting available for school plays will range from simple, general purpose room illumination to fairly sophisticated theatrical instruments and controls. This range also parallels the appropriate use of lighting technology from first through twelfth grade. While this element is strictly performance based, the pedagogical playwright should take it into consideration when composing the play. If one lacks the lighting ability to move between light and darkness, and one is doing a journey into the underworld or presenting a scene that happens at night, the playwright will have to communicate these changes through the spoken word.

Chapter 3
Composing a Performance Text

There are three stages to composing a performance text after selecting the story: sketching the plot, writing the scenario, and composing the text. The following example shows these steps for Dickens' *A Christmas Carol.*

Sketching the Plot:

One Christmas Eve Ebenezer Scrooge, a miser, is warned by the ghost of his dead partner that he will be visited over the course of that night by three spirits. The spirits appear, each in turn, and take him on a spectral journey, during which he witnesses poignant scenes of his past, present, and future. He is so moved by what he experiences on these journeys that he swears to change his ways. Thus, when he awakes on Christmas morning he is a reformed man; and profoundly appreciative of his salvation, he immediately sets out to correct his past wrongs through deeds of great generosity and compassion.

Writing the Scenario:

Scenarios allow the playwright to sketch how the raw plot will develop, scene by scene and act by act, into the working, detailed text. A scenario is especially valuable for identifying storytelling challenges in the plot and its staging. There follows a scenario for the first stave of *A Christmas Carol.*

Stave One: Prologue: Scrooge, Narrator & population of London.

A narrator, dressed as Dickens, appears before the closed curtain and speaks the opening words of the novel. The curtain opens on a London street tableau that suddenly comes to life. Scrooge enters up-right and makes his solitary way through the crowd, each character in turn telling something about Scrooge's personality as he passes. The scene ends with Scrooge entering his down-right office.

Scene 2: Scrooge's Office: Scrooge, Cratchit, Fred, Two Gentlemen

Scrooge and his clerk Bob Cratchit at desks, the latter trying to warm his hands by a candle. A clock strikes three. Fred, Scrooge's nephew, enters full of Christmas cheer. He invites Scrooge to Christmas dinner but Scrooge rebuffs him with a "Bah! Humbug!" so Fred, still cheerful, wishes Scrooge well and exits. Scrooge is again interrupted, by two gentlemen seeking charitable contributions. Each time they mention a different hardship Scrooge cynically rebuffs them, finally ushering them out with his coldest remark, that the poor should be left to die and thereby "decrease the surplus population."

Scene 3: Street: Narrator & population

Narrator and city's population move across stage describing the merriness of Christmas Eve.

Scene 4: Scrooge's Office: Scrooge, Cratchit, Cheerful Boy, Narrator.

A boy pops into the office and wishes Scrooge and Cratchit a Merry Christmas, which Scrooge meets with "Bah! Humbug!" Cratchit reminds Scrooge that since tomorrow is Christmas he won't be at work, and Scrooge calls Christmas "A fine day to pick a man's pocket." They close the office, and the Narrator describes Scrooge's evening meal and return home, where Scrooge sees Marley's face instead of a knocker on his door. Agitated, Scrooge exits through the door.

Scene 5: Scrooge's Apartment: Scrooge, Marley's Ghost. Lost Souls.

Scrooge enters, now in his nightgown with a single candle. He sits, suffering from indigestion. He becomes aware of the rattling and scraping of chains when suddenly his window flies open and Marley (a huge puppet) sweeps in, rattling chains and moaning horribly. They converse about Marley's life of business. (Abbreviate the novel's dialogue.) The conversation concludes with Marley warning Scrooge that his only hope to avoid sharing his fate is to heed the three visitors that will come to him that night. Marley then exits through the window, rattling and moaning, as Scrooge pleads for more information. The stage is then filled with the lost souls of the avaricious; they sweep about and exit through the auditorium as Scrooge faints, the lights go dark, and a bell tolls midnight.

Composing the Text:

The next stage is composing the performance text. Here is the prologue and opening scene fleshed out with dialogue and stage directions.

NARRATOR: *(In front of curtain)*

Marley was dead, to begin with. There is no doubt whatever about that. Dead as a doornail;

LONDONER 1: *(Putting head through curtain)*

Scrooge knew he was dead?

NARRATOR:

Of course, he did! Otherwise nothing wonderful can come of the story we are going to relate. He and Marley had been partners for who knows how many years, so after the funeral Scrooge never painted out old Marley's name. There it stood, years afterward above the warehouse door: Scrooge and Marley.

(CURTAIN opens to STREET CROWD going about business)
(ENTER SCROOGE: weaving through CROWD.)

ALL:

SCROOGE!

LONDONER 1:

Oh! He was tight-fisted!

LONDONER 3:
A squeezing,

LONDONER 2:
wrenching,

LONDONER 3:
grasping,

LONDONER 2:
scraping,

LONDONER 3:
clutching,

LONDONER 2:
covetous old sinner!

ALL:
SCROOGE!

NARRATOR:
The cold within him froze his old features,

LONDONER 5:
nipped his pointed nose,

LONDONER 4:
shriveled his cheek,

LONDONER 5:
and made his thin lips blue.

ALL:
SCROOGE!

NARRATOR:
He carried his own low temperature always about him.

LONDONER 7:
No warmth could warm;

LONDONER 6:
No wintry weather chill him;

LONDONER 5:
No wind that blew was bitterer than he;

LONDONER 8:
No falling snow was more intent upon its purpose;

LONDONER 9:
No pelting rain less open to entreaty.

LONDONER 8:
Foul weather didn't know what to make of him.

LONDONER 10:

Nobody ever stopped him in the street to say, with gladsome looks:

LONDONER 11:

"My dear Scrooge, how are you?"

LONDONER 10:

No beggars implored him, no children asked of him the time.

BEGGAR:

Even the blind man's dog, when it saw him coming on, would tug its owners into doorways as though to say,

NARRATOR:

"No eye at all is better than an evil eye, master!"

LONDONER 4:

But what did he care?

LONDONER 1:

It was the very thing he liked: to edge his way along the crowded path of life, warning all human sympathy to keep its distance.

ALL:

SCROOGE!

NARRATOR:

Then one Christmas Eve—of all the good days in the year—old Scrooge sat busy in his counting-house.

Working with Established Texts

Most class teachers, because of the tremendous amount of time and effort it takes to write a full length play, will chose to do one already written, especially in eighth grade. Almost all of the available plays from the legitimate theater, especially the well-made plays of the twentieth century, will require substantial editing. After making sure the content is appropriate for the students, the important thing is to reduce the play to a manageable length while not compromising its integrity. A good play, of course, cannot take too much editing before it begins to fall apart and no longer makes sense. Herein lies the difficulty in doing modern well-made comedies. They are tightly constructed, and every character is essential for the story. One simply cannot eliminate scenes or cut character. The best one can expect to do is to eliminate a subplot and shorten some speeches without doing any serious damage to the play as a whole. Eliminating subplots, however, will highlight for the teacher of a class larger than ten or so students the problem inherent in most well-made plays; they are very economically cast since anything written for the commercial theater has always needed to keep production costs low, especially actors' salaries. The class teacher who cuts scenes and, therefore, characters, easily winds up with neither enough parts for the students nor a play that makes sense.

Shakespeare in Eighth Grade

Doing Shakespeare in eighth grade has become traditional in some North American Waldorf schools. While the arguments against it are pedagogically sound and the arguments for it little more than the reasons for doing any other full-scale production at this age, the tradition is impacted like a molar in some schools' cultures and trying to stop the tradition is as easy and comfortable as self-administered oral surgery. That Shakespeare's language is too sophisticated and demanding for middle school students, and that his vision of humanity, even in the comedies, is too dark and too cynical for the grade matters little against this tradition. Leave Shakespeare to tenth or twelfth grades; but even then his plays require significant and careful editing. Fortunately, Shakespeare's dramaturgy is so luxurious that it is relatively easy to shorten without destroying the performance-worthiness of the plays.

Concluding Thoughts on Pedagogical Playwrighting

Everything about a play—its plot, its characters, its ideas, its words, its sound, and its appearance—must be appropriately sized, not just for the students who will be performing it but also the audience that will be watching it. If the pedagogical playwright-director cannot communicate his or her artistic intentions clearly and appropriately through these six elements to the students and then through the students to the audience, s/he will have failed; the resultant suffering in the theater will not be that of a god but of someone much more mortal.

Therefore, before writing the teacher-playwright must determine if the story:

- Is pedagogically appropriate for the class and audience
- Can be adapted for the stage
- Can be rehearsed and performed in the available time and space
- Will be received positively by the community.

Once each of these questions has been answered positively, then the teacher is ready to compose the text and produce the play.

Part III:
Producing the Play

Producing a play is far more complex and challenging than composing one. Whereas the writing of a play is essentially a solitary process, happening in the privacy of the playwright's mind, mounting a text onstage is a very social activity. When writing, one's follies and errors are known only to one's self, but when producing a play they are known to the students, one's colleagues, the audience, and the full school community. Therefore, this part of the book will not just describe the steps that are taken in moving a text to a performance but will focus, first, on how the teacher works inwardly with his or her own self; and second, how the teacher works as director-producer in a pedagogically appropriate manner with students of various ages.

Chapter 1
The Pedagogical Law

At the heart of Waldorf Education is the concept known as the Pedagogical Law.[23] In the second lecture of *Curative Education* Steiner stated:

> Here we encounter a law, of the working of which we have abundant evidence throughout all education. It is as follows. Any one member of the being of man is influenced by the next higher member (from whatever quarter it approaches) and only under such influence can that member develop satisfactorily. Thus, whatever is to be effective for the development of the physical body must be living in the etheric body—in an etheric body. Whatever is to be effective for the development of an etheric body must be living in an astral body. Whatever is to be effective for the development of an astral body must be living in an ego...

In short, the teacher's next higher body is always at work on the next lower body of the child.

Being a law, this principle exists universally in human relationships. Every parent, teacher, coach, or mentor who is working with another human being in a pedagogical capacity is continually working out of the Pedagogical Law, whether conscious of it or not. It is the responsibility of the Waldorf teacher (who by very definition is working proactively with the development of the whole child), to consciously use this law in his or her pedagogical work.

Therefore, every aspect of the process of producing a play is governed by the Pedagogical Law, ranging from introducing the story, distributing the text, and casting the parts through the sequence, rhythm, and content of the rehearsals and to the performances. When one hears students complain about the stress of rehearsing, especially during run-through week, or hears a teacher-director comment on how crazy and chaotic things are, you can bet ready money that the teacher-director is not working out of the Pedagogical Law. Working properly with the Pedagogical Law creates enthusiasm and joy for working and learning, especially when time is crunched and the challenges of bringing things together properly become demanding.

It is important to note that the Pedagogical Law works wholistically. While one can put a conscious emphasis on one particular type of interaction (say, how one's astral body affects the etheric bodies of one's students), one's etheric body and ego are still affecting the children. Imagine that you are in rehearsal and learn that someone has generated a conflict in the use of the performance space for the very day your tech rehearsal is scheduled. Naturally, you feel (the astral body at work) like enacting your own diva scale mini-drama in a way that would get you the space while making you legendary in the school. The only good option, however, requires that your ego flash your enflamed astral body and transform your agitation into equanimity. A hard task, but a necessary one. Not only will this consciously willed equanimity keep the students from getting agitated, but it will actually strengthen their ability to work in a well-tempered manner with the many components of habituated memory that a theatrical production requires. It will also—hopefully—have a positive effect on the colleague who generated the problem, and result in the conflict being resolved.

What is at work here is a highly refined form of transformed worthiness-to-be-imitated. Just as our physical, emotional, and intellectual skills develop through imitating what we observe and then practice, so do each of our bodies and the skills associated with them develop imitatively. But what differentiates the developmental imitation of the bodies from common, everyday imitation is that there is a metamorphic process involved, one that develops in an expansively concentric way, like tree rings, each earlier stage repeatedly giving birth to each successive one. Since pedagogical theater is not only about putting on a show, as would be the goal in professional or amateur theater, but rather about educating the young person on all levels of development (aesthetic, social, emotional, intellectual, and spiritual), consciously and creatively practicing the Pedagogical Law is a primary responsibility of the teacher.

Authority and expertise are closely related ego functions of the Pedagogical Law, the former arising from the child's impulse to imitate, and taking the pedagogical lead between the change of teeth and puberty, and the latter between puberty and adulthood. In the lower grades when the teacher announces that the class will be doing a play, the children's enthusiastic embrace of its promise comes out of a natural appreciation for the authority of the adult standing before them. They do not think, "Does this teacher know anything about theater?" Instead they feel, "Since this adult is our teacher we will gladly do a play." Starting in middle school, however, the child's desire to be led by authority transforms with the birthing astral body into a need to be led by expertise. The adolescent wants to know, "Does this person know what s/he's talking about? Does s/he walk her talk?"

Of course, worthiness of authority, like worthiness of imitation, is still at work in the middle school. Now worthiness of knowledge joins these previous two impulses for learning and becomes the leading force. I recently witnessed an instance of this development in a colleague's eighth grade class. She brought in a graduate of our high school to work as a director and acting coach for their class play. Using her authority as their class teacher, she made it clear that this young man, who was in his mid-twenties and had been trained as an actor in one of the finest college theater programs in the country, was an expert in all things theatrical and that she was honored to work with him. There were no confused or split loyalties. The class appreciatively embraced the authority of their teacher and enthusiastically embraced the expertise of the young man. It is important to understand, however, that the Pedagogical Law was functioning foremost through the teacher's authority and only secondarily through the young man's expertise. Not versed in the Pedagogical Law, he would not have been able to work effectively if the teacher's ego authority had not been working with thoughtful oversight on the astral bodies of her students.

In high school theater the students must sense three things about a teacher's work: first, expertise in the art as a whole; and where expertise might not exist in one of its component parts, such as lighting or music, an immediate willingness to work creatively with someone who has that expertise. Second, authority as the show's producer, which means, of course, the ability to work enthusiastically in the social processes of the art. And third, the worthiness to be imitated in the areas where the teacher-director is an expert, say in blocking, gesture, and/or speech. If the teacher consciously works in a way that allows for the creatively joyful and productive integration of these three forces, and uses the Pedagogical Law to guide their implementation, s/he will be practicing true pedagogical theater.

As mentioned earlier, Rawson and Richter describe a practice in some European schools of having a twelfth grade completely produce their senior play. This practice makes good sense with eighteen-year-olds in light of the above principles, in that it recognizes the need of adolescents to develop their own inner authority and expertise in preparation for the type of destiny-embracing decisions life will soon demand of them. Students who have benefited from an education that worked consciously with the Pedagogical Law, and teachers who understood and practiced their authority and expertise in light of this law, are fully capable of meeting the type of social, aesthetic, and consequential activity such a practice entails.

Chapter 2
Planning the Production

Once a text has been written or selected, the play's production needs to be fully planned since there are dozens of components, large and small, that must all be brought together within a limited period of time. Therefore, it is wise to establish the practice of planning out a show well in advance of its going into production, usually several months before the first rehearsal and ideally during a vacation period. Giving oneself such a generous amount of time ensures that one has a firm grasp of what will be needed and when it will be needed; and removes a significant number of potential problems, thereby making it much easier to work proactively during the production period. It also permits the work to fall asleep and then be reawakened, which facilitates the gestation and birthing of new ideas.

Designing the Set

Once a performance text is completed, it is a good practice to start planning the production by designing the set. This requires a thorough understanding of the physical action of the play and the performance space in which it will happen. Naturally, the set designed for a full-capacity theater to which one will have near exclusive access will be extremely different from a shared space or a traveling production. The former situation permits great luxury of design while the latter needs to be lean in the extreme, sometimes little more than gestural. A further, important consideration when designing a set is understanding the restraints of time and space that sharing the performance space with the rest of the school will entail.

First off, a set must support and communicate the key ideas of the play, whether the set design is literal or abstract. It needs to be easily constructed from readily available and economical materials, since school theater budgets are usually lean. In the lower grades it is always good if the students can work on it, and then in the middle school, build as much of it as their skills permit. In high school, the set should be designed so the students can build the whole thing, with adult supervision, of course. A set also needs to be easy to install and strike; and if there are scene changes, it needs to be easily, quickly, quietly, and ***safely*** moved (and perhaps even stored) in a very short period of time.

It is good to start with a floor plan of the performance space where the play will be presented. Making a large format graph paper template upon which the basic dimensions and features of the stage are represented is an excellent way to start, since one can then make multiple photocopies of this template for sketching the set plan. It is also handy to make simple footprint cutouts for things like flats, platforms, staircases, and whatever else the play requires, thereby helping in understanding the actual distances between the things onstage. And sketching in plan view on the bottom half of the paper permits direct projection of the set's elevation view directly above.

One also needs to imagine how the actors will move about the set and how they will enter and exit, and whether they are hidden or exposed to the audiences view at such times. If the set will be shifted during the performance, or if a significant set change is required, one needs to have figured out how this change will be done during the performance in the minimal amount of time and with the least amount of noise; and, who will do the scene changing. Ideally it should be the students, so one needs to plan for that as well. If the show is sharing the space with other school programs, one needs to determine how and where will things be stored during the production.

Once one is satisfied that the set is expressive and practical, it is good to finalize the design by making a set of plans, cartoons, and shop-drawings, examples of which can be found in the second appendix. In elementary school these drawings are generally simple since the set will not be very elaborate, given the limitations of the children's ability to build and manipulate it. But in high school, a full set of detailed shop drawings (understanding all the while that things will change during construction) are important for the students who are building the set and the adult supervising them; it is a pedagogical activity, essentially no different from any other lesson preparation. Drawings that are clearly detailed and contain an explanation of what the set will do onstage will be especially instructive to the students.

Just as the teacher needs to have a clear understanding of what exactly is needed for a main lesson block and its individual lessons, especially the work the students will do, so in a play production the same level of preparedness is essential for the first day of class. Nothing says more clearly to adolescents on the first day of a class that the work they and the teacher are doing is important and worth attention than a well organized package of materials; this is equally true for a theatrical production, especially one that is part of the core curriculum and not an elective or after-school activity.

Shop drawings are as important on the first day of rehearsal for the tech crew as the printed script is for the actors, sending them the clear message that their work is of equal importance as that of the actors. Just as the actors build a performance from a text, so will the tech crew build their role in the performance from the text and a set of drawings. Shop drawings also give the person conducting the technical part of the production an excellent opportunity for a first lesson'. S/he can gather the students, distribute the drawings and sketches (assuming everyone in the class has previously studied the play together) and go over what they will need to do and by what dates, providing not just a clear set of course expectations, but also the opportunity for practical questions and creative suggestions regarding how the drawings will be realized.

This way of preparing is much better than making some vague statement such as, "We need a room with windows and doors"; or "We need a sewer for Jean Valjean to escape through." A teacher would not conduct a geometry class by saying, "Make a bunch of pentagons and turn them into a dodecahedron," nor would s/he begin a research paper class by telling the students to "write a ten-page paper on history in three weeks." Students are in school to be educated, and in a pedagogical theater program, as in any other program, the teacher needs to have all the basic materials for a course ready when the course begins.

Preparing the Working Script

The need for well-prepared scripts for distribution on the first day of production is self-evident, but there is a way of publishing the script that proves most useful in planning and tracking the blocking and attendant stage business. Basically, it entails preparing two types of formatted scripts, one for the actors and the other for the director and light-sound board operators. Since it is important that everyone be on the same page and have plenty of space for notes, exactly parallel pagination and wide margins for both types are essential. For the students, double-sided, spiral, or comb bound scripts (not stapled), work well; and taking the time to put each character's name on a script helps greatly when they are found lying about. For the director and lighting/sound crew I use a formatting technique learned from a stage manager. The key difference from the student version is that the director's copy is single sided and has text on the left side of an open page spread and a blank sheet on the right, providing plenty of room for notes and blocking diagrams on the left page. This layout is for the right-handed people and should be reversed for lefties.

Whose Where When

When producing a longer play, especially one that will require individual students to play multiple roles, it is very helpful to have a quick reference chart for keeping track of which character (and thereby student) is onstage when, and how much time there is between any given student-character's time onstage. Trying to keep this information in one's head or in written notes leads to confusion and even chaos, so I have developed a visual tracking that is based on a "French Scene"† system that uses the cell-moving capacities of Microsoft Excel.

Basically, the chart, which can be found in the appendix, allows one to quickly see who is on or off stage when and for how long. It lays out the scene sequence horizontally, assigning three columns per page of text, thereby allowing enough room for indicating entrances and exits, as well as scene divisions. The characters are listed vertically and grouped in adjacent rows according to what roles are being played by the same student. This layout helps the director check several things easily and immediately: how well the multi-role casting works; what scenes share the same students and therefore can be rehearsed in the same period; and how to make quick rehearsal changes when somebody is absent. The chart is invaluable for the dressers, showing them how much

† A French scene is a convention of the French and not British/American theater for indicating scenes by when specific actors are onstage.

time they have for costume changes for the multi-role performers so they can plan their designs accordingly. I bind this chart in my master script, as well as hang large format copies in the wings and in the scene costume shops.

Assigning Roles: Actors, Musicians, and Tech Crew

Generally, the students will be assigned to one of two major categories: performers (actors, eurythmists, dancers and musicians); and tech crew (set, costuming and props, and lights). It is essential that every student in a class be fully and productively engaged in one or more of the aspects of a production. Just as a teacher cannot have students idle or causing distractions in a regular class, so no one should be idle or distracting during a rehearsal. Productive, creative work must be available for everyone.

In the lower school there will be little if any formal division between performer and tech roles. Everybody will have some role onstage, some as the principals and supporting roles, and others as the chorus and supernumeraries. The students who act as the musicians will most likely also have supporting roles. Generally, before seventh or eighth grade every student will have some type of acting role and rarely will anyone be assigned solely to set, costume, or lighting work. There are two reasons for not assigning students solely to a tech role. First, being onstage together reinforces social cohesion; and second, the level of skills and responsibility needed to operate the tools, machinery, and equipment is simply beyond the capacity of this age. Much of the tech theater equipment is dangerous and expensive, and whenever students are working with or around it they need experienced adult guidance and strict supervision.

Casting Actors

How a play is cast varies with the age of the students. In the lower grades, the teacher will take one of two approaches: either cast by how the personality of the student reflects the character, or how the character reflects whom the student should strive to be. In middle school, when class plays become more of a performance art, the credibility of a particular student in a part must also be a factor. In high school, where a class play is fully a performance art, the credibility of the actor playing a part becomes as important as the pedagogical reasons for casting. Just as a music teacher would allow only a highly competent horn player to play a solo in a high school concert, so should the pedagogical director hold the artistic integrity of the performance foremost.

As to formal auditioning, I have found it largely irrelevant. Class plays are part of the core curriculum, not electives, and one does not audition to participate in a main lesson block, so why should one audition for a play? The only exception I have found valuable was for a full-scale, all high-school musical in which auditioning was limited to the principal singing roles. And even in that case, the music faculty already had a very good idea of who wanted and could play these roles, since vocal and acting ability would be key for the student's and the production's success. The auditioning was largely to provide the opportunity to audition, to confirm the faculty's inclination, and quite frankly, to add a little pizzazz to the pre-production process.

The lower school casting method has its strengths and weaknesses. Casting by personality is easiest for the students; and for good or ill, it takes advantage of the show-off personality (an essential one in theater) and makes for the liveliest show. It is also a very good method for comedy. The "strive to be" method works well with serious pieces, especially if the theme of the play is idealistic and edifying, and the teacher wants to help a child develop a particular soul quality. This method gets tricky with the villain roles for self-evident reasons. Whichever method the teacher uses is discretionary, and it is good to alternate from play to play in the interest of avoiding categorizing the children. It is not good to hear Oswaldo lament in fifth grade, "Why do I always play a soldier?" or vain Francine to assert, "But I always play the queen!"

Even though the teacher has selected a play with the students in mind, it is wise in the lower and middle school grades to check one's assumptions by observing the students while reading them the play for the first time, thereby watching for any powerful connections to roles that may need to be satisfied. To do otherwise risks serious disappointment that could undermine the production. Starting in seventh or eighth grade a third casting technique is possible. After the script has been distributed and read, each student can be given a check-sheet that lists all the characters and tech roles and asks each student to cast the play according to these criteria: first, who would be good in a role; second, personal preference (the *egotism* factor); and third, the absolute best cast possible. One can then collect and collate these sheets. It is remarkable what this information reveals. On one hand it usually confirms most of the teacher's assumptions, but not always; it can reveal options that the teacher had not observed, since no one knows a class better as a working ensemble than the students themselves. It has been my experience that when the teacher and student preferences diverge it is wise to defer to the students, unless significant reasons inform against it.

In high school, after collecting the students' preferences, the teacher can draw up an ideal casting but not share it initially with the students. Then in the next class all the roles are listed on the board, stating which roles, along with names, enjoyed the greatest agreement between the "good for a role," the "personal preference," the "best cast," and the director's choice. If one is lucky, all the principals will cast perfectly; but, alas, there are always problems, usually because more students want some roles than is possible to accommodate. At this point, the horse trading begins. The teacher, of course, knows his or her preferred cast, but declines to divulge this information. Remember, feelings are at stake. After about twenty or so minutes of discussion and negotiation, the best possible cast is invariably realized. The great advantage of this method is twofold: first, the class, since it needs to work as a team when producing the play, needs to come to agreement; and second, each individual student has had the opportunity to present his or her personal preferences and desires, and weigh them against the good of the whole. When everyone has had a say, not just the teacher, the class as a whole is able to sign off on the final casting, thereby achieving the highest level of social and aesthetic cohesiveness possible.

Double casting of principals and even supporting roles is a common practice. While it is usually done because of large class sizes and the hope of satisfying as many students as possible, there are several equally important reasons. The first is practical; it allows the rehearsal process to move forward more efficiently, especially when a student is absent. But there is a creative reason as well; when two students play the same role they can develop characterizations and stage business much more effectively as they create and learn the part with each other. An equally productive, if trickier-to-manage variation is double-double casting. In this system not only are the principals double cast, but each of the principals also plays a key minor role that interacts with the principal in the same scenes. The effectiveness of this variation is that each principal experiences as an actor the other principal's playing the shared role, thereby increasing the opportunity for creative imitation and collaboration.

The Tech Crew

The tech crew is an integral part of the performance, carrying responsibility for all work related to sound and spectacle. As such it provides a serious aesthetic and educational experience for the students doing that work and for the audience experiencing the show. The students who want to work seriously in this area need the same level of instruction, creative opportunities, and support as those who will be performing onstage, this being particularly important in high school.

Those constructing the set will need the greatest amount of instruction, guidance, and supervision, especially regarding the legal and safe use of tools, and the economical use of materials. The costume crew, thanks to the handwork curriculum, is usually the group with the most highly established skills and can do much of their work independently; but they will need periodic supervision and guidance. Those designing and operating the lights and sound will need someone with expertise to guide and supervise their work; but once oriented and underway, they usually can work with a large degree of independence, checking in with their supervisor and director as needed. Of course, like the construction crew, any time this group is working directly with the lighting instruments, whether on the ground or overhead, safety, legality, and common sense demands the strictest supervision.

It is also important to have the key members of the tech crew, especially those designing the costumes, lighting, and sound, present at the first read-through and subsequent key rehearsals. It is easy for this group be become detached from how the play develops; so it is very important to give them opportunities to observe the actors' and director's work, thereby inspiring and connecting their creative thinking to the whole. A teacher-director should never forget that an ensemble is not limited to just the performers. A play, to be a true social-pedagogical activity, must include all the students and all the component arts.

That said, there will be a small number of students who treat plays as a carte blanche for idling. They should, of course, be kept occupied, ideally with some activity that is creative and productive; but the sad truth is that sometimes idlers exploit the open form of a play production, disrupting the work or wandering off, seeking whatever adventure the campus provides. Put simply, they need to be put to work elsewhere. The best solution is a study hall table where they can do their homework while being on immediate call for whatever needs doing. They should not be automatically assigned to the tech crew; it is not fair to the students on the crew who actually want to do something creative and productive to be distracted by idlers.

Scheduling

A well-run production schedule will bring all the various components of a play to completion in a sequence that supports each piece creatively supporting the others, thereby making for the least stressful and most rewarding pedagogical experience for students, teacher-director, and colleagues. As described previously, first, the play's text must be prepared with sufficient lead-time so the teacher-director can live with its ideas and design how it will appear onstage. Then the assistants need to be engaged, and the students assigned their roles. This first production phase will be followed by rehearsal scheduling: the read-through, blocking, characterization, memorization, set, props and costume construction, light and sound design and set-up, full act run-throughs, assembling the play and tech rehearsals; and finally running the play in real time, multiple times One cannot put too much importance on the calm and deliberate managing of this sequence.

Scheduling a production is really no different from planning a main lesson block or the scope and sequence of an all-year skills program. One establishes the pedagogical intention of the course, identifies and prepares the instructional components, arranges them in an appropriate order, and plans sufficient make-up time for the inevitable delays and surprises. Every well-prepared teacher does this type of planning, since it ensures the highest levels of proactive and reflective preparation and student success. The Waldorf teacher has the additional responsibility of doing this work through the Pedagogical Law. Without this type of full, conscious lesson planning (a class play is basically a sequence of lessons), it is nearly impossible to realize the pedagogical intentions of a play. The Pedagogical Law necessitates working out of equanimity; and the teacher who is faced repeatedly with the unexpected will become frazzled and thereby driven by the excitable impulses of astrality and not the calm, focused guidance of the ego. This results in the students not being able to work rhythmically and enthusiastically to establish the level of form that is demanded by a social and aesthetic process such as a play. To entertain the attitude that "they will pull it together in the end" is not a productive pedagogical attitude but rather the equivalent of high stakes testing without preparation.

It is also important at this point to address the proper role of scheduling in a play production to the rest of the school. There is a bad habit in schools to allow productions to get out of hand and dominate the students' school life for weeks on end. Having fallen into that pit in the early years of my career, I've crossed the river, so to speak, and now preach against it. School should be modeling for the students a socially hygienic balance between the different subjects and how they work together, not robbing Peter to pay Paul.

Producing theater is time intensive, and the amount of time made available for a play, like any subject, should be scheduled into the school-year, and the teacher should plan accordingly and not exceed it. In my experience, every minute of stage time requires an hour of rehearsal. If you have a fifteen to twenty-minute class play in the primary grades, its rehearsals can easily be worked into the periods a class teacher has available. But if you have a forty-minute play, you will need approximately forty periods. And if you have a ninety-minute play, you are going to need proportionally more periods. This time needs to be scheduled, just as any art block or main lesson would be. After all, a play should not supersede the math, English, science, modern languages, movement, music, or studio arts curriculum in an educational program that strives for balance in teaching.

In high school and sometimes in the middle school, teachers schedule additional rehearsals after school and on weekends. The reason given for the practice is that the students need the time. It is, nonetheless, pedagogically inappropriate. Yes, they do need time—for regular school work, for after-school activities, for jobs, for sports, and for family and personal time, not extra classes. If the scale of the play is appropriate, and the number of periods is available for scheduling, then such extra time is simply an intrusion on everyone. Of course, an emergency may arise; but that is an entirely different issue.

Deadlines

Another key aspect of scheduling is establishing deadlines for each part of the production. While some deadlines will be flexible, others must be absolute, even though last moment crises will arise, such as props breaking, costumes tearing, someone announcing three days before performance, "I need to make a college visit but will be back in time for the opening curtain." Every type of student responsibility, whether performance or technical, needs its deadlines. While the performers and tech crew will be on different schedules, there will be crossing points where their work comes together. Deliberately planning when these points happen will keep the various jobs coordinated, allowing each group to work in creative support of each other, and make the final run-through week more productive and satisfying for everyone.

For actors, their first major deadline should be their being mostly off-book about a quarter of the way into the rehearsal schedule and completely off-book no later than two-thirds of the way through. Except in a very short play, it is unrealistic to expect the principals to be fully off-book by one date. (Although I have known students playing major roles to come to the first read-through completely off-book). Rather, a sequence of dates, about a week to ten days apart is realistic. The supporting and minor roles should follow this same sequence. Children in the lower grades usually have no problem getting off-book, especially when they learn their lines orally through imitating their teacher—an instance of healthy authority at work. In middle and high school where memory forces are significantly challenged by the turmoil of puberty, a good technique for getting all the students off-book is to have them periodically sit in a circle and do a speed-through of the play, having them recite the lines as quickly as possible. When lapses of memory arise the student should simply call out "line" and be thrown the needed line. If someone is woefully unprepared, embarrassment will have its corrective effect.

Similarly, the music needs to follow the actors' schedule closely and become part of the rehearsals as early as possible, thereby providing the opportunity for it to become the integral part of the performance that it should be. Patching music in at the end only generates unproductive tensions; it is much healthier for everyone working with the living elements of the musical design to feel fully comfortable with each other. Such comfort also provides the opportunity for the music to evolve with the development of the performances.

Costuming is universal in pedagogical theater. Scheduling it well is essential. About a week into the production, the costume crew needs to submit a set of sketches for the full costuming. Once approved, they will need dates for several interim fittings, as well as opportunities to watch the actors rehearse in costume, leaving time for alterations. They will also need a date for the first close-to-full-dress rehearsals. Since the actual wearing of a costume helps the actor so much in developing a character, the sooner the majority of this work is finished the more creatively productive it will be. And understanding what can be made and what needs to be bought or rented is where the experienced supervision of a skilled seamstress is most helpful.

The initial technical designs of the production should be completed about a week into production. Having this work well scheduled will help greatly in avoiding problems in the final weeks of the production when available time grows increasingly precious. Even though sets, props, and costumes take a long time to build, they need be completed, except for adjustments and finish work, by the beginning of the run-throughs, thereby allowing the actors to get used to working with them. In this vein, it is wise to make sure the lighting crew has unfettered access to the stage and theater at least a week before the first performance, which will allow them to have the lights up and operating so the actors can rehearse with them during the run-throughs. The sound crew will not need similar access to the performance space; they simply need to be ready.

In most school situations, a full set cannot be erected onstage earlier than a week or two before the performance, although movable pieces such as furniture and platforms can and should be used much earlier. A simple set can be set up in a short time, but even a simple set will need modification when actually seen onstage from the auditorium. With a full or variable set, such as would be needed in the *Inspector General, Playboy of the Western World,* or *The Skin of Our Teeth,* it will take several days to get the whole thing assembled, finished, and tested. In such cases, one will need to anticipate everybody sharing the stage at once. This is the only time one should experience chaos in the production; but even then, the word chaos is only vernacular for lots of not-immediately-related things going on simultaneously in time and space.

When handled well, deadlines strengthen the ensemble working of a class. Each time a deadline is successfully met, the students strengthen their feeling of being an ensemble, thereby adding to the artistic success of their creative work together.

Giving Grades

Giving students individual grades for theatrical productions is inherently problematic because the type and amount of work each student can actually do varies from role to role, assignment to assignment, and thereby from student to student. A principal actor does very different work from a supporting actor; and an actor's work and performance is completely different from a member of the tech crew. Although I would delight in not being under an obligation to give grades for a high school class play, it is simply impossible to avoid it if the school gives grades and credits for everything. Therefore, the teacher-director needs to come up with a system of grading that establishes as much common criteria as possible but allows for the natural differences of roles and responsibilities.

One solution is to have a three-part grading system. One part is for meeting deadlines, such as being off-book for actors and having a prescribed amount of assigned work completed for the tech crew. A second part is for engagement with the work: how the individual actors participate in rehearsals to move the production forward and how much the individual members of the various tech crews actually accomplish. A third part is for quality of the performance itself. The first two parts are individual grades, while the third part is a group grade that reflects the social, collaborative nature of theater.

Chapter 3
Directing

Playwriting and directing are the fraternal twins of theater. Playwriting is solitary; it happens in a private space that allows for innumerable mistakes, changes, reversed changes, and expressions of frustration, none of which ever meets a critical eye. Directing is social; it happens in the public space of the rehearsal hall and before potentially critical eyes. The pedagogical playwright can spend days developing a scene, even weeks composing a whole play, then decide it is unfit and discard it without anyone's knowing or caring. The pedagogical director, however, is first and foremost a teacher; and, as such, is subject to the same type of scrutiny that would result from confusing assignments, ineffective teaching, poor classroom management, or over-excited behavior and remarks.

The director carries the artistic vision of a play, and directing is the art of taking a dramatic text, and through collaborative, creative work with performers, designers, and technicians, raising it into a performance. There are many styles of directing: some intellectual; some emotional; some imitative; some participatory; some prescriptive; some suggestive; some collaborative; some from the front of the house; some from the back, and some up onstage. All have value for pedagogical theater, but some should be used with much more caution and restraint than others.

Every director has a preferred style, so being prescriptive about how one should direct runs counter to directing's very nature. That said, there are some pedagogical guidelines that, when followed, help greatly in making a class play a valuable educational experience for the students. First, the teacher-director needs to enthusiastically inspire the students with his or her imagination of the play. Second, the directing, as in any class, must be dynamic and not static; it should develop out of activity and not talk. As a teacher, the pedagogical director needs to understand what the students need to do in class and not only what the director wants. And finally, the directing should create a space for the play itself to become manifest on the stage.

A director should not hold a play too tightly in the beginning; too firm and rigid a grasp will only stymie its development. It is better to begin the rehearsal process with only lightly held, guiding concepts of the play, leaving a generous amount of room for the complexity of its meaning to be revealed in rehearsals. Of course, one must study a play thoroughly beforehand and form vivid imaginations about how it will appear and sound onstage—how key pieces of action can be done with the available resources; how the actors will work within the set and what their physical location onstage will mean;

and how the mood of the different scenes should feel for the audience. But it is wise not to become too definite, too soon, for too many things; or one risks choking off the creative impulses that will manifest themselves in the rehearsals. The essential thing is to provide plenty of room for the play to grow, develop, and tell you, the director, what it is becoming.

A good rehearsal is a circle of interwoven, individual imaginations, whether the director and actors are consciously aware of this or not. If the rehearsal space provides generous openings for the collaborative imaginative work, the rehearsal will breathe, and through its breathing receive the inspirations that are necessary to raise the process to the level of art. Imagination and inspiration are spiritual faculties of the human being, the former being individual and seeding the future; and the latter being social and generously active in the process of collaborative creativity. When these two forces are working well, they invite a third spiritual force, intuition, to enlighten and reveal what needs to be done. All three forces working together are, I suspect, what the ancients experienced as the singing of the Muse.

Some imaginations that arise in the rehearsal process can be metamorphosed into a higher form and become part of the performance, while others simply exist briefly in their "how about this?" moment and are then discarded. Viable imaginations, time after time, whether from teacher or student, inspire and enlighten the forward movement of the creative process and bring the play closer to its realization. It is the pedagogical responsibility of the director to guide this creative dialogue so that the play, as with any school course, broadens and deepens the students' experiences as it progresses from day to day. Such a way of working creates a vessel for what lives in the play to become manifest. When this process is the most vital, the type of *theatrical moments* described earlier come into being. These are "aha!" moments that lift all theater above mere entertainment.

At the heart of good pedagogical directing is "reading" the students.† Carefully reading how a student moves, stands, gestures, watches, speaks, listens will reveal what type of direction the student needs and can actually and safely use. Thoughtful reading of students in rehearsal gives rise to directorial imaginations that would have been impossible if the director had allowed his or her initial imaginations to become too hardened. Those original imaginations were simply personal imaginations, seeds. If viable, these seeds need a medium and external forces to grow and bloom. In pedagogical theater, the medium and forces are the collaborative work of rehearsal as led by the director.

Practically, this "reading" technique can work as follows: after introducing the general action, idea, and blocking of a scene, the teacher-director stands onstage with the actors but slightly off to the side and behind them. If the director's position is static then

† This "reading" entails the same type of careful and reflective child observation that a Waldorf teacher practices as a fundamental part of his or her work. In rehearsal, however, there is a much more immediate and spontaneous component to this activity than in a classroom setting, since a rehearsal is not a presentation by the teacher but a shared creative process between the student-performers and the teacher-director.

the "reading" is far more limited than if she or he, as unobtrusively as possible, crosses from side to side, up and down, and occasionally downstage-front. The students very quickly become used to this movement and pay it little attention.

The reason for this placement and movement is two-fold. First, it allows the director to identify sympathetically with the physical situation of the scene and the actor within its space. The second reason is the more subtle and more important. By working from the "back-space," a sensitive director can sense reflected in him- or herself the unfolding effectiveness of the scene, sensing in his or her own physical body and voice the gestures, large and small, that the particular student could use. Since this technique entails the most careful, sensitive, and discreet imitative observation on the director's part, it is, I suspect, akin to the experience of a young child when creatively mimicking an activity. Only when a scene begins to "have legs" should the director move into the auditorium; but even then not only to one place but rather move about, watching and listening from a variety of locations, assuming now the perspective and sensitivity of the audience.

Since rehearsing is repetition, it is never good to repeat something that is not working well. Every time a line, gesture, movement, or interactions is made in rehearsal, the actors are physically and emotionally memorizing it. Therefore, it is important to correct such problems immediately. To this end, it is essential to establish a method of politely interrupting student-actors and offering alternatives in a way that does not cause them to feel set-upon or frazzled. And here is another advantage to working intensely from the actor's backspace: one becomes particularly sensitive to the student-actors' feelings and can sense when to interrupt appropriately. Directing from a seat in the front of the auditorium and talking is too passive and intellectual, getting in the way of sensitive, improvisational imaginative activity.

One actual example of this technique will suffice. In a recent tenth grade production of *Les Misérables,* the student who was cast as Marius' grandfather was having a great deal of difficulty breaking out of his normally very reserved manner of moving. His reserve was so severe that his scenes had no life. The assistant director who had been working on this scene was deeply troubled and at a loss for what to do. He had made suggestions, but nothing had worked, so he asked me what I suggested. I suggested nothing, but had the students run the scene while I sat in a chair in the same position as the boy, focusing on him and making myself a reflection of his presence onstage.

As I watched I noticed that his arms extended perpendicular from his torso and his hands lay flat and unmoving on the table. It was as if he was holding himself to the table with this gesture. It then came to me that he needed to be given a new gesture for his arms, a transformed and dynamic version of the static one. When the scene was finished I said, "Here, you stand next to me and watch; this might help." I sat exactly as he had while the other actors spoke their lines; then when the grandfather said, "As it should be. Who fouled your mind with such a vulgar tale?" I angrily flipped my hands and forearms upward on "As" and on "be" slapped them down loudly. I then asked the boy to do exactly what I had done, and he imitated me with great delight. From then on the scene worked. The key here is that he was able to use the tense rigidity of his earlier gesture to trigger and release an expressive gesture. From then on his voice also developed a new expressive character, lyrical and condescending, a manner of speech as remote from his normal voice as his original gesture had been from the new one. From then on he delighted in the role and being in a play.

Of course, if such a suggestion does not work, one should not press it but explore alternate, more comfortable gestures. By the student suggesting, the teacher-director modeling, and the student then imitating, the correct gesture will most probably appear. Work of this type should not be done with more than the fellow actors in the scene, and they should be discreetly told that patient support is being asked of them. Such work will take time, perhaps the best part of the rehearsal period; but the time spent will be worth it. It is also an important idea to review and rehearse in the very next rehearsal what was achieved in such sessions, even if it disrupts the established schedule. And of paramount importance, once the scene has some legs, have the actors perform it for the class so they can receive their classmates' heart-felt applause.

A key difference between grade and high school directing is that high school should strive for the highest possible standard for theater as a performing art. Therefore, it is important, primarily in senior year, to coax the students to take a play where it needs to go. The following examples from a production of Wilder's *The Skin of Our Teeth* will illustrate the value of pushing scenes. In the third act Mrs. Antrobus and her daughter Gladys are reunited with Sabina in the ruins of the Antrobus home after a terrible world war. When reading the following scene it is important to know that these two women have been nemeses throughout the play, but that Mrs. Antrobus had saved Sabina in the closing cataclysm of Act Two, even though Sabina had just attempted to steal her husband. Essentially Sabina is returning home.

SABINA'S VOICE: *(Off)*
Mrs. An-tro-bus!

MRS. ANTROBUS AND GLADYS:
What's that?!!

SABINA'S VOICE: *(Off)*
Glaaaadys! Mrs. An-tro-bus!

MRS. ANTROBUS:
Gladys, that's Sabina's voice as sure as I live.

[Enter Sabina]
—Sabina! Sabina! Are you alive?!!

SABINA:
Of course, I'm alive. How've you girls been? —Don't try and kiss me. I never want to kiss another human being as long as I live. Sh-sh, there's nothing to get emotional about. Pull yourself together, the war's over. Take a deep breath—the war's over.

MRS. ANTROBUS:
The war's over!! I don't believe you. I don't believe you. I can't believe you.

GLADYS:
Mama!

SABINA:
Who's that?

MRS. ANTROBUS:
That's Gladys and her baby. Gladys, Sabina says the war's over. Oh, Sabina.

SABINA: *[Leaning over BABY.]*
Goodness! Are there any babies left in the world! Can it see? And can it cry and everything?

The line "Oh, Sabina" began to become problematic; none of us could come up with an appropriate reading. It just stuck there until I noticed that on the "Oh" the actress playing Mrs. Antrobus, who was standing very close to Sabina, rotated towards "Gladys" and then back to Sabina, all the while holding her hands at her side. Then I saw the solution; Mrs. Antrobus was holding back the feeling needed (an appropriate gesture, mind you, for Mrs. Antrobus) for the line by keeping her hands lowered. "Take her hands," I said. The Mrs. Antrobus actress crumbled and said emphatically, "NO!" "Try," I coaxed; "it will be beautiful; you'll move the house to tears." "I can't." "Try it just once; if it doesn't work, drop it." "Okay." So she took Sabina's hands on the "Oh, Sabina" and Sabina began to cry natural tears and the actress playing Mrs. Antrobus embraced her with a great hug. "Well," I said, "Mrs. Antrobus doesn't show that much feeling." We all laughed, and I asked the reticent actress whether it worked for her. "Yes," she said; "it makes the line." Which it did, but not just the line or even the scene; it gave Mrs. Antrobus her dramatic climax and allowed the character to move graciously into her denouement.

The second example is from the closing of the second act which requires a very well-coordinated and violent hurricane soundscape over which the Antrobus family and Sabina must desperately find each other and reconcile their estrangements. In the rehearsals the sound crew was simply lackadaisical about hitting the cues just right. It began to become very frustrating as we ran the scene over and over again, since getting the timing exactly coordinated was essential or the scene would seem silly. Finally one of the sound board crew got annoyed and began to argue that the scene was too hard so why bother with it. He, fortunately, said, "And after all, it's just a play." At times a director needs to come down on such an attitude like a ton of bricks on the side of the actors and the show and, quite frankly, one's personal artistic visions and demand, "Then make it work!" Faced with no other choice, they became attentive and with each subsequent run-through the sound and light work became as brilliant as the acting on the stage. But the director must never forget that s/he has only one or two times when this can be done in a production.

And finally, in addition to the vision, design, and management of the play, the director carries responsibility for the physical and emotional well-being of the students.

Physical safety is largely a function of good stage-room management during rehearsals and performances, and is usually ensured by a safe set, classroom routines, and expectations that keep horseplay to an absolute minimum. Ensuring emotional safety is far more challenging and, as such, requires constant attention to the Pedagogical Law, as well as vigilance about how students are working with their characters, especially in emotionally intense or volatile scenes.

Chapter 4
Rehearsals

Rehearsals[24] are where the creative work of a play is done, for the students and the director. It is when the text is made actual through the creative dialogue of directing; when the students develop characterizations; when the various meanings of the text become manifest; and when the students practice working together as an ensemble. Rehearsals entail six components: orientation and warm-up, blocking, developing characterization, concentration, discovering and expressing emotions and meaning, and review.

Orientation and Warm Up

It is good to start every rehearsal period with a brief teacher overview of what was accomplished in the preceding rehearsal. Have the students share their impressions of how things are going, entertain questions, and then sketch out who will be doing what that day. Having everyone seated allows this to be done as efficiently as possible. This activity can be followed by warm-up exercises. All told, no more than ten to fifteen minutes, tops, should be spent in this work.

For their warm-ups many teachers have had great success in middle and high school with improvisational theater games, as found in Viola Spolin's *Theater Games for the Classroom* and *Theater Games for Rehearsal.* Having done games like these as a teenager in my acting training, I appreciate their value in a formal, drama school context, but find them unnecessary in a class that has been working as an ensemble for years, preferring instead three simple but powerful exercises: one from lower school opening exercises, one of my own devising, and the third borrowed from eurythmy. Because of the limited time scheduled for rehearsing, it is good to keep the warm-up short and potent.

In middle school and up, with variations according to age, class disposition, and real time available, I use the following set of exercises. We form a circle, establishing its roundness and even spacing. This exercise is usually the hardest since it entails taking mastery of one's self in the emotionally charged, overlapping spaces of adolescence. Once the circle is stable, we begin a simple expansion and contraction exercise, similar to what one might do with a class in second or third grade. The exercise develops into one step in, two steps out, three steps in, four steps out, then reverses. The goal of the exercise is to get back as close as possible to one's starting position. It is good to do this exercise several times; students generally like the challenge of overcoming their distraction and getting it right. If the activity has been successful, it is repeated with eyes closed, which is very challenging, and the class likes to see how well they did it together. The next exercise is a simple character exercise in which we step back from the circle, inwardly and silently identify our character in the play, and imagine the character as a heap, like clothing, on the floor before us. We then step forward and don the character, not just the clothing but the whole "costume" of temperament, personality, gait, body language, facial expression, and voice. We then wander about the stage greeting each other, always in character. The object here is to find one's character and exercise self-control over the silliness the activity can stimulate. The last exercise is adapted from eurythmy and consists of a set of variations on the long "e" and "u" tones using the words "me" and "you," accompanied by the respective eurythmy vowel gestures. We do all sorts of expressive variations, one proud, another humble, one sympathetic, another aggressive, one serious, the next humorous, expanding the circle with the "e" and contracting it with the "u." This last exercise was designed to remind everyone that theater is an art of emotive polarities, and one must hold these polarities consciously and respectfully, even when having fun. The exercises close with a quiet circle before everyone heads off to their jobs.

Blocking

Blocking is the precise physical and aesthetically meaningful movement of actors from location to location onstage and how they occupy those locations; it pertains not just to the two-dimensional plane of the stage's surface, but also to the stage as a three-dimensional performance space. In addition to establishing where and how the actors move and stand onstage, blocking, as with costuming and make-up, is a key aspect of the element of spectacle. Just as the tone and rhythm of speech express the feeling needed to support the meaning of the words spoken, so blocking further expresses and enhances the element of idea through the physically and aesthetically appropriate use of body movement, gesture, and the spatial relationships of the actors.

The surest way to learn blocking is to watch plays, lots of plays, and, ideally, experience theater as an actor. If neither of these are possible, then directing from the stage, as described earlier, will help the teacher-director develop sensitivity for and capability in the art, since every teacher needs to have a keen sensitivity to his or her personal space and its relationship to and effect on the personal space of the students. Similarly, blocking entails the same combination of clear and precise instructions, supported by encouraging visual signals, that is essential for effective instruction and good classroom management. And finally, blocking requires that the teacher-director be able to move, stand, and gesture in a way that the students can easily and comfortably imitate.

Establishing a system for the draft sketching and final recording of blocking is essential since it is so easy to forget, especially after long intervals between specific scene rehearsals. For this the director-script format described in the earlier section on preparing the script proves most useful. After sketching out my initial blocking ideas, I enter these sketches on the blank page facing the text. My sketches are modeled on the type of form choreography used by eurythmists and basketball or football coaches. First, I sketch simple indicator lines and shapes for the stage's boundaries and whatever set or furniture the scene contains. Then, referenced to the facing text, I sketch the two-dimensional movement of the actors as it would appear from above. And finally, I make a simple stick figure drawing of how the actors would appear from the audience. All this work is done in pencil and serves as the starting point for the actual blocking with the students.

Fortunately, learning blocking, like memorizing lines, is easy for Waldorf students. All the time they have spent moving in class, whether in opening exercises or eurythmy, not only makes following and learning blocking easy, but also gives the students an inner feel for working creatively with it.

With younger children, blocking largely consists of creating dynamic, ever-shifting choral tableaus that create the illusion of acting. These tableaus are human sculptural forms; and if visually interesting (and the performance space not too large), they replace scenery. From out of these tableaus the individual children step to speak and enact their parts, the other students moving in choreographed forms with and around them. In this way the performance is kept safely within limits of the children's abilities, while the audience, even if it is only the children themselves, is able to easily follow and respond to what is being presented. The blocking challenge here is to create a feeling of fluidity in what is essentially a fairly static technique. This illusion of tonal and gestural fluidity imparts life to the activity onstage and is the essence of what makes a lower-grades' class play theatrical.

The pedagogical intention behind this technique is social. First, it reinforces conscious spatial orientation and conscious purposeful movement of the individual within a group. Second, it serves as the foundation for class ensemble work, which is at the root of pedagogical theater. These fundamental ensemble skills are difficult to develop and require that each individual listen and speak, stand and move in a way that supports what is being developed within the group, as a class of individuals who are learning, through an artistic activity, how to carry a sense of personal and social responsibility for the whole.

From middle school on, blocking, while always a social activity, becomes more individually oriented. The student-actor must develop a much more self-aware sense of him- or herself in the performance space. The same technique for sketching out the blocking can be used, but now the student should develop a sense for why his or her character is moving where and as he or she does. Blocking from now on will change from its initial sketches to its final forms much more than in the earlier grades, as the creative dialogue between director and actors evolves. By senior year, the blocking sketches will serve simply as common, starting markers from which everyone branches out to discover the play's "being" in space.

Expressing credible action and emotions is one of the great challenges for student-actors. How the actor moves and stands is the foundation of this work, but that is only the broadest level of expression, the one that is used with younger children in the blocking method described above. Of equal importance are the more subtle and intimate aspects of expression, particularly what is communicated through the eyes and hand gestures. In professional theater these expressions would fall more under characterization than blocking; but in theatrical work with children and adolescents, it is best to treat them as a subtle form of blocking.

An audience is always tracking facial, ocular, and manual expressions, seeking in them deeper meanings than the text of the play can convey. Natural modesty, however, makes it difficult for children to know what to do with their eyes because eyes are so revealing of their inner being.[25] As a result, the teacher-director needs to sense what the student can do and model the appropriate expressions for the student's imitation. Here again the guiding principle of character as costume helps in tempering and even overcoming reticence.

Chapter 5
Characterization

Once the rough blocking is established, the work of characterization begins. It is a discovery process, and is the most intimate, revealing, and creatively enjoyable part of theater for everyone since we all like playing at or imagining being someone else. Characterization is basically the most living aspect of costume the actor wears when performing a part and is thereby the primary vehicle for the ideas of the plays. It is also the hardest with which to work since it is the most intimately connected to the individuality of the performer, being developed out of the actor's body, voice, and very way of moving. (Think how often we call a character by the actor's name.) And herein lurks the most challenging aspect of theater from a pedagogical perspective. Characterization is built on an imaginative imitation of a fantastical "someone else's" body and soul, founded in a literary text and created out of the student's maturing self-knowledge. Like all forms of metaphoric expression, it describes something by what it is not. In short, it is a truth-filled lie; and as such, must be handled with care.[26]

When directing children younger than fifth grade, the text itself and what the children imitate in the teacher should provide the characterization, and all that a teacher-director should expect is that the children appreciate their role's function in the story of the play, and understand their lines and speak them expressively. Of course, simple things like a change of voice or a different way of walking is important, especially when playing Loki, Thor, or the Queen of the Noise Giants, but the type of creative character building that can start in middle school is inappropriate and should be avoided in these lower grades.

There are two reasons for delaying direct work with characterization before middle school, one pedagogical and the other practical. Children before middle school are too young for the type of conscious emotional expression required by true characterization. It is an ability that comes into being with the birthing of the astral body. To awaken this astrality prematurely has no place in pedagogical theater. On the practical side, one of the basic realities of putting groups of young children onstage is that they can only go into character when they are actively doing something, speaking lines or moving deliberately, such as stamping around as noise giants. Otherwise, they can only stand onstage in a costume, unable to summon the type of artistic concentration that true theatrical characterization requires.

From middle school on, students can begin to move toward creating actual characterization. When this transition is handled properly, it is an excellent activity for exploring, as Steiner's "To Wonder at Beauty" verse states, "the width of the world" and "the depth of the soul." One of the key values of theater with adolescents, whether they are just entering adolescence or in its full sway, is that it provides an artistic platform for exploring, as do literature and history, the many ways we are human. Middle school students are just beginning to develop an ability to objectify events and experiences and practically emancipate themselves from subjectivity; but their thinking is still dominated by their feelings. As in all other aspects of Waldorf Education, theatrical characterization, working out of an age appropriate story and in support of an age appropriate idea, provides an avenue by which purposeful activity can connect children's will with their thinking through the feelings that an imaginative activity activates.

The developing of characterization in adolescence is psychologically complex and thereby potentially problematic. Since the costume of character is worn by the astral, or soul body, the director has to be particularly alert as to how the students create and work with their characterizations. An effective starting point is to begin by having the students establish a character-costume that includes a manner of speaking and a set of simple defining gestures, such as a distinctive way of standing, walking, or holding one's hands at rest. (Thus the reason for the warm-up exercises described earlier.) If a student is unable to come up with anything, just supply something and allow the student to personalize it. Then in rehearsal the teacher-director can intensify or tone down the characterizations, until each student has fully discovered how to express the role's character. The teacher all the while keeps a careful watch that individual students do not drift into or become overwhelmed by the fantastical nature of characterization.

Students should do homework with their characters that extends beyond merely memorizing lines. They need to work-up specific types of inflections and gestures, listening carefully to their own voices and observing closely their gestures. When building a character, one is essentially dressing oneself in a mask and costume of character; and practicing gestures before a mirror can be helpful for some students, but not for others. Simply speaking with the students about how they feel before the mirror will guide the teacher as to whether the practice should be encouraged or discouraged. In this way the student-actors begin to emancipate themselves from being just rote imitators of their teacher. By bringing this individual homework into rehearsal and joining it with the homework of the other students, the class is fulfilling one of the purposes of pedagogical theater—learning how to be true collaborators out of one's own creativity in an artistic, social process. The director's job, of course, is to keep all this work balanced and healthy.

In the earlier section on casting, the three methods of pedagogical casting were addressed. One method utilized how some aspect of the personality of the student reflects the character; a second how the character reflects who the student should strive to be; and the third what character a particular student-actors can credibly play. Creating characterizations reflects whichever method is used, and most plays will allow for a combination of these methods, even though one will naturally predominate over the others, depending on the students' age.

Adaptations of Dickens are a rich source for middle and high school class plays. In terms of characterization, few authors, other than Shakespeare or Hugo, provide as rich an opportunity to utilize all three casting-characterization methods. And *A Tale of Two Cities* is one of the richest in this regard. There are the nobly idealized characters such as Sydney Carton, Lucy and Doctor Manette, and Mr. Lorry. There are morally ambiguous characters such as Monsieur DeFarge. There are the monstrous characters such as Madame DeFarge, the Marquis Evrémonde, and The Vengeance. And there are the vast array of grotesques and caricatures, such as Jerry Cruncher and Miss Pross, that populate Dickens' world. *Oliver Twist* and *A Christmas Carol*, along with Hugo's *Les Misérable*, Shakespeare's *A Midsummer's Night Dream*, and Gogol's *Inspector General*, present a similarly broad range for different types of casting and characterization.

From the twentieth century dramatic canon, we get a similar if more restrained range. Synge's comedy *Playboy of the Western World* is a wonderful play for twelfth graders in that it allows them to play characters who are very close to their own ages, resulting in the students' being able to play, in the broadest meaning of the word, some aspect of themselves while feeling a safe, comic remove. Another aspect of *Playboy* that appeals to twelfth graders is that, like *A Midsummer's Night Dream*, it is about what happens when astrality breaks free of social restraints. Brecht's *Caucasian Chalk Circle* and *The Good Person of Szechuan* provide high school students the opportunity to play highly objectified, archetypal characters, providing a safe distance between themselves and their characters, while still mining their own self-knowledge for the characterization.

Concentration

Concentration is essential for an effective performance. While it is an aspect of characterization, it is good to comment on it briefly in its own right. There are two type of stage concentration. The first is staying in character, especially when not speaking or doing a piece of character-related stage business. The second type is using one's concentration either to focus the audience's attention on the central action of a scene, or to deliberately distract their attention for a dramatic purpose. Once again, Waldorf students have an excellent foundation in this regard, having done a wide variety of concentration work since first grade in eurythmy class and the opening exercises of main lesson.

Before puberty, group activity provides concentration, and herein lies another reason for short scene play architecture; choral speaking that alternates between different groups and individuals; and the alternating choreography-tableau style of blocking. These techniques disguise the near impossibility for young children to concentrate individually in a way that gives the audience the illusion of focused action, feeling, and thought. With eighth grade and up, the need for each individual student-actor to concentrate on staying in character onstage becomes a responsibility akin to staying on pitch and rhythm in a chorus or orchestra, or keeping one's eye on the ball in a sporting event.

Staying in character requires having something to do onstage, either outwardly through speaking, gesturing, or active listening to other characters; or inwardly through a silent monologue that is characteristic of the role and pertinent to the action of the scene. It is good to practice the inward type of characterization in the rehearsal warm-up and have the students also practice it at home and among themselves when learning lines, since learning a role involves repetitive rehearsal. If an actor learns a role without concentration, that will be what s/he will carry into rehearsals and have to unlearn.

With high school students, there are two concentration exercises that can be done within the rehearsing of scenes. Both should start very early in the rehearsal process, since their power exists in their repetition. They are called *Freeze* and *Center*. In the first one, the director approaches a student-actor during a run-through and places his or her hand on the student's head and says, "Freeze!" Everyone freezes in mid-motion as in the children's game Red Rover. Then the director asks the selected actor, "What is your *character* thinking?" The actor must tell what the character's thoughts are. Naturally, there is little to say the first time the game is played. But as the students become familiar with the exercise, they realize that their character needs to have something to say. Such an exercise, when practiced randomly in rehearsal, stimulates concentration. *Center* has a similar effect. Anywhere in a scene the director calls out, "Center!" All the actors then point to the focal point of the scene's action. As with Freeze, which develops individual concentration, this exercise encourages, develops, and strengthens ensemble concentration. The ultimate goal of these exercises is that the students stay in character and thereby work together theatrically.

Discovering Meaning and Expressing Emotions

Meaning is first discovered by reading and thinking about the text; and second, by repetitively rehearsing the text and leaving oneself open to the inspirations that can only become manifest through enactment.

When an actor enacts seeing and gesturing what the character sees and does, the audience will read the action as intended, suspend their natural disbelief, and accept the imagination of the play. In this way, characterization is at the heart of the type of communication and understanding that theater creates. Two examples from two widely different age groups illustrate this principle.

If, for instance, Moses needs to stab the Egyptian overseer, there is really no need for a rubber prop knife unless the visual image of the brandished knife is important. All that needs to happen is that both the assailant and the victim "see" the knife; then the gestures of stabbing and falling are convincingly portrayed. Similarly, the same holds for that most uncomfortable piece of stage business, the kiss. In *Les Misérables* just as Marius is leaving Cossette for the barricades, the story demands that they kiss. Now, when the students read this in the script one couldn't hear a canon go off over the cries of "Oh, my god!" and "I won't do that!" and "I quit!" Sure, one solution would be to have Marius take her in his arms and upstage the "kiss" so that "nothing happened" will not be seen by the audience. But that type of business will still be awkward. The best thing is to have Cossette cry out, "One kiss!" reaching longingly to Marius, who is reaching toward her; then just as their fingers are about to touch, fill the theater with the sound of gunfire from the barricades, and have Marius break free and exit. You can bet good money that most of the middle school girls in the audience will swear that they saw the kiss.

Review

Review is an integral part of the rhythmic sequence of lessons from day to day in Waldorf Education. In theater the review, or notes, generally happens when the director and stage manager go over with the actors all the notes taken in that rehearsal. The intention is to give immediate feedback so that the actors can practice what is needed in preparation for the next rehearsal. This process is very time-consuming, and has limited value immediately after a rehearsal with middle and high school students who are tired and impatient and need to get on to the next thing in their day. It is one of the necessary conventions of the theater that does not translate well to a school situation involving a class of students who have varying degrees of interest in the process. Yet, review is necessary.

Before middle school it is best done at the beginning of each rehearsal. The teacher can simply reiterate with the children what went well and why, and then explain, equally briefly, what will be done that day to make the play better. No criticism should be involved, simply a generous sprinkling of compliments designed to generate enthusiasm for the rehearsal. In middle and high school, post-rehearsal reviews can be done, but it is essential to keep them very short and succinct. I've found a simple explanation of what is going well and what needs work to be sufficient; longer explanations go largely unheard. The important thing is to present what needs to be done prior to the next rehearsal; in other words, the homework. Given the busyness of a student's day and all the different things that need to be kept organized and completed each night, I've found it to be more effective to give specific instructions about character or stage business at the beginning of a rehearsal, just after the opening exercises. At this time the students are most attentive and able to apply what has been suggested. To expect the average middle or high school student to remember notes overnight or over a weekend is unrealistic.

Neither is it a productive use of valuable time to spend a lot of time sharing notes during the final days of a production. It is much more valuable to have brief discussion about what the students felt about the previous rehearsal's strengths and weaknesses, and what they as a class need to do in light of their observations. High school students need to engage in this type of productive, self-critiquing work, and they need to do it out of themselves, assisted, of course, by their teacher's guidance and encouragement. They know what was strong and weak in their work; and most importantly, they know that the remedy is working together in support of each other as a class. In short, they know what it means to be an ensemble.

Speaking Onstage

Well-formed speech is at the heart of the class play. It must enliven, rather than deaden its listeners to the beauty and meaning of the story. In well-crafted language a creative partnership exists between its rhythms and tones, and its images and ideas. The imagistic nature of language awakens thoughts and sharpens consciousness while its rhythmic-tonal nature elevates consciousness into its imaginative state. Well-crafted and well-spoken language brings these qualities into a lively dynamic tension, and each sound, syllable, word, phrase, and line when well spoken faithfully serves what the text strives to express.

Children need to be taught how to speak verse properly, and this is especially true when speaking in unison. The best method of instruction in the art of articulate and expressive speaking is imitation. The teacher speaks the lines as they should be spoken, and the children repeat them imitatively. It is key that the teacher presents the tempo, volume, tone, and meaning of the words and phrases in a way that encourages the children to imitate his or her manner of speaking the text appropriately. One should never forget that each time something is repeated poorly, it is learned poorly; and that each time something is repeated well, it is learned well.

In the middle school, the students' speech often becomes careless. It is of the utmost importance, therefore, that they continue to receive speech training, especially in how to modulate the tones and rhythms of speech and how to articulate metaphoric language. It is sad to hear middle-schoolers recite mechanically and dully, giving only the slightest indication of what their words are expressing. Daily recitation, accompanied by textual interpretation, is the best way to train their voices for the delivery of a theatrical text. Once articulate speaking skills are developed, they can be taught how to use different speech patterns for verse or prose to create the voices of the characters they are playing. By eighth grade, it is important that they understand that the rhythms of the language are like the rhythms of breath and pulse; they are always there, carrying life, but rarely brought up to wakeful consciousness, except during the extraordinary circumstances of artistic expression.

High schoolers present their own set of challenges. Most adolescents hold their voices within their mouths and have difficulty appreciating how they sound. The pedagogical director, therefore, needs to work patiently with overcoming this problem; or quite frankly, they will not be heard or understood by an audience. The key here is doing speech exercises that teach the students how to form their voices and place them effectively and expressively outside of themselves. In addition to speech formation exercises that develop articulation, a good exercise for learning how to project the voice is to pick a spot in the house and have each student repeatedly practice "aiming and throwing" his or her voice towards it. Students should also practice hearing their own voices larger than normal but not shouting in the performance space. Using a ninth grade theater skills class is an excellent place to start, but the exercises should also be a preliminary part of every production.

Chapter 6
The Performance

About three weeks before the first performance, individual scenes and sequences of scenes start to "stand upright" and move forward on their own accord, and one feels that the play is developing its own gait. Part of this "having legs" is that the teacher-director and student-actors begin to discover things about the play that had been previously hidden, and their original vision not only becomes clearer, but also undergoes a metamorphosis. The teacher-director may even feel that there is still time to experiment with different ways of playing lines and even blocking scenes. In truth, there isn't. Nothing new should be added from this point forward. Attention should be on strengthening and deepening what has already been developed, and the director has to understand that the really hard work, the work most critical for the students' feelings of creative accomplishment (and thereby the play's artistic success), is just beginning.

For many students, either the second to last and penultimate week is the hardest, especially in middle and high school. Some grow bored and lose enthusiasm; others feel that finishing will be impossible and not worth the effort. Occasionally, someone will even suggest postponement of performance or outright abandonment of the production. Either way, the dramatic arc of the production, just like the arc of a play, has reached its point of maximum tension. The production is passing through a hurricane, and it is the teacher's responsibility to pilot the class calmly through it by not speeding up the pace but actually slowing it down. By demonstrating confidence that everything will come together without some hysterical rush to the finish line, the teacher-director is practicing the pedagogical law.

It is a good rule of thumb, particularly with high school students, to dedicate the next to last week of the production to uninterrupted run-throughs of whole acts. Then as the week progresses, alternate the run-throughs with the final details of prop, costume, and set building. If possible, it is good to give the actors an early dismissal one afternoon; director and tech crew will have plenty to do with this free access to the stage, and the actors will come to the next rehearsal eager to get back into the forward momentum of the production. Such an alternation provides the opportunity for in-breathing and out-breathing, and brings a much-needed rhythmic balance to the work, transforming anxiety into healthy, creative, and goal-oriented tension. And finally on the Friday of the next to last week, the play should be made to run, even if stumbling, from start to finish, with as many props, costumes, and pieces of the set as possible.

From this penultimate Friday onward, the best thing is to let the play run and thereby to permit the students to feel their collaborative, creative efforts moving it toward performance. It has to become their play. But before a play can run gracefully, it must stagger, even stumble a bit. But to stagger and stumble is good; it allows the students to know out of their own perceptions where their work is strong and where it is weak. Of equal importance with letting the play run is for the director to step back from the role of director, and to assume instead that of audience, and ultimately supervising stage manager. Anxious or inexperienced directors (or those who have not managed their rehearsal time effectively) feel that they must continually add suggestion upon suggestion right up until the first performance. In truth, students can do little with these suggestions other than grow confused or anxious. The best thing for a class is to experience their work's strengths, and fix its weaknesses, through their own collaborative efforts. Without this independent social activity by the students themselves, the production has not been effective pedagogical theater.

But the most important thing that a play needs to come alive is an audience; a real audience, one that makes noise as it enters the theater, and grows silent in anticipation as the house lights dim. Only when a class feels the expectant excitement of their audience will that flood of creative forces, which have been existing only in potential, burst forth and propel performers and audience alike forward, inspiring them to achieve together that highest of theatrical moments: the luminous communion of performer, audience, and being of the play.

Part IV: Plays

This final part of the book consists of a collection of representative plays for performance by children and adolescents at all grade levels from first through twelfth grades. The plays range from short circle plays for the primary grades to full-length, main-stage productions for high school. All the plays written for grades one through four are representative of the traditional Waldorf School Curriculum and are thereby illustrative of the stories that would serve as the subject matter of the main lesson language arts or history curricula. Starting in fifth grade and then extending into the middle school the plays are more reflective and derivative of a given grade's language arts and history curricula, not literally representative of a story that would have been worked with in class. These middle school plays include several original variations on mythic stories or dramatic genres. The high school plays fall into one of three categories: two adaptations of nineteenth century novels; one recasting of Gogol's The Inspector General *into a mid-twentieth century context; and the last set being plays in German and Spanish written by colleagues for high school student performance for the elementary school.*

Chapter 1
Plays for the Primary Grades

First Grade

In first grade, children should not be placed before an audience. The *play-acting* of a story is primarily for themselves, and the play should be "performed" in the round. This orientation is natural only in that it reflects the orientation of *play-acting*. Just as in free *imaginative play,* individual or small groups of children step inward, to enact the various episodes and, when done, step back into the embracing whole. There is no need to rush the children into the world of stage conventions.

Once the play has been fully prepared and can be enthusiastically and effectively presented, parents and maybe another class can be invited into the classroom to watch. In a classroom presentation where the audience can be seated around the class, performing in the round is the best arrangement. An auditorium presentation is strongly discouraged, but if a larger space than the classroom is used, a slightly closed crescent is a good option, even though shape defeats the power of the circle form by increasing the self-consciousness of the children, which is pedagogically inappropriate. For this reason, it is best not to present a play in an assembly until second grade.

The first play is the very first play I wrote for children. The English fairy tale *The Three Sillies* was so popular with my first class in first grade that for several days after I told the story, the children playacted it over and over, providing me with my first inspiration as a pedagogical playwright. The play is about 250 words long and takes less than ten minutes to present. Since the children had already worked out most of the blocking in their playacting, it was easy to "produce" and make stage-worthy. Thirty-three years later I can still hear those six-year-olds delightfully lamenting the dangerous potential of the mallet.

Second Grade

In second grade, the class can begin working with the theatrical conventions of facing forward and projecting to an audience. Other than this change, the development of the plays out of playacting remains the same as in first grade. The running time, however, can be a little longer, say fifteen minutes, as opposed to the ten, but brevity is still a virtue second only to enthusiasm. Few things are more tedious than long choral narrations, delivered by stationary blocks of monotonously chanting children who periodically wave their arms or shift positions to indicate action.

The fable and saint legend plays that follow represent the basic polarity of the second grade language arts curriculum. The first play enacts the classic fable of *The Ant and the Grasshopper* and, being the simpler of the two, was designed for use early in the school year for classroom presentation for only the parents. *The Legend of Saint Odelia* is based on a widely used story from the second grade curriculum, which can be found in Ursula Synge's wonderful book *The Giant at the Ford and Other Legends of the Saints.* The focus of this play is on the themes of pride, anger, and repentance. The story also has high entertainment value, being exciting and having strong, vivid characters; dramatic confrontations; an exciting change of circumstances (the miracle); a chase, and a spectacular conclusion—all sure crowd-pleasers. It was designed for school assembly presentation.

The Odelia play also originated in watching my class playacting the story as part of the review during a language arts main lesson block. They were particularly fond of the parts when Aldaric drives his daughter away, when Odelia confronts him on the drawbridge of his castle, and when the rocks snap shut to aid her escape from her father's wrath. In the playacting they devised a "London Bridge is falling down" way of representing the snapping rocks, having great fun playing the scene over and over. Other children liked the part where Odelia regains her sight and goes from nun to nun, touching their faces. That business was fun because they could get to touch each other.

The play's dramatic structure is much more complex than that of the earlier plays. First, there is Aldaric's castle, used twice; then there is the nunnery where the miracle of her restored sight takes place; and finally there is the mountainside. The plot requires the mountainside to split open and then close miraculously around the fleeing Odelia. It is completely unnecessary to attempt to physically represent any of these settings with a set; they can all be called forth through narration and choreographed tableaus.

The Three Sillies

A Play for First Grade (1982, revised 1990)

Characters:

Squire	Farmer	Wife	Daughter
Man	Old Woman	Chorus	Villagers

CHORUS:

Each evening as the sun dipped low
To a farmer's house a squire rode.
Yet tasty as his meal would be,
The daughter only he wished to see.
Red were her cheeks, rosy and round:
The fairest maid for miles around.

One evening when the meal was done,
And after many songs were sung,
The cider jug . . . empty stood!
The squire frowned.

SQUIRE:

This isn't good.

FARMER:

Daughter! Quickly fetch some more!

WIFE:

The squire thirsts; his throat grows sore!

(Daughter goes to fetch cider.)

CHORUS:

While drawing cider she chanced look up:
Above a beam a mallet was tucked;
With dust and webs it was all covered;
So on the floor she sat and blubbered:

DAUGHTER:

Supposing he did marry me
And a handsome son we had;
And once while drawing cider,
That horrid, horrid mallet
Fell off that beam
And killed the poor boy dead.

CHORUS:

Upstairs their throats grew dry as dust;
The squire, thirsty, was feeling gruff.

SQUIRE:

Where is that cider?

CHORUS:

He loudly wondered,
So off the mother went to find her.

WIFE:

Daughter, daughter, don't delay?
The squire thirsts; I heard him say;
Hurry or he'll ride away.

DAUGHTER:

Supposing he did marry me
And a handsome son we had
And once while drawing cider
That horrid, horrid mallet
Fell off that beam
And killed the poor boy dead.

(Farmer's wife sits and blubbers.)

SQUIRE:

Farmer, farmer, I grow so dry,
Without sweet cider I'll surely die.

CHORUS:

So quickly as a slamming door
The farmer ran to get some more.

FARMER:

Daughter, wife, why this delay?
Hurry, or he'll ride away.

DAUGHTER/WIFE:

Supposing he/she did marry me/him
And a handsome son we/they had
And once while drawing cider
That horrid, horrid mallet
Fell off that beam
And killed the poor boy dead.

(Farmer sits and blubbers.)

SQUIRE:

Where, oh where, can those three be?
I think I'll have to go and see.

What! Cider's flowing everywhere,
And you just sit blubbering there?

DAUGHTER/WIFE/FARMER:
Supposing you did marry me/her
And a handsome son we/you had
And once while drawing cider
That horrid, horrid mallet
Fell off that beam
And killed the poor boy dead.

SQUIRE:
Oh, never ever did I see
Such silly people as you three!

CHORUS:
Then up he reached and down he took
The horrid mallet from its nook.

SQUIRE:
I'll not marry you until I find
Three people sillier than your kind.

(They blubber louder as Squire rides off.)

CHORUS:
Around the land the squire rode,
But none so silly ever showed
Until a woman he did see
Who, pleading on her bended knee,
Beseeched a cow to mount a roof.

OLD WOMAN:
Climb this ladder; use your hoofs!
There's grass up there for you to eat!
Don't you want a scrumptious treat?!

SQUIRE:
Woman, you climb up and throw it down.

OLD WOMAN:
Shush, you fool! or I'll knock your crown.

SQUIRE:
One silly this will be,
But two more sillies I must see.

CHORUS:
Around the land the squire rode,
But no more sillies ever showed
Until a fellow he did find
Who surely must have lost his mind.
He'd hung his trousers on a hook
Then with a run a leap he took
But on the floor he'd only land
And never in the hanging pants.

(Man tries jumping into pants repeatedly.)

SQUIRE:
Good man, that will take all your day.

MAN:
You think you know a better way?
Shush, you fool! I'll knock your crown
Then drive you forth from this town!

SQUIRE:
Two sillies that will be.
Just one more silly must I see.

CHORUS:
So on he rode for a long long time,
But no more sillies did he find
Until one night when the moon was high
Around a pond a crowd he spied
Who beat the water and loudly cried
As if they feared someone might die.

(Crowd beats water with sticks.)

SQUIRE:
What's the matter, who's fallen in?
Is there no-one who can swim?

VILLAGERS:
The moon, the moon!
It's gonna' drown!
Onto the water
It's fallen down.

SQUIRE:
Look above you; no need for fright;
That's not the moon, it's just its light.

VILLAGERS:
You be quiet and leave our town,
Or in you go until you drown.

SQUIRE:
That's more than three!

CHORUS:
The Squire cried.

SQUIRE:
Now it's time to claim my wife!

CHORUS:
So back he rode with ring in hand
And the silliest daughter?
He took her hand.

The Ant and The Grasshopper

A Play for Second Grade (1982)

Characters:

Ant Grasshopper Chorus

CHORUS:
The summer sun so warm and bright
Smiled down upon the earth;
A green grasshopper sang a song
And fiddled with great mirth.
Just then with great and heavy load
An ant trudged toward his hill;
He never paused to dance or sing.
His larder he would fill.
At the sight of this good fellow
The hopper sang out bright:

GRASSHOPPER:
Oh lookey here, here comes that ninny!

CHORUS:
He laughed with all his might.

CHORUS:
The worthy ant put down his load
And shook a strong hard claw.

ANT:
Oh, you'll be sorry, you lazy fellow
When summer's here no more.

GRASSHOPPER:
Ha, ha, you boring, dull old fool,
What can you teach to me?
Look at the sky; it is so blue,
And green leaves fill the trees.
The day's as warm as warm can be,
And the sun shines down on me.

CHORUS:
The ant just huffed and swung his load
Up on his sturdy back
And trudged ahead with steady pace
Against the coming cold.

ANT:
Harder, harder I must work;
Summer's almost gone.
The days grow short;
The nights grow long,
And soon will come the frost.

GRASSHOPPER:
What lovely days...

CHORUS:
...the hopper sighed

GRASSHOPPER:
What wonders there are to see!
The colors change; bright leaves dance
Across the fields for me!
Isn't it a fine parade!
It's days like these
That make me glad
I never went to work.
I'll just lean back and play a tune;
How ever could that hurt?

CHORUS:
Now in the place where people eat
The ant had found a feast:
Biscuits, puddings and cider lakes,
And many kinds of sweets.

GRASSHOPPER:
Oh, here he comes, old bony legs.
What do you say today?
Is not this fair October
As good as merry May?

ANT:
Your tune will change soon enough
When all is white with snow.

GRASSHOPPER:
Oh, go away you boring ant
Who cares if that is so!

CHORUS:
A week or two of fine bright days
Then autumn quickly passed.
And lo, the winds blew from the north!

GRASSHOPPER:
OH! Brrrrrrrrrrr....

CHORUS:
...he cried
And off he hopped
To find a warmer place.

GRASSHOPPER:
The ant...

CHORUS:
...he thought....

GRASSHOPPER:
...will help me out
And share his winter's space.

O, let me in, my dearest friend;
My jibes were but a joke;
I'll sing you songs and play gay tunes
And dance the Miggey Moke.

ANT:
Go away; I've worked so hard
To barely have enough.

GRASSHOPPER:
Oh, just one crumb is all I ask;
This cold is cruel and gruff.

CHORUS:
The thrifty ant tossed out one crumb;
The hopper snatched it up.

GRASSHOPPER:
One more....

CHORUS:
...he cried....

GRASSHOPPER:
....or else I'll die.

CHORUS:
The ant said...

ANT:
...THAT'S ENOUGH!

The Legend Of St. Odelia

A Play for Second Grade (1983)

Characters:

Odelia	Aldaric	Wife	Chorus	Holy Sisters
Abbess	Bishop	Chorus	Prince	Soldiers
Hunters	Baying Dogs	Baby		

(Aldaric, Wife & Soldiers come forward.)

ALDARIC:
A lord most terrible am I;
Oppose me? Just you try;
My wrath is felt by young and old,
All who fail to do as told.

CHORUS:
A tale we tell of fearful pride,
Of father and daughter, and their lives,
Each stubborn as any soul could be,
But softened by love's charity.

SOLDIERS:
Aldaric was a great and fearsome man;
With sword and threat he ruled his lands.
He only wanted for a son
To rule the lands his wrath had won;
So when his wife at last gave birth
He stomped his foot upon the earth.

ALDARIC:
Wife, come to me
Lift my son for me to see.

WIFE:
My lord, your wish I shall obey,
But a daughter, bright as summer day,
Is born .... without the gift of sight,
She's doomed to days as dark as night.

ALDARIC:
Away, I say, this cannot be;
No child of mine cannot see!
Take it away; it brings me shame.
I thing so worthless deserves no name.
So I command, far and wide,
If any name her, he shall die.

(Soldier takes away child.)

WIFE:
Far away my child they took
To hide her from my lord's cruel look,
And I to sorrow was resigned, for love
And joy were no more mine.

(Wife & Aldaric withdraw.)

CHORUS:
By holy sisters the babe was raised,
And as she grew she earned high praise
For all she did she did with skill
And never-tiring strength of will.
And so with time the girl became
A fair bright maid who bore no name
Until one day the bishop arrived,
And called the sisters to his side.

(Bishop comes forward.)

BISHOP:
An angel told me just last night
To hurry here and set wrong aright,
"Name the girl, who since her birth
Without a name's been cruelly cursed."

ABBESS:
A dreadful death has been declared
For one who names this maid so fair.

BISHOP:
I fear but God; His will alone obey.
(Odelia knells;Bishop touches & names her.)
I name you Odelia; Arise I say.

HOLY SISTERS:
As storm clouds part on blackest days
And bathe the earth with golden rays,
Thus blindness flees from this girl's eyes;

She sees God's earth and humbly cries.

ODELIA:
Creation's goodness I behold,
As fair and fine as I was told;
Good sisters let me guess thy names.

CHORUS:
And so the girl began a game:
Voices with faces she surely fixed,
And not a one she missed or mixed.

(Odelia goes from sister to sister.)

ODELIA:
Mary, it's thee, I'm sure,
Who always helps the sick and poor.
I know thee by thy kindly look
That comes from reading the holy book.
And Rachel, I am certain from thy hands,
It's thee who loves to work God's land
And plant the seeds that give us fruits:
The grains, flowers, and nourishing roots.

Some say my father's a wicked man.
Then with God's help I'll take his hand
And warm his heart with God's mercy
So thus the right way he will see.

I'll make him love me as his child,
And tame his heart some think so wild.

BISHOP:
Her will, good sisters, it must be stayed.

ABBESS:
Odelia, dearest, listen, pray.
Aldaric's a cruel and heartless man;

HOLY SISTER I:
He'll crush you with his pitiless hand.

ODELIA:
But strength of will is mine also,
So to his castle I shall go.

(Bishop, Abbess and Holy Sisters withdraw.)

CHORUS:
Across deep valleys and rocky ground,
Odelia rode until she found
His tall strong fort with walls so high
That all who near are seen for miles.
At the moat she reined her horse,
Declared herself, and sought to cross.

ODELIA:
Odelia's my name; my father I shall see,
Unbar this gate and grant entry.

(Soldiers come forward.)

SOLDIERS:
Listen to this foolish girl!
Do you think you rule the world?
Go back! You are not welcome here!
Our lord is childless; best take fear,
For soon he rides out through this gate
And grind you down beneath his hate.

(Aldaric comes forward. He raises his arm to strike her, but she stands firm.)

ALDARIC:
A soul more brave I'll never see.
Only a child of mine could so be.

CHORUS:
So they ruled, side by side,
Till a prince ,who sought a bride,
The fair Odelia asked to wed.

(Prince comes forward & bows before Aldaric, who tries to give him Odelia's hand.)

ALDARIC:
Yes!

ODELIA: *(Pulling free)*
I'll not marry him, or any other.
I've vowed to serve the Holy Mother.

ALDARIC:
What! You dare to disobey!
Bow down! Submit! Do as I say!

ODELIA:
Never father; I've made a vow.
Only to God will I bow.

(Odelia withdraws.)

CHORUS:
Blinded by rage he stormed away,
And from his land she fled that day.
But when he learned that she was gone
His face grew dark, wild as a storm.

ALDARIC:
Soldiers, hunters, dogs of war!
Find this girl who grieves me sore;
I'll bring her back in chains so tight
That n'er again she'll scorn my might.

(Odelia flees and hides.)

CHORUS:
They chased her to a mountaintop
And there she scrambled up the rocks,
But as the dogs snapped at her feet
And towering cliffs blocked her retreat.
The cliff split open then closed around,
Drawing her safely underground.

ALDARIC:
O God, O God! Pity me
To lose my child is agony.

I swear to heaven a solemn pledge
No man will she ever wed
If thou, my Lord, my child return,
Pride and anger I'll henceforth spurn.

CHORUS:
The stones split open and out she stepped,
And arm in arm they humbly wept.
Two souls who'd been so full of pride
Now humbly rejoiced side by side.

Chapter 2
Third Through Fifth Grade

In third and fourth grades the children are able to work as an ensemble for the first time. They are also old enough to take on more individualized parts. The narrative chorus, however, still retains a central role in the storytelling and essentially has two functions. First, it allows large stretches of story to be handled within the time constraints of a short play. And secondly, it provides a safe way for shy and overly self-conscious children to participate in a theatrical presentation by shielding them from the full force of an audience's attention. The plays also become longer. They have more substantial individual speeches and longer dialogue exchanges. They also can include more complex blocking and dramatic choreography. Eurythmy, as well as instrumental and vocal music, can also play a much larger role. Actual theater is beginning to emerge.

Third Grade

The story of Joseph and his brothers is superbly suited for a third grade play. First, its subject matter is one of the key stories in the language arts curriculum,. The story is full of moral conflict; and with its broad array of characters, the story provides the opportunity for everyone in a class to have at least a small speaking role. And it has a "wow" finish when Joseph not only reveals himself to his brothers, but also proclaims that their sin has provided the opportunity for the Lord God's providence.

Fourth Grade

If Waldorf pedagogical theater has a greatest hit, a play that almost all teacher-playwrights cover, it is the story of the Norse god Thor's journey, dressed as a bride, to the land of the noise giants to retrieve his hammer. It is simply great fun to produce, especially when the noise giants get to declaim, "We stomp and smash and hoot and HOWL!!!!!" The version that follows in this section runs about twenty minutes.

Fifth Grade

Fifth grade is possibly the richest year in the Waldorf school curriculum for stories that can be turned into plays, its scope ranging from ancient India to classical Greece. While fifth grade is sometimes referred to as the golden period of childhood, a period when the child lives in a balanced harmony of body and soul, it is also an important threshold year for the development of a sense of individual responsibility regarding how one will lead his or her life, as the child draws rapidly closer to the capacity for causal thinking.

He Who Saw the Deep tells the Gilgamesh story. It is as closely modeled on the structure of Greek tragedy as the Gilgamesh story permits. As such, it requires the students to use all the theatrical devices experienced in previous grades while introducing a new thematic intensity as well as expecting much more demanding ensemble work than before, especially with individual and choral speaking and the eurythmy. It does not, however, require any real acting from the students, allowing instead the language itself to carry the characterization. It runs for about fifty minutes, depending on the amount of eurythmy.

Joseph and His Brothers

A Play for Third Grade (December 1991; Revised December 1997)

Characters:

Joseph (boy)	Joseph (adult)	Jacob	Naphtali
Dan	Gad	Levi	Issachar
Zebulun	Rueben	Judah	Asher
Simeon	Potiphar	Potiphar's Steward	Lackeys
Pharaoh	Butler	Baker	Guard #1
Guard #2	Joseph's Steward	Benjamin *(mute)*	Ishmaelite
Merchant	Egyptian Captain	Egyptian Soldiers & Courtiers	

ACT I: Scene I: *Field near Jacob's tents.*

NAPHTALI:
Look yonder, brothers, see who comes.

DAN:
Why, if it isn't our father's favorite son.

ISSACHAR:
His little darling, his heart's sweet dear.

ZEBULUN:
What brings that lap dog sniffing near?

GAD:
Quick, let us gather up our stuff,
Of that pup I've had enough.

LEVI:
I hate to be in any place
Where I must look upon his face.

SIMEON:
That's the truth; can't he see
Why from him we always flee?

(They rise to leave.)

JOSEPH:
Brothers wait. Hear my dream.
Wisdom, like sunshine, from it beams.

As we were working in a field
We stopped and gathered for a meal;
Our sheaves of wheat were circled round,
Then all but one bowed to the ground,
And in the center just one stood,
Tall, majestic, golden, good.

JUDAH:
Your dream is nonsense; who cares, I say.

ZEBULUN:
Now little pup, be off; go away.

ISSACHAR:
Why look; he's right; we're circled round!

(They play a tripping game till Joseph falls)

GAD:
Careful now, don't fall down.

JOSEPH:
Your insults do not bother me,
But I'll tell father, then we'll see
Who stands tall and who bows low,
And who within his favor grows.

GAD:
Run to father now, if thou can.

(Kicks at Joseph)

ZEBULUN:
Stop yelping, be a man.

JUDAH:
You think he'll always fall for lies?

LEVI:
Soon comes the day ....

SIMEON:
...when thou can't hide

DAN:
Behind the curtains of the women's tent.

HALF OF THE BROTHERS:
Then we'll see . . . .

HALF OF THE BROTHERS:
. . . . what your dreams really meant.

JOSEPH:
My dreams are sent from God on high,
To the heart of one He finds most wise.

(Joseph scrambles off; brothers give chase.)

RUEBEN:
Stop brothers, just forget the boy.
Those dreams are nothing but his toys.

Scene II: *Jacob's Tent*

JACOB:
Oh, dearest son, it grieves my soul
To learn thy brothers are so bold
To do such wicked, hurtful things
And on your father such shame bring.

JOSEPH:
I share thy sorrow, hand in hand;
My brothers are a shameless band,
They bring disgrace to our line
That reaches back to Abram's time.

JACOB:
But quiet now, thy brothers come;
I'll have no quarreling amongst my sons.

(ENTER the brothers)

Welcome sons and take your place
Around my feet and share God's grace,
Let's lift our blessings for this meat
By which the Lord lets us feast.
Praised be God for all His gifts,
And to His glory our voices lift,
And thank Him for our family strong
And save my sons from sin and wrong.

(They bow their heads and pray)

RUEBEN:
O father, what lies hidden in thy words?
Has some ill news just been heard?

JACOB:
Yes, indeed, my first born son,
Who's lost thy birthright to one so young!
Great is the shame thou hast brought
By turning from what thou wast taught
About the things which please the Lord.
Thou bowed to idols! Thy sins do bore
Into my heart and bring me shame!
On thee now falls all my blame.

LEVI:
Father, what hast my brother done?
Why must thou heed this sneaky one?
Believest thou his every tale;
His lies can make a fish a whale.

SIMEON:
Yes, dear father, what did he say?
I swear we're guiltless as the day
When Adam in the garden walked;
These slanders are but jealous talk.

JACOB:
Listen sons, and mark my words:
I know the truth when it is heard.
Joseph's words — they cut me through —
Confirmed for me what I knew.
But each of ye I still love dear,
That, though you sin, I'll keep thee near
And clasp thee close unto my side,
To feast beside me until I die.

JOSEPH:
Father, thou speaketh well;
Now listen to the dream I tell,
And let it heal my brothers' hearts,
Though it might sting them like a dart.

GAD:
A dream! . . .

NAPHTALI:
. . . A dream!

ISSACHAR:
. . . . Another dream!
More likely some vile, bragging scheme.

DAN:
He seeks to scold us, cause us fright
With his strange visions from the night.

ASHER:
I'll stop my ears with my fists

Before I'll hear more of this
Nonsense which he heaps on thee;
Enough of his vile trickery.

JACOB:
Dearest son, what hast thou seen
Of our future in thy dreams?

JOSEPH:
The sun and moon and starry lights
Were gathered in the field of night,
And there I stood, and they did bow
Before me, surely as thou sees me now.

RUEBEN:
What are these stars of which thou speaks
That bow so humbly and so meek?

JUDAH:
Are they thy father and his sons?

JACOB:
Shame on thee, hold thy tongue.
Remember that I too once did dream,
And heavenly splendors I have seen.
Like Joseph, the angels to me have shown
Those wonders God wished were known.

Scene III: *A distant field*

DAN:
What say you, brothers? I've had enough
Of Joseph's tattles. I will not trust
The little whelp; he's full of plots;
I'll bear no more; it has to stop.

SIMEON:
Agreed! my brother; the boy's a pest,
Always scurrying from mess to mess.

LEVI:
And like a pest he should be treated
And not by father highly seated.

SIMEON:
Then like a pest he should die . . .

RUEBEN: *(Interrupting quickly)*
. . . Put such evil thoughts aside.
Hast thou forgot the sin of Cain
And by that anger what became
Of his poor soul and all his line,
How they've been marked for all of time?

LEVI:
Hast thou forgot, Leah's son,
What thou hath lost to this favored one.

ZEBULUN:
Had he a thought for thy brotherly love
When by his tattling he climbed above
His rightful station on this earth
And pushed thee from thy place of birth?

RUEBEN:
Thou speakest the truth, indeed;
But it's a sin to harm our father's seed.

SIMEON:
The boy's a weed, that I say;
I yearn with passion for the day
When I might break his shameless pride
And whip some sense into his hide.

ISSACHAR:
But look, my brothers; here he comes;.
Oh, how I hate this chosen one.

ASHER:
He'll run to father, the tattle-tale.

SIMEON:
Oh no he won't. Where's my flail?
Join me brothers; we have the might
To rid ourselves of this blight.

(Joseph enters.)

JOSEPH:
This is not where thou should be;
Give me something, or I'll tell on thee.

(They set to beating him.)

Have mercy, brothers, can't you see
I beg ye on my bended knee.
Spare my life, release your hold,
Or else our father will be told.

ASHER:
What did he say? . . .

SIMEON:
. . . He begs for more.

GAD:
Then, answer him, as before.

(They beat him harder.)

RUEBEN:
I fear the Lord for what we've done.
How can this end when so begun?

SIMEON:
The ending's clear, can't thou see
One can't turn back from what must be.

RUEBEN: *(Pulling them off Joseph)*
Shed not his blood, use thy wits;
Think clearly brothers. There's a pit;
We'll cast him down into its depths
And let the snakes sting him to death.

LEVI:
A good idea; let it be done;
The snakes will finish what we've begun.

(They drag Joseph off, then return.)

ISSACHAR:
He's finished; let's rejoice!

ASHER:
What joy to never hear his voice!

RUEBEN:
I'll fetch some wine to celebrate
Our freedom and our brother's fate.

(EXIT to side)

DAN:
Here's the cursed coat he loved so much;

SIMEON:
Smear it with blood, . . .

LEVI:
. . . tear it up.

ZEBULON:
But if father learns what we have done?

SIMEON:
We'll say wild beasts killed his fav'rit son.

RUEBEN: *(From the side)*
Dear Joseph, I'll pull thee from that pit
And see that thou art well and fit.

(Exit Rueben)

ASHER:
A brother's death's the mark of Cain.

JUDAH:
Quick, let us raise him up again.

DAN:
Let not his blood be on our hands.

LEVI:
Let's sell him into Egypt's land.

SIMEON:
Not far from here the slavers pass;
That way we'll profit from the lad.

(They pull up Joseph and exit.)

ACT II: Scene 1: *Egypt: Potiphar's House*

ENTER Guards

LACKEYS:
Great is the might of our master;
We bow to him every day.
Great is the might of our master;
From birth we were born to obey.
Weak are the slaves of our master;
We grovel like dogs at his feet.
Weak are the slaves of our master;
We'll die if that's what he seeks.

(ENTER Potiphar with great pomp, yawning, followed by steward and merchant.)

POTIPHAR:
What bargains are there here for me?
How stale and dull my life has grown;
I yearn for something fresh to see.

ISHMAELITE MERCHANT:
Then I've a little Hebrew here with me —
A radiant boy whose wit is known
To cure whatever might be ailing thee.

POTIPHAR:
Then bring him here for me to see
That I might judge, and I might know
If you are speaking honestly.

(Joseph is brought. Potiphar examines him.)
Hebrew child, see that vine that grows?
Now tell me, male or female, which it be?

JOSEPH:
Tis both; male in the pride of its growth,
And female in the fruit it boasts.

POTIPHAR:
He's as you say—bright as the sun.
I'll take him. Steward, pay the fee.

It is a shame you have just one.
I think I'll like his company.

(EXIT Potiphar, followed by his marching guards. His steward takes Joseph and pays the merchant who exits.)

STEWARD:

And so was Joseph brought to that house,
And he rose in standing until the spouse
Fell in love with the handsome lad.
And sought to break the trust he had,
But he refused, this faithful youth,
Then she betrayed him, despite all truth.

(Casts Joseph down and exits.)

Scene 2: *Prison*

(Joseph in prison; guards enter with royal butler and baker.)

GUARD 1:

Into this cell, the two of you,

GUARD 2:

And languish here until we're through
Deciding your just punishment

GUARD 1:

Or whether we'll be lenient.

BAKER:

I swear it is but some mistake

BUTLER:

I never could his trust forsake.

BAKER:

I worship Pharaoh; he is my god!
I kiss the ground where he has trod.
I swear I never fouled his bread;
And sooner would myself be dead.

GUARD 1:

That's what you'll be if it proves true
That such a thing you tried to do.

BUTLER:

He could have done so vile a thing
But never me. I serve my king
And put not flies in his wine
I'd sooner die than commit that crime.

GUARD 2:

Enough; I'm sick already of your talk;
Let this Hebrew hear you squawk.
With time the truth will all come out,
Who lives, who dies, without a doubt.

BUTLER:

Hebrew slave; I've heard it told
Those of your tribe the future know.
I pray thee tell what shall become
Of me since nothing have I done.

JOSEPH:

Your hearts I'll fathom and your fates:
But for one I sense it is too late,
Of a treasonous crime he stands accused,
Since trusted office he's abused.
The other one for Pharaoh great
Is like a fly before his face;
He'll notice you, if so inclined,
And let you buzz another time.
Until he stirs, you'll languish here,
And I, your watcher, sitting near.

(Lights dim to denote a passing night.)

Scene 3. *As before*

BAKER AND BUTLER:

Watcher, mighty visions filled our sleep,
Their meanings were so strange and deep
That we can't fathom what they mean.
Can you read for us our dreams?

JOSEPH:

God shows his will in dreamy visions,
Revealing what till then lay hidden.
Yes, I am skilled in reading them,
And learning thus the fates of men.

BUTLER:

Then hear mine first. It goes like this:
Once more I stood in Pharaoh's midst
And right beside me stood a vine.
Three branches grew, strong and fine,
And as I watched dark grapes sprang forth,
Then with my hand, as I was taught,
The fruit I pressed into fine wine
That Pharaoh drank as he dined.

JOSEPH:
This dream is simple, easily read.
In three days time he'll raise your head
Up high and give you back your place
So you with joy may praise his grace.

BAKER:
The Butler's dream sounds good to me.
Now hear my dream, and let me see
The happy day that it foretells
When I am freed from this dark cell.
Three baskets were upon my head,
And each contained the finest bread,
Then screeching birds swooped down low
And lifted up the choicest loaves.

JOSEPH:
This dream is simple to understand.
In three days time will Pharaoh's hand
Raise up your head so very high
It leaves your shoulders, and you die.

BAKER:
You lie; you lie; this cannot be!
You're like the rest; stop mocking me.

JOSEPH: *(To Butler)*
Remember me when such is done,
And tell great Pharaoh I'm the one
Who read the visions sent from high
And knew who'd live and who would die.

BUTLER: *(Addressing audience)*
So it did happen as the Hebrew said,
And I was lifted from the dead
And stood in honor by Pharaoh then
And held his golden cup again.
But in my joy I did forget
The Hebrew slave who languished yet
Until great Pharaoh had a dream
That broke his sacred rest serene.

Scene 4: *Pharaoh's Palace*

PHARAOH:
Bring me the Hebrew slave who reads
The dreamy script writ cross the night,
And let him part the clouds for me
That hide its meaning from my sight.

JOSEPH:
(Bowing low before Pharaoh)
Radiant master, thou art the sun
That shines above all mortal ones.

PHARAOH:
Two dreams I had that broke my rest,
Both strange and filled with irony,
But neither one, I must confess,
Is understood by me.
At first the Nile did deeply flood
And fields grew green and thick to see,
Then seven cows rose from the mud
And peacefully began to feed.
Then seven more appeared in turn,
As thin and gaunt as death;
They ate the first; the sun did burn
Them wasted, stripped of flesh.
The second dream contained a stalk
With seven golden grains of corn.
It proudly held its head aloft,
So perfect was its form.
And then another, withered, dry,
Beside the first appeared,
And as they touched the first did die,
Then I awoke in fear.

JOSEPH:
Thy dreams, great king, are the same :
The seven cows and seven grains
Mean seven years of plenty,
Followed by seven more so empty
That all the bounty of the first
Will be devoured by famine's curse.

PHARAOH:
I sense great wisdom in thy words.
What must we do to save our land,
Since there is truth in what we've heard,
How, Hebrew, would thou plan?

JOSEPH:
I know a way, most mighty king.
Build granaries and to them bring
All the bounty of Egypt's earth
And store it safely till times are worse.

Then all the nations in their need
Will come to Pharaoh and bow to thee
And seek our grain to make their bread
And pay our price in fear and dread.

PHARAOH:
And who will guide this awesome task?

JOSEPH:
The wisest servant that thou hast.
Give mighty powers to this man,
But keep him lower than thy hand.

PHARAOH:
In all my land there's none but thee
Who I would trust to so serve me,
So from thy bondage I set thee free,
Now all of Egypt, Hebrew, oversee.

Act III Scene 1: *Jacob's tent*

JACOB:
Sons, gather round, for I must speak:
Our great wealth withers; we grow weak.
This famine has consumed our plenty,
Our herds grow few that once were many.
Rise up and take a chest of gold,
And all the wealth thy camels hold,
And go down into Egypt's land,
And purchase grain from Pharaoh's man.
Your parting fills my heart with sadness;
Return home safely; restore its gladness.
Not since my dear son Joseph's death,
Have I from sorrow known rest.
Yet leave young Benjamin here with me;
His youth will keep my sad heart company.

Scene 2: *Joseph's Palace*

JOSEPH'S STEWARD:
My Lord, we watched the Hebrew border
And questioned all according to thy orders,
And finally found the spies you sought,
Arrested them, and before you brought.

(Jacob's sons are brought in before Joseph.)

CAPTAIN:
We know you kind, you Hebrew spies,
Speak truthfully, forsake your lies,
So brilliant is our master's sight
That he can make the darkness bright.

RUEBEN:
Our father's Jacob, an honest man;
He sent us out of hunger to this land.

JOSEPH:
You lie! You seek the weakness of this place,
Treachery is written across thy face.

RUEBEN:
We're honest men; we swear to you
That no such evil would we do.

JOSEPH:
Are you this Jacob's only sons?

RUEBEN:
With him he's kept his favorite one.

JOSEPH:
His favorite one? What's he called?

RUEBEN:
Benjamin. . . .

JOSEPH:
. . . Is he all?

RUEBEN:
There was another, lost long ago;
Alive or dead; we do not know.

ASHER:
Tis true; we swear full faithfully.

SIMEON:
Our hearts bear no treachery.

JOSEPH:
Seize that man; the lies fly out
Each time he starts to move his mouth.
Take and throw him in some pit
For such an end he's best befit.

(Guards seize Simeon.)

ISSACHAR:
O, mighty master, Pharaoh's hand,
Have mercy on our wretched band.
Spare our brother from that fate.

JOSEPH:
Silence! Or even worse you'll face.

RUEBEN:
I fear we pay for Joseph's blood;
Judgment pours forth like a flood.

JOSEPH:
Begone. Give them what they need.
Let none say Pharaoh failed to feed
The low and wretched in their plight,
But this hostage will I hold, as I might,
Until this Benjamin you bring as proof
That what you told me was the truth.
Now hurry back to your father's tents
And bring the boy for whom I've sent.

Scene 4: *Jacob's tent*

JACOB:
Again my sons, you wound my soul.
Why must this happen to one so old?
First, it was Joseph that thou lost.
Now Simeon is the awful cost
Thou hast paid for a bag of feed,
And now my dearest thou dost need.

DAN:
Dear father we beg that we might go
And take young Benjamin to show
The mighty gov'nor we're honest men;
We'll free our brother, and return again
With all the sons that thou hast sent.

JACOB:
Alas, if only Joseph had that way went.

Scene 5: *Joseph's Palace*
So you Hebrews have obeyed.
Is this the boy who you say
Is thy father's favorite son?

JUDAH:
Yes, master, he is the one.

JOSEPH:
He has a sweet and lovely smile.
Was the lost one like this child?

RUEBEN:
Fairer, great lord; his beauty shone
As radiant as a prince upon a throne.

JOSEPH:
Give these beggars what they need;
Release their brother to their company.

(Joseph rises suddenly and flees the room. As the brothers leave he says to a servant.)
Fill to brimming their empty sacks,
And hide this cup among their packs,
And then, a little after they have left
Arrest that boy for my cup's theft.

(Servants leave; Joseph sits back on his throne and waits.)

Scene 6: *Joseph's Palace*

(The brothers are dragged-in, bound, and cast before Joseph.)

JOSEPH:
Is there no gratitude for what I've done?
But Pharaoh's just, so only one
Among you thieves shall be my slave.
Seize the boy. The rest of you are saved;
Take yourselves back to your father
And tell him never again Egypt bother.

JUDAH:
Great Lord, let your anger turn
From our brother; . . . .

GAD:
. . . but if it burns,
Direct it towards the sins we've made;
Don't drive our father towards his grave.

ASHER:
To take that boy will break his heart.

LEVI:
He cannot bear again to part
From the son he loves the most;

ZEBULUN:
The poor man will become a ghost.

SIMEON:
O Lord, an awful thing has come to be
Because we sold our brother into slavery.

NAPHTALI:
Joseph was our father's dearest boy;
We envied him our father's joy.

ISSACHAR:
And to our envy fell on him;
Punish us for our sins.

JOSEPH: *(To Egyptians)*
Clear the room, leave us alone.
Sons of Jacob, approach my throne.

(Rising and proclaiming in grand voice as brothers bow before him.)

I am Joseph, the brother who once you lost,
And terrible might have been your envy's cost
If the Lord God had not redeemed your deed,
And by His wisdom sent me to feed
The seed of Abraham so it might multiply.

Return to Canaan and before our father's eyes
Confess thy sins, then bring him here
To be united with his son most dear.

Thor, The Bride

A Play for Fourth Grade (1985)

Characters:

Norns (Spinners of Fate)
Loki (Shapechanger: half Aesir, half Giant)
Odin (Supreme Aesir)
Freya (Aesir of Love)
Idun (Aesir of Eternal Youthfulness)
Gazack (A nasty noise giant)
Kazzapim (A nasty noise giant)
Trok (A nasty noise giant)
Thor (The Thunder God)
Tyr (Aesir of Law & Heroism)
Frigg (A Wife of Odin)
Heimdahl (Watcher for Aesir)
Thrym (King of the Noise Giants)
Tjzecknir (A nasty noise giant)
Blazzapp (A nasty noise giant)

PROLOGUE

NORNS:
Deep down beneath the great ash tree
The ageless Norns forever weave
The Fate of all, for joy or woe,
For hope or dread, none may know.
Their shuttle is the passing time,
Life's treads they weave, course or fine.
But comes the time when each will break,
Then Doom appears and sweet life takes.

SCENE I: Odin's hall in Asgard

(Thor asleep after a feast. ENTER Thrym & using great magic steals Thor's hammer, Mjollnir. Loki, watching, laughs to himself as Thor awakes to find his weapon gone.)

LOKI:
A thief I saw slip from this place;
The prize he took, I'd dare not take;
But sport I'll have before I'm done
And by my wits have Thor undone.

THOR: *(Awakening & rising)*
Safe should I slumber circled by kinsmen,
But dreams of dark danger like rumbling thunder,
Crept near a coward to take treasure from me,
Afraid to face combat by cunning he plundered.
Could only be Loki! I'll crush that vile creeper!

LOKI:
Oh mercy Thor, so wise and strong;
Why do you rage? I've done no wrong!
No ill 'gainst you would I dare do,
Yet wrath towards me like storm clouds grew.

THOR:
Halt your hollow honeyed words.
Your tongue is twisted like your lips.
To tell your tricks no wits are wanted.
Hand here my hammer or feel my fury!

LOKI:
Thy hammer gone?! Let me think
And from my words truth you'll drink.
Who'd seek to rob you of your power
Except foul giants in dark cold towers?
Give me but a *fair* disguise
And all their wastelands I will spy
Till Thor's great weapon I will find
And whisk it back from Jotenheim.

TYR:
What troubles the night awaking all Asgard?

LOKI:
Trouble in plenty, woe upon woe!
Against bright Asgard is struck a blow!

Our noble Thor's great hammer's taken
And down our walls may soon be shaken
Unless fair Freya's feathered cloak might fit
A form so fair despite its twist.

FRIGG:

To truth-words do we listen or sly Loki's crawling lies?

THOR:

That twisted trickster's talk is true.

FREYA:

Let this alight upon thy twisted frame.
May its sun-brightness fill thy shadowed heart.
Fair-feathered goodness make fast his flight.

(EXIT Loki, towards Jotenheim.)

ODIN:

Aesirs watchful be; from shapechangers no good comes.
Danger, Dread, Doom and Death
Keep council with our carelessness.

(EXIT Odin, leading Aesir off.)

SCENE II: *Thrym's Hall in Jotenheim*

NOISE GIANTS

We stomp and smash and hoot and HOWL!!!!!
Here's never silence; we find it foul!
Let those worthless gods talk nice,
For we'll be rude and not think twice!
We'll cut you off and pay no heed.
Of gentle manners we have no need.
And if some Aesir dared say please.....
We'll have him begging on his knees!

TROK:

Agh! Hear that crashing noise!
Such ugliness gives us joy.
The icy mountains quake with fear
'Cause master Thrym is stomping near!

THRYM:

You worthless wretches crawl for me;
Look what I took from sleeping Thor.
Not even in a dragon's hoard
Is geld so great that you could see!
Now stash it deep 'neath solid stone,
Eight miles deep in hardest rock.
My greatest joy will be to mock
Some begging Aesir from my throne.

(They carry it away, rejoicing and arguing.)

GAZACK:

Oh, brother Thrym, so loud and cruel,
Looky see, some Aesir fool.

THRYM:

Cousin Loki, how goes it friend?

LOKI:

Not well; after a thief I'm sent,
Yet I who watch while others sleep
Spied a crafty brute who creeps,
Saw him steal from sleeping Thor
A mighty thing you'd quake before.

THRYM:

Ha, I saw your sneaky eyes on me
But Mjollnir costs a pretty price,
Something Aesirs won't find nice....
Bring Freya as a bride to me.

SCENE III: *Odin's hall in Asgard*

FREYA:

Which ill is worse I dare not say:
Mjollnir lost or monster mate?

ODIN:

Doom awaits either choice.

HEIMDAHL:

All-Father hear my council;
Send another, not so fair,
In Freya's place.

THOR:

Too much talk I'm bored with banter.
Sword-sharp deeds settle scores!

LOKI:

Quiet, mountain mover; I see his scheme.
Oh! what a lovely girl you'd seem —
A silky veil, a bright white dress —
A dainty bride so sweet and fresh!

FREYA:
And Loki, oh, what cleverness
That puts you too into a dress.

IDUN:
Since Thor must be the blushing bride
Then you're the bridesmaid at his side.

(They dress Thor and Loki merrily.)

ALL:
So as they dressed the Aesir two,
Mighty Thor planned what he'd do.
Around his hammer his hand he'd wrap
And bring down Thrym with a thundering clap.

SCENE IV: *Thrym's hall*

BLAZZAPP:
Oh looky, looky, looky here;
The dainty Aesir bride draws near.

(Thrym howls in anticipation of his `bride'.)

KAZZAPIM:
Great master Thrym howls with delight,
So loud that mountains quake with fright.

TJZECKNIR:
A thund'ring chariot Freya rides!
Go get the feast for master's bride —
Fat slabs of meat, great tubs of mead.
Quick get ready; tonight we feeds.

(Gazack greets "bride" and "bridesmaid.")

GAZACK:
Great brother Thrym waits on his throne,
But listen, hear that lovely groan —
That's tables 'neath the tasty treats.
No finer husband could you meet.

THRYM:
Welcome Freya to Clamor Hall.
T'will be your home forever now.
Safe you'll be in its walls proud.
With you inside, they'll never fall.
But later my shrewd plans, so foul;
Get you here at my side,
Fetch some grub for my bride.
Can't you hear her stomach growl?

(They bring great plates of food that "Freya" devours instantly.)
Such gobbling for a dainty maid?

LOKI:
Great Noise Lord Thrym, no bite she ate
Since last we saw high Asgard's gate.

GAZACK:
Lucky master, such a pretty bride.

THRYM:
I'll take my kiss.....AH!!! WHAT EYES!!!!!
They glow like goals in fire bright!
For a maid this don't seem right.

LOKI:
It's true they burn . . . with love for thee!
But first THE GIFT she must see.

THRYM:
Oh! what a gift I gots for you.
Wretches bring Thor's hammer here!
Stupid Thor we'll never fear;
With Freya ours, what can he do!!

(Mjollnir placed on "Freya's" lap. "She" rises, holds it high, casts off "her" veil. The giants howl in horror and try to flee.)

THOR:
Joyful my fingers when Mjollnir feels them,
And full its fell fury falls on my foes.
Feel now my vengeance my caress and my kiss,
And may Doom dark and dreadful be your wedding bliss.

(He swings the great hammer. Loki ducks, and all the giants fall dead.)

He Who Saw the Deep

A Play for Fifth Grade (2013)

Adapted from the Gilgamesh Epic of Sin-lige-unninni

Characters:

Trapper	Trapper's Son	Enkidu
A deer	Head Magi	Chorus of Magi (male)
Gilgamesh	Humbaba	Ishtar
Anu	Scorpion Man	Scorpion Woman
Siduri the Refresher	Urshanabi the Ferry Man	Utnaphishtim the Ancient One
Utnaphishtim Wife	The Lion of the Earth	

Chorus of People (male & female)
Chorus of Disciples of Lady of the Wild Cow (female)
High Priestess of Ninsun (Lady of Wild Cow; aka Gilgamesh's mother
Chorus of the Sea of Death

Setting: Ancient Mesopotamia
Scenery: Dual level platform mid center stage; sliding flats for mountains & realm of Utnaphishtim
Performance Space: Thrust apron stage
Music: Voices, flute, percussion, possibly lyres
Eurythmy: Speech eurythmy for choral odes
Costuming: Akkadian in gesture

PROLOGUE:

TRAPPER, TRAPPER'S SON, ENKIDU, DEER

Setting: The forest, some distance removed from Uruk

ENTER fleeing deer, pursued by HUNTER and HUNTER'S SON who stop center stage.

TRAPPER:
Stop! Stop, my Son!
My heart trembles; Danger's lurking near!
Relax thy arm! Restrain thy spear.

TRAPPER'S SON:
Stop? Why!? My father!
My eye cries out, "There, there; the target's clear!"
My arm cries out, "Release, release thy eager spear!"
Look there, my father, there!
The quarry trembles, sensing Death is near!

TRAPPER:
Yes, my Son. Death is near,

But it is ours, not the deer's.

TRAPPER'S SON:
Why father, such alarm?
Help me understand

TRAPPER:
This is the beast-man's land.
Whoever seeks to do his creatures harm,
He tears to pieces with his mighty hands.
Restrain thy spear; relax thy arm.
A god warns, "Fly, Death draws near."
My heart, my son, bursts with fear.

TRAPPER'S SON:
What can subdue him?

TRAPPER:
The Power of Women.

TRAPPER'S SON:
Not King Gilgamesh?

TRAPPER:
Not even King Gilgamesh,
But fly, my son; again the god cries;
"Fly swiftly, or you will die!"

EXIT TRAPPER and TRAPPER'S SON.

ENTER ENKIDU. He aggressively searches for them. When he finds their trail, he lets loose an angry howl and EXITS in pursuit.

PARADOS:

CHORUS OF MAGI, HEAD MAGI, CHORUS OF PEOPLE, CHORUS OF DISCIPLES

Setting: The Gates of Uruk

ENTER CHORUS of the PEOPLE, dressed as all walks of life. They gather in anticipation, leaving center open. Some anxious w/joy, others with dread.

ENTER CHORUS of MAGI, led by HEAD MAGI, immediately after CHORUS of PEOPLE, chanted lines alternating with CHORUS of PEOPLE. They process ceremoniously, stopping center stage in a formal, forward-facing arrangement, flanked by CHORUS of PEOPLE.

HEAD MAGI: *Leading procession of CHORUS of MAGI*
Gilgamesh! Gilgamesh!
Two-thirds god,
One-third mortal.
Tremble before him!

CHORUS of MAGI: *Chanting as they process*
Gilgamesh! Gilgamesh!
He walks out in front,
He walks at the rear,

Supreme above all kings!
Protector of Uruk!
We tremble before him!

CHORUS of PEOPLE: *Chanting in response*
We tremble before him!

ENTER CHORUS OF DISCIPLES, led by HIGH PRIESTESS. Ceremoniously, stopping center: formal, forward-facing, before two choruses.

HIGH PRIESTESS: *Stepping* to *front*
Gilgamesh! Gilgamesh!
Son of the Wild Cow.
Son of the Young King,
Tremble before him!

CHORUS of DISCIPLES: *To Heaven*
Gilgamesh! Gilgamesh!
Strong as the wild bull,
Strong to perfection,
Fierce as the piercing horn
That gores its rival.
We tremble before him.

CHORUS of PEOPLE: *Chanting in response*
We tremble before him!

HEAD MAGI & HIGH PRIESTESS:
Gilgamesh! Gilgamesh! (HM & HP)
He channels the flood (HM)
That rages against us! *(*HP*)*
He digs the deep wells (HM)
That give us sweet water! (HP)
Tremble before him! (HM & HP)

CHORUS of MAGI & DISCIPLES: *To Heaven*
Gilgamesh! Gilgamesh!
He builds the great wall (CM)
That guards our homes! (CD)
We tremble before him! (CM & CD)

CHORUS of PEOPLE: *Chanting in response*
We tremble before him!

SCENE 1: *As before*

GILGAMESH, ENKIDU

ENTER GILGAMESH, on top of gate.

ALL:

Gilgamesh! Gilgamesh! Gilgamesh!
We tremble before thee!

GILGAMESH:

Arise, my children, and behold thy lord, son of heaven's queen.
Behold my works: the strong protecting walls, great beyond compare;
The mighty dikes that keep the flood at bay.
All this and so much more, I, Gilgamesh, Ninsun's Son,
Hath made for thee, hath given thee, hath done for thee.

MAGI:

Gilgamesh! Our Lord!
We hold thee mighty above all kings!
All others bow before thy word;
All others quake before thy eye.
Command, and we obey;
Our lives are thine.

GILGAMESH:

My heart rejoices at your praise and loves you as it loves itself.

HIGH PRIESTESS:

Before thy majesty I humbly bow.
Greatness hast thou brought thy people,
The gifts of Heaven hast thou dispensed,
No Lord of Earth is thy compare.
But dreadful words, I must speak,
Dreadful words I fear to speak,
Dreadful words beyond compare,
Dreadful words, doom filled words,
Words not heard before:
Thy equal, Lord Gilgamesh,
Thy *equal*, Lord Gilgamesh,
Walks this earth;
Nears the city.

GILGAMESH: *Imperiously*

Speak mortal woman, slave of Fear, why should I dread your words?

HIGH PRIESTESS: *Defiantly*

Ninsun, thy mother, has revealed to me
Thy equal now draws near.
See, here he comes, thy match.

ENTER ENKIDU, from crowd. GILGAMESH leaps from gate, and they struggle to a draw.

GILGAMESH:
My Brother, my yearned for other self, embrace me as Heaven embraces Earth.

ENKIDU:
My Brother, my god-like self, I embrace thee as Life embraces Self.

GILGAMESH:
Great the gods made me; now greater greatness do they bestow through thee.
What on earth can match our power? Nothing! Only a god
Could cause our strength to falter, could bring us to our knees.

MAGI: *Bowing; all but Enkidu bowing with him.*
Thou speakest truly, O god-like king.

GILGAMESH:
Know thou any who dares to be our equal? Reveal him; expose him to our wrath.

HIGH PRIESTESS: *Fearlessly*
Humbaba.

(A groan of terror ripples through crowd.)

HIGH PRIESTESS:
The faintest rustle in his forest;
He can hear a hundred leagues away.
His footfall fills the earth with terror
As he stalks his hapless prey.

Even thou, Gilgamesh, Great King of Uruk,
Even thou will tremble when he draws near.
Even thou, Enkidu, beast-man of the forest,
Even thou will tremble, gripped by fear.

ENKIDU:
Humbaba, his roar the raging flood!
Humbaba, his mouth consuming fire!
Humbaba, his breath Death itself!

GILGAMESH:
Why fear such goblin stories, told to frighten children.
Must not all mortals die? So why fear Death
When only Glory lives forever?
Come, my brother,
Arm in arm, defying danger! Arm in arm we'll slay Humbaba!

EXIT ALL, cheering & following GILGAMESH & ENKIDU, but HIGH PRIESTESS & MAGI & male/female EURYTHMY CHORUS (6-8 performers).

STANDING SONG 1:

HIGH PRIESTESS & MAGI

MAGI: *accompanying eurythmy*
What cannot kings do for glory,
For immortality bestowed by words,
To live forever through a story
That by the countless generation's heard!

HIGH PRIESTESS: *accompanying eurythmy*
Are not such stories like the wind?
Rush loudly past, then silent fall,
As lasting as a passing whim,
Glorious for a moment, then no more?

EXIT ALL, revealing Gilgamesh & Enkidu asleep on lower platform.

SCENE 2: *The mountainside, before Humbaba's forest*

GILGAMESH, ENKIDU

(Brief musical interlude signifying sleep.)

GILGAMESH: Waking
O Enkidu, a dread-filled dream invades my sleep:
A mountain crashes down, crushing me
Beneath its weight.

ENKIDU:
Take heart, my brother,
The omen's good. Humbaba is the mountain
That is destroyed.

(Brief musical interlude signifying sleep.)

GILGAMESH: Waking
O Enkidu, a second dream,
Invades my sleep:
The heavens rain down fire,
Burning earth to ash.

ENKIDU:
Take heart, my brother,
The omen's good. It is Humbaba, burned to ashes,
That is destroyed.

(Brief musical interlude signifying sleep.)

GILGAMESH: *Waking*
O Enkidu, a third dream,
Invades my sleep:

a raging bull from heaven
Gores all to death.

ENKIDU:

Take heart, my brother,
The omen's good. It is Humbaba, gored to death,
That is destroyed.

(Brief musical interlude signifying sleep.)

Arise, my brother, let us enter
Great Humbaba's forest. Do not tremble, be strong, my brother;
Enkidu walks at thy side.

GILGAMESH & ENKIDU enter imaginary forest. Each carries two axes.

Montage 1:

HIGH PRIESTESS & MAGI, EURYTHMY CHORUS

ENTER MAGI, HIGH PRIESTESS on platforms, eurythmy/pantomime CHORUS on floor.

MAGI & HIGH PRIESTESS: *Alternating unison & solo narration*
Vast the forest spread around them, towering high above their heads;
Dark the shadows that engulfed them, silence stretching mile on mile.
Suddenly they heard Humbaba, thundering through the fearful dark,
Crashing through the trees and bracken, rushing closer, closer, closer,
Till the forest heaved and shuddered, great trees falling, crashing round them.

Then Humbaba loomed above them, laughing loudly, laughing cruelly,
Contemptuous of the puny mortals. "Tremble now you little insects!
Humbaba is my dreadful name. Only gods may look upon me, only gods
May enter here, only gods live to leave here, only gods escape
My wrath. Wretched death I'll pile upon you."

Gilgamesh, great king of Uruk, stood undaunted, fury surging
Through his muscles, through his muscles pride and courage
Bursting forth to strike the monster, strike him down, again, again.
Enkidu, right beside him, blow on blow he battered down,
Battering down the great Humbaba till he cowered in defeat.

"Mercy!" cried the trembling monster, "Mighty king, show thy mercy!"
Then Gilgamesh was filled with pity, pity for the trembling monster
Crying weakly in defeat. "No, my brother," cried the beast-man,
"Kill him! Kill him! Kill him now! Kill him with thy fearsome weapons!"
So the king swung his axes, chopping off Humbaba's head.

(Gilgamesh & Enkidu, holding high Humbaba's head, process triumphantly.)

SCENE 3: *Before Uruk*

ENTER ISHTAR.

ISHTAR: *Blocking their way*
O Gilgamesh, Ishtar greets thee!
O king most mighty,
Be my husband.

ENKIDU: *Blocking her*
O brother, ignore this goddess;
Push right past her. All men know
She will betray you.

She'll treat you like a toy.
And once she's done, she'll
Cast you right aside.

ISHTAR:
O puny beast-man, shut your mouth!
Great King, most handsome.
Behold my beauty.

GILGAMESH: *Imperious*
Be gone, foolish goddess.
I care nothing for your wiles?

EXIT GILGAMESH & ENKIDU, pushing past her triumphantly.

ISHTAR: *Outraged*
O careless mortal! Dare to mock me!
Floods! Plagues! Drought! Fleas! These
I shall release!

ENTER ANU.

ANU: *Scolding*
O Ishtar, vain, immortal daughter,
Control thy anger!

ISHTAR: *Outraged*
No, Anu,
Divine father! The Bull of Heaven
Must be unleashed!

ANU: *Commanding*
O Ishtar,
That may not happen; Control thy anger!
Rein in thy wrath.

ISHTAR: *Outraged*
Then all the dead

From graves I'll free to swarm the earth
And kill mankind

ANU: *Submitting*

O Ishtar,
That can not be. The Bull of Heaven
I shall release.

ANU & ISHTAR ascend to upper platform.

Montage 2:

HIGH PRIESTESS & MAGI, EURYTHMY/PANTOMIME CHORUS.

MAGI & HIGH PRIESTESS: *Alternating unison & solo narration*
Down towards earth the Bull of Heaven, snorting, roaring, boldly charged.
Vicious horns swinging wildly, piercing, goring, cleaving stars.
Madly charging down from Heaven came the Bull, his eyes ablaze,
Blazing like eternal fires, blazing with eternal rage,
Down to Earth the Bull descended, smashing all things in his way.

Bravely Gilgamesh stood between him and the people of his land;
Bravely Enkidu stood beside him, weapons gleaming in their hands
Instantly the Bull was on them and instantly they thrust their swords;
Deep into the Bull they plunged them, all their might the monster bore
Till he shuddered, stumbled, humbled, falling dead, fierce no more.

GILGAMESH & ENKIDU:
There vain goddess lies your husband;
With mortal men your charms have failed.

ISHTAR: *Livid with rage*
Father Anu, smite these mortals,
The Bull of Heaven
They've destroyed . . .

ANU: *Exasperated*

. . . Stop your blubbering!
You got your way, and here's its cost.
But if mankind must be punished
Then all the gods in lofty council
Will say who pays for death with death.

EXIT ANU & ISHTAR down rear platform steps; GILGAMESH, ENKIDU & CHORUS to side.

STANDING SONG 2:

HIGH PRIESTESS & MAGI

MAGI: *Accompanying eurythmy*

What will not mortals do for glory,
For immortality bestowed by words,
To live forever through a story
That by the countless generation's heard?

HIGH PRIESTESS: *Accompanying eurythmy*
Are not such stories like the wind?
Rush loudly past, then silent fall,
As lasting as a passing whim,
Glorious for a moment, then no more?

EXIT MAGI & HIGH PRIESTESS.

SCENE 4: *The Palace at Uruk*

ENTER GILGAMESH & ENKIDU on lower of platform.

ENKIDU:
Agh, Gilgamesh, agony overwhelms me!
Death battles with life within my very bones!
Must I crouch beneath the throne of Death
Never to feel the brightness of the sun,
Never to see my Gilgamesh again?

Agh, Gilgamesh, I see a young man
Whose face is dark, whose arms are clad
In blackest feathers. He comes to sweep me
Down the one way road to Death,
Where dust is food and tears the only drink.

GILGAMESH:
Agh, Enkidu, your pain within me echoes!
Agh, Enkidu, do not leave thy brother;
Agh, Enkidu, madness stalks my heart;
Agh, Enkidu, madness overwhelms me!

(GILGAMESH descends to stage; dons a dog skin in his madness & takes a spear.)

Montage 3: *Gilgamesh's madness & journey through mountains*

ENTER MAGI, HIGH PRIESTESS, EURYTHMY/PANTOMIME CHORUS.

MAGI & HIGH PRIESTESS: *Alternating unison & solo narration.*
Madness gripped his soul with terror, Gilgamesh, a king once mighty
Madly raved, howled in sorrow, hurling curses at the gods,
Casting down his crown and weapons, raving, fleeing
Mad with sorrow across the plains and to the mountains,
Destroying life where he found it, destroying all before his wrath.
High into the barren mountains fled the man more beast than man.
There he found a barren dwelling, the Scorpion-Man and his woman.

People unlike any other, they blocked his way with upraised hand:

ENTER SCORPION MAN & SCORPION WOMAN.
EXIT MAGI, HIGH PRIESTESS, EURYTHMY/PANTOMIME CHORUS.

SCORPION MAN:
Stop! Intruder. We guard the Gateway of the Sun. None may pass
Into the tunnel that he uses for his journey through the night.

SCORPION WOMAN:
Why intruder are you wailing like a woman for a child?

GILGAMESH:
Bitter is my lamentation. Fearing Death, I seek its meaning,
The hidden meaning of life and death.

SCORPION WOMAN:
Dark that passage, blinding,
Darkness!

SCORPION MAN:
All your passage must be finished ere the Sun-God
Ends his journey down the sky-road into night.

EXIT GILGAMESH, SCORPION MAN & SCORPION WOMAN.

(Musical interlude describing passage through mountain.)

SCENE 5: *Siduri's Lodge: confluence of world's rivers at Celestial Ocean's edge*

SIDURI, GILGAMESH, URSHANABI

ENTER SIDURI veiled and with Jug of the World's Rivers.

ENTER GILGAMESH.

SIDURI:
Surely this one wants to murder
Whoever stands in his way.
Against this man I'll bar my door.

(She withdraws behind a barrier. Gilgamesh lifts his spear.)

GILGAMESH:
Unbar your door, wise Siduri; sweet Refresher of the Gods
Unbar it now or I'll break it down. Only you the god's cupbearer,
Who pours the waters of life eternal, only you can share
What's needed to cross the wide Celestial Water
To Utnaphishtim and learn from him why men must die

SIDURI:
Gilgamesh, great is your folly.
You'll never find what you seek.

Since creation the lot of man
Has been to die. So fill your belly
With life's pleasures. Rejoice; be merry
All night and day. Rejoice; be merry
In feasting, dancing, singing, playing.
Array yourself in splendid clothes;
Wash your hair; bathe your body;
Attend the child who's in your care.
Love your wife and help your neighbor.
For that is all Man gets from life.

GILGAMESH: *Brandishing his spear*
That's not enough. Shall I, like Enkidu my brother, lie down
And never rise again. Shall a worm fall from my nose.

SIDURI: *Unafraid*
Then Gilgamesh, seek Urshanabi,
For he alone knows the channel
That leads across the timeless deep.

GILGAMESH:
How then, may I find him?

SIDURI: *Pointing*
Put down your spear for there he stands.
He shall lead you o'er the Sea of Death.

(Gilgamesh hesitates then lowers his spear to the ground.)

ENTER URSHANABI, signaling to follow.

EXIT SIDURI.

Montage 4: *Crossing the Sea of Death*

ENTER CHORUS of the SEA OF DEATH.

Gilgamesh & Urshanabi pantomime crossing the sea.

CHORUS of the SEA of DEATH:
Launched upon the deathly waters, forbidden waters it's death to touch,
Gilgamesh and Urshanabi pole by pole slowly crossed
Far beyond the realms of sunlight, far beyond day and night
Till they came to Utnaphishtim, in the land before the Flood.
There they found him by the seashore, silently upon his couch.

EXIT CHORUS OF SEA OF DEATH

SCENE 6: *Land From Before the Flood*

ENTER UTNAPHISTIM & WIFE. He lies on couch & sleeps; his wife stands in waiting.

ENTER GILGAMESH & URSHANABI.

(Gilgamesh & Urshanabi approach couch. Gilgamesh bows; Urshanabi stands behind him.)

UTNAPHISHTIM: *Not bothering to look or get up*
Mortal man, why did thou bother
To make your away across the sea?
Turn back; thy trip was futile.

GILGAMESH: *On knees*
O great and wise grandsire, Survivor of the Flood,
My friend is stiff, fallen silent; a worm dropped from his nose.
We two had conquered great Humbaba; the Bull of Heaven
We brought low. We chased the panther, slew the lion,
Sped like wind across the steppe! Yet still a worm dropped from his nose.
So still, my friend, so cold, so silent. He runs no more
At my side. Oh why, great grandsire, must men die?

UTNAPHISHTIM: *As before*
It is willed, willed forever:
Mortal man must suffer death.

GILGAMESH: *On knees*
O great and wise grandsire, Survivor of the Flood,
I cannot bear that answer. There must be more.

UTNAPHISHTIM: *As before*
So it's willed, willed forever.
Mortal man must suffer death.

UTNAPHISHTIM'S WIFE:
Husband, this one has made a journey
Greater than man ever made before.
Show pity; test him, test if he is worthy
To hear the council of the gods.

UTNAPHISTIM: *Sitting up*
Then test him.

UTNAPHISHTIM'S WIFE:
O Gilgamesh, for six days and seven nights
Thou may not sleep but must keep watch.
Only then may the gods find thee worthy
To teach thee more than man may know.
Crouch there, upon thy haunches.

(Gilgamesh does as commanded and immediately falls asleep.)

UTNAPHISHTIM: *As before*
Look, wife, so soon unworthy.
Sleep breathes on him like rain in mist.

UTNAPHISHTIM'S WIFE:
O, touch him, husband, so he awakes
And may return across the Celestial Sea.

UTNAPHISHTIM: *As before*
Mankind's wicked, crafty deceivers.
When he awakes he'll say he didn't sleep.
Place a little cake by his head
Then on the morrow place another;
For seven nights place the cakes.
Only then shall I awake him.

(She places the cakes one by one beside his head. A musical interlude delineates each passing day. After the last one's placed Utnaphishtim wakes Gilgamesh.)

GILGAMESH: *Waking*
Not yet had sleep crept up on me before thy touch drove it away.

UTNAPHISHTIM: *Laying down as before*
As I said, so men behave.

Look there, Gilgamesh, crafty liar:
Seven little cakes:
The first dried out;
The second bad;
The third soggy moist;
The fourth turned white;
The fifth all mold;
The sixth still fresh;
The seventh warm.
One for each day you slept.
Tell no more lies; the truth is clear.

(Utnaphishtim turns to Urshanabi.)

Urshanabi, may the landing place reject you.
Urshanabi, may your crossings heave with storms.
Urshanabi, you have ferried the unworthy.
Urshanabi, you will suffer for this wrong.
Take this liar from me.
So I may once again lie down
And dream the dreams the gods
Bestow on those found worthy.

(Urshanabi, dejected, leads Gilgamesh away but is stopped by the Wife.)

UTNAPHISHTIM'S WIFE:
O husband, the mortal looks so weary,
His trials were great, his suffering greater.
Show pity; reveal to him, at least,
The Secret of the Deep
So he may give it to Mankind.

UTNAPHISHTIM: *Lying on his back as before*
Of that and only that *may* he prove worthy.
Urshanabi, take him to the Navel of the Deep.
Then have him plunge down through the tunnel,
Through the dark and deathly waters,
And pluck the flower of eternal youth.

EXIT UTNAPHISTIM & WIFE; GILGAMESH & URSHANABI opposite.

Montage 5: *Plunging the Deep & the Lion of the Earth*

ENTER CHORUS OF THE SEA OF DEATH & THE LION OF THE EARTH.

CHORUS of SEA of DEATH: *Pantomime or eurythmy*
Down he plunged into the tunnel, heavy stones tied to his feet,
Down he plunged, sinking, sinking, sinking to the ocean's floor
Where he found the precious flower, grasped it, felt it prick his finger.
Felt he then youth within him, surging brightly through his veins,
So he cut the stones that bound him, surging upward, to life again!

Then upon the shore they landed, and Gilgamesh thanked the gods,
Rejoiced with all his heart to heaven that he'd found the sacred plant
Whose power brings youth eternal. "This I'll bring to my people,
Give to them this priceless gift." Then by a pool of living water
He stopped to bathe and put the precious flower down.

Stealthily came the serpent, the cunning Lion of the Earth,
Gliding silent through the grasses, drawn by the flower's promise;
Then it came upon the flower, that cunning Lion of the Earth,
And cunningly the snake devoured the joy and hope of Gilgamesh,
Leaving just its cast-off skin.

EXIT CHORUS OF THE SEA OF DEATH

GILGAMESH: *Lamenting*
O Urshanabi, for what has been all my labors?
For what has been my heart's blood spent?
For what have I, the greatest mortal, seen the deep?
Not for myself, nor for my people have I gained a single thing.

But look, rising mightily before us, the walls of Uruk!
Behold, Urshanabi, the mighty city's walls and towers,
Its dikes and dams.

ENTER MAGI & HIGH PRIESTESS & EURYTHMY CHORUS

Climb up and walk upon them, Urshanabi.
Are they not great? Only this can mortals wish for; this alone
Can give them fame. This alone makes life worth living.

EXODOS:

GILGAMESH & URSHANABI, HIGH PRIESTESS, MAGI & CHORUSEs

MAGI & HIS CHORUS:
What will not mortals do for glory,
For immortality bestowed by words,
To live forever through a story
That by the countless generation's heard?

HIGH PRIESTESS & HER CHORUS:
Are not such stories like the wind?
Rush loudly past, then silent fall,
As lasting as a passing whim,
Glorious for a moment, then no more?

EXEUNT

Chapter 3
Plays for Middle School

Students from sixth grade on want something new. Their expectations, while still very much those of children, are turning toward the future, and their sense of identity is beginning to orient itself towards adolescence. Although historical plays are a conventional (and safe) option for the teacher-director, they are not as much fun as a robust, theatrically challenging, and slightly sassy comedy. The essence of comedy is that it allows us to laugh at ourselves, and the finest comedies allow performers and audience to experience safely the ridiculousness of the human condition. Everybody—parents, teachers, and especially the students themselves—needs a good-natured laugh at what it means to be human. Where tragedy brings the light of understanding into the darkness of suffering, comedy reveals the darkness that lies hidden within the security of normalcy. While tragedy is the disaster from which we cannot escape, comedy is the same disaster made ridiculous and averted. Comedy is like an atmosphere charged with threat, throwing everyone into a mad panic, only to pass with just some thunder and a few drops of rain. It is a wildly sparking high voltage transformer that, when safely shut down, reveals itself to have been no more than a gigantic but harmless sparkler display.

One of the great pleasures of comedy is that it is paradoxical, complicated yet transparent; qualities that appeal greatly to adolescents. As the characters fall deeper and deeper into comic adversity, the audience is allowed to feel pleasurable anxiety at their misfortunes. At any moment someone could stand up and shout, "Don't do that! Can't you see you're being fooled?" But nobody ever does, and the problems only continue to deepen, careening ever closer to disaster. Comedy allows us to safely watch and take a detached, superior pleasure in the awful things that happen to others, something that is forbidden in everyday life. Similarly, misunderstandings abound in comedy, and everything is torn loose from its moorings. The simplest actions go astray, and complexity and disorder are the norm. The world of comedy progressively tumbles out of control. Comedy creates its own ridiculous universe, safely parallel to our own, and one into which we could easily fall if we were not so clever and wise (and safely situated in our seats).

Comedy has many subgenres, and farce is one of its greatest. Everything about a farce must be carefully designed; it must run like a well-tuned, high-speed machine. Each part must support the work of every other part; and, at its most absurd and unbelievable moments, it must neither falter nor permit the audience to object to its total implausibility. The plot must work perfectly, even if it becomes temporarily lost in the comic situations exploding on the stage; and most importantly the absurdity of its characters' actions must be completely believable within the little world of the play. This meticulous attention to detail might at first appear mechanical and pedantic, but it is essential if comedy is to succeed on an artistic level. The key to exquisite comedy, especially farce, is strong, self-confident ensemble work.

Comedy meets a great soul need for the turbulence of adolescence. Through it, middle school and high school students can artistically experience human folly, the mishaps this folly generates, and its ultimate resolution. They can feel also the comic paradox of pretending to be free of themselves while still glorying in who they actually are. Comedy permits them to poke fun at their most sacred vanities—striving to be cool, petulance, and indignant self-righteousness. They can act out their fantasies of ridicule and triumph over the oppressive authority of the adult world through a good comic play.

A good comic starting point is the stereotypic comedy developed by the Romans, which has evolved into modern situational comedy. To this day almost every comic device (generational conflict, mistaken identities, faithless and beguiling servants [employees], miserly and gullible masters [employers], run-away lovers and distracted parents, long "dead" siblings who suddenly appear, dithering patriarchs and rebellious, overconfident youths, cowardly soldiers, and insufferable braggarts) can be found in their prototypical form in these comedies. Slapstick and cross-dressing abound, and the jokes, to everyone's titillating delight, are insulting and off-color. The Roman comic playwrights stocked the shop, and playwrights and comedians have been buying there ever since.

This Way and That was written for sixth grade, but is suitable for all adolescents. When composing the play, I chose the classic device of mistaken identities and twins, modeling it on Shakespeare's *A Comedy of Errors* and Plautus's *The Twin Menaechmi*. In the mistaken-identity play, much is pre-established. There should be twins (the more the merrier) who have been separated at birth. These twins must unwittingly find themselves in the same place at the same time, and everyone they meet must confuse one for the other. Aggravating this confusion there must be a generational and masculine/feminine conflict, a romantic subplot, a master/servant or similar authority relationship, and a broad array of supporting characters who propel the confusion forward. Some cross-dressing helps. The play should be universal and contemporary, and everything that happens must make the audience laugh.

This Way and That, like other plays, was rooted in observation of a specific class of students. Each day at recess a group of my girls would form into a line and go through endless repetitions of a then current music-video-style dance routine. This routine was the most important thing in their lives, and its constant repetition aggravated and fascinated the boys to no end. There was also an ongoing friendly but physically aggressive rivalry between a boy and girl in the class, and another boy's constant bragging about anything and everything under the sun had become a running class joke. As I watched these and other behaviors, I began to associate the students and their various relationships with the stock characters and situations of Roman farce, a genre I had wanted to explore for years.

Although the creative, collaborative nature of rehearsal is key in lifting any play off the page and making it a theatrical experience, it is especially true for farce. For farce to work, the students must be disciplined in working to achieve the effects needed, and the teacher-director must always be open to spontaneous inspirations that will make themselves visible through the imaginations of the students. One afternoon, fairly late in the production schedule, we were rehearsing a classic slapstick routine in which too many people, trying to enter and exit the same door simultaneously, crash together at high speed. It was a wild scene, preceded by the braggart warrior, Bombasticus, trying to trim another character down to size with his six-foot sword. We had gotten everything down pretty well and were running it for speed when one of my students, cried out, "Mr. Pittis, let's have an instant replay!" "Yeah, in slow motion," cried another. "With a rewind," screamed a third. The suggestions were perfect, exactly what the scene and the timing of the play needed. Getting this business down was difficult work and took us hours of careful blocking, but in the performance it was a showstopper and defined the whole play.

This Way and That

A Farce for Young Adolescents In Three Fits (1995)

CHARACTERS: *In Order Of Speaking*

Astralus (son of Maximus Secundus)
Maximus Primus (a traveling jeweler, twin to Secundus)
Devius 1 (a slave-twin to Devius 2)
Minutus (a traveling merchant)
Maladia (a matchmaker)
Bombasticus (a bragging captain)
Maximus Secundus (a pig merchant; twin to Primus)
Flirtia (friend of Astrala)
Prissilia (friend of Astrala)
Gigglia (friend of Astrala)
Spacia (friend of Astrala)
Fortissima (housekeeper to Secundus)
Astrala (long-lost daughter of Primus)
Devius 2 (a slave-twin to Devius 1)
Pesta (a wine merchant)
Quackquintius (a doctor)
Queen Hyperpericulia (Queen of Bohemia)

Scene: A town on the coast of ancient Bohemia.

Set: Two building fronts, one a house, the other an inn; each with door, in between a courtyard, accessible from each. All entrances and exits through building doors, courtyard and stage right (the harbor) or left (the forum).

Casting Note: The same student can play Devius 1 & 2, needing only a stand-in for the final recognition scene. Flirtia, Prissilia, Gigglia, Spacia & Astrala are Roman style Valley Girls or whatever is the affectation held in disdain at the time.

ACT I, scene 1

ENTER PRIMUS & ASTRALUS FROM HARBOR

ASTRALUS:

Take heart uncle; things could be worse.

PRIMUS:

Worse, Astralus, what could be worse? For thirty years I've plied my trade as an honest jeweler in every port from Egypt to Spain. But now I'm completely ruined! Falsely accused by that Egyptian king of dishonest trade! Our goods all confiscated! Put on some leaky ship full of murderous thieves and dumped at their whim by night on some unknown shore! What could be worse?

ASTRALUS:

We could be dead.

PRIMUS:

Death would be welcomed compared to this. If it wasn't for the sacred oath I swore to your father, Maximus Secundus, I'd gladly die. We were twins; no two salty tears were ever more alike than he and I. From the moment of our births we never once were parted. We looked so much alike that not even our own mother could tell us apart. And when we were married we wanted so many of the same things in a wife only twins could satisfy us. Only our personalities were not the same; he was harsh while I've been mild.

I swore upon my soul if anything ever happened to him that I'd live solely for you, his only child. And he swore the same for my dear sweet daughter Astrala, may her soul be at peace. *(Weeping)* You were too young to know her, but she was as like you as I was like my brother, her mother like your mother.

ENTER DEVIUS 1 FROM HARBOR

DEVIUS 1:

Ah, masters; there you are!

PRIMUS:

Loyal Devius, what have you learned? What is this land called?

DEVIUS 1:

Ask a different question, master, and I'll tell you what you'd like to hear.

ASTRALUS:

Stop this riddle, slave; answer quick.

DEVIUS 1:

Master Maximus, let the boy beat me since I refuse.

PRIMUS:

I'll never beat you; come, tell us where we are.

DEVIUS 1:

We've been here before, fifteen years ago, but never set foot upon its shore, only heard the roar of waves upon its stormy beach. Heaven wept that night; *(Weeping)* We both lost our brothers that night; like you I lost my twin, but great as my loss was it was nothing next to yours. You lost your lovely little girl to that storm.

PRIMUS:

Oh cruel Bohemia! I curse that name!

ASTRALUS:

But Uncle, it's just a place, and not that bad from what I've heard. People say the women are famous for their friendliness, especially to strangers. I like it here. We're lucky being dumped in a place where the women don't greet us with a stick.

ENTER MINUTUS FROM FORUM

PRIMUS:

Good day, friend; Is this Bohemia?

MINUTUS:

It is. If you're strangers, beware! The queen Hyperpericulia has just learned the army she sent against Egypt has been destroyed. She seeks revenge and has hired the great captain Bombasticus to wipe the Egyptians off the earth.

All men between the ages of fifteen and thirty-five must serve or be put to death. As foreigners you'll serve as galley slaves.

ASTRALUS:

Things are worse.

DEVIUS 1:

And what becomes of those too old or weak to row?

MINUTUS:

Condemned as spies and their heads chopped off.

DEVIUS 1:

And their servants?

MINUTUS:

Too terrible to say. Take my advice; leave on the tide. There's a smuggler named Clandestus who'll help you for a price.

PRIMUS:
Thank you, friend; if ever you're in Athens, ask for me, Maximus; I'll help you in your need.

MINUTUS: *Preparing to leave*
Maximus? I've heard that name before. *(Turning)* One last word, the women in this town are too friendly; stay away from them.

EXIT MINUTUS TO HARBOR

ASTRALUS:
Doomed!

PRIMUS:
What will we do?

DEVIUS 1:
Let's get off this street; here's an inn; have we enough to rent a room? Quick, wrap Astralus' toga around him like a dress; he'll be safer as a girl, and a little of this red dirt will rogue his cheeks. . . .

ASTRALUS:
. . . but uncle; this isn't fair.

PRIMUS:
Stop whining; do you want to die a galley slave?

DEVIUS 1:
And some of this yellow straw, soaked and wrapped around his head, should make a wig and be enough to disguise him as a girl.

PRIMUS:
I hear some voices from the neighboring house!

EXIT PRIMUS, DEVIUS 1 & ASTRALUS TO INN

ACT I, scene 2
ENTER MALADIA & BOMBASTICUS FROM HOUSE

MALADIA: *(To within)*
Yes sir, Maximus, you couldn't make a better match; your niece Astrala is a lucky girl; when it comes to husbands, I've arranged the best. (*To Bombasticus)* It's signed and sealed. The girl is yours.

BOMBASTICUS:
She's a lucky one, gettin'me. A woman can't help but be happy when she gets a Man's Man. I should know; I've had lots of wives. Marry 'im young, and they learn faster than a dog. Take my first wife. She was fourteen. I loved her like my sword, a shame she died. Some plague. But I got a second one, but she only lasted a couple of days, fainted and fell under a chariot's wheels. (*Confidentially*) The excitement of worshiping me made her swoon.

MALADIA:
I'm sure.

BOMBASTICUS:
So I got another right away. I tell ya; I can pick 'im. People gossiped she was over seventy, but she looked good to me. Unless ya got up real close, you'd swear she was sixteen. And was she rich! Mountains of rings on her fingers and so many gold chains she needed a cane to stand up straight. And a lucky thing she got me when she did. Within two days she fell into the lion pit at the games. I jumped in to save her, but it was too late, so I slew the beast. The crowd went wild. That's the soldier's life.

MALADIA:
Maximus' niece has been brought up right, not like these modern girls who turn their husbands into wives. She's everything you want—dutiful, adoring, beautiful and young, only sixteen.

BOMBASTICUS:
Your words are like the cries of the wounded. But the wedding gift? I can't accept a penniless bride.

MALADIA:
A gift of 100 silver coins. . . .

BOMBASTICUS:
. . . 100 silver coins! I expected more!

MALADIA:
More, for so desirable a bride. What do you think I've found? Some crippled hag, hobbling on a cane? Astrala's been raised the old fashioned way. You'd lose her for some change?

BOMBASTICUS:
No, no, not at all. But when will I get...

MALADIA:
...hmm . . . .

BOMBASTICUS:
...the wedding gift?

MALADIA:
The bride you mean?

BOMBASTICUS:
That's what I said.

MALADIA:
It's all arranged. Maximus has promised to pay this afternoon. But listen closely, he's a tight-fisted man, never's let a penny get away. If you didn't have me he'd take you for a bag of wooden coins.

BOMBASTICUS: *(Swinging sword)*
Let him try. No one cheats Bombasticus.

MALADIA:
Just leave it to me, and everything will be fine. Remember the motto:

Matrimonial services
A modest fee.
Perpetual excitement guaranteed.

ENTER SECUNDUS FROM HOUSE

ENTER DEVIUS 2 FROM REAR OF YARD, Watching

SECUNDUS:
Devius! Where's that worthless slave?

MALADIA:
Ah, Maximus; I was just telling Bombasticus what a match we've made.

(Throughout Devius play acts everything Secundus says.)

SECUNDUS:
Where's that slave? It breaks my heart to let her go. She was my twin brother's only child. Devius! Born the same day as my poor drowned boy. I saved her life, you know, when our ship was lost. I tell you, never count on a slave. It was a terrible night, waves like mountains tossed our ship. Everyone wept and prayed, but I was busy saving . . .

DEVIUS 2: *(Simultaneously)*
. . . gold.

SECUNDUS:
Devius! My brother, Maximus Primus, held the little ones, but when I saw the babes sucked from his arms I dropped everything . . . .

DEVIUS 2: *(Aside)*
Gold sinks faster than a child.

SECUNDUS:
. . . and struggled toward the children.

DEVIUS 2:
. . . like a drowning man for straw.

BOMBASTICUS:
I'd've done the same.

MALADIA:
Gentlemen; this evening there'll be time to share your tales, . . .

DEVIUS 2:
When each has nearly drowned in wine.

MALADIA:
. . . but now you both have many things to do before the wedding rites.

SECUNDUS:
Yes, you're right; Devius! Where's that slave?

EXIT SECUNDUS TO HOUSE

MALADIA:
I've business at the harbor. Love never takes a break.

BOMBASTICUS:
I'll walk with you.

MALADIA:
It's just a little way.

BOMBASTICUS:
I saw some men who'll swell my ranks.

DEVIUS 2:
Since the plague the harbor's full of limping sickly men who'll gladly sell their lives for a better way to die.

MALADIA:
But why would a man's man as great as you need help; I've heard you once killed ten thousand men just by looking at them.

BOMBASTICUS:
I don't like to boast, but it's true. I'll tell you, as a friend, I don't need troops to fight. They're simply there for show. The heavy work I do myself. *(Swings sword)* My men take the body count and tell the world how many millions I've slain.

EXIT MALADIA & BOMBASTICUS TO HARBOR

DEVIUS 2:
Millions, MILLIONS! The fool, either he kills his own men or the same man twenty times. How else explain the body count. "Stand up; fight like a man! Take that! Now die again, you bag of bones!"

ENTER SECUNDUS FROM HOUSE

SECUNDUS:
Oh, they're a crafty pair. I must be careful, or they'll get my money and leave me with the girl. *(To audience)* Did you know the cost of raising a girl is twice the price of just one breeding pig?
There you are! Now listen closely. I'm finally rid of my niece; what a drain! It was hard, but Maladia's found a match. But will it cost! Bombasticus has insisted on 100 silver coins, plus the girl! Can you believe the cost!?! But still that's cheaper than her yearly keep.

Now here's my plan. I have those worthless rings that you took for a load of pigs; here's your chance to fix that deal. I've polished them till they shine. That wine merchant, Pesta, has a pickled brain; she'll take them off my hands. Tell her they're really fine, but because I love my niece—And I'm low on cash. I'll take half their worth. Do this right, and there's wine in it for you *(Secundus weighs & gives sack of rings)*

DEVIUS 2:
Oh, master; never has a slave been as fortunate as I. *(Puts out hand for rings)*

SECUNDUS:
Don't give me that. Make the deal. *(Withholds rings)* I'll tell Astrala the news.

DEVIUS 2:
She doesn't know?

SECUNDUS:
Why should she? The rings are mine. *(Rubbing his hands)* The lucky dear.

EXIT DEVIUS 2 TO FORUM
EXIT SECUNDUS TO HOUSE

ACT I, scene 3

ENTER FLIRTIA, PRISSILIA, GIGGLIA, SPACIA FROM FORUM

GIGGLIA:
Oh, wow!

FLIRTIA:
And then what?

PRISSILIA:
So I said, "Just try; see if I care." And Daddy said, "I don't care what you say; the answer's no!"

FLIRTIA:
Oh, wow!

GIGGLIA:
And then what?

PRISSILIA:
So I just threw myself on my bed and cried.

SPACIA:
Oh, wow!

GIGGLIA:
And then what?

PRISSILIA:
My maid came.

FLIRTIA:
Oh, wow!

SPACIA:
And then what?

PRISSILIA:
I threw myself on the floor, pulled my hair and sobbed.

SPACIA:
Oh, wow!

FLIRTIA:
And then what?

PRISSILIA:
The house slaves came.

GIGGLIA:
Oh, wow!

SPACIA:
And then what?

PRISSILIA:
I ripped the curtains from the wall, threw the furniture into the atrium, and screamed.

FLIRTIA:
Oh, wow!

GIGGLIA:
And then what?

PRISSILIA:
The kitchen slaves came.

GIGGLIA:
Oh, wow!

FLIRTIA:
And then what?

PRISSILIA:
I grabbed a little bottle I'd prepared for the occasion, held it high and cried "it's poison; apologize right away, or I die!"

GIGGLIA:
Oh, wow!

FLIRTIA:
And then what?

PRISSILIA:
He went and bought the little silver leash I needed for my parakeet.

SPACIA/GIGGLIA:
Oh, wow!

FLIRTIA:
And then what?

PRISSILIA:
I did my hair.
(A blood curdling scream from within)
ENTER ASTRALA FROM HOUSE

ASTRALA: (Seeing girls)
I'll die! I'll drink poison! I'll stab myself to death with my finger nails!

GIRLS:
Oh, wow!

ASTRALA:

I'm doomed! I'll die before I marry Bombasticus!

FLIRTIA:

That grinning brute who struts around . . .

GIGGLIA:

. . . dragging that huge sword

SPACIA:

. . . and trying to kiss every girl he sees?

ASTRALA:

The same!

GIGGLIA:

Whose first wife caught the plague so she could die when he tried to kiss her?

ASTRALA:

The same!

FLIRTIA:

Whose second wife threw herself beneath a chariot's wheels when he tried to kiss her?

ASTRALA:

The same!

SPACIA:

Whose third was a hundred and five and jumped to the lions at the games when he tried to kiss her?

ASTRALA:

The same! And I'm the fourth!

GIRLS:

Oh, wow! Did he try to kiss you?

ASTRALA: (*Makes sour face, wails.*)

What will become of me? Flirtia, please, strangle me with my hair.

ENTER FORTISSIMA FROM HOUSE

FORTISSIMA:

Oh, you poor dear! First you lose your loving father in a storm, then you're saved by your uncle Maximus, and now you have to marry that bragging boar!

ASTRALA:

Oh, why didn't Uncle Maximus just let me drown. Why, Fortissima, why?

FORTISSIMA:

A handsome profit hidden somewhere, but he'll take a loss and regret this scheme.

ASTRALA:

That's disloyal!

FORTISSIMA:

Big deal! He never cared for you a bit.

ASTRALA:

He saved my life.

FORTISSIMA:

You washed into his arms.

GIRLS:

Oh, wow!

FORTISSIMA:

How many times have I heard the old buzzard complain about how much you've cost.

Less than an hour ago I heard him tell Maladia, "If only Astrala were a slave, I'd have sold her for a handsome price, but now she costs me a dowry and a wedding feast."

He's the twin that should've drowned. Just this morning as I was throwing crumbs to the birds, he cried, "Don't waste that food; it'll feed Astrala for a week."

GIRLS:

Oh, wow!

ENTER DEVIUS 2 FROM FORUM

DEVIUS 2:

The deal's arranged. The wine merchant Pesta really does have a pickled brain; she's just dying to get my master's rings. What's this? I'll listen in. Maybe some profit can be made.

ASTRALA:
Please, help me; you're my only friends.

GIGGLIA:
My aunt lives in Thebes; she'll hide you there. When she was young Maximus courted her; but when he learned how much a wife would cost, he dropped her like a burning coal. She never forgot the shame.

FLIRTIA:
But if we're caught?

GIRLS:
Bombasticus!

SPACIA:
Oh, wow!

FORTISSIMA:
Your plan sounds fine.

DEVIUS 2:
And profitable too.

FORTISSIMA:
But how will we get her there?

DEVIUS 2:
One hint to Maximus of this, and I'll have a barrel of wine.

FORTISSIMA:
Disguise her as a boy! I'll get Maximus to believe what we want by telling the cook that you're off to town to spread the joyous news. She'll run to him right away and blather all she's learned.

EXIT FORTISSIMA TO HOUSE

GIRLS: (*Alternating*)
Like oh, my god / She just got a manicure; / A boy I swear / We've gotta change her gorgeous hair. / A boy, a boy, a girl, a girl; / Take some sissors to those curls. / Go, go, dress right; / Gee, I hope she looks all right. / Oh wow, / oh wow, / oh wow!

DEVIUS 2: *(Dancing with girls)*
Oh wow, oh wow; This is worth a lake of wine; Oh wow, oh wow. . . .

ENTER FORTISSIMA FROM HOUSE (Grabs Devius 2)

FORTISSIMA:
. . . Insect! What've you heard?

DEVIUS 2:
Nothing I couldn't forget if the price was right.

FORTISSIMA:
(Punches alternately) Here's a price that's right, and the left too.

DEVIUS 2: (Crying)
Oh, my little mouse; you tenderize me; it was just a joke.

FORTISSIMA:
Then, laugh. *(Swats him harder)*

DEVIUS 2:
Oughaahaoughhaaougha.

FORTISSIMA:
I'll tell our master about those pigs you said had died. He'll beat you to a pulp and then I'll tell about that barrel of wine.

DEVIUS 2:
Please, my mouse; I've already forgotten what I heard.

FORTISSIMA:
You slithering worm; you'll not forget what we've said; you're gonna help us make our plans. Now listen careful. Clandestus smuggles people who need to escape; arrange with him for our escape.

DEVIUS 2:
But that costs! How will I pay?

FORTISSIMA:
You have your ways. Girls, you have brothers; teach Astrala how to be a boy. *(To Devius)* Now.

DEVIUS 2:

Yes, my mouse.

EXIT FORTISSIMA TO HOUSE

EXIT FLIRTIA, PRISSILIA, GIGGLIA, SPACIA, ASTRALA TO FORUM

DEVIUS 2:

I've been in worse trouble before and always turned trouble into gain. *(Rubs his fingers)* And here's trouble enough to make me rich.

It's not just the money I want. I want to pay my master back, . . . for all he's given me; . . . each whipping, cuffing, clubbing and cruel word. I've the ambition of the slave—get revenge and run away! Maximus should foot the bill. But I can't say, "Generous master, your niece and household slaves plan to run away and humiliate you in front of all the town; give us a hundred silver coins." "Certainly, Devius; here's my purse; take what you need."

Here's Pesta for my master's rings. Oh, thank you gods! Here's some fun for a moment or two. Watch.

Act I, scene 4

ENTER PESTA FROM FORUM

DEVIUS 2:

It's about time, Pesta. What took you?

PESTA:

No help from anybody; the streets are swarming with so many bill collectors I almost didn't make it here. There was one lying wait for me at every corner.

DEVIUS 2:

It's a lovely day.

PESTA:

Fair enough . . .

DEVIUS 2:

. . . Wouldn't you say that it's a shame that slaves can't enjoy a day like this.

PESTA:

I couldn't say . . . Have you the rings?

DEVIUS 2:

. . . Rings? There are so many. The *ding dong ding*, or the *dong ding dong*, or the *ding ding dong*, or, AH!, the *dong dong ding*? Now my master prefers the *chingle, chingle chingle* . Just this morning I heard him say, "Nothing beats the *chinkle, chinkle chinkle* of a fat purse full of coins." Which do you like?

PESTA:

I wouldn't say. Now enough of your chatter and give me the rings?

DEVIUS 2: *(Singing tones)*

Ding, dong, ding. Dong ding ding. Ding ding dong.

PESTA:

The rings!

DEVIUS 2:

What do you think those were?

PESTA:

That's not what I want.

DEVIUS 2:

Ah! You must want *Dong, dong, dong, dong, dong, dong, dong* . . .

PESTA: *(Interrupting)*

No; your master's rings.

DEVIUS 2:

My master's rings? Ah! *(Singing inanely)* Chingle, chingle, chingle!

PESTA:

I mean . . .

DEVIUS 2:

. . . Mean? No, my master's not that kind.

Why, just this morning when he was beating me, he went to grab his whip and cried out, "No, I'm not that kind!" And grabbed a chain instead. Ah, did that ring: *clang, clang clang*, clang, clang! No pitiful ding, ding, ding, but a mighty *CLANG CLANG CLANG.*

PESTA:

I mean . . . I mean . . !!!

DEVIUS 2:

Don't shout.

PESTA:

Agh! The half price rings!

DEVIUS 2:

Ding dong? You couldn't mean half a ring?

PESTA:

Agh! The half price rings!

DEVIUS 2:

What kind of master do you take Secundus for? A half wit? Imagine: *(Singing) ong ding*? Or, *ing dong*. He enjoys more full bodied sounds, like "*Clang*! Agh! *Clang*! Agh! *(Miming a beating)* He's not that kind.

PESTA:

Agh! No! the finger rings, the kind he means to give his neice Astrala!

DEVIUS 2:

His neice! Now, she's a *RRRRINGA DING DING*! No, puny *ding dong ding*. Today's her wedding day, you know? Ah, *(Ringing to the tume of "Here Comes the Bride" Ding, ding, ding-dong..."*

PESTA:

Agh! Enough!

DEVIUS 2:

Enough? That's hardly enough. My master wouldn't cheat his neice. You know how much he resents when people say he's a selfish, nasty, tight-fisted miser who'd deny a thirsty man a sip of water because it costs to wash the cup?

PESTA:

Hm; that's true.

DEVIUS 2:

Would you want people to think my master Secundus thinks she worth only a "Ding ding ding?". You have to help him; help people change, their minds, or else he'll have to live his life a lonely, despised man. Ah! I know what we can do! *(Grabbing her with great enthusiasm)* I'll I bring her to your shop and you cry out in a voice that can be heard across the harbor, "So you've come for your chingle, chingle chingle!" Then give her a hundred silver coins. Count them out, one by one, then count them out again, at least three times, each time louder than the last.

PESTA:

Now, at least, you're making sense counting one by one at least three times; that's your master's way.

DEVIUS 2:

Ah, you see; it all makes sense; this is the way he shows his love.

PESTA:

It's true; people only judge you by what you've spent. *(She turns to go then stops.)* But the rings?

DEVIUS 2:

Ding ding, ding-dong! Ding, ding, ding-dong! Hurry; she's on her way this very moment. *Ding, DING, ding, ding, DING, ding ding, ding ding ding, ding ding ding ding-dong!*

EXIT PESTA TO FORUM (Muttering & shaking head)

DEVIUS 2:

Now I've only got to get those rings, and

then the coins, and we're gone. And if it fails? I'll get a beating, spend some time in chains. But a slave is born to chains, and beatings are his fate. But a master always needs a slave for some devious scheme, and I'll soon be free and about my ways. What do I know about Clandestus that might shave his price?

EXIT DEVIUS 2 TO HARBOR

ACT II, scene 1

ENTER SECUNDUS FROM HOUSE

SECUNDUS:

Merchants and servants rob me blind. Fortissima! Fortissima! Where's that slave? I've spent a fortune keeping her, and now when I have to spend another fortune on a wedding feast she's nowhere to be found. But at least I'll finally be rid of Astrala. For a while there when she began to scream I was worried. Thought I'd have to chain her to the bed. A nasty scene—dragging a screaming bride to the nuptial rites. Who knows what that could've cost? Bombasticus could've easily demanded twice the price! Fortissima! Where is that wench?

EXIT SECUNDUS TO YARD

ENTER DEVIUS 1 FROM INN

DEVIUS 1:

Oh, where can my dear master be? He should've been back from making the arrangements for our escape by now. No sooner had I wrestled Astralus into his wig than he heard some girls giggling in the street and started bellowing like a calf. I need some help; oh dear, where can Maximus be?

ENTER SECUNDUS FROM YARD

SECUNDUS:

That worthless Fortissima's nowhere to be seen. Devius; everything arranged?

DEVIUS 1:

I've done just like you asked, but Astral . . .

SECUNDUS:

. . . Don't worry. Take this *(Tosses sack of rings)* and don't get cheated this time. Fortissima! Where is that wench?

EXIT SECUNDUS TO YARD

DEVIUS 1: *(Looking in bag)*

Thank god! We've something after all.

EXIT DEVIUS 1 TO INN

ENTER ASTRALUS FROM INN as girl, throwing down a rope

ENTER PRIMUS FROM HARBOR

PRIMUS:

Everything's set; we leave on the tide. *(Astralus flirts; Primus is shocked and disgusted.)*

EXIT PRIMUS TO INN

ASTRALUS:

Whew! That was close. This disguise is useful after all. They'll see the pillows heaped beneath the sheets and think I'm asleep. Where are those girls?
Great gods! Uncle Maximus again! How did he get over there? Darn!

EXIT ASTRALUS TO INN

ENTER SECUNDUS FROM YARD

SECUNDUS:

Nowhere to be found. I have to do everything myself.

EXIT SECUNDUS TO FORUM

ENTER PRIMUS & DEVIUS 1 FROM INN

PRIMUS:

Don't worry Devius; let him sleep. This town is as dangerous and crazy as we were warned. Just now I saw three youths hauled off by some beast of a warrior. Then he fell upon me, called me by name and bragged endlessly about all sorts of intimate things. No sooner did I get away than another raving fool latched onto me; she claimed she knew me and jabbered about some wedding. I'm glad when we're gone. But first I have to find someone named Pesta; Clandestus the smuggler said she collects antique jewelry and will pay whatever I ask for my ring. Be ready when I return.

DEVIUS 1:

Be careful master, and please stay away from the women like we were warned.

PRIMUS:

Don't worry Devius, I saw one already; they're too ugly for me. Getting enough money for our escape is my only concern.

EXIT PRIMUS TO FORUM

ENTER FORTISSIMA FROM HOUSE

FORTISSIMA:

"Fortissima! Fortissima!" He barks just like a dog. I've better things to do than jump at his command.

(Aside) Here's Devius. He looks like something's up; I better check him out; you never know what plan he has of his own. I'll treat him nice; see what that shows. *(Smiles and flirts)*

DEVIUS 1: *(Aside)*

Just like the merchant warned! *(Smiles back)*

FORTISSIMA: *(Aside)*

He is too nice; something's wrong. Like some lunch? *(Smiles back)*

DEVIUS 1:

No, thank you ma'am; I'm not hungry.

FORTISSIMA: (*Aside*)

There's a lie. *(Brandishes fly swatter)* Get inside.

DEVIUS 1: (*Aside*)

The woman's mad; she'll start a scene. *(Smiles and nods to FORTISSIMA*) I'd love some lunch.

FORTISSIMA:

Get inside.

EXIT FORTISSIMA & DEVIUS 1 TO HOUSE

ACT II, scene 2

ENTER FLIRTIA, PRISSILIA, GIGGLIA, SPACIA, ASTRALA AS BOY FROM FORUM

GIGGLIA:

Now remember everything you've learned about being a boy, or you'll give yourself away.

FLIRTIA:

First, how do you speak?

ASTRALA:

In a loud and barking voice.

PRISSILIA:

And never wait your turn.

FLIRTIA:

And when you enter a room?

ASTRALA: (Swaggering like a boy)

Throw myself into the best chair, scratch my butt and burp.

SPACIA:

Oh, wow!

PRISSILIA:

Good, and don't forget to drape yourself across its arms . . .

GIGGLIA:

. . . and scrape some mud onto the floor.

FLIRTIA:

And if you don't like what your told?

ASTRALA:

Mutter "so fake" in a sarcastic tone.

GIGGLIA:

Good, and when food is served.

ASTRALA:
Grab for the meat and eat it with my hands.

PRISSILIA:
And when you're told to stop?

ASTRALA:
Say I wasn't told?

SPACIA:
Oh, wow.

ASTRALA:
Is this really how your brothers act?

FLIRTIA:
Worse, but you haven't time to learn.

GIGGLIA:
Prissilia, put on Astrala's shawl and wrap it around your face so Maximus will be fooled.

PRISSILIA:
But what should I do?

FLIRTIA:
Just what a man expects—giggle and fix your hair; if they see that they won't look for anything more.

PRISSILIA:
But . . . but . . . what about the wedding ceremony?

SPACIA:
Oh, wow!

GIGGLIA:
We didn't think of that!

FLIRTIA:
Here's what you do—if you get to the altar, throw a fit and scream.

PRISSILIA:
And if it doesn't work?

GIRLS:
Bombasticus!

ENTER DEVIUS 1 FROM HOUSE

DEVIUS 1:
Thank god I'm free of that bossy wench and her lousy food; I thought I'd have to eat until I'd puke.

SPACIA: *(Just noticing)*
Wow, what a disguise.

DEVIUS 1: *(Seeing Astrala, mistaking her for Astralus)*
There you are! I've been worried sick. Are you mad, going around as a boy?! *(Grabs Astrala's hand)*

EXIT DEVIUS 1 & ASTRALA TO INN

FLIRTIA:
The slave's mad.

SPACIA:
Oh, wow.

EXIT FLIRTIA, PRISSILIA, GIGGLIA, SPACIA TO HOUSE, SHRUGGING SHOULDERS & DANCING INTO HOUSE.

ACT II, scene 3

ENTER ASTRALUS FROM YARD (Wig in hand)

ASTRALUS:
Where are those girls? Oh, darn; what girl will want to talk to me in this stupid dress! *(Reacts to voices, hides)*

EXIT ASTRALUS TO YARD

ENTER PESTA AND MALADIA FROM HARBOR

ENTER PRIMUS FROM FORUM

MALADIA:
Ah, Maximus; you clever fox. What a scheme! Our friend was just telling me how you'll show your niece how much you care. She'll be impressed.

PESTA:
But, friend, it's not wise to let a girl whose head is filled with dreams of married bliss carry so great a sum. Here, take the payment now for the rings; send your slave Devius with them later on.

PRIMUS:
But . . .

PESTA:
I know; I know; how will she know your love? I've thought of that. In my shop I have some ornamental coins, big as dishes. They're next to worthless but will impress a child. When you send the girl, I'll count those out. Rest assured she'll think you're a prince.

EXIT PESTA AND MALADIA TO FORUM

ENTER DEVIUS 2 FROM HARBOR

PRIMUS:
This place is crazed! But somehow I must find this woman Pesta; she's nowhere to be found. Faithful Devius; Thank god! Everything ready for our escape?

DEVIUS 2: *(Terrified, plays along)*
Whatever you say.

PRIMUS:
I swear that once we're safely away from here I'll set you free, with all the money you'd ever need.

DEVIUS 2:
Freedom? Wealth? (*Aside*) Now who's crazed?

PRIMUS: *(Shouting)*
Yes, good Devius, and whatever else you'd want. Guard these coins; some lunatic shoved them into my hand. Now run inside and get Astral . . .

DEVIUS 2 PUTS A FINGER TO HIS LIPS

PRIMUS: *(Whispering)*
What a friend. I'm off to the harbor to see that Clandestus does not leave until we're all aboard. (gives hug and kiss) Wealth and Freedom, and whatever else you want!

EXIT PRIMUS TO HARBOR

DEVIUS 2:
Master's gone insane. *(Opens sack)* And here's the money that I schemed to steal. Wealth and freedom have come my way. For years I've worked by stealth and wit to steal such things and now a fortune drops into my hands. Where's the sport? What will become of mischief in this world!

ENTER ASTRALUS FROM YARD (Sees Devius & tries to turn)

DEVIUS 2:
What! still a girl?! Don't you know we've got to go. *(Takes a couple of coins and tosses the rest to Astralus)* Wait here; don't move an inch. I'll get my things.

EXIT DEVIUS 2 TO YARD

ASTRALUS:
My uncle and Devius are such bores, and they act so strange. I haven't met a single girl. What's this? Money! *(Sees girls)* Okay, now I'll have a good time.

ENTER FLIRTIA, GIGGLIA, SPACIA FROM HOUSE

FLIRTIA:
Still a girl?!

GIGGLIA:
What's wrong with you?

SPACIA:
Wow, you look strange!

FLIRTIA:
Hurry! What's wrong with you?

GIGGLIA:
Bombasticus will soon be here!

GIGGLIA: (Grabbing her)
Come on; we'll take you to your room . . .

FLIRTIA:
. . . and make you a man.

ASTRALUS:
Oh, wow!

ENTER DEVIUS 1 FROM INN

DEVIUS 1: (*Pulling Astralus aside)*
Young master! Why did you leave your

room? Don't you realize the women in this town have no shame, and here you are, the center of a scene.

FLIRTIA: (Grabbing Astralus)
She's ours; we're making her a man.

ASTRALUS:
Please, Devius; it's my only chance.

ENTER FORTISSIMA FROM HOUSE

DEVIUS 1:
Great gods!

FORTISSIMA:
Devius, be a "hon" and get my things.

DEVIUS 1:
Your things?

FORTISSIMA:
For our escape. *(Takes his arm)*

DEVIUS 1:
See what I mean.

EXIT DEVIUS 1, FORTISSIMA, ASTRALUS, FLIRTIA, GIGGLIA, SPACIA TO HOUSE

ENTER DEVIUS 2 FROM YARD (with sack)

DEVIUS 2:
Where's that girl? Oh, great gods; I better hide.

EXIT DEVIUS 2 TO INN

ENTER SECUNDUS FROM HARBOR

SECUNDUS:
Where's that slave; he was just here?

DEVIUS 1: *(*Within*)*
I don't know what you're talking about; I never saw you before this morning.

FORTISSIMA: *(Within)*
Insect; how can you say that; are you mad?

SECUNDUS: (Hand on Inn door)
I swear he ducked in here, but now I hear him over there.

EXIT SECUNDUS TO HOUSE

ENTER ASTRALA & DEVIUS 2 FROM INN

DEVIUS 2:
What were you doing in there?

ASTRALA:
You took me in.

DEVIUS 2:
No way!

ASTRALA:
But you . . . , my uncle comes!

DEVIUS 2:
How can this be? He just was right here! An evil spirit is afoot that carries him this way, then that. *(Grabs Astrala's arm)*

EXIT DEVIUS 2 & ASTRALA TO YARD

ENTER PRIMUS FROM HARBOR

PRIMUS:
Where are they? The tide's changed; we must set sail.

EXIT PRIMUS TO INN

ENTER DEVIUS 2 AND ASTRALA FROM YARD

DEVIUS 2:
What!?! I just gave you the sack of coins!

ASTRALA:
Coins? No, you didn't!

DEVIUS 2:
How can you . . . I should throw you to your uncle and Bombasticus.

ASTRALA:
(Screams & faints; Devius 2 catches her)

DEVIUS 2:
Great gods protect us! *(Turns to flee into house, hears Fortissima, turns again to flee)*

FORTISSIMA:
Insect!

DEVIUS 2:
. . . Roasted or fried? *(Faces Bombasticus)*

ENTER BOMBASTICUS FROM FORUM

BOMBASTICUS:
Halt slave! Or I'll run you through. Where's your master?

DEVIUS 2:
Hahahaha.

BOMBASTICUS:
I heard he's here; I want my wedding gift. Who's the whoosh?

DEVIUS 2:
Aah, Aah. . . Astralus! A friend of mine.

BOMBASTICUS:
A stranger to these parts?

DEVIUS 2:
No, no, born here and raised.

BOMBASTICUS:
I'll be back to sign you up, but not today; I'm getting married to Maximus' little niece. One lucky doll, gettin' me. Now where is that master of yours?

DEVIUS 2:
Ahlulululu. . .

BOMBASTICUS:
Well, he's not that way, so he must be this.

EXIT BOMBASTICUS TO HARBOR

ASTRALA:
All's lost.

ENTER MALADIA FROM FORUM

MALADIA:
Where's Maximus? I want my payment now; I know he has the money; I saw him give it to Pesta with my own eyes. Who's the boy? New around here?

DEVIUS 2:
Oh no, just arrived.

MALADIA:
Well, if you need help with a good match, and by his looks he will, just drop by. *(Gives Astrala her card)* Maximus!

EXIT MALADIA TO HOUSE

DEVIUS 2:
Quick, while we've a chance. *(Start,stop)*

ENTER PRIMUS FROM INN

PRIMUS:
There you are. I've been worried sick. Everything's arranged. Still a boy? *(Grabs Astrala's arm)* Quick Devius, get the bags. Clandestus won't wait long.

ASTRALA:
Uncle, not so hard.

PRIMUS:
It's not so soft being a galley slave, come on.

EXIT PRIMUS AND ASTRALA TO HARBOR

DEVIUS STUPID WITH CONFUSION, BEGINS TO SPIN AROUND

ENTER PESTA FROM FORUM

PESTA:
You worthless slave! Where are my rings?

DEVIUS 2:
Ahlulululu. . . .

PESTA:
. . . I should have known it was just another of Maximus' miserly schemes to cheat me. I'm settling this once and for all.

DEVIUS 2: *(Flapping his arms)*
Ahlulululu. . .

PESTA:
Fool!

EXIT PESTA TO HOUSE (Explosive shouting is heard from within house.)

DEVIUS 2:
Oh. . . ; I think it's time we take a break; there's refreshments in the lobby if you like. As for myself I'd best be scarce. Back with the pigs there's a barrel of Maximus' wine; if I drink it all before I'm caught my beating won't hurt half as much. But remember to come back to see how I untie these knots.

EXIT DEVIUS 2 TO YARD

INTERMISSION

ACT III, scene 1

ENTER SECUNDUS FROM HOUSE

SECUNDUS:
A thief! I know your kind. How dare you call me a thief? You're the thieves, preying on honest men. Police! Police! Police!

ENTER MALADIA, PESTA, FORTISSIMA FROM HOUSE

MALADIA:
Police! Police! Police!

PESTA:
Police! Police! Police!

MALADIA:
Swindler!

PESTA:
I gave you the money right here on this street.

SECUNDUS:
You're in cahoots! Swindlers! I swear upon my ancestors' graves I never saw a cent.

PESTA:
I'll have you in court for this; no one cheats me.

MALADIA: *(Waving contract)*
I have my reputation to uphold. Bombasticus will hear of this.

SECUNDUS:
You think I'm scared? That puff of wind!

MALADIA:
Right here; *(Pointing to contract)* see what it says. The girl is mine if you don't pay.

SECUNDUS:
Parasite! *(Tries to grab contract; Pesta holds him back)*

MALADIA:
Ha! She's mine!

SECUNDUS:
No! She's mine!

MALADIA:
Hahaha; tell it to the judge!

ENTER FLIRTIA, GIGGLIA, SPACIA, ASTRALUS DEVIUS 1 FROM HOUSE

FORTISSIMA:
Run, while there's a chance.

SPACIA:
Oh wow; what's happenin' here?

PESTA:
There's the culprit! *(Grabs Devius 1)*

MALADIA:
Ah; now she's mine! *(Grabs Astralus)*

SECUNDUS:
Give her back! Devius! Help me you wretch, or its a month in chains!

(Grabs Astralus: tug of war)

GIRLS:
("Shall we dance; boom, boom, boom" routine; everyone's shocked; they release prisoners.)

DEVIUS 1:
Young master! Here's our chance!

(Grabs Astralus, towards harbor, sees Bombasticus, freezes, bolts into yard)

EXIT ASTRALUS & DEVIUS 1 TO YARD

ENTER BOMBASTICUS FROM HARBOR, WAVING GIANT SWORD AT SECUNDUS WHO JUMPS AND DUCKS; VALLEY GIRLS CHEERLEAD

BOMBASTICUS: *(Snarling war cry)*
You can't humiliate Bombasticus and live another day! SIR! do you deny that you just saw me, and, SIR! didn't you run away? And SIR! where is my bride!

SECUNDUS:
I didn't do anything; I'm innocent!

BOMBASTICUS:
I saw you, SIR! and some girl walking by the dock. I was courteous and polite, SIR!

and greeted you. But you, SIR! turned and ran, shouting, "Flee; he's insane!"

SECUNDUS:

I did not; I swear upon my ancestors' graves I haven't laid eyes on you since I saw you here this morning.

SPACIA:

Wow, weird.

BOMBASTICUS:

Lying dog; prepare to die!

PESTA:

See! What did I say; he's a liar and a thief!

BOMBASTICUS:

Off with his head!

Secundus breaks free, crashes through screaming girls.

SECUNDUS:

I'll have justice from the queen!

EXIT SECUNDUS TO FORUM

FORTISSIMA:

The swine!

BOMBASTICUS:

To arms! *(Blows trumpet)*

(Girls sit down and begin to meditate.)

EXIT BOMBASTICUS, MALADIA, PESTA, FORTISSIMA TO FORUM

ENTER ASTRALUS AND DEVIUS 1 FROM YARD

ASTRALUS:

Please Devius; the girls! It's my only chance.

DEVIUS 1:

Your uncle waits! *(Drags Astralus away)* But first our things!

EXIT DEVIUS 1 & ASTRALUS TO INN

ACT III, scene 2

ENTER SECUNDUS FROM YARD

SECUNDUS:

Hunted like a lion! They're everywhere!

EXIT SECUNDUS TO AUDITORIUM

ENTER BOMBASTICUS, FORTISSIMA, MALADIA AND PESTA FROM FORUM

BOMBASTICUS:

There! In that crowd!

FORTISSIMA:

He's mine!

MALADIA:

No, mine!

PESTA:

Just wait!

(Fortissima waves hand in front of girls but can't bring them back to earth.)

EXIT BOMBASTICUS, MALADIA, PESTA TO AUDITORIUM

ENTER DEVIUS 1 & ASTRALUS FROM INN

DEVIUS 1:

Great gods; the whole town's gone insane. Quick, young master, hide in that chicken coop. I'll sacrifice myself and lead them away. *(Hides Astralus behind him)*

BOMBASTICUS: *(From auditorium)*

There's the slave!

FORTISSIMA:

Insect!

EXIT FORTISSIMA TO HOUSE (to get giant fly swatter)

PESTA:

It's all his fault!

ENTER SECUNDUS FROM HARBOR

SECUNDUS:

Devius; help me; I'm doomed!

DEVIUS 1:

Astral. . .

SECUNDUS:

Who cares?

EXIT SECUNDUS AND DEVIUS 1 TO HOUSE

ENTER BOMBASTICUS, PESTA, MALADIA FROM AUDITORIUM

MALADIA: *(Pointing to harbor)*
There!

PESTA: *(Pointing to forum)*
There!

BOMBASTICUS: (Pointing to *audience*)
There!

EXIT BOMBASTICUS TO AUDITORIUM

FORTISSIMA: (Within)
They're here!

SECUNDUS:
Aagghh!

DEVIUS 1:
Aagghh!

ENTER SECUNDUS AND DEVIUS 1 (tripped and grabbed) AND FORTISSIMA FROM HOUSE

PESTA: *(Grabbing Secundus)*
Now you'll pay!

FORTISSIMA: *(Putting giant knife to Secundus' neck)*
Off the pigs!

SECUNDUS:
This isn't fair!

MALADIA:
No, no, no; wait; what if they're insane? If we spill their blood it might spread and infect us like the plague!

GIRLS: *(Stop dancing)*
Wow! A plague.

(Everyone jumps back, Secundus and Devius panting, at bay)

MALADIA:
Is there a doctor in the house?

PESTA:
Quackquintius will know what to do!

MALADIA:
Get him quick!

FORTISSIMA:
Girls, fetch him here!

GIRLS:
AUUWWGGHH.

FORTISSIMA:
Now.

EXIT FLIRTIA, PRISSILIA, GIGGLIA, SPACIA TO FORUM

MALADIA:
Get some rope and tie them up before they escape.

EXIT FORTISSIMA TO HOUSE

PESTA: *(Pointing finger at them)*
Sure glad I'm not you.

MALADIA:
Yeah; Maximus you're gonna' pay.

SECUNDUS:
Just wait until I'm free. I'll sue you for everything you're worth.

PESTA:
Yeah?!

ENTER FORTISSIMA FROM HOUSE (With noose; ties them)

SECUNDUS:
I'll take your homes and businesses and slaves, everything, even your ancestors' graves!

FORTISSIMA:
Ah, shut up.

PESTA:
Get some gags.

(Maladia stuffs rags in their mouths)

SECUNDUS:
Humffff!

MALADIA:
Where's Astrala? *(Removes gag)*

SECUNDUS:
Hahaha, that's for me to know and you to . . . *(Regags him)*

PESTA:
What's gonna happen to them?

MALADIA:
Mad house for sure, or maybe the lions at the games.

FORTISSIMA:
Yeah, the games!

ENTER QUACKQUINTIUS FROM FORUM (Insane, with a giant syringe; Pesta, Maladia and Fortissima bow; Devius 1 and Secundus terrified.)

QUACKQUINTIUS: (Sings and dances soft-shoe style)
A doctor loves to help the sick.
A little cough? Call him quick.
There's nothing like a plague to fix.
A doctor loves to help the sick.
A doctor loves to show his skill
With powders, potions, little pills,
With scalpels, saws and buzzing drills
A doctor loves to show his skill.
A doctor loves to make you well,
Especially when you start to swell
Or gag or cough or even smell;
A doctor loves to make you well.
A doctor loves to treat you kind,
Especially when his fee you find;
(Puts out palm; Maladia gives coin)
He'll take your money any time;
A doctor loves to treat you kind.

QUACKQUINTIUS:
Take them in, and I'll begin. First I'll take a slice of skin.
(Secundus & Devius 1 try to bounce away.)
You're in good hands with Doctor Man.

SECUNDUS:
A dollar for anyone who sets me free!

EXIT FORTISSIMA, MALADIA AND PESTA TO HOUSE (DRAGGING SECUNDUS AND DEVIUS 1)

QUACKQUINTIUS:
Everybody well? If not, be smart, don't tell.

EXIT QUACKQUINTIUS TO HOUSE

ACT III, scene 3

ENTER BOMBASTICUS, DRAGGING PRIMUS AND ASTRALA, FROM HARBOR

PRIMUS:
Let us go; what do you want with us?

BOMBASTICUS:
It's hopeless to resist. You'll learn to love me, if you have the time. Women can't get enough. How about a kiss?

ASTRALA:
Scream!

BOMBASTICUS:
As for you, you lying pig; I'll teach you who to cheat. You're not even fit for a galley slave. I think I'll feed you to my dogs; your bones might last a week.
But this sweet little thing. Hey baby *(Flexes muscles)* pretty good, ey! what'a'ya think?

ASTRALA:
Scream!

BOMBASTICUS:
Hahaha. Well, Maximus; here's your house; I'll get my wedding gift then take you to the queen.

ENTER SECUNDUS AND DEVIUS 1 (knocking down Bombasticus, Primus and Astrala)

SECUNDUS:
Run! We're free!

ASTRALA:
Please, uncle, wait for me!

EXIT SECUNDUS & ASTRALA TO FORUM

PRIMUS:
Run, Astralus! We're free!

DEVIUS 1:
Wait master! Wait for me!

BOMBASTICUS:
What's happening here? I'd like to see them try that again!

OFFSTAGE VOICE:
Rewind.

(Scene runs backward to "I'll get my wedding gift from the queen." Everyone speaks lines as in very fast, distorted gibberish. Then it goes forward in very slow motion in drawn out distorted form to the following entrance of Fortissima.)

EXIT PRIMUS AND DEVIUS 1 FOR HARBOR

ENTER FORTISSIMA with giant fly swatter, MALADIA AND PESTA FROM HOUSE

FORTISSIMA:
I'll fix that slave!

MALADIA: *(To Bombasticus)*
Which way did they go?

PESTA: (Pointing to forum)
This way!

BOMBASTICUS: *(Pointing to harbor)*
No, that!

MALADIA:
How could they go this way and that?

PESTA:
They split in half!

BOMBASTICUS:
They must be spirits or devils or worse! How else could they escape from me!?!?

FORTISSIMA: *(Brandishing giant fly swatter)*
Stop yakking; time for attacking!

EXIT MALADIA TO HARBOR

EXIT BOMBASTICUS TO FORUM, BLOWING HORN

EXIT FORTISSIMA TO AUDITORIUM

EXIT PESTA TO YARD

ENTER FLIRTIA, SPACIA, GIGGLIA FROM FORUM

ENTER QUACKQUINTIUS FROM HOUSE (In tatters, squirting syringe; girls see him, terrified; he wanders out, chortling)

GIRLS:
Astrala? You inside? *(Timidly knocking on house door)*

ENTER ASTRALUS FROM YARD (Pulling off dress and wig)

ASTRALUS:
Those chicken's really stink, how will I ever meet those girls like this.

FLIRTIA:
Where have you been?

SPACIA:
Wow; you stink!

GIGGLIA:
Come with us to the baths; we'll wash you up.

ASTRALUS: *(Aside)*
Can you believe this?

EXIT FLIRTIA, SPACIA, GIGGLIA, ASTRALUS TO FORUM

ENTER PRIMUS AND DEVIUS 1 FROM HARBOR

PRIMUS:
Oh gods! Where's Astralus? He's not here! I've failed my oath!

DEVIUS 1:
Please, master; perhaps he's at the ship.

EXIT PRIMUS AND DEVIUS 1 TO HARBOR

ACT III, scene 4

ENTER QUEEN AND BOMBASTICUS FROM FORUM

QUEEN:
Who was that young man with the noble girls?

BOMBASTICUS:
A future rower in your fleet, your hininess; I'll arrest him right away.

QUEEN:
Your Highness, PLEASE! . . . *(Regaining her composure)* What you say is very strange; if half of what you say is true; it means a plague of madness has seized my land. Let me see if I understand. Maximus, the pig dealer, promised you his niece Astrala as your wife. This was arranged by Maladia, the matchmaker?

BOMBASTICUS:
Yes, your hininess; that's what I said.

QUEEN:
YOUR HIGHNESS, PLEASE!! . . . *(Regaining her composure)* And Maximus promised to give you 100 silver coins as a dowry for the girl, and this money was to come from Pesta, the wine merchant, who, you say, was seen by the whole street giving it to Maximus.

BOMBASTICUS:
Yes, your hininess, every word.

QUEEN:
YOUR HIGHNESS, PLEASE!! . . . *(Regaining her composure)* But then Maximus and his slave went insane and denied ever having seen you or receiving the coins?

BOMBASTICUS:
It's true, your hininess.

QUEEN:
YOUR HIGHNESS, PLEASE!!!!!!! . . . *(Regaining her composure)* And they tried to escape? But you caught them, including the niece, trying to board a ship. You brought them back and Dr. Quackquintius tried to drive the evil spirits from them, but the spirits were too strong for his medicine, and Maximus escaped again.

BOMBASTICUS:
Yes, your hininess; I swear it's true.

QUEEN:
!!!!!!!YOUR HIGHNESS, PLEASE!!!!!!!
. . . *(Regaining her composure)* Now, here your tale becomes truly strange. You say Maximus and his slave each split into two identical men and a chariot drawn by two dragons rose out of the sea and carried them away?

BOMBASTICUS:
I swear upon my sword, your hininess, every single word is true. How else can this be explained?

VOICES: (From all around and within)
He's here! He's there! No, over here! Insect! He'll pay! The pig!

ENTER PRIMUS & DEVIUS 1, FOLLOWED BY MALADIA, FROM HARBOR

ENTER SECUNDUS AND ASTRALA, FOLLOWED BY PESTA & FORTISSIMA, FROM FORUM

(Bombasticus tries to defend Queen, but they all meet in a mighty crash at her feet. Fortissima swats Devius 1 with fly swatter as he is getting up.)

FORTISSIMA:
Insect!

MALADIA: *(Grabbing Astrala)*
She's mine!

(Bombasticus reaches and pulls up Primus and Secundus.)

BOMBASTICUS:
See, your hininess; just like I said; they split into two identical men!

(The crowd gasps; Primus and Secundus face each other, stunned.)

SECUNDUS:
Primus!

PRIMUS:
Secundus!

QUEEN:
What does this mean?

SECUNDUS:
My long lost twin! *(Embraces Primus)*

PRIMUS:
My long lost twin! *(Embraces Secundus)*

ASTRALA:
Father! *(Embraces Primus)*

PRIMUS:
Astrala! Can this be? *(Embraces Astrala)*

SECUNDUS:
Don't I get a son?

DEVIUS 1:
Don't worry Maximus Secundus; he's here somewhere.

(Screams from forum)

ENTER FLIRTIA, SPACIA, GIGGLIA FROM FORUM

GIRLS:
SHE'S A MAN!

ENTER ASTRALUS FROM FORUM (With towel around waist)

ASTRALUS:
I meant no harm! *(Sees twins and freezes)* Uncle? Who is this man?

PRIMUS:
Your father who was lost but now is found.

ASTRALUS:
Dad! *(Embraces Secundus)*

QUEEN:
This ***is*** truly strange, and by it everything's explained. A day of rejoicing I here declare to celebrate the reuniting of these twins.

BOMBASTICUS:
But your hininess; where is my bride?

QUEEN:
Enough about my hininess or your hininess will sorely pay.
Maladia, find another bride for this man's man. Astrala will not marry him and ruin such a happy day.

ASTRALA:
My queen! *(High fives with valley girls)*

QUEEN:
Come, let the feast begin.

EXIT QUEEN, FOLLOWED BY PRIMUS, ASTRALA, SECUNDUS, ASTRALUS, FLIRTIA, SPACIA, GIGGLIA, PESTA, BOMBASTICUS, MALADIA TO FORUM

DEVIUS 1:
My lot in life, I'm still without my twin.

FORTISSIMA:
Don't worry; like bad luck he'll show up.

ENTER DEVIUS 2 (Raving drunk) FROM YARD

DEVIUS 2: (*Played by stand in*)
Get your whip! I won't feel a thing! Great gods, who's him?

DEVIUS 1:
Oh, Devius; it's me, your twin!

DEVIUS 2:
Devius!

(They embrace.)

EXIT DEVIUS 1 & DEVIUS 2 TO YARD

FORTISSIMA:
So, friends; our play is done.
Applaud our efforts, everyone.

EXIT FORTISSIMA TO HOUSE

FINIS

Chapter 4
Puppet Theater in Middle and High School

Artistic vanity is an unfortunate by-product of theater, and it is good to counterbalance it with a play in which no student is an actor but all are artistic technicians. Puppet theater is the perfect antidote in that no one is onstage showing-off except the puppets; therefore no one feels him or herself to be the center of attention. A further benefit of puppet theater is that it requires a complete integration of performing and technical arts, and is therefore ideally suited for seventh grade when mechanics is first introduced. And if puppet theater is anything, it is artistically applied mechanics. The practical pedagogical value of the students' building the different types of puppets (string, hand, rod, and shadow) and then having to learn to operate and fix them is unequaled by any other activity.

The Sacred Flame play was written and designed for seventh grade and performed semi-kindergarten style with fully visible puppeteers and Waldorf-doll style marionettes that the students made in the handwork classes over the course of the year. The handwork teacher and I had discussed working together at the end of the preceding year and decided to intimately coordinate these curricula.

The crazy thing about this play was the choice of story, which served as a teacher's lesson in theatrical vanity. In the story the protagonist carries a lighted candle from Jerusalem to Florence while riding backward on a horse—not easy to do for a horseman, much less a marionette. The impulse behind this choice was the type of over-excited can-do-anything imagination that sometimes takes hold of class teachers. After the initial idea that a puppet play would integrate the language arts, theater, handwork, and mechanics curriculum, I thought, "Why not toss in the electricity part of the physics curriculum as well! We can use grain-wheat-bulbs for the candle, whether it's being carried or placed on the ground; conductor wires as part of the strings; battery packs on the manipulation-cradle; little switches to turn the various lights on and off as the candle is passed from character to character." Easier said than done. At least, I had better sense than to try to incorporate the seventh grade chemistry program, which is built on combustion, into the show.

The students loved the complexity of the process, especially the practical problem-solving puppets presented. Since so many problems arose in a show this complicated there was an opportunity for every type of talent to come forward. One student had a marvelous ability to solve three-dimensional puzzles and could untangle strings in a moment when someone accidently dropped a puppet. Another very phlegmatic student loved fixing the electrical circuits (always buy good switches, not cheap ones!) and he became skilled with soldering. And another quickly mastered the acrobatics of getting the rider puppet back and forth onto the horse.

One of the most wonderful things pedagogically about puppet theater, especially marionettes, is that because of the physical constraints of the medium, everyone has to work far more closely together than in a conventional play, thereby enhancing the social aspect of the pedagogical experience. For instance, onstage it is simple for a character to cross in front of or behind another character. But because marionettes have strings, the challenge arises as to how one puppeteer moves his or her puppet across the stage without it's becoming a clumsy mess. There are two solutions, both of which require a lot of coordination, cooperation, and patient rehearsal. The first involves the puppeteer being "crossed" to hunch into as small a space as possible while the other "crossing puppeteer" reaches over and from behind. Both puppets, of course, have to continue their normal movement. The second method is harder, but necessary if there is no room for the puppeteers to move; it involves passing the puppet's cradle to another puppeteer. While the passing is easy, the trick is keeping the puppet's movement continuous. Countless other technical-performance challenges arose, and letting the class figure out how to meet them was the great pedagogical lesson of puppet theater.

The version of *A Christmas Carol* that follows was originally composed as a seventh grade puppet play for performance at the school's Winter Faire. As a puppet play it was performed in a jewel house puppet theater built for the occasion, and used three types of puppets: traditional marionettes, rod puppets, and shadow puppets. Because I was teaching woodworking at the time, the puppet-making happened in those periods over the course of the fall; and once the puppets were completed, we used those periods for rehearsals. The art teacher helped with painting the miniature sets, and a parent who was an award-winning doll maker designed the patterns for most of the clothing, which the students made at home. There was also a small tech crew of students who ran the lights and curtain.

Puppet theater can also be done in high school. Once upon a time there was a tenth grade that was loathe to do a class play, and they whined endlessly about how they couldn't be made to do one. Needing to overcome this sentiment (since cancelling was impossible), I one day realized that the conventions of classical Greek tragedy were well suited for Bread and Circus style back-pack puppets; that the school's new auditorium had an excellent sound system that could be used for radio theater style speaking; and that there was a student in the class who was profoundly talented in fabrication skills, having worked since boyhood in his father's custom car business.

I worked with most of the students building the puppets while my assistant did the vocal direction with the students who would speak the roles when the puppets were onstage. I directed the puppeteers (who, you understand, were inside the giant puppets) while the speakers standing at their microphones accompanied their characters. Again, years of eurythmy made this arrangement seem perfectly natural once the feeling of disembodiment that comes with working radio style was overcome.

The economy of text that puppet theater requires also helps to distill a story or pre-existing text to its essence, which, of course, makes a play easier and more effective to produce. All three plays, *The Sacred Flame*, *A Christmas Carol*, and *Antigone* also worked well as actor-carried plays, requiring only changes of stage directions and minor text-expansion. *The Sacred Flame* is the puppet text, while *A Christmas Carol* is the actor version, which is more useful to more teachers. Anyone interested can request the puppet text from me, as well as both *Antigone* texts, the stage version having been adapted so the chorus could be played by eurythmists.

The Sacred Flame

A Puppet Play for Seventh Grade

Adapted from the Selma Lagerloff short story. Dedicated to Jens Bjørneboe and Joe Martin.

Characters:

Narrator	Servant	Francesca
Rogue Knights (2)	Raniero (A ruthless knight)	Jester
God's Voice	Giovanni (Raniero's servant)	St. Peter's Voice
Robbers (3)	Innkeeper	Pilgrims (2)
Troubadour	Old Woman	Poor Woman
People in Street	Odo	Bishop

Prologue

Sung to Renaissance instruments.

SERVANT:

Some say that love's a golden cloth
Of hope and joy it's made.
Some cherish every single thread,
Despite some being frayed.

FRANCESCA:

Raniero is my dear love's name
I thought his love was true
But then he left and went away
To seek adventure new.

SERVANT:

He gathered up a gang of rogues
To plunder holy lands,
Yet still you pray that God will keep
Him safely in his hands?

FRANCESCA:

My love is like a golden cloth,
But torn and stained and frayed.
We try to mend it thread by thread
With every passing day.

Scene I:

Raniero is sitting on bench with his candle; he is tired and a cup of wine hangs from his hand. The two knights enter stage left, laughing and celebrating, without seeing Raniero.

KNIGHT 1:

Over the top he went and onto the defenders; like a madman without a care for himself.

KNIGHT 2:

After the prince, the first to scale the city's walls.

KNIGHT 1:

One thing's certain; Raniero has good reason to celebrate tonight; he's won the greatest glory anyone can have— the first to light his candle at Christ's tomb.

RANIERO: *Standing*

And rightly so; where were you cowards when I was defeating a city?

KNIGHT 2:

Right behind you.

KNIGHT 1:

Like we always are.

RANIERO:

And always will be—right **behind**. What entertainment have you found?

KNIGHT 1:

A jester.

ENTER Jester.

RANIERO:
You, earn your keep; make me laugh.

JESTER:
Be careful how you address your Lord.

KNIGHT 2:
Hear that?

KNIGHT 1:
His Lord?

RANIERO:
Lord; he's bold.

JESTER:
No, master; I know what's good for me, and you would too if the Lord and Saint Peter were always at **your** side.

RANIERO:
What do you mean . . .

Jester produces two hand puppets: God and St. Peter. Knights roar with laughter.

JESTER: ST. PETER'S VOICE:
Stand back, good knight; don't you recognize me? You'll be seeing me soon enough if you don't mend your ways.

KNIGHT 2:
It's St. Peter himself, with his keys to Heaven's gate.

KNIGHT 1:
Oh, we better behave ourselves;

KNIGHT 2:
He might not let us in.

RANIERO: *Laughing*
And who's that on your other hand? God, I suppose?

JESTER:
Now you understand.

JESTER: GOD'S VOICE:
What's all this noise, disturbing such a beautiful night?

JESTER: ST PETER'S VOICE:
It's just Raniero and his pack of knights.

JESTER: GOD'S VOICE:
Then you should be pleased.

JESTER: ST PETER'S VOICE:
Pleased with them? Look at the mounds of corpses they've made today. And don't you hear the wretched moans of the wounded filling the night?

JESTER: GOD'S VOICE:
You're always looking for the worst. These good knights risked their lives to give me back this city.

KNIGHT 1:
Yeah!

KNIGHT 2:
That's right!

JESTER:
Shh. Not so loud; you might offend the Lord.

RANIERO: *SCOFFING*
The Lord.

JESTER: ST PETER'S VOICE:
I beg your pardon, your supreme holiness, but these knights are just rogues who've tried to turn murder into piety.

RANIERO:
Watch yourself.

KNIGHT 1:
Wait master; let's see if the Lord speaks in our defense.

JESTER: GOD'S VOICE:
Thank you, good knight.

KNIGHT 2:
Yeah; obey the Lord.

RANIERO:
Of course, the Lord.

He mockingly bowing his head

JESTER: GOD'S VOICE:
I will concede that they're not the gentlest looking sort, but there's one whose looks

strike me as special.

JESTER: ST PETER'S VOICE:
Which one?

JESTER: GOD'S VOICE:
That one there; the big one with the scar.

JESTER: ST PETER'S VOICE:
Him! He's the cruelest of them all!

KNIGHT 1:
Ha, ha, ha.

KNIGHT 2:
Ha, ha, ha.

JESTER: GOD'S VOICE:
No, he has a kind and noble soul.

JESTER: ST PETER'S VOICE:
I beg your pardon, God.

JESTER: GOD'S VOICE:
Look; he's as gentle as a little child.

KNIGHT 2:
Ha, ha, ha.

JESTER: ST PETER'S VOICE:
A little child?

JESTER: GOD'S VOICE:
Yes, see; his candle's still burning; the one he lighted from my tomb. Everyone else's has gone out, but see how he shelters it with his hand from every little breeze. That simple deed shows the purity of his soul.

KNIGHT 1:
Purity . . .

KNIGHT 2:
Don't go soft on us, boss, it's just a flame. Who knows how you'll act next time a slave begs for his life.

KNIGHT 1:
I'm moved to tears.

RANIERO: *Cold Brittle Voice*
Go on.

JESTER:
You want me to finish, master?

RANIERO:
I've paid for a laugh.

JESTER: GOD'S VOICE:
You might laugh now, my friends, but soon Raniero will help the poor, care for the distressed, and show as much love for the most wretched beggar woman as he now does for his little flame.

KNIGHT 2:
His little flame.

Jester: God's Voice:
Where else do goodness and gentleness spring from if not my tomb?

RANIERO: *Leaping Up*
I've had enough!

JESTER:
Watch the flame!

EXIT Jester, fleeing. Raniero follows but stops to protect candle flame.

RANIERO:
Ah, I'll find him at dawn.

KNIGHT 2:
Watch the flame.

RANIERO:
Wouldn't you?

KNIGHT 1:
One thing's for sure; you won't be sending your most precious thing back to the Madonna at home this time.

RANIERO:
Why?

KNIGHT 1:
How could you send that flame all the way from Jerusalem to Florence?

RANIERO:
You'll see!

He calls for his servant.

ENTER Giovanni
Giovanni!

GIOVANNI:
Yes, master.

RANIERO:
Make ready for a long journey. Tomorrow you'll carry this flame back to Florence and place it on the Madonna's altar with all my other gifts.

GIOVANNI:
Please, master. How could anyone carry a candle flame all the way to Florence? Nobody could! It will blow out the instant I leave this tent.

RANIERO:
Coward, get out! Knight, you carry the flame.

KNIGHT 1:
You joke, master; who could ever do as you ask?

RANIERO:
Worthless knave. You take it, and say Raniero sends this gift.

KNIGHT 2:
It can't be done.

RANIERO:
Cowardly dogs. This candle will go to Florence. I'll carry it myself. Now, where are your laughs? For a man like me it is but child's game.

Scene II:

The Road to coast.

NARRATOR:
That night Raniero took pains to make sure the sacred flame did not go out, and in the morning, having gathered up a great bundle of extra candles, he set out for the port on the coast. He could take passage on a ship to Italy, and once safely in his cabin, it would be easy to keep the flame lit until he had arrived at the port of Pisa; from where he could continue to Florence. At most it would take a month, then he could return to Jerusalem and show those doubters what a resolute man could do.

There was a heavy, still mist when he left before dawn. No one even noticed him, except the moths that attacked the flame, but he easily kept them away. But at sunrise, a breeze arose, and he had to slacken his pace. He tried covering the flame with his cloak, but that was futile, so he had to turn in his saddle, riding backwards, his great body sheltering the tiny flame.

After only a few miles, he came to a narrow valley and found himself surrounded suddenly by a band of robbers. They were pitiful men. At any other time he could have slain them in a second, but now he was helpless.

ENTER robbers & Raniero on horse puppet, opposite

FIRST ROBBER:
Look at the madman.

SECOND ROBBER:
Riding his horse backwards.

THIRD ROBBER:
But dressed pretty good.

SECOND ROBBER:
What a *pazzo*!

FIRST ROBBER:
A real madman!

FIRST ROBBER:
Get'im.

SECOND ROBBER:
Eh, why always me.

FIRST ROBBER:
'Cause I'm the boss, wanna make something of it?

SECOND ROBBER:

Hey you, *pazzo*, yeah, you, madman; I'm talking to you. Stay right there if you know what's good for you. Toss down everything you have.

Raniero throws down his saddle bags, taking care to protect flame.

FIRST ROBBER:

Can you believe it; the *pazzo*'s really listening to him.

THIRD ROBBER:

Look at this stuff.

FIRST ROBBER:

Nice dagger, give it here.

THIRD ROBBER:

The armor's mine.

SECOND ROBBER:

No, it's mine.

FIRST ROBBER:

A purse. Gold; well, this is mine.

THIRD ROBBER:

That horse looks pretty good; mine's almost dead.

SECOND ROBBER:

Back off; I'll take the horse.

THIRD ROBBER:

No, I didn't get nothing yet.

FIRST ROBBER:

Stop fighting. What's this? Candles!

THIRD ROBBER:

The candles are mine. All of them; hand over that one too.

RANIERO:

Touch this candle and you're dead.

THIRD ROBBER:

What's so special about the candle? Made of gold?

RANIERO:

The flame comes from Christ's tomb; would you like to be the one to put it out? Because if you do, it will be the last flame you ever extinguish. I'm carrying this flame back to Italy to place before the Madonna's statue.

THIRD ROBBER:

Maybe we should leave him his horse.

FIRST ROBBER:

You're the *pazzi*, now; take the horse and it's yours, I'm out of here now.

EXIT robbers & Raniero opposite

Scene II:

Rainero on horse puppet riding across stage; pilgrim's hymn hummed.

NARRATOR:

He was furious. If not for the flame he could have fought them. But what was worse, they would brag, and it would not take much for people to realize it was Raniero they had robbed. He consoled himself, however. Once he finished his mission he would return and pay them back.

As the sun rose higher the road from the coast filled with people, hurrying to Jerusalem. The sight of Raniero riding backwards filled them with cruel delight. "Look at the madman, the *pazzo*!" Some threw stones, and once he was even knocked from his saddle. The candle rolled into the ditch and went out, but the flame ignited the dead grass, and Raniero was able to save it and continue on his way.

A knight on horseback could make the coast in a single day, but by nightfall Raniero found he still had miles to go, so he stopped at an inn and huddled himself over his tiny flame.

ENTER Raniero and huddles over the flame. ENTER Innkeeper enters.

INNKEEPER:
Hey fellow, watch that flame. Can't you see there's straw about. You could set us all on fire. Put it out.

RANIERO:
It cannot be put out, not by my hand, nor yours.

INNKEEPER:
Whose inn is this anyway?

RANIERO:
Be warned; I will defend this flame even with my bare hands, but do not worry; I will not let it burn your stable.

INNKEEPER: *ASIDE*
He's mad; I'll watch from a safe distance, and when he falls asleep take care of that flame.

Raniero falls asleep and the Innkeeper approaches. He goes to put out the flame but decides against it. Instead he takes the candle and EXITS. A musical interlude passes & Raniero awakes.

RANIERO:
The flame! My flame! It's gone. So that Jester was wrong. How could I have taken it all that way? I must have been mad.

ENTER Innkeeper with candle.

INNKEEPER:
Good morning. I feared you'd burn us all up, so I took your candle.

RANIERO:
It was wise to extinguish it.

INNKEEPER:
I did nothing of the sort. It seemed so precious to you that I let it burn. Here.

He gives Raniero the candle.

RANIERO:
Thank you, sir. This is the will of God, and so I must obey.

EXIT Raniero & Innkeeper, opposite.

Scene III:

Shadow puppet, narration and musical accompaniment

NARRATOR:
Raniero now realized that without money all hope of travelling by sea was gone. He would have to make the long journey by land. But he did not despair; he was now the servant of the flame. His every action would be devoted to its care, and his every thought would be for it. Neither wind nor rain nor human deed must ever put it out.

A month passed and he had used all the candles he had brought, but this was no bother. Whenever he came to a village he told them the story of the flame, and the villagers freely gave him candles so he might continue on his way. But eventually he came to a wild and lonely mountainous place where no village could be found. He rode silently as his candles all burned down.

Finally, when left with just the butt, he found a place safe from the wind and dismounted to watch the death of his flame.

ENTER Rainero

RANIERO:
This is as good place as any for my journey to end.

NARRATOR:
Suddenly, the sound of singing floated up the trail; it was pilgrims, but he did not move, not even when they gathered about him, looking wondrously at this a great bulk of man, crouched over a little flame.

ENTER Pilgrims, singing hymns

RANIERO:
Stand back; be careful of my flame.

PILGRIM 1:
He's mad.

PILGRIM 2:
He just stares at it. Let's get on.

TROUBADOR:
What troubles you, friend?

RANIERO:
I'm guarding this flame; it mustn't go out.

TROUBADOR:
Why?

RANIERO:
It's from Christ's tomb.

PILGRIM 1:
In Jerusalem?

Raniero just nods.

PILGRIM 2:
How can that be; that's months away.

TROUBADOR:
You've carried it this far?

RANIERO:
Every step of the way.

TROUBADOR:
But certainly it has gone out many times before?

RANIERO:
I've never let it die.

TROUBADOR:
How did you manage such a feat? Was it hard?

RANIERO:
I cannot think, or dream, or have a moment's rest. I must always be alert, for even the slightest breeze or drop of rain could snuff it out.

TROUBADOR:
I too carry a flame, but mine burns in my heart. It is the flame of song; and from this day I'll sing of your praise.

PILGRIM 2:
Here; I've found the way.

TROUBADOR:
Farewell friend; I wish you God's speed on your way.

RANIERO:
My journey's done; I go no further.

TROUBADOR:
Why?

RANIERO:
Because this is my last candle; when it is burned the flame will die.

TROUBADOR:
Has anyone a candle for this noble man?

PILGRIM 2:
Not I.

PILGRIM 1:
Nor I, but a holy man dwells nearby; perhaps he has some to spare.

TROUBADOR:
Come with us friend; there's still hope.

Raniero rises to follow, but the Old Woman collapses.

RANIERO:
Let me help you.

OLD WOMAN:
It's no use; my life is dying like your flame.

RANIERO:
No, no; do not despair; you must live. I'll carry you.

OLD WOMAN:
How will you shield your flame?

He hesitates. puts the flame down.

TROUBADOR:
God will provide.

He hands down the candle and they lift the Old Woman onto the horse.

Scene IV:

NARRATOR:

The path was steep and dangerous. A light rain began to fall. How Raniero suffered in his heart; surely the flame would die. But when they reached a hermit's cave, and the holy man gave him candles, Raniero saw only the bitterest irony in his success.

But God in his infinite mercy had sent tiny birds to shield the tiny flame. They flitted here and there, catching every rain drop on their backs.

Raniero lights candle and continues.

His devotion to the flame sealed him off from all else in the world, as if in a trance until the desperate sobs of a woman woke him.

ENTER Poor Woman, begging.

POOR WOMAN:

Pilgrim, please, give me a light. My fire has gone out.

RANIERO:

This flame is not for that. Ask another.

POOR WOMAN:

I beg you. My children freeze.

RANIERO:

This flame is sacred; it's not for things profane.

POOR WOMAN:

What could be more sacred than the flame of the my children's lives?

RANIERO:

Here.

He gives her a light and she EXITS.

NARRATOR:

As night was falling, he rode into a village. It was getting cold, and a peasant stood in the road. When he saw Raniero shivering and hunched over his little flame, the peasant flung an old sack at him, laughing.

PEASANT:

Hey, *pazzo*, this will keep you warm.

EXIT Peasant

NARRATOR:

The sack extinguished the flame, and Raniero cried in pain and rage but then remembered the poor woman to whom he had given a light.

Raniero rides back

ENTER Poor Woman

RANIERO:

I've come to beg a flame.

POOR WOMAN:

Take what you need; come in and get warm.

RANIERO:

I cannot stay. *Hesitating.* You say your flame is the life of your children, tell me then what name my flame bears?

POOR WOMAN:

Whence lighted?

RANIERO:

Christ's tomb.

POOR WOMAN:

Gentleness and Love.

RANIERO:

How strange. Of all the warriors in this world I was chosen to bear this gift. Truly, the flame has given me a new life.

EXIT both opposite

Scene V:

Florence

NARRATOR:

The road passed through rich fields and prosperous towns. People gathered and cheered him on. Finally he found himself at Florence's gate. A mob of urchins and young thugs ran before him, mocking and pelting him with stones. He saw his old self in their twisted faces; he heard his old voice in their jeers. But now he felt no anger, only sorrow, mixed with shame.

ENTER CROWD & Raniero opposite

THUG 1:
Go back!

THUG 2:
We don't want crazies in this town!

THUG 3:
Put him out of his misery!

THUG 1:
Hey, look, look he's got a candle!

THUG 2:
It's mine!

THUG 3:
No, mine!

ALL:
Mine! Mine! Mine!!

THUG 1:
Pull him down!

THUG 2:
Knock over that scrawny horse!

THUG 3:
Here; I've got some bigger stones!

NARRATOR:
Raniero felt desperate; they were everywhere, leaping and trying to extinguish his flame.

RANIERO:
Is this the end of my journey?

THUG 2:
Aim for the flame!

THUG 1:
Yeah, the flame!

THUG 3:
Look, the *pazzo* is trying to stand.

Francesca and her servant appear on balcony as Raniero stands in his saddle. He holds the flame high above him, swatting at the crowd with his free hand. Francesca reaches down and takes flame. The crowd cheers.

THUG 1:
Look; she got the flame!

ALL:
Yay!!!

Raniero looks up at his empty hand and falls to the ground

THUG 3:
He's done.

THUG 2:
Let's get on.

EXIT crowd

ENTER Francesca, opposite

FRANCESCA: *Bending Down*
Here, pilgrim; here's your candle. What do you need?

RANIERO:
Take me to the cathedral.

FRANCESCA:
Then come with me; I am on my way to mass.

RANIERO:
I know you from my past.

FRANCESCA:
Are you Raniero, come home at last?

RANIERO:
And you Francesca?

FRANCESCA:
Hurry; it is Easter Eve, and soon the service will start.

Scene VI:

Florence Cathedral

NARRATOR:
As they entered the great church, Raniero saw that row upon row of candles stood

unlighted on the altar, a symbol of mourning for Christ's suffering on the cross.

ENTER Bishop

RANIERO:

Your grace, I am Raniero di Raniero, returned with this sacred flame. I have carried it all the way from Christ's tomb in Jerusalem. I wish to give it to the Mother of God.

FRANCESCA:

Oh, God! This is greater happiness than I can bear.

BISHOP:

Citizens of Florence, let the pilgrim pass. He bears the sacred flame from Christ's tomb. Approach and light the candles .

RANIERO:

Mother of God, I have brought this sacred flame from Christ's tomb in Jerusalem. Not once has it been extinguished, and many miraculous deeds has it performed. It is my most precious thing; I give it to the Mother of our Lord.

ENTER Odo

ODO:

Fraud!

BISHOP:

Who dares?

ODO:

I, Odo; father of the boy this cruel man hounded to death. What proof do you have this flame comes from Jerusalme? Where are the witnesses?

RANIERO:

God help me! I rode alone. Only desert wastes and frigid mountainsides could bear witness for me.

ODO:

You expect us to believe such nonesense from a man whose fame is built on cruelty and pride? Citizens of Florence! Let us extinguish this faker's flame.

Odo rushes Raniero; he holds the flame up high. Suddenly a bird flies into the church and extinguishes flame.

ODO: *Triumphantly*

So God wills.

FRANCESCA:

Oh, God; the bird's aflame!

RANIERO:

Someone help it!

SERVANT:

Look it's flying towards the Altar.

The burning bird flies across the unlit candles and drops upon the altar. One by one the candles flicker to life.

BISHOP:

God's will! God has testified!

RANIERO:

My gift has been delivered!

BISHOP:

May this flame shine as a symbol of our city, and may its light shine forth to illumine the world.

The End

Chapter 5
Plays for High School: The Canon and Language Plays

Although most plays produced in high school are abridged versions of works from the theatrical canon, occasionally the teacher-director will write an original play or adapt a novel for the stage or completely rework a piece to fit the pedagogical or performance needs of the high school theater. The first play that follows is an adaptation of Dickens' *A Christmas Carol.* This script was originally composed for a seventh grade puppet play, as described above and was later expanded for performance by a tenth grade at the Austin Waldorf School's Winter Faire. The next two plays, *Edelmiro II y el dragón Gutiérrez* and *Die Rabe*, were adapted or written by the AWS high school language teachers, Giannia Guardia-Hayes and Ann Coltman, for performance by the eleventh grade before the whole student body of the school. The final play is this author's transposing of Gogol's masterpiece *The Inspector General* to contemporary times for twelfth grade performance.

Eleventh Grade: The Modern Language Play

After the Austin Waldorf School's high school finished its pioneer phase we turned our attention to strengthening and deepening programs. Part of this work was to make the modern language programs equal to the math and English programs. But we very quickly realized that to achieve this goal the students who did not go abroad on an exchange needed a more intensive, artistically based immersion experience in the respective languages than was possible in a traditional classroom setting. To this end, we substituted German and Spanish language children's theater for the traditional eleventh grade scene work from Shakespeare that we had been doing.

Ann Coltman, the high school German teacher, wrote the first play, *Die Rabe*, from the Brothers Grimm story, and Giannina Guardia-Hayes, the Spanish teacher, adapted Fernando Lalana's Spanish language play, *Edelmiro II y el dragón Gutiérrez.* Both plays were performed in February of 2012.

Twelfth Grade

The final play in this book is an adaptation of one of the greatest pieces in the western theatrical canon, Gogol's *The Inspector General*, also known as *The Government Inspector* or, most literally, *The Revizor*. It is a difficult play to do successfully in its original form for an American audience. Many of the jokes, cultural references, and social satires require an understanding of early to mid-nineteenth century Russian provincial society in the backwaters of the empire. There is also a fair amount of misogynistic and violent humor that would only be tolerated as museum theater by a contemporary theater-going audience. And the period costuming would be a nightmare given a school's resources. That said, the play's plot, constellation of characters, and themes are brilliant, so I decided to adapt it completely by setting it in near-contemporary small town America.

Such an undertaking is a form of translation and, as such, tricky. One must always keep in mind the Italian pun/adage: *traduttore, tradittore*—translator, traitor. To succeed in such an endeavor one must have the greatest respect for the playwright's artistic intention and its relation to the play's historical and cultural context, as well as the target society and period into which the play is being cast. One should not substantively change its plot, set of characters, theme or tone but rather find their equivalencies. Just as every line of dialogue needs to be translated into its new context, so every action, character and idea needs to be true to the source and target.

The pedagogical reasons for doing this play lie in several areas. Most superficially, the play is Russian literature, usually a part of the twelfth grade Waldorf curriculum. It is also unique in terms of literary genre, being a tragedy clothed in the costume of a five-act comedy. Theatrically, it also gives the students an opportunity to work with elements of farce, which require some of the most sophisticated timing and stagecraft. But its true value lies in its characterizations and moral themes. Each character, although based on a stock comic type, is essentially tragic, and thereby requires sensitive and thoughtful characterization by the students. The only exception is the antagonist, Khlestakov, a simpleton who is mistaken for a high government inspector. He is almost a demonic figure, sent by Fate to expose and to punish corruption and human folly. But most importantly from a pedagogical perspective, in order to play the roles properly, the student-actors must develop a sympathetic relationship to the characters, despite their being worthy of disdain; and through this sympathetic feeling an appreciation for what it most profoundly means to be human.

Although my abridgment of Synge's comic masterpiece, *Playboy of the Western World, is not* included because of space limitations and the fact that it can be easily found on-line, it is one of the grandest plays that can be done with a twelfth grade. The story is a simple one: a fugitive, Christy Mahon, arrives one night at a tavern in a village in the west of Ireland, claiming to have killed his fearsome father with a potato spade, thereby becoming a great celebrity. Everyone is impressed by this bloody deed, especially the women who begin to compete against each other for his attentions, the two major competitors being the tavern keeper's daughter, Pegeen Mike, and the Widow Quinn, who has herself killed a husband. Over the course of one night and day, Christy rises to heroic stature, wins Pegeen Mikes' love, but soon falls from his exalted position when his "murdered" father appears, raving mad and fit to be tied, and exposes Christy as a hollow braggart. The villagers, furious in their disappointment and assisted by the father, reject Christy, who again "murders" his father. But this time he is not seen as hero, only a gruesome killer. But once again, the father fails to die, coming instead to his son's aid, father and son scorning the villagers for their credulity as they march off in triumph, realizing they have happened upon a livelihood well suited to their abilities. Besides its being an exciting play to rehearse and perform, full of grand speeches, flirtation and romance, and exquisite stage violence, twelfth graders love the play because most of the characters are about their own age, providing a wonderful opportunity to develop characterizations that are both close to heart, and yet safely removed. Another great advantage of the play is that there is an equal balance of good male and female parts.

A Christmas Carol

Adapted from Charles Dickens Novel (1998, 2008)

For Middle and High School

CHARACTERS:

Narrator	Ebenezer Scrooge	Boy Scrooge
Young Scrooge	Fan	Dick
Fred	Fred's Wife	Topper
Eunice	Miners	Lighthouse Keepers (2)
Mr. Fezziwig	Mrs. Fezziwig	Belle
Belle's husband	Bankrupt Man	Bankrupt Woman
Ship's Captain	Sailors	Ship's Lookout
Gentleman 1	Gentleman 2	Banker
Broker	Merchant,	Bob Cratchit
Mrs. Cratchit	Peter Cratchit	Martha Cratchit
Polly Cratchit	Tiny Tim Cratchit	Jacob Marley
Christmas Past	Christmas Present	Christmas Yet to Be
Old Joe	Charwoman	Laundress
Londoners	Goose Boy	Blind Man
Dancers	Dance master	Musicians
Ignorance & Want		

STAVE ONE: Prologue

I: 1: Introduction

[ENTER NARRATOR before Curtain.]

NARRATOR:

Marley was dead, to begin with. There is no doubt whatever about that. Dead as a door-nail;

LONDONER 1: *[ENTERING]*

Scrooge knew he was dead?

LONDONER 6: *[ENTERING]*

Of course he did!

NARRATOR:

Otherwise nothing wonderful can come of the story we are going to relate. He and Marley had been partners for who knows how many years, so after the funeral Scrooge never painted out old Marley's name. There it stood, years afterward above the warehouse door: Scrooge and Marley.

[CURTAIN OPENS}

[ENTER SCROOGE & STREET CROWD]

ALL:

SCROOGE!

LONDONER 2:

Oh! he was tight-fisted!

LONDONER 3:

A squeezing,

LONDONER 2:

wrenching,

LONDONER 3:

grasping,

LONDONER 2:

scraping,

LONDONER 3:

clutching,

LONDONER 2:
covetous old sinner!

ALL:
SCROOGE!

NARRATOR:
The cold within him froze his old features,

LONDONER 5:
nipped his pointed nose,

LONDONER 4:
shriveled his cheek,

LONDONER 5:
and made his thin lips blue.

ALL:
SCROOGE!

NARRATOR:
He carried his own low temperature always about with him.

Londoner 7:
No warmth could warm;

LONDONER 6:
No wintry weather chill him;

LONDONER 5:
No wind that blew was bitterer than he;

LONDONER 8:
No falling snow was more intent upon its purpose;

LONDONER 9:
No pelting rain less open to entreaty.

LONDONER 8:
Foul weather didn't know what to make of him.

LONDONER 10:
Nobody ever stopped him in the street to say, with gladsome looks:

LONDONER 11:
"My dear Scrooge, how are you?"

LONDONER 10:
No beggars implored him, no children asked of him the time.

BEGGAR:
Even the blind man's dog, when it saw him coming on, would tug its owner into doorways as though to say,

NARRATOR:
"No eye at all is better than an evil eye, master!"

LONDONER 4:
But what did he care?

LONDONER 5:
It was the very thing he liked. To edge his way along the crowded path of life, warning all human sympathy to keep its distance.

ALL:
Scrooge!

NARRATOR:
Then one Christmas Eve—of all the good days in the year—old Scrooge sat busy in his counting-house:

I: 2: Scrooge's Office: Fred & Charitable Gentlemen

[A dreary office, two desks, candle on each. Feeble fire flickers. SCROOGE at high table, writing. CRATCHIT warming hands on candle.]

[Clock strikes 3. Door opens, fog rolls in]

[ENTER FRED.]

[SCROOGE & CRATCHIT look up; SCROOGE glares at CRATCHIT who instantly returns to work.]

FRED:
A merry Christmas, uncle! God save you!

SCROOGE:
Bah! Humbug!

FRED:
Christmas a humbug, uncle! You don't mean that, I am sure?

SCROOGE:
I do. Merry Christmas! What reason have you to be merry? You're poor enough.

FRED:
Come now; what right have you to be dismal? You're rich enough.

SCROOGE:
Bah! . . . Humbug!

FRED:
Don't be cross, uncle!

SCROOGE:
What else can I be, when I live in such a world of fools as this Merry Christmas! Out upon merry Christmas. What's Christmas to you but a time for paying bills. If I had my will every idiot who goes about with "Merry Christmas" on his lips would be boiled in his own pudding.

FRED:
Uncle!

Scrooge:
Nephew! Keep Christmas in your own way; let me keep it in mine.

FRED:
Keep it! But you don't keep it.

SCROOGE:
Let me leave it alone then.

[Turning back to his work.]

Much good that it's ever done you.

FRED:
There are many things that are good but earn me no profit.

SCROOGE: *[Writing furiously.]*
Bah.

FRED:
Christmas among them. I have always thought of Christmas as a good time; a kind, forgiving, charitable, pleasant time. The only time of the year when men and women open their shut-up hearts freely and share the goodness that lives within. Though it has never put a scrap of gold or silver in my pocket, it has done me good, and *will* do me good, so I say, God bless it!

CRACHIT:
Hurrah!

SCROOGE:
Another sound from you.

FRED:
Don't be angry, uncle. Come dine with us tomorrow.

SCROOGE:
Good afternoon. [*Escorts FRED to door.*]

FRED:
I am sorry. . .

SCROOGE:
. . . Good afternoon.

FRED:
. . . sorry with all my heart . . .

SCROOGE:
. . . Good afternoon!

FRED:
So a Merry Christmas then uncle.

[FRED crosses & shakes hands with CRATCHIT.]

SCROOGE:
Good afternoon. [Holding door.]

FRED:
And a happy new year.

[EXIT FRED.]

SCROOGE:
Bah! Humbug! There's another fellow, my clerk, with fifteen shillings a week, and a wife and family, talking about a merry Christmas. I'll retire to the mad house.

[SCROOGE returns to his work.]

[ENTER TWO GENTLEMEN. One is carrying a large flat book; the other has papers. Cross to SCROOGE'S desk & present papers.]

GENTLEMAN 1:
Have we the pleasure of addressing Mr. Scrooge or Marley?

SCROOGE:
Marley's dead, been so for seven years, this very night.

GENTLEMAN 2:
We have no doubt his generosity . . .

GENTLEMAN 1:
. . . is well represented in his surviving partner.

[SCROOGE pushes back the papers and resumes his work.]

GENTLEMAN 1:
At this festive season of the year it is more than desirable that we should make some slight provision for the poor and destitute ...

GENTLEMAN 2:
. . . who suffer greatly at the present time.

GENTLEMAN 1:
Many thousands are in want of the most common necessities. . .

GENTLEMAN 2:
. . . hundreds of thousands of common comforts . . .

SCROOGE: *[Looking up]*
. . . Are there no prisons?

GENTLEMAN 1: *[Laying down his pen.]*
Plenty.

SCROOGE:
And workhouses? Are they still in operation?

GENTLEMAN 1:
They are.

SCROOGE:
And the Poor Law is in full force?

GENTLEMAN 1:
Sadly; it still is.

SCROOGE:
Oh! I was afraid from what you said that something had occurred to stop them in their useful course. *[Resuming his work.]*

GENTLEMAN 2:
But they scarcely bring cheer. We have chosen this time . . .

GENTLEMAN 1:
. . . when Want is keenly felt . . .

GENTLEMAN 2:
. . . and Abundance rejoices to buy some meat and drink and warmth for those in greatest need.

GENTLEMAN 1:
The most wretched of the poor.

GENTLEMAN 2:
What shall we put you down for?

SCROOGE:
Nothing!

GENTLEMAN 1:
You wish to be anonymous?

SCROOGE:
I wish to be left alone. Since you ask me what I wish, gentlemen, that is my answer. I don't make merry myself at Christmas, and I can't afford to make idle people merry. I support the places I have mentioned—they cost enough. Those who are badly off; let them go there.

GENTLEMAN 2:
Many can't . . .

GENTLEMAN 1:
. . . and many would rather die.

SCROOGE:
Then let them do it and decrease the surplus population. They're not my business. Good afternoon, gentlemen. *[Pleased, takes up work vigorously.]*
[EXIT TWO GENTLEMEN.]

I: 3: Street on Christmas Eve 2

[The clock strikes four.]

LONDONER 2:

The fog and darkness thickened.

LONDONER 3:

Foggier yet, and colder! Piercing, searching, biting cold.

[ENTER CROWD.]

NARRATOR:

Yet the streets of the great city were a glorious pageant of brightness and warmth. Shops, where holly sprigs and berries crackled in the lamp heat of the windows, made pale faces ruddy as they passed. And these merry souls, jovial and full of glee, greeted each other cheerfully,

LONDONER 4:

humming, . . .

LONDONER 6:

or whistling, . . .

LONDONER 4:

or bursting into song.

[The CROWD bursts into a building Christmas song & reel dance in the street.]

I: 4: Scrooge's Office II: Closing Office & Dinner

[ENTER BOY.]

Boy:

[Pokes head into SCROOGE's office & attempts a cheerful refrain of] "God Rest Ye Merry Gentlemen".

SCROOGE:

Bah!

[Boy flees. Clock strikes five and lights rise on counting-house. Puts down his pen.]

You'll want all day tomorrow off, with pay, I suppose?

CRACHIT:

If convenient, sir.

SCROOGE:

It's not convenient, and it's not fair.

CRACHIT:

It's only once a year.

SCROOGE:

Once a year! A poor excuse for picking a man's pocket every twenty-fifth of December! But I suppose you must have the whole day. [Crachit rises.] But be here all the earlier the next.

CRACHIT:

God bless you, sir, and Merry Christmas.

SCROOGE:

Bah! . . . Humbug.

[Scrooge locks office, makes his way, through the foggy streets, to his dining place, where he lingers over books before heading home. Narration pauses at ellipsis.]

NARRATOR:

Scrooge put his desk in order, triple-locked his door, double-checked his locking. and stepped into the foggy street.

Then, as he did every other evening of the year, took his melancholy dinner in his usual melancholy tavern. And having beguiled away the evening with his banker's books, he went home to bed. . . .

But tonight it was so dark, and the fog and frost so black that even Scrooge, who knew every stone like his own hand, was forced to grope his way towards his door.

[EXIT SCROOGE around back of set.]

Now let any soul explain to me how it happened that Scrooge, having his key in the lock, saw in the knocker not a knocker, but his dead partner's face.

[Projection of MARLEY'S face on door.]

I: 5: Marley's Ghost

[ENTER SCROOGE through opening doors.]

SCROOGE: *[Turns & looks back at knocker.]*

Marley*!* Humbug*!*

[SCROOGE double-locks the door, searches the room, then takes off jacket & puts on night shirt, then sits in the chair, hunched over the fire.]

Something I ate; nothing more.

[Eating gruel.]

[Bell begins to ring incessantly. Bells from all around ring in response. The distant sound of dragging chains can be heard off; SCROOGE leaps up & hides behind chair.]

Only humbug! I won't believe it!

[The fire flares up, lighting the whole stage.]

[ENTER MARLEY'S GHOST.]

What do you want with me? *[Caustically.]*

MARLEY:

Much!

SCROOGE:

Who are you?

MARLEY:

Ask me who I *was*.

SCROOGE:

Who *were* you then?

MARLEY:

In life I was your partner, Jacob Marley. You don't believe me.

SCROOGE:

I don't. You could be a slight disorder of my stomach, or an undigested bit of beef, a crumb of cheese, a fragment of an underdone potato. There's more of gravy than of grave about you, whatever you are! Humbug, I tell you; humbug!

MARLEY: *[Approaching.]*

Aaauuugghh!!

SCROOGE: *[Falling on his knees.]*

Mercy! Dreadful apparition, why do you trouble me? Why do you walk the earth, spirit, and come to me?

MARLEY: *[Sits and unties kerchief, dropping jaw into lap.]*

It is required of every man that the spirit within him should walk abroad among his fellow men; but if that spirit does not go forth in life, it is condemned to do so after death; doomed to wander through the world—oh woe, is me!—and witness what it cannot share, but *might* have shared on earth, and turned to happiness! Aaauuugghh!! *[Shakes chains.]*

SCROOGE:

You are chained; tell me why?

MARLEY:

I wear the chain I forged in life. Link by link, yard by yard, by my own free will. Is its pattern strange to *you*? Do you know the weight and length of the one you yourself wear? You have labored long on it. It is a ponderous chain!

SCROOGE:

Jacob!! Speak comfort to me, Jacob!

MARLEY:

I have none to give. Mark me, Ebenezer, my spirit never walked beyond our money counting hole; and weary journeys lie before me! No rest, no peace. Incessant torture and remorse! Aaauuugghh!! My life's opportunities were misused. Oh! not to know that any mortal spirit working kindly in its little sphere will find its life too short for all the good it might do. Not to know that no amount of regret can make amends for opportunities misused! Yet such was I! Oh! such was I!

SCROOGE:
But you were a good man of business, Jacob.

MARLEY:
Business! Mankind was my business. The common welfare was my business. Charity, mercy, and kindness were all my business. *[Rattles chain.]* At this time of the rolling year, I suffer most. Why did I walk through crowds of fellow beings with my eyes turned down and never raise them to that blessed Star which led the Wise Men to a poor abode? Hear me! My time is almost gone!

SCROOGE:
I will. But don't be hard on me.

MARLEY:
I am here tonight to warn you, Ebenezer, that you have yet a chance and hope.

SCROOGE:
You were always a good friend to me, thank'ee.

MARLEY: *[Ties up jaw and rises.]*
You will be haunted by Three Spirits. Without them you cannot hope to escape the path I tread. Expect the first . . .

SCROOGE:
. . . Couldn't I take 'em all at once, and have it over, Jacob? . . .

MARLEY:
. . . when the clock strikes one. Remember, for your own sake, what I've said.

[EXIT MARLEY. SCROOGE]

[ENTER GHOSTS, driving SCROOGE downstage.]

[Percussive cacophony. Stage is full of chained ghosts, moaning & swirling about in a great display of misery & anguish in chains. Some linked together. None free. Their misery is clear: they seek to interfere, for good, in human matters, & have lost the power forever. SCROOGE rushes through them towards audience.. He swoons and falls. Church bells strike 12 midnight; GHOSTS disperse.]

STAVE TWO: Christmas Past

II; 1: Appearance of Ghost of Christmas Past

[Dim light: SCROOGE warily rises.]

NARRATOR:
When Scrooge awoke it was still very foggy and extremely cold.

[A loud church bell tolls One.]

SCROOGE:
The hour itself. *[Listens intently.]* Bah! Nothing!

[A powerful ruddy light streams out from under the curtain, growing stronger and stronger in intensity. SCROOGE peeks between curtains and it flys open.

[ENTER GHOST OF CHRISTMAS PAST, carrying a light that grows in intensity as IT approaches. SCROOGE steps back in fear.]

SCROOGE:
Are you the Spirit, sir, whose coming was foretold?

GHOST OF CHRISTMAS PAST:
I am!

SCROOGE:
Who, and what are you?

GHOST OF CHRISTMAS PAST:
I am the Ghost of Christmas Past.

SCROOGE:
Long past?

GHOST OF CHRISTMAS PAST:
No. Your past.

[SCROOGE, shielding his eyes from the intense light, backs down onto main stage and motions to the Spirit, who follows, to cover his head with his candle snuffer hat.]

GHOST OF CHRISTMAS PAST:
What! Would you put out the light I give so soon? Is it not enough that you, in your passion, have made this cap and forced me for years to wear it low upon my brow?

[Scrooge gestures "no."]

SCROOGE:
What is your business, Spirit?

GHOST OF CHRISTMAS PAST:
Your welfare! Your reclamation! Take heed!

[Puts out his strong arm and clasps SCROOGE'S arm.]

Walk with me!

[Fog rolls across the stage. SPIRIT begins to lead SCROOGE across stage, which glows as SPIRIT gestures toward it. Fog intensifies, blowing upward.]

SCROOGE:
Where are you leading me! I am only mortal; I will fall!

GHOST OF CHRISTMAS PAST: *[Laying hand on Scrooge's heart.]*

Bear but a touch of my hand here and you shall be upheld in more than this!

[EXIT SCROOGE & SPIRIT. Laughter, jingling bells, & falling snow.]

II; 2: Boyhood School

[ENTER BOYS & SCHOOL MASTER. The BOYS throw snowballs & knock off MASTER'S hat; he pursues them.

[ENTER SCROOGE & GHOST OF CHRISTMAS PAST.]

SCROOGE:
Good Heavens! I was a boy here! My school! So long forgotten, so long, long ago!

GHOST OF CHRISTMAS PAST:
You remember the way?

SCROOGE:
I could walk it blindfolded.

GHOST OF CHRISTMAS PAST:
Strange to have forgotten it for so many years! These are but shadows of the things that have been. Your lip is trembling, and what is this upon your cheek?

SCROOGE:
A snow flake. [Spirit touches cheek.]

GHOST OF CHRISTMAS PAST:
I see. The school is not quite deserted. A solitary child is left there still.

SCROOGE:
I know.

[ENTER BOY SCROOGE, sits, reading.]

GHOST OF CHRISTMAS PAST:
Poor boy; alone but for his books.

SCROOGE:
I wish. . . *[Drying his eye with his sleeve]*. . . but it's too late now.

GHOST OF CHRISTMAS PAST:
What is the matter?

SCROOGE:
Nothing; nothing. There was a boy singing a Christmas Carol at my door last night. I should like to have given him something: that's all.

GHOST OF CHRISTMAS PAST:
Nothing? Let us see another Christmas!

SCROOGE: *[In wonder & sorrow]*
The room is becoming a little darker and more dirty. The panels shrink, the windows crack; fragments of plaster fall out of the ceiling, and the naked laths show instead. There I am, older now yet alone again, when all the other boys have gone home for the jolly holidays.

[BOY SCROOGE paces. The doors opens.]

[ENTER FAN, a pretty young girl. She embraces BOY-SCROOGE and kisses him.]

FAN:

Dear brother, dear brother; I have come to bring you home, dear brother.

BOY SCROOGE:

Home?

FAN:

Yes, home; for ever and ever.

BOY SCROOGE:

But father?

FAN:

He's so much kinder than he use to be; home's like Heaven. You're never to come back here, never again, and you're to be a man, but first we're to be together all Christmas long, and have the merriest time in the world.

BOY SCROOGE:

You're quite a lady, little Fan!

[EXIT BOY-SCROOGE & FAN, through doors, joyfully, laughing. Scrooge, deep in thought, crosses down left, followed by Spirit.]

GHOST OF CHRISTMAS PAST:

Always a delicate creature, whom a breath might have withered, but she had a large heart!

SCROOGE:

So she had.

GHOST OF CHRISTMAS PAST:

She died a woman and had, I think, children?

SCROOGE:

One child.

GHOST OF CHRISTMAS PAST:

True; your nephew, Fred.

SCROOGE: *[Whisper.]*

Yes.

II: 3: Fezziwig's Christmas Party

[The scene changes to a busy city street. The STREET CROWD is humming carols & hurrying home.]

[ENTER FIDDLER MR. & MRS. FEZZIWIG w/ BELLE, MUSICIANS (fiddle, tambourine & squeeze-box), FRIENDS.]

GHOST OF CHRISTMAS PAST:

Know it?

SCROOGE:

Know it! Was I not apprenticed here?

SCROOGE: *[Happily agitated.]*

Why, it's old Fezziwig! Bless him! It's Fezziwig, alive again.

FEZZIWIG:

Yo ho, there! Ebenezer! Dick! No more work tonight. Hilli-ho!Christmas Eve, Ebenezer. Clear away, my lads; let's have plenty of room here! Hilli-ho! Tonight we dance!

*[**ENTER** YOUNG-SCRG & DICK close the shop. Fiddler starts dance tune; couples pair off & dance ensues. BELLE & YOUNG-SCROOGE dance. BELLE is a superb dancer; YOUNG SCROOGE is clumsy but lovable. Halfway through the dance the floor clears & MR. & MRS. FEZZIWIG dance to everyone's delight. When dance ends, there is a refreshment break, allowing for SCR & Xmas-Past dialogue.]*

GHOST OF CHRISTMAS PAST:

A small matter to make these silly folks so full of gratitude.

SCROOGE: *[Challenging.]*

Small!

GHOST OF CHRISTMAS PAST:

Why! Is it not? He has spent but a few pounds of your mortal money. Is that so much?

SCROOGE:
It isn't that; the happiness he gives is almost as great as if it cost a fortune.

GHOST OF CHRISTMAS PAST:
What is the matter?

SCROOGE:
Nothing.

GHOST OF CHRISTMAS PAST:
Something, I think.

SCROOGE:
No, no; just that I should like to be able to say a word or two to my clerk just now.

GHOST OF CHRISTMAS PAST:
My time grows short. Quick!

[Music & dancing resume and fade as party-goers exit.]

[EXIT FEZZIWIGS & DANCERS/ MUSICIANS as music fades.]

II: 4: Belle: Engagement & Family

SCROOGE:
Again he saw himself; in a garden this time. He was older now, a man in the prime of life. His face had begun to wear the signs of care and avarice.

[BELLE & YOUNG SROOGE sitting on a bench.]

BELLE:
I matter little to you, Ebenezer, very little. Another idol has displaced me and will cheer and comfort you in my place.

YOUNG SCROOGE:
What idol, Belle?

BELLE:
A golden one.

YOUNG SCROOGE:
This is the fair dealing of the world! There are no two things it condemns in a man so harshly as poverty or the pursuit of wealth.

BELLE:
You fear the world too much. Deny what I say if you can, but I have seen all your nobler aspirations fall one by one until your master passion, Gain, engrosses you.

YOUNG SCROOGE:
What does it matter if I am wiser? I am not changed towards you, Belle.

BELLE:
Our marriage contract is an old one, and I will not hold you to it against your will.

YOUNG SCROOGE:
Have I sought release?

BELLE:
Not in words but in your looks. Tell me truthfully; would you now seek out a penniless girl who'll bring no Gain with her marriage?

YOUNG SCROOGE:
You think so?

BELLE:
Heaven knows, I would think otherwise, yet the truth is plain . . .

SCROOGE: *[Picking up her speech from memory.]*
. . . This may hurt you, but in a very, very brief time you will forget me, like an unprofitable dream from which you gladly wake.

BELLE: *[Rising.]*
May you be happy in the life you have chosen.

[EXIT BELLE, YOUNG SCROOGE alone.]

SCROOGE:
Show me no more! Conduct me home. Why do you delight in torturing me!

GHOST OF CHRISTMAS PAST:
One shadow more!

SCROOGE:

No more! No more! I don't wish to see it! Show me no more!

[ENTER HUSBAND, carrying Christmas presents. Happy children rush across stage to him. . He swings them in laughter.]

[ENTER BELLE, taking off apron; she embraces HUSBAND.]

BELLE'S HUSBAND:

Belle, I saw an old friend of yours this afternoon.

BELLE:

Who?

BELLE'S HUSBAND:

Guess!

BELLE:

How can I? *[He makes a sour face.]* Mr. Scrooge?

BELLE'S HUSBAND:

Mr. Scrooge it was. I passed his office today. His partner lies upon the point of death, I'm told, and there he sat alone, quite alone in the world, with not a soul to comfort him in his loss. But worse I doubt he even cared.

SCROOGE:

Spirit! Remove me from this place.

GHOST OF CHRISTMAS PAST:

They are but shadows of what has been; they are what they are, do not blame me!

SCROOGE:

Remove me! I cannot bear it! Leave me! Take me back! Haunt me no longer!

[SCROOGE struggles with Xmas-Past; its light grows brighter as it retreats until squeezes out light. SCROOGE staggers back and collapses as the stage goes dark.]

STAVE THREE: The Ghost of Christmas Present

III: 1: Appearance of Christmas Present

[Clock strikes 2; long resonance. A powerful ruddy light streams under the curtain. SCROOGE cautiously approaches it.]

[Booming voice from back of auditorium; SCROOGE spins around.

[ENTER GHOST OF CHRISTMAS PRESENT.]

GHOST OF CHRISTMAS PRESENT:

It is I you seek! Come! and know me better, man! I am the Ghost Of Christmas Present. Look upon me! You have never seen the like of me before!

[SCROOGE bows reverentially.]

SCROOGE:

Never.

GHOST OF CHRISTMAS PRESENT:

Have you never walked forth with the younger members of my family, meaning (for I am very young) my elder brothers born in former years?

SCROOGE:

I'm afraid not. Have you many brothers, Spirit?

GHOST OF CHRISTMAS PRESENT:

More than eighteen hundred.

SCROOGE:

A tremendous family to provide for. Spirit, conduct me where you will. I went forth before under compulsion and learned a lesson which is working now. Tonight, if you have anything to teach me, let me profit by it.

GHOST OF CHRISTMAS PRESENT:

Touch my robe!

III: 2: Christmas Day Present

[SCROOGE touches XMAS-PRES' robe, & CURTAIN opens, revealing a street scene; fog rolls & blows around the feet of the many hunched, desperate figures.]

NARRATOR:

They stood in the city streets. The sky was gloomy, and the streets were choked with a dingy mist, half thawed, half frozen. There was nothing cheerful in the climate or the town.

ALL:

Except it was Christmas morn.

[Bursting to life as more people stream with a great cheerful busyness, bells ringing & crowd greeting each other & singing carols. SCROOGE & XMAS-PRES move among them, XMAS-PRES sprinkling good cheer from his torch. A fight interrupts song. The Spirit sprinkles fighters; they stop, & song resumes.]

GHOST OF CHRISTMAS PRESENT:

It's such a shame to quarrel on Christmas Day.

LONDONER 1:

And so it is! God love it, so it is!

SCROOGE:

Is there a peculiar flavor in what you sprinkle from your torch?

GHOST OF CHRISTMAS PRESENT:

There is. My own.

SCROOGE:

Would it apply to any kind of dinner on this day?

GHOST OF CHRISTMAS PRESENT:

To any kindly given, but to a poor one the most.

SCROOGE:

Why a poor one?

GHOST OF CHRISTMAS PRESENT:

Because it needs it the most. We're here.

III; 3: Cratchit Christmas Dinner

[Cratchit home on platform: simple table w/ benches and a hearth. Children are playing. PETER & POLLY setting table.]

[ENTER MRS. CRATCHIT.]

MRS CRATCHIT:

Where's your father and Tiny Tim? And Martha? She warn't as late last Christmas!

POLLY:

Here's Martha! We've such a goose!

[*ENTER* **MARTHA.**]

MRS CRATCHIT:

Why bless your heart alive, my dear, how late you are!

MARTHA:

We'd a deal of work to finish up last night and clear away this morning, mother.

MRS CRATCHIT:

Well, never mind as long as you've come.

POLLY:

There's father coming! Hide Martha, hide.

[MARTHA hides.]

[ENTER BOB CRATCHIT w/TINY TIM on his shoulder. Puts TIM down. He walks to the hearth, tapping his crutch.]

CRACHIT: *[Looking around.]*

Why, where's our Martha?

MRS CRATCHIT:

Not coming.

CRACHIT:

Not coming? Not coming on Christmas day?!

[MARTHA rushes forward & embraces him, then sets about getting food.]

POLLY:

Come Tim, hear the pudding.

[EXIT POLLY; ENTER TINY TIM, up right.]

MRS CRATCHIT:
And how did little Tim behave?

CRACHIT: *[Sitting.]*
Good as gold, and better. Somehow he gets thoughtful, sitting by himself so much, and thinks the strangest things. He told me that he hoped the people saw him in the church, because he was a cripple, and it might be pleasant to them to remember, upon Christmas Day, who made lame beggars walk and blind men see.

[ENTER TIM, MARTHA w/goose, and TWINS, tapping of his crutch heard.]

MARTHA:
Mother, father! The goose is so fine!

[They all sit & bow their heads for grace.]

CRACHIT:
There never was such a goose. I don't believe there ever was such a goose cooked. Its tenderness and flavor, size and cheapness . . . .

MRS CRATCHIT:
. . . were the themes of universal admiration. Yet only by being eked out with apple sauce and mashed potatoes was it sufficient for the whole family; . . .

[Notices people are finished eating and quickly proclaims.]

But now it's time to bring in the pudding.

[EXIT MRS CRATCHIT.]

POLLY:
Suppose it isn't done!

MARTHA:
Or breaks in the turning out!

PETER:
Or someone has got over the wall . . .

PETER/MARTHA/POLLY:
. . . and stolen it?

[ENTER MRS. CRATCHIT triumphantly w/steaming pudding.]

ALL:
Hurrah!

CRACHIT:
A Merry Christmas to us all, my dears. God bless us!

All:
God bless us all!

TINY TIM:
God bless us, every one!

[They toast and celebrate.]

SCROOGE:
Spirit, tell me if Tiny Tim will live?

GHOST OF CHRISTMAS PRESENT:
I see a vacant seat and in the chimney corner a crutch without an owner, carefully preserved.

SCROOGE:
No, No! Oh, no, kind Spirit, say he will be spared.

GHOST OF CHRISTMAS PRESENT:
If these shadows remain unaltered by the Future, the child will die. What then? If he is to die, let him do it, and decrease the surplus population.

[SCROOGE hangs his head in shame and despair.]

Man, if man you be in heart, forbear such wicked thoughts until you have discovered what the surplus is, and where it is. Will you decide what men shall live, what men shall die? It may be that in the sight of Heaven you are more worthless and less fit to live than millions like this poor man's child. O God! to hear the insect on the leaf pronouncing on the too much life among his hungry brothers in the dust!

CRACHIT: *[Raising glass.]*
Mr. Scrooge! I give you Mr. Scrooge, the Founder of the Feast!

MRS CRATCHIT:
The Founder of the Feast, indeed! I wish I had him here; I'd give him a piece of my mind to feast upon!

CRACHIT:
My dear, the children! Christmas Day!

MRS CRATCHIT:
It could only be Christmas Day when one drinks the health of such an odious, stingy, hard, unfeeling man as Mr. Scrooge.

CRACHIT: *[Mildly.]*
My dear, Christmas Day.

MRS CRATCHIT:
I'll drink his health for your sake, and the day's, not his. Long life to him! A merry Christmas. He'll be very merry and very happy, I have no doubt.

[All drink sullenly.]

CRACHIT:
They drank the toast, but there was no heartiness in it.

PETER:
Scrooge was the Ogre of the family. But after it had passed they were ten times merrier than before, . . .

POLLY:
. . . from the mere relief

CRACHIT:
Why so gloomy on Christmas day; come, let's have a song!

MRS CRATCHIT:
Yes, the one about the Good Shepherd. That's my favorite.

[Bob finds the note.]

ALL:
The night t'was so dark; the snow so deep,
That the little lost boy did cry.
"I fear in this blizzard I've lost my way,
And tonight I'll surely die."
But the good shepherd heard the crying boy
And hurried to his side
And bundled him up in his fleecy cloak,
"Now, now, my lad, don't cry."

[Bell strikes 10 as TIM finishes song. Spirit sprinkles them w/his torch.]

MRS CRATCHIT: *[To audience, in self justification.]*
They were not a handsome family; they were not well dressed; and their clothes were scanty.

[Tiny Tim returns to get his mother, followed by Martha who, having heard what her mother said, kisses her & speaks to audience.]

MARTHA:
But, they were happy, grateful, pleased with one another, and contented with their time.

SCROOGE:
And as they faded, Scrooge had his eye upon them, and especially on Tiny Tim, until the last.

[EXIT CRATCHIT FAMILY. SCROOGE watches TINY TIM fondly.]

III; 4: Christmas Night Montage I

NARRATOR:
By this time it was getting dark, and snowing pretty heavily; but the brightness of the roaring fires in kitchens, parlours, and all sorts of rooms, was wonderful. Then, without warning, they stood upon a bleak and desert moor,

[Howling wind. Speakers must shout.]

GHOST OF CHRISTMAS PRESENT:
[With prickly tones.]
. . . where nothing grows

SCROOGE:
but moss

GHOST OF CHRISTMAS PRESENT:
and thorns,

SCROOGE:

and coarse, rank grass.

[A cheerful company huddling and singing a Christmas song in voices that seldom rise above the howling of the wind.]

SCROOGE:

What is this place?

GHOST OF CHRISTMAS PRESENT:

Where miners live, who labor in the bowels of the earth, but see they know me. Hold my robe.

NARRATOR:

And passing on above the moor, they sped toward the darkened horizon.

SCROOGE:

Not to sea?

NARRATOR:

To Scrooge's horror, he saw the last of the land, a frightful range of rocks, behind them; and his ears were deafened by the thundering of water, as it rolled, and roared, and raged.

LIGHTHOUSE KEEPER 1:

Built upon a dismal reef of sunken rocks, there stood a solitary lighthouse.

LIGHTHOUSE KEEPER 2:

But even here, two men who watched the light had made a fire, that through the loophole in the thick stone wall shed out a ray of brightness on the awful sea.

LIGHTHOUSE KEEPERS 1 & 2:

Joining their horny hands over the rough table at which they sat, they wished each other Merry Christmas.

[Ship rigging, roaring wind, humming sails.]

NARRATOR:

Again the Ghost sped on, above the black and heaving sea—on, on—until, being far away from any shore, they lighted on a ship.

SHIP'S CREW:

And stood beside the helmsman at the wheel,

SHIP'S LOOKOUT:

the look-out in the bow,

SHIP'S CAPTAIN:

the officers who had the watch;

SHIP'S CREW:

dark, ghostly figures in their several stations.

SHIP'S CREW/CAPTAIN/LOOKOUT:

But every man among them hummed a Christmas tune,

SHIP'S CAPTAIN:

or had a Christmas thought,

SHIP'S LOOKOUT:

or spoke below his breath to his companion of some bygone Christmas Day.

III: 5: Fred's Christmas Party

[Scene changes to glowing light. Voice off, laughing merrily.]

[ENTER FRED, WIFE, TOPPER & EUNICE.]

FRED:

He said that Christmas was humbug, as I live! He believed it too!

ALL:

Ha, ha! Ha, ha, ha!

FRED'S WIFE:

More shame on him, Fred!

FRED:

He's a comical old fellow; that's the truth; and not so pleasant as he might be.

FRED'S WIFE:

I'm sure, but he is very rich, Fred!

FRED:

What of that, my dear; his wealth is of no use to him. He doesn't do even himself any good with it.

FRED'S WIFE:
I have no patience with him.

FRED:
Oh, I have! I am sorry for him; couldn't be angry if I tried. Who does he hurt? Himself, always. Here, he takes a dislike to us, and he won't come and dine. What's the consequence? He loses a fine meal.

TOPPER:
Here, here! A fine meal indeed!

FRED: *[Raising a toast as the music ends.]*
Hurrah!

FRED'S WIFE:
A merry Christmas to all!

FRED:
And specially my uncle Scrooge, wherever he is!

EUNICE:
Ha, ha!

FRED:
He wouldn't take it from me, but let him have it, nevertheless. Uncle Scrooge!

ALL:
Uncle Scrooge!

EUNICE:
Now Topper, sing us a song.

[Bell strikes 11.]

FRED'S WIFE:
Yes, Topper, a song!

EUNICE:
No excuses now; give us a song.

[WIFE sits at harp, while TOPPER assumes a singing position. As TOPPER starts to sing, SCROOGE hums along in croaking voice.]

NARRATOR: *[After part of a verse.]*
While this strain of music sounded, all the things that Ghost had shown him came upon his mind; he softened more and more and . . .

SCROOGE:
Spirit, may we stay?

GHOST OF CHRISTMAS PRESENT:
No, we must be on.

III: 6: Montage II.

NARRATOR:
Much they saw, and far they went, and many homes they visited, but always with a happy end. The spirit stood beside sick beds,

SCROOGE:
And they were cheerful.

NARRATOR:
By struggling men.

SCROOGE:
And they were patient in their greater hope.

NARRATOR:
By poverty.

SCROOGE:
And it was rich.

NARRATOR:
In poorhouse. Hospital. And jail.

SCROOGE:
In misery's every refuge, the Ghost sprinkled the blessings of his torch.

[CHRISTMAS PRESENT staggers. SCROOGE goes to comfort him.]

SCROOGE:
Spirit; you've grown gray. Is your life so short?

GHOST OF CHRISTMAS PRESENT:
My life upon this globe is very brief; it ends tonight.

SCROOGE:
Tonight!

GHOST OF CHRISTMAS PRESENT:
Tonight at midnight. Hark. *[Bell strikes.]* The time is drawing near.

SCROOGE:

Forgive me if I ask, but I see something strange, protruding from behind your skirts. Is it a foot or claw?

GHOST OF CHRISTMAS PRESENT:

[Sorrowfully.]

It might be a claw, for the flesh there's left upon it. Look here!

[XMAS-PRES reveals IGNORANCE & WANT.]

GHOST OF CHRISTMAS PRESENT:

O Man! Look here! Look, look, down here!

SCROOGE: *[Stammering.]*

Spirit! are they yours?

GHOST OF CHRISTMAS PRESENT:

They are Man's, and they cling to me. This boy is Ignorance. This girl is Want. Beware of them both, and all of their kind, but most of all beware of this boy, for on his brow I see written Mankind's Doom.

SCROOGE:

Have they no refuge or resource?

GHOST OF CHRISTMAS PRESENT:

Are there no prisons? Are there no workhouses?

[Bell strikes 12]

[EXIT XMAS-PRES].

[SCROOGE collapses, exhausted, center stage.]

STAVE FOUR: Ghost of Christmas Yet to Come

IV; 1: The Ghost Approaches

[ENTER a phantom slowly, gravely, silently approaches from up right, crossing down the full depth of stage. It is stately, tall, & in deep black; it is back -lit, and everything about it is concealed except one outstretched hand. At first it is distant, then as it comes closer it shadows the huddled figure of SCROOGE]

SCROOGE:

Am I in the presence of the Ghost of Christmas Yet to Come?

[GHOST OF CHRISTMAS YET TO COME points onward w/hand.]

Are you to show me shadows that have not yet happened but will happen in the time before us?

[GHOST OF CHRISTMAS YET TO BE nods solemnly.]

Ghost of the Future! I fear you more than any specter I have seen. But as I know your purpose is to do me good so I might live as another man from what I was, I will bear your company with a thankful heart.

[GHOST OF CHRISTMAS YET TO BE points.]

Lead on! Lead on!

[SCROOGE follows, here as afterwards, in the shadow of SPIRIT.]

IV: 2: Cynical Business Men

[ENTER BUSINESSMEN talking on street.]

NARRATOR:

They found themselves in the heart of its business district, among merchants and bankers, who hurried up and down, and clinked the money in their pocket, and looked at their watches, and conversed thoughtfully in groups.

MERCHANT:

No, I don't know much about it, only that he's dead.

BANKER:

When did he die?

MERCHANT:

Last night, I believe.

BROKER:

Why, what was the matter with him? I thought he'd never die.

MERCHANT:
God knows.

BANKER:
What has he done with his money?

BROKER:
Left it to himself, I suppose.

MERCHANT:
Well, he hasn't left it to me; that I know.

ALL:
Ha, ha, ha!

BANKER:
Likely be a cheap funeral, for, upon my life, I don't know anybody who'd go.

BROKER:
If they feed me lunch!

ALL:
Ha, ha, ha!

BANKER:
Well, I care nothing for lunch; I'll go, if anybody else will too. When I come to think of it I probably was his only friend.

MERCHANT:
Friend?! How so?

BANKER:
He spoke to me whenever we met.

BROKER:
Pray tell, whatever did he say?

BANKER:
"G'bye; G'bye."

ALL:
Ha, ha, ha! Good day. Good day.

IV; 3: Old Joe's Rag Shop

[A vile street scene: solicitations, fighting, drinking, thieving. SPIRIT & SCROOGE, in terror, moves amidst it]

NARRATOR:
They left the busy scene, and went into an obscure part of the town. The ways were foul and narrow, the shops and houses wretched, and people drunken, slip-shod, ugly. Alleys and archways, like so many cesspools, disgorged their offenses of smell, and dirt, and life, upon the straggling streets; and the whole quarter reeked with crime, with filth and misery.

[ENTER OLD JOE, a filthy old man; he sits and counts money.

[ENTER CHARWOMAN and LAUNDRESS from a burst of fighting on the street.]

CHARWOMAN: ***[Off.]***
I'm first; get y'gone, or I'll bite y'ear right off y'ed.

[ENTER Charwoman & Laundress, each w/a bundle. OLD JOE hurries them.]

LAUNDRESS:
Ha, ha! 'Ear y'talk; get'y'back b'for y'dead.

OLD JOE:
Stop y'mouths till I shut the door. Want to be drawing attention. Come into the parlor. Come in, me darlings; come in. Now whatta'y'ave for Old Joe t'night?

[CHARWOMAN puts her small bundle on the table. JOE rifles it.]

OLD JOE:
Sheets, towels, two silver teaspoons, three boots, one badly worn; Three and six, not a penny more; I always give too much to ladies. it's a weakness of mine. Someday I must repent of being so liberal.

LAUNDRESS:
And now undo my bundle, Joe. [She puts a large bundle on the floor; JOE kneels down & undoes it, pulling out a large, heavy roll of some dark stuff.]

OLD JOE:
Whatta'y'ave'ir? Bed-curtains?!

LAUNDRESS: *[Crossing arms.]*
Ah! Bed-curtains!

OLD JOE:
Y'don't mean t'say y'took'em down, rings an'all, with'im lying there?

LAUNDRESS:
Yes, I do; why not?

OLD JOE:
You were born t'make yr fortune.

LAUNDRESS:
I sh'nt hold my hand when I can get something in it just by reaching it out.

OLD JOE:
His blankets?

LAUNDRESS:
Whose else? He isn't likely to take cold without'em.

OLD JOE:
I'ope he didn't die of anything catching? Eh?

LAUNDRESS:
I ain't so fond of his company to hang around'im for such a thing, if he did. Ah! look through that shirt till your eyes ache, but you won't find a hole in it. It's the best he had. They'd'ave wasted it, if not for me.

OLD JOE:
Whatt'ya call wasting it?

LAUNDRESS:
Putting it on'im t'be buried in it. Somebody was fool enough to do it, but I took it off again. If calico an't good enough for such a purpose, it isn't good enough for anything. It's quite as becoming to the body. He don't look uglier in what I left'im in than he did in that one!

OLD JOE: *[Paying out money.]*
Ha, ha, ha! Yer a precious one, y'ar.

LAUNDRESS:
This is the end of it, you see! He frightened every one away from him when he was alive, to profit us when he was dead! Ha, ha, ha!

SCROOGE:
Spirit! I see, I see. This unhappy man might be me. Merciful Heaven, what is this?

IV: 5: The Grave

[A terrible scratching and the screeching of cats. A bed with a sheet over a corpse. The GHOST OF CHRISTMAS YET TO BE motions to SCROOGE to approach. SCROOGE retreats.]

SCROOGE:
Spirit? What if this man could be raised up now, what would be his foremost thoughts? Avarice, hard dealing, griping cares? They have brought him to a rich end, truly! What do they want in this room of death? Spirit! I have learned my lesson; let us go!

[GHOST OF CHRISTMAS YET TO BE continues to point at corpse.]

I can't; I can't. Spirit; I beseech you, if there is any person in this world who mourns this man's death, show me, Spirit, I beseech you!

[GHOST OF CHRISTMAS YET TO BE spread his cloak like a great set of wings.]

IV: 6: The Bankrupts

[A woman in despair w/baby. ENTER a Man.

BANKRUPT WOMAN:
What is the news? Good or bad?

BANKRUPT MAN:
Bad.

BANKRUPT WOMAN:
Then we are ruined?!

BANKRUPT MAN:
No, there still is hope.

BANKRUPT WOMAN:
Will *he* relent and give us time to pay the debt?

BANKRUPT MAN:
He is past relenting. He is dead.

BANKRUPT WOMAN:
Dead! Thank God! . . . *[Shocked with herself.]* What have I said? How far we've fallen! To whom will our debt be transferred?

BANKRUPT MAN:
I don't know, but by then we'll have the money.

SCROOGE:
Let me see some tenderness connected with this man's death.

[The SPIRIT conducts SCROOGE through vile streets.]

IV: 7: Cratchit Home in Mourning

[MRS. CRATCHIT is sitting at table in despair. Tiny Tim's crutches are clearly visible in the chimney corner. PETER, reads Bible.]

PETER: *[With difficulty.]*
"And he took a child, and set him in the midst of them."

MRS CRATCHIT:
It must be near the time your father comes home from work.

PETER:
Past it, but I think he walks a little slower than he used, these last few evenings, mother.

MRS CRATCHIT:
I have known him to walk with . . . *voice breaks* . . . I've known him to walk with Tiny Tim upon his shoulder very fast indeed.

PETER:
And so have I. Often.

POLLY:
And I.

MRS CRATCHIT:
But he was very light to carry, and your father loved him so, that it was no trouble—no trouble. And here's your father now!

[MRS. rises to meet CRA. PETER sets tea for him, and POLLY sits on his knee. CRATCHIT is cheerful with CHILDREN.]

CRACHIT: *[Growing solemn, then weeping.]*
I went today; how I wish you could have gone. It would have done you good to see how green a place it is. *[Breaks down.]* My little, little child! My little child!

[FAMILY gathers around and comforts him.]

Guess who I met on the street today. Mr. Scrooge's nephew. He saw how down I was and asked what distressed me. And when I told him he took my hand and said, "I am heartily sorry for it. If I can be of any help in any way," and he gave me his card and said, "that's where I live." It really seemed as if he had known our Tiny Tim, and felt with us.

MRS CRATCHIT:
I'm sure he's a good soul.

CRACHIT:
You can be sure of it, my dear. I wouldn't be surprised if he got Peter a better situation.

SCROOGE:
Specter, something tells me that our parting moment is at hand. Tell me who was the man we saw lying dead.

[SPIRIT points to next scene.]

IV; 8: Scrooge's Revelation

[A tombstone.]

SCROOGE:
Before I draw nearer, answer me one question. Are these the shadows of the things that Will be or are they shadows of the things that May be only?

[The GHOST OF CHRISTMAS YET TO BE only points at the stone. On it appears the name Ebenezer Scrooge.]

Am *I* that man? No, Spirit! Oh, no, no! I am not the man I was, nor will I ever be him again. Why show me this; am I beyond all hope?

[GHOST OF CHRISTMAS YET TO BE'S hand begins to shake & continues to do so until scene's end.]

Oh Good Spirit, tell me how I may wipe away the writing on this stone!

[SCROOGE grabs the GHOST OF CHRISTMAS YET TO BE'S hand but the GHOST OF CHRISTMAS YET TO BE pushes him back. SCROOGE falls over, raising his hands in supplication as GHOST OF CHRISTMAS YET TO BE EXITS.]

I will live in the Past, the Present, and the Future. O Jacob Marley! Heaven and Christmas-Time be praised for this!

[Lights fade slowly.]

STAVE FIVE: Christmas Morning Redeemed

V; 1: Christmas Morning

[SCROOGE, pulling dressing gown over nightshirt, looks out at audience.]

SCROOGE:

I am here! The shadows are dispelled! I'm as light as feather, as happy as a schoolboy. A merry Christmas to everybody! A happy New Year to the world!

[Church bells. ENTER CROWD, hurrying, laden with gifts and packages.]

SCROOGE:

Merry Christmas! Merry Christmas! Merry Christmas! Oh, glorious, heavenly sky; sweet, fresh air; merry bells! Boy! What's today?

GOOSE BOY: *[Taken aback]*

Eh?

SCROOGE:

Yes, today, my fine fellow!

GOOSE BOY:

Why, Christmas Day!

SCROOGE:

Christmas Day! I haven't missed it! Boy, do you know the butcher on the next street? You know the prize Turkey that was hanging up there? Not the little prize turkey, but the big one?

GOOSE BOY: *[Aside.]*

Merry Christmas! *[To audience.]* It's as big as me!

SCROOGE:

What a delightful boy! Yes, that's the one! Go and buy it! Merry Christmas! I'm in earnest! Merry Christmas! Go and buy it and tell the butcher to bring it to Bob Cratchit's! He sha'nt know who sends it! But I must get ready; there's so much to do! Merry Christmas!

[SCROOGE rushes from person to person, greeting, patting their backs and wishing them a Merry Christmas.

[ENTER CHARITABLE GENTLEMEN.]

SCROOGE:

Good morning, sir! A merry Christmas to you) My dear sir, how do you do? I hope you succeeded yesterday. A merry Christmas to you, sir!

GENTLEMAN 1:

Mr. Scrooge?

SCROOGE:

That is my name, and I fear it may not be pleasant one to you. Allow me to ask your pardon. And will you have the goodness . . .

[SCROOGE whispers in his ear. GENTLEMAN is startled.]

GENTLEMAN 2:
Lord Bless me!

GENTLEMAN 1:
My dear Mr. Scrooge, are you serious?

SCROOGE:
Not a penny less, and a great many back payments are included, I assure you, and there will be more. Come and see me. Will you come and see me?

GENTLEMAN 1 & 2:
We will!

SCROOGE:
Thankee. I am much obliged. He walked about the streets, and watched the people hurrying to and fro, and patted the children on the head, and questioned beggars, and looked down into the kitchens of houses, and up to the windows, and found that everything could yield him pleasure. Merry Christmas! Merry Christmas! Merry Christmas!

[ENTER FRED & WIFE. They are shocked; WIFE wants to turn away but FRED approaches SCROOGE kindly.]

FRED:
Uncle Scrooge? Why bless my soul!

SCROOGE:
It's I. Your Uncle Scrooge. May I still come to dinner. Will you let me in, Fred?

FRED:
Let you in! Why nothing would give us greater pleasure!

[As SCROOGE moves to shake hands of others he crosses and speaks directly to audience. Everyone gathers, watching curiously & exchanging remarks of delight.]

It is a mercy he didn't shake their arms off. Nothing could be heartier. It was a wonderful party, wonderful games, wonderful happiness! But he was home early because he had to be up and at the office early the next morning.

Oh, he was early, long before nine! If he could only catch Bob Cratchit coming late! That was the thing he had set his heart upon.

V; 2: Finale: Scrooge's Office

[SCROOGE sits at his desk, trying to write carefully but unable to restrain his delight. All the characters are gathered around, pretending that they are not watching. Clock strikes 9.]

[ENTER CHRATCHIT; he passes through the crowd, who wag their fingers at him, looking at their watches.

SCROOGE: *[Growling.]*
Hallo! What do you mean by coming here at this time of day?

CRACHIT:
I am very sorry, sir. I *am* late.

SCROOGE:
Yes, I think you are. Step this way, sir, if you please.

CRACHIT:
It's only once a year, sir. It shall not be repeated.

SCROOGE:
Now, I'll tell you what, my friend; I am not going to stand this sort of thing any longer. *[He grabs and pulls CRATCHIT toward him.]* Therefore, I am about to . . . raise your salary!

CRACHIT:
Mr. Scrooge! Are you gone mad?

SCROOGE:
A merry Christmas, Bob! A merrier Christmas, Bob, than I have given you for many a year! I'll raise your salary, and assist your struggling family, and your boy

Tiny Tim, rest assured, I'll care for him. Now Bob. Make up the fire, and heap it high before you dot, Bob Cratchit, another ***i***!

CRACHIT: *[Crossing down to main stage.]*
Scrooge was better than his word. He did it all, and infinitely more;

PETER:
And to Tiny Tim

TINY TIM:
He did NOT die.

[SCROOGE swings TINY TIM up onto his shoulder.]

MRS CRATCHIT:
He was a second father.
[Putting arm around Bob and rest of family.]

GENTLEMAN 1:
He became as good a friend and as good a man as the old City knew,

GENTLEMAN 2:
or any other good old city, town, or village in the good old world.

SCROOGE:
And it was always said of him, that he knew how to keep Christmas well, . . .

FRED:
. . . if any man alive possessed the knowledge.

MRS CRATCHIT:
May that be truly said of us, all of us!

MARTHA:
And so as Tiny Tim observed.

TINY TIM:
"God bless Us,

ALL:
EVERY ONE!"

[EXEUNT, singing "God Bless Ye Merry Gentlemen."]

Edelmiro II y el dragón Gutiérrez

por Fernando Lalana

adaptado por G. Guardia-Hayes (2012)

Personajes

La Narradora	Benito:	El Rey Edelmiro II
La Reina Felisa	La Pregonera	El Dragón Gutiérrez
La Tesorera Real	Espectador (2)	El Dragonero
El Caballero Tiburcio	La Bruja Matilde	Dos Guardias Reales
Criado (3)	Ciudadano 1 / Fofano	Ciudadano 2 / Oveja
Ciudadano 3 / Otro Fofano		

Empieza la acción

NARRADORA:

¡Señoras y señores! ¡Amigos y vecinos! ¡Público en general! ¡Escúchenme todos! Quiero contarles una historia sensacional, llena de misterio y emoción. Tiene muchos personajes: unos serán buenos, buenísimos; otros serán malos, malísimos; otros no serán ni buenos ni malos; y es posible que uno sea bueno y malo al mismo tiempo. Ustedes van a ser un elemento muy importante dentro del teatro; sin un público no es posible el teatro. Esta historia va a ser un desastre y es muy importante que ustedes presten mucha atención, porque si no, es posible que no entiendan nada. Así, pues, ¿están listos? ¿Tienen los ojos abiertos? ¿Tienen los oídos limpios? ¿Listos?

EL PÚBLICO:

¡Síííííííííí!

NARRADORA:

¿Listos?:

EL PÚBLICO:

¡Síííííííííí!

NARRADORA:

¡Excelente! Entonces, adelante. ¡Acción! *(Sonido: fanfarrias. El narrador se va al fondo del escenario y por la izquierda aparece Benito, un señor con bigote y uniforme azul marino.)*

BENITO:

¡Hola a todos! Me llamo Benito y soy la más alta autoridad del país de Fofa.

ESPECTADOR:

¿Cómo, cómo? ¿Del país de qué?

BENITO:

¡Fofa! Mi país se llama Fofa. ¿No conoce el país de Fofa?

ESPECTADOR:

Pues mire que no. Nunca jamás…

BENITO:

¡Vaya, hombre, siempre igual! Nadie sabe nada de Fofa. Y es que, claro, es un país tan pequeñito que no aparece en ningún libro ni en ningún mapa. Será por eso que no viene ni un solo turista…

ESPECTADOR:

¿Y usted es el rey de Fofa?

BENITO:

¿Yo? ¡Qué va! Fofa es tan, pero tan pequeño que ni siquiera tiene rey. Yo soy el que más manda en Fofa y soy solamente policía. Pero, mire, precisamente ahora andamos buscando un rey. Escuche, escuche….

PREGONERA:

(Sale por la izquierda, con el pregón en una mano y una flauta en la otra.)

¡Atención, atenciooooón! Por orden de don Benito, policía de Fofa, se hace sabeeeer: ¡Que el país necesita con urgencia un rey de buena calidad! Se ofrece un buen sueldo, trono de roble y marfil y entradas gratis para el cine todos los saaaaábados. Se exige buena presencia, corona y manto propios y experiencia en cargo similaaaaar! (*Se va por la derecha.*)

(Entra en ese momento de la calle, con una gran maleta en la mano. Se acerca al escenario dando voces por el pasillo central del patio de butacas.)

EDELMIRO:

¡Eh! ¡Aquí, aquí! ¡Pssst! ¡Oiga!

BENITO:

¿Qué ocurre? ¿Qué pasa por ahí? ¿Quién hace tanto ruido?

EDELMIRO:

¡Soy yo! ¡Soy yo!

BENITO:

¿Quién es usted? ¿Y qué quiere?

EDELMIRO:

(*Consigue subir al escenario, resoplando como una locomotora.*) ¡Buf! ¡Arf! ¡Bof! Es que acabo de oír el pregón y vengo corriendo para ver si me contratan. ¡Yo soy rey!

BENITO:

(*Incrédulo.*) ¿Usted, rey? Pues, la verdad, no tiene un aspecto muy real, que digamos…

EDELMIRO:

Es que estoy sin trabajo desde hace seis años y, claro, se pierde la forma. ¡Pero soy rey! Se lo aseguro. Rey diplomado.

BENITO:

¿De veras?:

EDELMIRO:

Mire, mire. Aquí traigo mi título, perfectamente en regla.

(Saca de la maleta un precioso diploma, con una banda roja que lo cruza en diagonal.)

BENITO:

A ver… ¡Ah, pues sí! Es usted rey. Rey diplomado. Pero verá… Nosotros queríamos un rey alto y guapo y ancho de espaldas; y usted; perdone que le diga, pero de eso, nada. Lo que se dice nada, ¿eh?

EDELMIRO:

(*Un poco triste.*) Ya, ya lo sé. Soy bajito y más bien feo, tiene usted razón. Pero a cambio de eso…

BENITO:

¿Qué?

EDELMIRO:

De pura casualidad estoy casado. Así que, por el mismo precio puede tener usted un rey y una reina. (*Grita, en la dirección en que vino.*) ¡Felisa! ¡Felisa! ¡Ven que te presente a este señor tan simpático!

(Por la puerta del fondo de la sala aparece la Reina Felisa, a los acordes de una marcha real. Avanza por el pasillo central saludando al público, que le aplaude enfervorizados. Llega por fin al escenario.)

EDELMIRO:

Aquí, mi señora, la reina Felisa. Felisa, te presento a don Benito.

BENITO:

Encantado, majestad.:

FELISA:

El gusto es mío, Benito.

EDELMIRO:

(A Benito) Bueno, ¿qué? ¿Qué le parece?

BENITO:

(*Sinceramente impresionado por lo ventajoso de la oferta.*) La verdad es que está muy bien. ¡Pero que muy requetebién! Resulta muy económico. Dos por el precio de uno. Eso cambia completamente las cosas.

EDELMIRO:

Entonces... ¿Nos aceptan?:

BENITO:

(*Tras pensárselo un poco.*) ¡De acuerdo! Queda usted contratado como el rey del país de Fofa.

EDELMIRO:

¡Estupendo! ¡Muchas gracias!

BENITO:

Por cierto... ¿Cuál es su nombre?

EDELMIRO:

Me llamo Edelmiro Segundo.

BENITO:

¿Edelmiro Segundo? ¡Caramba! ¿No será usted hijo del famoso rey Edelmiro Primero?

EDELMIRO:

Pues no, no señor. Mi papá se llamaba Ramón y no era rey, sino que equilibrista en el circo Atlas. Lo que ocurre es que me llamo Edelmiro de nombre y Segundo de apellido: Edelmiro Segundo. ¿Comprende?

BENITO:

¡Ah, ya! Pues nada, hombre. Reinará usted con el nombre de Edelmiro II, que lo encuentro muy apropiado.

(Benito y Edelmiro se abrazan y quedan estáticos, formando cuadro. Inmediatamente, el Narrador, que ha estado observando la escena desde el fondo, se acerca a la batería.)

NARRADORA:

Y así, de aquella sencilla manera, Edelmiro II se convirtió en rey del país de Fofa. Y para celebrar el acontecimiento, se decretó en todo el reino un día de fiesta, y todo el mundo se mostró muy contento de tener un rey nuevo.

(Efectivamente, la escena se ha iluminado por completo. Unos aldeanos han hecho su aparición por ambos laterales y bailan y cantan muy contentos.)

UN ESPECTADOR:

¡Viva el rey Edelmirooooooo!

TODOS:

¡Vivaaaaa!

OTRO ESPECTADOR

¡Viva la reina Felisaaaaaa!

TODOS:

¡Vivaaaa!

NARRADORA:

(*Haciéndose oír por encima del follón, que ya va cesando.*) Ese mismo día, el rey Edelmiro subió al balcón más alto del palacio para dirigir su primer discurso al pueblo de Fofa.

(Mutación: ahora el decorado representa la plaza ante la fachada principal del palacio real de Fofa. Aparece Benito en el balcón.)

BENITO:

¡Pueblo de Fofa! ¡Con ustedes, su rey: Edelmiro II!

TODOS:

¡Bieeeen! (*Aplausos.*)

EDELMIRO II:

¡Ejem, ejem! ¡Querido pueblo! ¡Ciudadanos y ciudadanas! ¡Fofos y fofas!

UN CIUDADANO:

¿Eh?

OTRO CIUDADANO:

Pero, ¿qué dice?

OTRO MÁS:

¡Nos insulta!

Y OTRO:

¡Insolente! ¡Fuera, fuera!

(La muchedumbre empieza a increpar a Edelmiro "ad libitum".)

BENITO:

(*Aparte, a Edelmiro, asustado*). ¡Señor, señor! ¡Majestad!

EDELMIRO II:

¿Qué ocurre? ¿Por qué se enojan conmigo, Benito?

BENITO:

Es que los habitantes de Fofa no se llaman fofos. ¡Se llaman fofanos!

EDELMIRO II:

¡Uy, madre! ¡Vaya error! Desde luego, ya, ya... (*Al pueblo.*) ¡Ejem! ¡Perdón! Quise decir: ¡Queridos fofanos y fofanas!

TODOS:

(Con alivio.) ¡Aaaaaaah!

EDELMIRO II:

La reina Felisa y yo queremos que Fofa sea un país tranquilo y agradable. Pondremos jardines y parques llenos de árboles por todas partes. Obligaremos a los circos venir por aquí más a menudo y bajaremos el precio de las entradas al cine y del teatro. A partir de este momento nos pueden comunicar todos sus problemas, que yo les prometo hacer lo posible por solucionarlos. He dicho.

(Hace ademán de regresar al interior del palacio, pero una voz le detiene.)

UN FOFANO:

¡Rey! ¡Rey Edelmiro! ¡Majestad!

EDELMIRO II:

¿Qué ocurre, querido súbdito?

FOFANO:

Resulta que ya tenemos un problema muy grande.

EDELMIRO II:

¿Cómo? ¿Tan pronto? ¡Qué mala suerte! ¿Y de qué se trata el problema?

FOFANO:

Se trata del dragón. Tiene que librarnos del malvado dragón Gutiérrez, que nos tiene atemorizados desde hace ciento once años.

EDELMIRO II:

¿Cómo? ¿Un dragón? Pero... ¡Oiga, Benito! Cuando se me ofreció el empleo no se mencionó en ningún momento a ese dragón.

BENITO:

(*Haciéndose el despistado.*) ¿No se lo dije? Vaya, hombre... Seguramente se me olvidó. En realidad, tampoco hay que preocuparse demasiado. El asunto no tiene demasiada importancia. Total: un simple dragón de siete mil kilos.

EDELMIRO II:

¿Siete mil ki...ki... kilooooos?

BENITO:

Eso, si es que no está más gordo. Pero la verdad es que casi todo se le va a la cola y los cuernos.

EDELMIRO II:

¿Cu ...cu... cuernoooooos? ¿Que tiene cuernooooooos?

BENITO:

Sí. Tiene ocho cuernos.

EDELMIRO II:

(*Asustadísimo.*) ¡Mi abuelo!, y seguro que echa fuego por la boca.

BENITO:

¡Bah...! Muy poquito. Muy poquito...

OTRO FOFANO:
Si quiere demostrar que es un buen rey, lo primero que debe hacer es librarnos del dragón.

TODOS:
¡Eso, eso! ¡Sí! ¡Que nos libre del dragón!

(Frases similares "ad lib")

EDELMIRO II:
(*Tratando de poner orden*). Bueno, calma, calma. (*Como no le hacen ni caso, lanza un berrido descomunal*). ¡Silenciooooo, carambaaaa! (*Callan todos*). ¡Bien! Puesto que es tan importante, ahora mismo vamos a poner manos a la obra. ¡Que venga el tesorero real!

(Dentro se van oyendo sucesivas voces reclamando al tesorero real y por fin aparece este con un cofrecito en las manos).

EL TESORERO:
(*Ha aparecido en el balcón contiguo*). ¡Diga, majestad!

EDELMIRO II:
Tesorero. ¿Cuánto dinero hay en las arcas reales?

EL TESORERO:
(*Abre el cofrecito y, a tiempo, consulta unos papeles que saca del bolsillo*). Unas mil monedas de oro, majestad. Se iban a utilizar para construir el nuevo estadio de fútbol.

EDELMIRO II:
¿Fútbol? ¡Nada de fútbol! Desde hoy queda abolido el fútbol en todo el país. El que quiera jugar algo, que juegue a las canicas. Esas mil monedas las vamos a utilizar en la guerra contra el dragón, que es mucho más importante. ¡Pregonera!

(Desaparece el Tesorero y aparece en el balcón la Pregonera)

PREGONERA:
Majestad…

EDELMIRO II:
Pregona ahora mismo a los cuatro vientos que aquel que sea capaz de acabar con el temible dragón Gutiérrez, será recompensado con la suma de mil monedas de oro. Envía telegramas a los reinos cercanos para que también allí se conozca nuestra oferta.

PREGONERA:
Al momento, Majestad.

(Mutación: el decorado representa ahora la Sala del Trono. Edelmiro II y la Reina Felisa están sentados en sendos tronos reales).

NARRADORA:
(*Adelantándose hasta la batería*). Y así, en muy poco tiempo empezaron a llegar al país de Fofa los más extravagantes personajes, dispuestos todos a acabar con el dragón Gutiérrez y a ganarse las mil monedas de oro prometidas por el rey Edelmiro. (*Vuelve al fondo*).

REINA FELISA:
¿Viste, amado esposo? El recibidor de palacio está lleno de valientes caballeros que quieren acabar con el dragón.

EDELMIRO II:
¡Ah! ¿Sí? Pues que pasen en el orden que llegaron. ¡Que pase el primero!

UN CRIADO:
¡Que pase el primero!

VOZ DE OTRO CRIADO:
(*Dentro*) ¡Que pase el primero!

VOZ DE OTRO MÁS:
(*Más adentro*) ¡Que pase el primero!

EL DRAGONERO:
(Entra por la izquierda. Es un tipo muy extraño. Viste bata blanca y lleva gafas. Parece un científico despistado. Hace gestos

muy raros y tiene tics nerviosos).
¡Buenos días a todos! Querido rey Edelmiro... Querida reina... Querido pueblo de Fofa... ¡Tengo una solución para su problema! ¡Una solución científica, radical y definitiva! Soy el exterminador oficial de dragones del reino vecino de Mecachis y vengo a ofrecerles mi último invento: la dragonera.

TODOS:
¿La dragoneraaaaaa?

EDELMIRO II:
¿Qué es eso?

EL DRAGONERO:
Como indica su nombre, la dragonera no es ni más ni menos que una ratonera para dragones.

BENITO:
¿Piensas cazar un dragón con una ratonera? ¡No me hagas reír!

EL DRAGONERO:
Es que no se trata de una ratonera normal, caballero. ¡Es una ratonera gigante!

REINA FELISA:
¿Gigante?

EL DRAGONERO:
Ahora mismo van a verla. (*Llamando a alguien fuera de escena*). ¡Vamos! ¡Tráiganla aquí!

(Entre dos pajes meten en escena la dragonera, tirando de ella con unas cuerdas. Efectivamente, es parecida a una ratonera con ruedas y del tamaño de un automóvil.)

TODOS:
(*Al verla*). ¡Oooooooh!

EDELMIRO II:
¡Caramba! Es impresionante. ¿Cómo funciona?:

EL DRAGONERO:
Es un mecanismo sofisticado y eficaz, majestad. En este receptáculo se coloca el cebo, cuando el dragón se acerca, dispuesto a llevárselo...¡zas!, se dispara automáticamente atrapando irremediablemente al monstruo.

BENITO:
¿Y qué piensa poner como cebo?:

EL DRAGONERO:
Llevo años estudiando el problema y he llegado a la conclusión de que el mejor cebo que puede usarse es un gran trozo de... ¡queso!

EDELMIRO II:
¿Queso?:

EL DRAGONERO:
Sí, sí. ¡Queso!

REINA FELISA:
Pero.... ¿qué es eso del queso?

EDELMIRO II:
Eso, eso. ¿Qué es el queso?

EL DRAGONERO:
(*Confuso*). Pues el queso es eso: ¡queso! (*Asombrado*). ¿No saben lo que es el queso?

TODOS:
Noooooo...

EL DRAGONERO:
Esta sí que es buena. Verán: el queso se hace con leche...

REINA FELISA:
¿Leche? ¿Qué es leche?

EL DRAGONERO:
Pero... ¿no saben lo que es la leche?

TODOS:
Nooooo....

EL DRAGONERO:
La leche es lo que dan las vacas.

REINA FELISA:
¿Vacas? ¿Qué son las vacas?

EL DRAGONERO:
(*Desesperado*) Pero… ¿tampoco saben lo que son las vacaaaaas?

TODOS:
Tampocoooooo….

EL DRAGONERO:
¡Vaya! Esto sí es un problema. Francamente no contaba con ello. Pero no perdamos la calma. Habrá que ir paso tras paso. En primer lugar, será preciso comprar una vaca en algún país vecino. Luego, ordeñarla para que nos dé leche. Y con la leche, hacer queso. Más tarde, poner el queso en la dragonera. Y esperar entonces a que caiga el dragón, y a continuación…

EDELMIRO II:
¡Basta, dragonero! Lo siento, pero su sistema es demasiado lento y complicado. Nos llevaría demasiado tiempo. Vuelva cuando tenga perfeccionado el invento.

EL DRAGONERO:
Pero…

EDELMIRO II:
Adiós. (*Dos soldados reales acompañan al Dragonero a la salida y retiran la dragonera de escena*). ¡Que pase el siguiente!

CRIADO:
¡El siguienteeeee!:

OTRO CRIADO:
(*Dentro*). ¡El siguienteeeee!:

OTRO MÁS:
(*Más adentro*). ¡El siguienteeeee!:

EL CABALLERO FEROZ:
(Entra a caballo. Mide metro cincuenta de alto y metro setenta y cinco de ancho. Usa bigote estilo morsa y tiene una cara de bruto que asusta a las piedras. Realiza unos saltos ecuestres y, por fin, se presenta).
¡Hola! Soy Tiburcio de Trasmoz, el caballero feroz. Esta es mi espada Dorada. (*Efectivamente, es dorada*). Esta, mi armadura oscura. (*Se golpea el pecho bravamente*). Y este, mi escudo peludo. (*El escudo está cubierto por una abundante caballera*). Con sólo estos instrumentos, voy a enfrentarme a la fiera y verán de qué manera la liquido en un momento. Prepare la recompensa, querido rey Edelmiro. Manejando a mi Dorada jamás me permito un fallo y acabaré con el bicho en menos que canta un gallo. ¡Con Tiburcio basta y sobra! ¡Despidan a los demás! Antes de caer la noche ¡lo convertiré en foie-gras!

REINA FELISA:
(*Aparte, al rey*). ¡Qué horror!

EDELMIRO II:
¡Es un guerrero terrible!, ¿verdad?

REINA FELISA:
Los que son terribles son sus versos. ¡En mi vida los había oído tan malos!

EDELMIRO II:
Al menos, parece más rápido y eficaz que el anterior.

EL CABALLERO FEROZ:
¡Basta de conversación! Dígame sin tardar dónde encontraré al dragón con el que debo acabar.

BENITO:
(Conteniendo a duras penas la risa ante los ripios de Tiburcio).
Es muy fácil: el dragón Gutiérrez vive en una cueva de las afueras, cerca del molino. Si coge el carruaje de la línea treinta y dos, lo dejará casi en la puerta.

EL CABALLERO FEROZ:
Sólo tengo una última duda: ¿reconoceré al dragón si le echo la vista encima? No me gustaría equivocarme y, por una

confusión, acabar con una oveja pensando que es el dragón.

REINA FELISA:
No se preocupe por eso, valiente Tiburcio. Precisamente tenemos aquí una fotografía del dragón Gutiérrez, tomada por un turista el verano pasado. ¡Mire! (*Le da una foto 18x24*).

EL CABALLERO FEROZ:
¡Hum! A ver... (*Al mirarla, cambio de tonos: de tono de piel, pues se pone amarillo, y de tono de voz, pues se le pone temblorosa y ya no vuelve a intentar ningún ripio*). ¡Vaya! ¡Qué feo es!

REINA FELISA:
Sí. ¡Es horrible!

EDELMIRO II:
¡Horriblísimo!

BENITO:
¡Horriblisísimo!

LA PREGONERA:
¡Horriblisisísimo!

EL CABALLERO FEROZ:
Y además...es muy grande. ¡Mucho más grande de lo que yo pensaba!

REINA FELISA:
Sí. ¡Es grandísimo!

EDELMIRO II:
¡Grandisisísmo!

BENITO:
¡Grandisisisísimo!

LA PREGONERA:
¡Grandisisisisísmo!

EL CABALLERO FEROZ:
Y esos cuernos tan afilados...

REINA FELISA:
¡Afiladísimos!

EL CABALLERO FEROZ:
Y esas escamas tan gordas...

EDELMIRO II:
¡Gordísimas!

EL CABALLERO FEROZ:
Y esa piel verdusca...

BENITO:
¡Verdusquísima!

REINA FELISA:
Pero... feroz Tiburcio. ¿Qué le pasa? ¡Está amarillo! ¿Se encuentra mal? Parece tener miedo.

EL CABALLERO FEROZ:
(*A punto de desmayarse de miedo*). ¿Miedo? ¿Miedo, yo? ¡Ja, ja! Lo que pasa es que... que comí huevos para el desayuno y seguro estaban malos. ¡Eso es!

REINA FELISA:
¡Pobrecito! ¿Quiere una taza de té? ¿O Pepto Bismol? Le ayudaría.

EL CABALLERO FEROZ:
Pues ahora que me lo dice... Sí, creo que tengo el estómago un poco revuelto.

EDELMIRO II:
¡BENITO! Acompañe a este "valiente" caballero a las cocinas, que le den una taza de té y una cucharada de Pepto Bismol. Y luego, que se vaya a casa. (*Salen ambos. Benito ayudando a Tiburcio, que no hace más que lamentarse*). ¡Que pase el siguiente!

UN CRIADO:
¡A ver! ¡El siguiente!

OTRO CRIADO:
(*Dentro*). ¡El siguienteeeee!

OTRO MÁS:
(*Más adentro*). ¡El siguienteeeee!
(*En medio de una nube de humo aparece La Bruja Matilde. Más fea, imposible.*)

LA BRUJA MATILDE:
¡Jia, jia, jia! Han fallado todos, ¿verdad?

¡Jia, jia, jia! Nadie ha conseguido acabar con el dragón Gutiérrez. ¿A que no?

REINA FELISA:
No. Nadie lo ha hecho hasta ahora.

LA BRUJA MATILDE:
Yo lo haré, no se preocupen. ¡Jia, jia, jia!

EDELMIRO II:
¿Quién es usted?:

LA BRUJA MATILDE:
¡Jia, jia, jia! ¡Soy la bruja Matilde, naturalmente!

LA PREGONERA:
(*Aparte, al rey.*) Tenga cuidado, majestad. La Bruja Matilde está loca.

EDELMIRO II:
¿Cómo? ¿Está loca?

LA PREGONERA:
¡Completamente chiflada!

EDELMIRO II:
¡Ejem! Dígame, Matilde. ¿Cómo piensa acabar con el dragón Gutiérrez?

LA BRUJA MATILDE:
Tengo un plan infalible: ¡magia!

TODOS:
¿Magiaaaa?:

LA BRUJA MATILDE:
Sí, magia. ¡Jia, jia, jia! He aprendido un conjuro para convertir a los dragones en ovejas.

EDELMIRO II:
¡Caramba! Eso sí que sería una buena solución.

LA BRUJA MATILDE:
¡Sí! ¡Jia, jia, jia! Pero hay un pequeño problema.

REINA FELISA:
Siempre hay un pequeño problema. ¿Cuál es el problema?

LA BRUJA MATILDE:
Como el dragón Gutiérrez es tan grande, grandísimo, grandisisísimo, el conjuro tiene que resultar muy potente, potentísimo, potentisísimo. Y la única solución para que salga así de potente es... ¡que lo hagamos todos a la vez! ¡Jia jia jia!

REINA FELISA:
¿Todos a la vez?

LA BRUJA MATILDE:
¡Sí! Todos nosotros y todos los habitantes de Fofa y todos los que han venido al teatro hoy. ¡Todos! (*Se dirige al público*). Presten atención, que les voy a enseñar el conjuro. ¡Jia jia jia! Hay que hacerlo sentado en una silla. (*Ella se sienta en un taburete que le trae un paje*). Este es el primer movimiento. (*Lo hace: hay que darse una palmada con las manos en la parte delantera de los muslos*). Este es el segundo movimiento. (*Lo hace: es una palmada normal*). Y este es el tercer movimiento. (*Lo hace: extender el brazo derecho hacia delante y chasquear los dedos*). ¡Jia, jia, jia! Pero, además, hay que decir las tres sílabas de la palabra mágica a la misma vez que los movimientos. Así: char-les-tón. ¿Escucharon? ¡Jia, jia, jia! ¡Pues, vamos a ensayarlo! Una, dos, tres... (*Todo el teatro se palmea los muslos, da una palmada y chasquea los dedos diciendo char-les-tón.*) ¡Pero aquí no acaba la cosa! ¡Jia, jia, jia! Para que haga efecto hay que repetirlo tres veces. Cada vez más deprisa y cada vez más fuerte. ¿Entendido?

TODOS:
¡Síííííííí!

LA BRUJA MATILDE:
Entonces, vamos a hacerlos cuanto antes. ¿Están preparados?

TODOS:
¡Síííííííí! (*Sonido: redoble de tambor*).

LA BRUJA MATILDE:
¡Allá vamos! A la una ... a las dos....y a las...¡tres!

TODOS:
Char....les....tón. ¡Char! ¡Les! ¡Tón! ¡¡CHAR!! ¡¡LES!! ¡¡TON!!

LA BRUJA MATILDE:
(*Cuando cesa el jolgorio*). ¡Jia, jia, jia! ¡Estupendo, chicos y chicas, estupendo! Bueno, rey Edelmiro, ¿qué le parece?

EDELMIRO II:
¡Beeeeeeee!

REINA FELISA:
¿Eh?

La **PREGONERA:**
¡Ahí va!

UN FOFANO:
¡Guau!

LA BRUJA MATILDE:
(*Muerta de risa*). ¡Jia, jia, jia, jia! Pero, ¿qué pasa aquí?

REINA FELISA:
¿Que qué pasa? ¡Que en lugar de al dragón, usted ha convertido en oveja a mi esposo, el rey!

EDELMIRO II:
(Efectivamente, se ha convertido en una hermosa oveja blanca, con un lazo rosa al cuello y un pequeño cencerro). ¡Beeeeeeeee!

LA BRUJA MATILDE:
¡Anda! Pues es verdad. ¡Jia, jia, jia! ¡Qué divertido! ¡Jia, jia, jia!

REINA FELISA:
¿Cómo? Encima le parece divertido. *(Se levanta del trono hecha una furia, agarra la porra de uno de los guardias cercanos y se dirige a probarla en la cabeza de la bruja. Pero antes de hacerlo, aparece corriendo Benito).*

BENITO:
¡Escúchenme! ¡Escúchenme todos! ¡Qué cosa más horrible!

REINA FELISA:
¿Qué ocurre, Benito?

BENITO:
¡Algo pasmoso! Estaba el feroz caballero Tiburcio tomándose una taza de té cuando de repente.... ¡se convirtió en oveja!

REINA FELISA:
¿Cómo? ¿También él?

LA BRUJA MATILDE:
(*Desternillándose de risa*). ¡Jia, jia, jia! ¡Divertidísimoooooo! ¡Jia, jia, jia!

BENITO:
Pero no solo él. También se han convertido en ovejas todos los caballeros que estaban esperando su turno en el recibidor.

LA BRUJA MATILDE:
(*Tirándose literalmente por los suelos.*) ¡Jia, jia, jia! ¡El colmo de la risa! ¡Jia, jia, jia! ¡El colmo de los colmos!

REINA FELISA:
(*Se dirige hacia Matilde y la agarra por el cuello con una mano*). ¡Esto es demasiado! ¡Haga que todos ellos vuelvan a su estado normal ahora mismo!

LA BRUJA MATILDE:
(*Calmándose un poco y secándose las lágrimas*). ¿Yoooo? ¡Jia, jia, jia! De eso nada. Tienen que hacerlos ustedes.

REINA FELISA:
¿Nosotros?

LA BRUJA MATILDE:
¡Claro! ¡Jia, jia, jia! Ustedes hicieron el conjuro y sólo ustedes pueden deshacerlo.

Es muy sencillo: basta con repetirlo todo... ¡al revés!

REINA FELISA:

¿Todo al revés? ¡Ya comprendo! Entonces... en lugar de decir char... les... tón, habrá que decir: ton...les...char.

LA PREGONERA:

(*Metiendo baza.*) ¡Claro! Y los tres movimientos hay que hacerlos en el orden contrario.

REINA FELISA:

Y habrá que repetirlo todo tres veces, como antes. Pero ahora hay que gritar cada vez menos y hacerlo cada vez más despacio.

LA PREGONERA:

(*Al público*). ¡Tienen que ayudarnos a salvar al rey Edelmiro y a todos los caballeros convertidos en ovejas! ¿Están dispuestos?

TODOS:

¡Síííííííí!

REINA FELISA:

Atención, pues. ¿Están preparados? A la una, a las dos y a las ... ¡tres!

TODOS:

(*Haciendo los movimientos*). ¡¡TON!! ¡¡LES!! ¡¡CHAR!! ¡Ton! ¡Les! ¡Char! Ton... les... char

EDELMIRO II:

(*Tras unos relámpagos y explosiones lo vemos de nuevo en su estado normal*). ¿Dónde estoy? ¿Quién soy? ¿Cómo me llamo? ¿Qué pasó? ¿Por qué estoy en cuatro patas? Me siento raro, como lanoso... ¡me pica todo!

REINA FELISA:

Ya te lo explicaré más tarde, querido esposo. ¡Guardiaaaaaas!

LOS GUARDIAS:

(*Son dos tipos enormes, que se mueven y hablan siempre a la misma vez*). ¡¡Sí, majestad!!

REINA FELISA:

Agarren a la bruja Matilde, quítenle su varita mágica y enciérrenla en un calabozo para que no vuelva a hacer más bromas pesadas.

LOS GUARDIAS:

¡¡A la orden, majestad!!

REINA FELISA:

¡Y que no le den de comer más que macarrones!

LOS GUARDIAS:

¡¡Macarrones, majestad!! (*Agarran a la bruja Matilde y la levantan en volandas*).

LA BRUJA MATILDE:

¡No! ¡Eso no! ¡Odio los macarrones! ¡Los odio con toda mi alma! ¡No los puedo ni veeeeeer!

REINA FELISA:

Pues macarrones para almorzar y macarrones para cenar.

LOS GUARDIAS:

¡¡Macarrones, majestad!!

LA BRUJA MATILDE:

¡No! ¡Macarrones no! ¡Aborrezco los macarrones!

REINA FELISA:

¡Y macarrones para desayunar!

LOS GUARDIAS:

¡¡Macarrones, majestad!!

LA BRUJA MATILDE:

¡Aaaaaag! ¡Me las va a pagar! ¡Me vengaré! ¡Cuando recupere mi varita mágica los convertiré a todos en macarrones! (*Por fin, Los Guardias se la llevan*).

EDELMIRO II:

(*Sin dejar de rascarse nerviosamente todo el cuerpo*). Bueno… Demos por terminado este incidente. ¡Hagan que pase el siguiente caballero matadragones!

UN CRIADO:

¡El siguienteeeeeee! (*Pero no aparece nadie, ni se oyen las habituales voces de los otros criados*). ¡Ejem! He dicho: ¡El siguienteeeeeeeeee! (*Nada*).

EDELMIRO II:

¡Vaya a ver qué ocurre! (*El criado desaparece y regresa al cabo de tres segundos y siete décimas*).

UN CRIADO:

¡Majestad! ¡Majestad! ¡Ya no hay más voluntarios para acabar con el dragón!

EDELMIRO II:

¡No es posible! ¡Si estaba el recibidor lleno hace un momento!

UN CRIADO:

Es que cuando la bruja Matilde los convirtió en ovejas, salieron todos a comer pasto a los campos, y ahora… ¡quién sabe donde están!

EDELMIRO II:

¡Vaya! Esto sí que es una faena.

BENITO:

Mucho me temo que sí, majestad. Porque ahora sólo le queda una solución.

EDELMIRO II:

¿Cuál?

BENITO:

Que usted mismo se enfrente al dragón Gutiérrez.

EDELMIRO II:

(*Horrorizado ante semejante perspectiva*)

¿Quién? ¿Yo? ¿Es una broma, Benito? ¿No ha visto lo grande que es el dragón? ¡Me convertiría en puré! ¡En pico de gallo! ¡En carne molida! ¡Ni soñarlo!

BENITO:

En ese caso, sintiéndolo mucho, tendrá que dejar el trono. Habrá que encontrar otro rey más valiente.

EDELMIRO II:

¿Dejar el trono? Hombre… Ahora que ya le estaba cogiendo cariño.

BENITO:

Lo lamento mucho, pero no hay más remedio. ¡Pregonera! Vaya a pregonar a los cuatro vientos que necesitamos otro rey.

EDELMIRO II:

¡Eh, eh! ¡Espere! No tan deprisa… (*Pasea nerviosamente por escena, sin dejar de rascarse*). ¡Está bien! Si no hay más remedio… ¡iré!

UN FOFANO:

¡Viva el rey Edelmirooooooo!

TODOS:

¡Vivaaaaaaaaa!

EDELMIRO II:

(*Correspondiendo a los vítores*). Gracias, gracias, querido pueblo. Pero ahora dejen de gritar y tráiganme rápidamente un cañón bien grande.

BENITO:

(*Con aire de fastidio*). Majestad, no está bien eso de ir a combatir dragones con cañones. No es digno de un rey. ¡Hay que hacerlo a la antigua! Agarre su armadura, su lanza, su espada y su escudo. ¡Y vaya por él!

TODOS:

¡A por él!

EDELMIRO II:

¡Mamá! Quiero ir con mi mamaaaaaaá….

OSCURO:

(Durante el oscuro, que servirá para cambiar el decorado, se pone música de Tchaikovsky. Por desgracia, a los diez o doce compases se estropea el tocadiscos, con lo que se podrán escuchar perfectamente los martillazos de los tramoyistas, las voces de uno de ellos pidiendo más clavos, las maldiciones del empresario porque no encuentra las llaves de su oficina y el berrido de un luminotécnico cuando recibe un calambrazo de 220 voltios al cambiar una lámpara).

(Fin del oscuro)

(La escena representa ahora la antesala de la cueva del Dragón Gutiérrez. Fondo izquierda, forillo que representa el exterior, donde se ve el poste de una parada de carruajes de la línea 32).

NARRADORA:

Así que el rey Edelmiro, con más miedo que siete viejas, tomó sus armas y se encaminó hacia aquí, la cueva del dragón Gutiérrez. Miren: precisamente ahora llega.

(Entra Edelmiro II, totalmente embutido en su armadura. Entra en la cueva y avanza hasta la batería. Se mueve con mucha dificultad. La armadura se adivina pesadísima y chirría siniestramente a cada paso).

EDELMIRO II:

(*Con voz metálica*). ¡Oigaaan! ¿Hay alguien por aquí? ¿Me pueden decir dónde estoy? (*Para sí*). ¡Mecachis en la mar! Si es que no veo nada metido aquí dentro... (*Gritando de nuevo*). ¡Busco la cueva del dragón Gutiérrez! ¿Alguien me puede decir dónde está?

(En ese momento, entre el regodeo del público, aparece a espaldas del rey el Dragón Gutiérrez. Mide cinco metros treinta de alto, y aunque tiene un aspecto horripilante, debe inspirar cierta ternura. No olvidar los ocho cuernos).

EL PÚBLICO:

¡El dragón! ¡Ahí está el dragón! (*O cosas por el estilo*).

EDELMIRO II:

(*Sin volverse*). ¿Cómo? ¿Qué dicen? ¡No oigo ni torta con este yelmo!

(El Dragón, que viste de bata y zapatillas de felpa, se ha puesto a tender en un cordel que cruza el foro una enorme camiseta de manga corta con la inscripción "I LOVE FOFA". Cuando termina su trabajo, se marcha por donde ha venido, sin apercibirse de la presencia del rey. Ni este de la suya.)

EDELMIRO II:

(*Dándose pesadamente la vuelta cuando ya es tarde*). ¡Yo no veo ningún dragón! Bueno, a decir verdad, no veo nada de nada. ¡Y ya estoy harto de esta armadura!

(Deja caer el escudo, la lanza y la espada. Luego, intenta quitarse el yelmo de la cabeza, pero en sus esfuerzos trastabilla, rueda por el escenario y termina cayendo al foso de la orquesta con gran estrépito. Varios empleados del teatro acuden en su ayuda).

¡Ay! ¡Ay qué golpe, madre mía! Quítenme esto. Quítenme esta armadura de encima o me va a dar un infarto.

(Los empleados le ayudan a despojarse de las piezas metálicas y se las llevan).

¡Uf! Menos mal: me estaba asfixiando ahí dentro. (*Mirando a su alrededor*). ¡Atiza! Pero si esto parece... ¡La cueva del dragón!

(Tras Edelmiro II, con más ropa para tender, ha vuelto a aparecer Gutiérrez. Ambos se dan la espalda. El rey, atemorizado, va retrocediendo paso a paso hasta topar con el dragón. Quedan los dos inmóviles un instante y, al

descubrirse, lanzan un grito cada uno y salen corriendo en direcciones opuestas).

EL DRAGÓN:

¡Auxiliooooooo! (*Se va por el lateral*).

EDELMIRO II:

¡Mamaaaaá! (*Se esconde tras una roca, en primer término*).

EL DRAGÓN:

(*Se asoma, temeroso*). ¿Quién anda ahí? ¿Quién es usted?

EDELMIRO II:

(*Sin asomar ni la punta de la oreja*). ¡Nadie! ¡No soy nadie! Soy… ¡Soy el cobrador del gas!

EL DRAGÓN:

¡Mentira! Yo no tengo gas en la casa.

EDELMIRO II:

(*Para sí*). ¡Vaya, hombre! Ya he vuelto a meter la pata.

EL DRAGÓN:

O me dice quién es inmediatamente o llamo a la policía.

EDELMIRO II:

(*Para sí*). ¡Vaya situación! ¡Estoy perdido! Creo que lo mejor será dar la cara y ver qué pasa. (*Al Dragón*). Está bien. ¡Soy Edelmiro II, rey de Fofa!

EL DRAGÓN:

¡No me lo creo!

EDELMIRO II:

De verdad.

EL DRAGÓN:

Entonces, enséñeme la corona real.

EDELMIRO II:

(*Asoma la cabeza y se señala con el dedo la corona*). ¿La ves?

EL DRAGÓN:

(*Entrando ya en escena*). Majestad… Disculpe que me haya asustado de esta forma. Como recibo tan pocas visitas… Es un verdadero honor tenerlo aquí.

EDELMIRO II:

¿Cómo? ¿Me tenías miedo? ¡Vamos!

EL DRAGÓN:

Pero no se quede ahí, tras esa roca. Pase, pase. Como si estuviera en su casa.

EDELMIRO II:

Muchas gracias. Con permiso…

EL DRAGÓN:

¿Quiere algo de tomar? ¿Quiere una limonada? Yo mismo la hago. Es la receta de mi abuela.

EDELMIRO II:

¿Limonada? Hombre….digo, dragón. Sí, sí. Me gustaría mucho.

EL DRAGÓN:

Enseguida se la preparo. (*Va hacia un rincón donde tiene una cristalería con los vasos del tamaño de papeleras*). ¡Ah! Tenga cuidado de donde se pone, no le vaya a pisar sin darme cuenta. Es que no veo muy bien.

EDELMIRO II:

(*Tratando de ser amable*). Tiene usted una cueva muy bonita. Está decorada con mucho gusto.

EL DRAGÓN:

Gracias, se hace lo que se puede. Y dígame: ¿por qué anda por aquí?

EDELMIRO II:

Pues, había venido a…. (*Queda sin saber qué decir*).

EL DRAGÓN:

¿A qué?

EDELMIRO II:

No…. ¡A nada, a nada! ¡Je, je! De visita.

EL DRAGÓN:

¿Y siempre que va usted de visita lleva esa

lanza tan gorda y esa espada tan afilada?

EDELMIRO II:

Pues sí. ¡Digo no! ¡No, no, no! ¡Qué va! Es que… las encontré mientras venía hacia aquí. Algún despistado, que las habrá perdido. ¡Caramba! Esa limonada se ve muy deliciosa…

EL DRAGÓN:

¡Ya verá qué rica está!

(Bajan las luces, aunque no del todo. El Narrador se adelanta y es iluminado por un cañón de luz).

NARRADORA:

Mientras el rey Edelmiro se encontraba en la cueva del dragón, todo el pueblo de Fofa esperaba angustiado en el exterior. Esperaron durante más de una hora. Por fin, convencidos todos de que el rey había sido devorado por la fiera, se armaron y, dirigidos por Benito, decidieron atacar ellos mismos al monstruo.

(Vuelve la luz. En el mismo momento, por todas partes aparecen todos los personajes armados con palos y espadas y dando gritos de ¡muerte al dragón!).

EDELMIRO II:

(*Poniéndose de pie*). ¡Alto! ¡Quietos todos! ¿Se puede saber adónde van?

REINA FELISA:

¡Esposo mío! ¡Estás vivo! ¡Qué alegría! (*Corre a abrazarlo*).

EDELMIRO II:

¡Claro que estoy vivo! ¡Estoy perfectamente bien!

TODOS:

¡Viva el rey Edelmirooooo! ¡Vivaaaaa!

EDELMIRO II:

¿Y Benito? ¿Dónde está Benito?

BENITO:

(*Saliendo del grupo*). ¡Aquí! ¡Aquí estoy, majestad!

EDELMIRO II:

(*Algo enfadado*). Oiga, Benito. ¿De dónde rábanos se han sacado ustedes que este dragón era malo y cruel? ¡Si prepara la mejor limonada que he probado en mi vida!

BENITO:

(*Asombrado*). ¿Qué?

EDELMIRO II:

Y tiene Fofa-opoly y otros juegos de mesa.

TODOS:

(*Asombradísimos*). ¿Cómooooooo?

EDELMIRO II:

Lo que escuchan. Tiene otros juegos como Jenga también.

BENITO:

Pero si es tan feo…

LA PREGONERA:

Y tan grande….

REINA FELISA:

Y tan verde…

LOS GUARDIAS:

(*A la misma vez*). Y tiene ocho cuernos…

UN FOFANO:

Y echa fuego por la boca…

EDELMIRO II:

Bueno, sí. ¿Y qué? Él no tiene la culpa de ser así, igual que Benito no tiene la culpa de tener la nariz torcida. Pero díganme, ¿el dragón se ha comido a alguien alguna vez?

TODOS:

Noooo….

EDELMIRO II:

¿Le ha prendido fuego a una de sus casas?

TODOS:

Noooo…..

EDELMIRO II:

¿Los ha mordido? ¿O arañado?

TODOS:

Noooo.....

EDELMIRO II:

¡Entonces! ¿Por qué quieren matar al pobre Gutiérrez?

UN FOFANO:

En todas las historias los dragones son malos y hay que matarlos.

EDELMIRO II:

Pues, miren a Gutiérrez. Él no es malo. Es muy simpático y agradable. No es justo juzgarlo por cómo son los otros dragones en los otros cuentos. Así que, mientras yo sea el rey de Fofa, nadie le hará daño a Gutiérrez. ¿Está claro?

TODOS:

¡Sí, majestad!

EDELMIRO II:

¡Tesorero!

TESORERO:

(*Saliendo del grupo. Siempre con su cofrecillo*). Aquí estoy, majestad.

EDELMIRO II:

Como la lucha con el dragón ha terminado, declaro que en el país de Fofa vuelve a permitirse jugar al fútbol, y las mil monedas de oro se destinarán a la construcción del nuevo estadio, tal y como estaba planeado antes.

TODOS:

¡Bieeeeeeen!

(Estalla gran bullicio. Todos cantan, ríen y juegan al pelotón. También Gutiérrez se une a la celebración, bailando con cuidado para no escachiflar a ningún fofano. Desde una esquina del proscenio, el Narrador contempla la escena sonriente y se dirige al público por última vez).

NARRADORA:

En el país de Fofa volvió a reinar la felicidad. Los fofanos empezaron a visitar al dragón Gutiérrez asiduamente y le perdieron el miedo. Es por esto que no podemos juzgar a las personas y a las cosas en primera instancia. Como dicen en inglés: "Don't judge a book by its cover." No todos los dragones son malos, como nuestro querido Gutiérrez, el único dragón del mundo que sabe preparar limonada.

Die Rabe

"Die Rabe" von den Gebrüdern Grimm erarbeitet als 11.

Klasse Theaterspiel 2012 von Ann Coltman

Spieler:

Die Königin	Die Rabe/Prinzessin	Der Mann
Die alte Frau	Der kleine Riese	Der grosse Riese
Die Räuber: 1, 2, 3		

Die HelferSzene i:

Schloss. Königin mit Baby.

(Das Baby schreit. Raben fliegen um das Schloss herum.)

KÖNIGIN: *(singt)*

Schlaf, Kindlein, schlaf,
Der Vater hüt die Schaf,
Die Mutter schüttelts Bäumelein,
Da fällt herab ein Träumelein.
Schlaf, Kindlein, schlaf!

(Baby schreit. Mutter versucht es zu berühigen.)

KÖNIGIN:

Schlaf, Kindlein, schlaf,
Am Himmel ziehn' die Schaf,
Die Sternlein sind die Lämmerlein,
Der Mond, der ist das Schäferlein,
Schlaf, Kindlein, schlaf!

(Das Baby schreit. Raben fliegen um das Schloß herum.)

Mutter:

Ach!!! Ich wollte, du wärst eine Rabe und flögst fort, so hätt' ich Ruhe!

(Baby ist verwandelt und fliegt fort. Mutter fällt zum Boden und weint.)

Szene ii: Wald. Viele Jahre später. Rabe und der Mann.

RABE: *(Ruft)*

MANN: *(Geht der Stimme nach)*

RABE:

Ich bin eine Königstochter von Geburt und bin verwünscht worden. Du aber kannst mich erlösen.

MANN:

Was soll ich tun?

RABE:

Geh weiter in den Wald. Dort wirst du ein Haus finden. Darin sitzt eine alte Frau. Diese wird dir Essen und Trinken reichen, aber du darfst nichts annehmen: wenn du etwas isst oder trinkst, so verfällst du in einen Schlaf und kannst mich nicht erlösen. Im Garten hinter dem Haus ist ein großer Steinhaufen. Darauf sollst du stehen und auf mich warten. Drei Tage lang komm' ich jeden Mittag um zwei Uhr in einem Wagen zu dir. Wenn du aber nicht wach bist, sondern schläfst, so werde ich nicht erlöst.

MANN:

Ich verspreche dir alles zu tun, was du verlangt hast.

RABE:

Ach, ich weiß es schon, du wirst mich nicht erlösen! Du wirst etwas von der Frau annehmen.

MANN:

Nein, nein. Ich verspreche dir, ich werde

nichts anrühren, weder von dem Essen noch von dem Trinken. Ich werde dich erlösen!

RABE:
Dann sehen wir uns bald. Ich komme bald zu dir und du erlöst mich. Auf Wiedersehen.

MANN:
Auf Wiedersehen.

Szene iii: Wald. Haus. Alte Frau, Mann, Rabe.

ALTE FRAU:
Armer Mann, was seid Ihr abgemattet! Kommt und erquickt Euch, esset und trinket.

MANN:
Nein, ich will nicht essen und nicht trinken.

ALTE FRAU:
Wenn Ihr dann nicht essen wollt, so tut einen Zug aus dem Glas. Einmal ist keinmal.

MANN: *(Zögert, aber dann)*
Na gut. Sie haben recht: Einmal ist keinmal. *(Trinkt.)*

(Alte Frau ab.)

(Glocke: Zwei Uhr)

(Mann geht in den Garten und wartet. Er wird auf einmal müde. Er legt sich ein wenig nieder, doch will er nicht einschlafen. Aber kaum hat er sich hingestreckt, fallen ihm die Augen von selbst zu, und er schläft ein.)

RABE:
Ich weiß, dass er schläft. (*... erblickt ihn ...)* Ich wusste es, ich wusste es! Wer erlöst mich dann! (*Schüttelt ihn und ruft ihn an, aber er erwacht nicht.)* Wach auf! Wach auf! Mann! *(Weint. Ab.)*

MANN:
Wo ist sie? Ach, ich habe geschlafen! Nein! Ich hätte nichts trinken dürfen!
(Mond und Sonne überqueren die Bühne.)

ALTE FRAU:
Armer Mann, was seid Ihr abgemattet! Kommt und erquickt Euch. Esset und trinket. Sie müssen etwas trinken und essen!

MANN:
Nein, nein, ich will nichts annehmen.

ALTE FRAU:
Wenn Ihr dann nicht essen wollt, so tut doch noch einen Zug aus dem Glas. Einmal ist keinmal.

MANN: *(Zögert, aber dann.)*
Na gut. Sie haben schon recht.
Einmal ist Keinmal. Aber nur einen Zug! *(Trinkt.)*

(Glocke: Zwei Uhr.)

(Mann geht in den Garten und wartet, aber ... er fällt in einen tiefen Schlaf.)

RABE:
Ach, ich weiß, dass er schläft. (*... erblickt ihn ...*) Ich wusste es, ich wusste es! Er schläft doch. Wer erlöst mich dann? (*Geht zu ihm hin, aber er liegt im Schlaf und wacht nicht auf.)* Mann! Mann! Wach auf! Wach doch endlich auf! *(Weint. Ab.)*

MANN:
Nein, nicht schon wieder! Ich bin doch eingeschlafen! Wo ist sie? Nein! Sie hat mich gewarnt und ich habe doch getrunken! Ich hätte nichts trinken dürfen!

(Mond und Sonne überqueren die Bühne)

ALTE FRAU:
Was ist los? Sie trinken und essen nichts! Wollen Sie sterben?

MANN:

Ich will und darf nicht essen und nicht trinken.

ALTE FRAU:

Aber, schau. Hier habe ich eine Schüssel mit Essen und ein Glas Wein. Riech mal! Wie es duftet! Und wie es schmeckt! Hmmmm…. *(Kostet)* Koste doch! Einmal ist doch noch keinmal!

MANN:

Ich halte es nicht aus! Es duftet so gut! Ich muss es kosten. Aber nur einen klitzekleinen Zug! *(Trinkt.)*
(Glocke: Zwei Uhr.)

(Mann geht in den Garten und wartet … schläft ein.)

RABE: *(zu sich)*

Bitte, bitte … lass ihn noch wach sein! … Ach ich weiß, dass er schläft und mich nicht erlösen kann. *(Erblickt ihn, rüttelt ihn und ruft ihn aber er aufwacht nicht.)* Mann! Mann! Wach auf! Bitte, bitte wach auf. *(Überlegt.)*

Hier habe ich ein Brot …. und hier ein Stück Fleisch, und eine Flasche Wein. Sie haben alle magische Kräfte: du kannst von allem so viel nehmen, wie du willst, es wird nicht weniger. Und hier ist mein goldener Ring. Mein Name ist darauf eingeprägt. Und hier ist ein Brief, worin steht, „Das Brot, das Fleisch und der Wein – sie haben magische Kräfte. Sie werden nie alle. Ich sehe wohl, dass du mich hier nicht erlösen kannst. Willst du mich aber noch erlösen, so komm nach dem goldenen Schloss von Stromberg. Es steht in deiner Macht, das weiß ich gewiss.“ *(Fährt traurig ab.)*

MANN:

Ach nein, jetzt habe ich wieder geschlafen! Gewiss ist sie eben vorbeigefahren, und ich habe sie nicht erlöst. Aber, was ist das? Ein Brot …. und ein Stück Fleisch … und eine Flasche Wein? Sie war doch hier! Und ich habe sie nicht erlöst! Ich habe geschlafen! Ich dummer Trottel!!!

Und hier ist ihr goldener Ring … und ein Brief! Was? Das Brot und das Fleisch und der Wein sind verzaubert? Sie werden nie alle? Egal wie viel ich davon esse? …*(Isst fleißig.)* Und was steht hier? Ich kann sie doch erlösen! Ich muss nur zum goldenen Schloss von Stromberg! Aber wo liegt das Schloss? He! Alte Frau!

ALTE FRAU:

Was ist? Habt Ihr Hunger? Wollt Ihr doch was essen?

MANN:

Nein, nein. Wisst Ihr wo das goldene Schloss von Stromberg liegt?

ALTE FRAU:

Aber nein. Aber hier könnt Ihr bleiben. Bleib bei mir!

MANN:

Nein, ich bleibe nicht. Ich werde das goldene Schloss von Stromberg finden! Und ich werde die Prinzessin erlösen!! *(Ab.)*

Szene iv. Wald. Mann, 2 Riesen.

RIESE: *(Heulen und Jammern.)*

Ich habe Hunger! Wir haben nichts zum essen! Ach, ich habe solchen Hunger! Nichts, nichts haben wir. Schüssel leer, Teller leer, Schränke leer …. Ich könnte ein Schaf essen! Oder einen Baum! Oder einen Stein! Oder ein…

MANN: *(Zu sich)*

Gehst du hinein und der Riese erblickt dich, so ist es leicht um dein Leben geschehen. …. Aber vielleicht weiss er wo das goldene Schloss von Stromberg liegt? Ich muss mich wagen ...*(Traut sich nicht).*

RIESE 1:

Hunger! Hunger! Ich habe Hunger! Ich könnte einen Bär essen! Oder einen Elefanten! Oder einen Tiger! .... Oder ...

MANN:

Eeem ... Entschuldigung ....

RIESE 1:

Oder einen MANN!! Mmmmmm. Es ist gut, dass du kommst, ich habe lange nichts gegessen. Ich will dich gleich zum Abendbrot verschlucken!

MANN:

Lass' das lieber sein! Ich lasse mich nicht gerne verschlucken! Verlangst du etwas zu essen, so habe ich genug, um dich satt zu machen.

RIESE 1:

Wenn das wahr ist, so kannst du ruhig bleiben. Ich wollte dich nur verzehren, weil ich nichts anderes habe.

MANN:

Schau – ich habe Brot ... und Fleisch ... und Wein. *(Sie setzen sich an den Tisch.)*

RIESE 1:

Das gefällt mir wohl. *(Beide essen. Riese rülps.)*

MANN:

Jetzt hast du keinen Hunger mehr. Kannst du mir sagen, wo das goldene Schloss von Stromberg ist?

RIESE 1:

Ich sehe auf meiner Landkarte nach; darauf sind alle Städte, Dörfer und Häuser zu finden. *(Zieht die Landkarte heraus. Schaut.)* Stromberg, Stromberg, wo liegt Stromberg? Ich finde es nicht! Es steht nicht darauf.

MANN:

Na gut. Dann muss ich weiter suchen. Ich muss das goldene Schloss von Stromberg finden. Ich muss die Prinzessin erlösen.

RIESE 1:

Aber warte doch! Mein Bruder kommt bald nach Hause. Er wird bestimmt wissen wo Stromberg liegt.

MANN:

Na gut. Dann warte ich noch.

RIESE 2:

Schwesterherz! Hier habe ich Essen mitgebracht! ... Aber, du hast auch Essen!

RIESE 1:

Ja, hallo Bruderherz! Wir haben hier verzaubertes Essen! Das Brot, das Fleisch, der Wein, es wird nie alle, egal wie viel wir essen. Das hat uns dieser Mann geschenkt. Er möchte nur wissen wo das goldene Schloss von Stromberg liegt.

MANN:

Ja, ich muss das goldene Schloss von Stromberg finden! Ich muss die Prinzessin erlösen!

RIESE 2:

Wenn ich gegessen habe und satt bin, dann will ich es auf der Karte suchen. *(Isst. Alle essen und rülpsten.)* Jetzt bin ich richtig satt! Jetzt suchen wir das goldene Schloss von Stromberg! *(Holt seine Landkarte ... sucht)* Goldene Schloss von Stromberg ..... goldene Schloss von Stromberg .... Wo liegt ... Stomboli, Spumoni, Spaghetti - hmmm *(Isst.)* Stromberg Stromberg... ... aha,aha, aha! Hier liegt es! Aber es ist viele viele tausend Meilen weg.

MANN:

Wie werde ich bloß dahin kommen?

RIESE 2:
Zwei Stunden hab' ich Zeit, da will ich dich bis in die Nähe tragen, dann aber muss ich wieder nach Haus, um unser Kind zu füttern.

RIESE 1:
Auf Wiedersehen! Viel Glück! Danke für's Essen!

MANN:
Auf Wiedersehen. Danke!

RIESE 2: (*Trägt Mann bis etwa hundert Stunden vom Schloss.*)
Den übrigen Weg kannst du wohl allein gehen.

MANN:
Danke! Vielen Dank!

RIESE 2:
Auf Wiedersehen.

(Mann läuft und läuft. Mond, Sonne. Mond, Sonne.)

Szene v: Vor dem goldenen Schloss Stromberg auf einem gläsernen Berg. Rabe reitet um das Schloss herum.

MANN:
Hallo! Hallo, Prinzessin! (*Versucht hinaufzusteigen aber er rutscht immer wieder herunter.*) Ach, das geht nicht! Ich komme nicht weiter, weil das Glas zu glatt ist! *(Betrübt.)* Ich will hier unten bleiben und auf sie warten.

MANN:
Baut sich eine Hütte und sitzt davor. Monate vergehen.

(Januar bis Dezember gehen vorbei.)

Szene vi: Vor dem Schloss Stromberg. Mann, 3 Räuber mit Pferd, Stock, Mantel.

RÄUBER 1:
Das ist meins! Gibs her!

RÄUBER 2:
Nein, das ist meins! Das gehört mir! Aua!

RÄUBER 3:
Aua! Lass los! Das ist meins!

MANN:
Gott sei mit euch!

RÄUBER 1-3: *(Still. Schauen sich herum, sehen niemand, fangen wieder an sich zu schlagen.)*

RÄUBER 1:
Das ist meins! Gib's her!

RÄUBER 2:
Nein, das ist meins! Es gehört mir! Aua!

RÄUBER 3:
Aua! Lass los! Es ist meins!

MANN:
Gott sei mit euch!

(Räuber 1-3: Still. Gucken sich an, gukken sich um. Sehen niemand.)

RÄUBER 1:
Hast du was gehört?

RÄUBER 2:
Nein. Du?

RÄUBER 3:
Nein. Du?

RÄUBER 1:
Nein. Du?

RÄUBER 2:
Nein. Du?

RÄUBER 3:
Ach, das ist Unsinn. Sei still und sprich kein Wörtchen mehr!

MANN:
Gott sei mit euch!

(Räuber 1-3: Still. Gucken sich an, gucken sich um.)

MANN: *(Zu sich)*
Du musst sehen, was die drei vorhaben.

RÄUBER 1-3:

Fangen wieder an sich zu schlagen.

RÄUBER 1:

Das ist meins! Gib's her!

RÄUBER 2:

Nein, das ist meins! Das gehört mir! Aua!

RÄUBER 3:

Aua! Lass los! Das ist meins!

MANN:

Na ihr drei Räuber! He! Ihr da!! Was habt ihr Schönes?

RÄUBER 1:

Ich habe einen verzauberten Stock gefunden. Wenn ich damit wider eine Tür schlage, so springt sie auf. *(Demonstriert.)*

MANN:

Verblüffend!

RÄUBER 2:

Und ich habe einen Mantel gefunden. Wenn ich den umhänge, so bin ich unsichtbar!

(Demonstriert – alle suchen ihn, vergebens.)

Mann:

Donnerwetter!

RÄUBER 3:

Ich habe ein Pferd gefangen. Damit kann ich überallhin reiten, sogar auf den gläsernen Berg hinauf.

MANN:

Wunderbar! Und warum streitet ihr euch?

RÄUBER 1-3:

Wir wissen nicht, ob wir sie in Gemeinschaft behalten sollen oder ob wir uns trennen sollten.

MANN:

(Hat eine Idee.)

Die drei Sachen will ich euch eintauschen: Geld habe ich zwar nicht, aber andere Dinge, die wertvoller sind! Doch muss ich vorher eine Probe machen, damit ich sehe, ob ihr auch die Wahrheit gesagt habt.

RÄUBER 1:

Gute Idee! Was ist doch wertvoller als Geld?

RÄUBER 2:

Sehr gute Idee! Gold ist wertvoller als Geld!

RÄUBER 3:

Prima Idee! Aber Essen ist wertvoller als Gold!

(Sie lassen ihn aufs Pferd sitzen, hängen ihm den Mantel um und geben ihm den Stock in die Hand. Als er alles hat, können sie ihn nicht mehr sehen. Da gibt er ihnen tüchtige Schläge.)

MANN:

Ihr Bärenhäuter, da habt ihr, was euch gebührt: seid ihr zufrieden?

RÄUBER 1:

Aua! Das tut weh! Mein Stock!

RÄUBER 2:

Aua! Mein Mantel!

RÄUBER 3:

Aua! Mein Pferd!

(Mann reitet weg. Die Räuber suchen und ab.)

Szene vii: Mann, Rabe/Prinzessin.

(Mann reitet zum Schloss. Schlägt mit dem Stock an das Tor, und es springt auf. Er geht die Treppe hinauf bis oben in den Saal. Da sitzt die Jungfrau und sie hat einen goldenen Kelch mit Wein vor sich. Sie kann ihn aber nicht sehen, weil er den Mantel umhat. Und als er vor sie kommt, zieht er den Ring vom Finger und wirft ihn in den Kelch, so dass es erklingt.)

RABE:

Das ist mein Ring, so muss auch der

Mann da sein, der mich erlösen wird!

(Sie sucht im ganzen Schloss und finden ihn nicht. Er geht hinaus, setzt sich aufs Pferd und wirft den Mantel ab.)

(Sie kommt vor das Tor und sieht ihn.)

RABE:

Hurrah! Du hast es geschafft! Du hast mich erlöst!

(Er steigt ab und nimmt die Königstochter in die Arme.)

MANN:

Prinzessin! Jetzt bist du erlöst!

RABE:

Ja, jetzt hast du mich erlöst! Ich danke dir!

MANN:

Bitte sehr… gern geschehen!

RABE:

Willst du mich heiraten?

MANN:

Ja, natürlich.

RABE:

Dann morgen wollen wir unsere Hochzeit feiern. *(Jubel.)*

The Inspector General

A Play for Twelfth Grade (2003, 2011)

Adapted from Nikolai Gogol's 1836 "The Government Inspector"

Characters: ***(In order of appearance)***

Amos Lynch, *County Judge*
Lubby Snatch, *Director of Public Works*
J.R. Dumpsker, *Mayor*
Lola Mae Bobsie, *a gossip*
Anna Dumpsker, *the mayor's wife*
Reba, *the mayor's housekeeper*
Vera Peech, *a waitress*
Bobby Joe Wump, *a merchant*
B.B. Baines, *a merchant*
Old Woman #2
Gert Winshelwypa, *a hairdresser*
A State Trooper
Thelma Grind, *Director of Human Services*
Madge Snipperi, *Superintendent of Schools*
Dolly Crust, *Postmaster*
Lola Mae Dobsie, *a gossip*
Mary Jane Dumpsker, *their daughter*
Jimmy Dean Khlestakov, *a data entry clerk*
Charlie Boy Klepp, *Sheriff*
Robin Snook, *a merchant*
Old Woman #1
Scratchy Winshelwypa, *a taxidermist*
Aligaita Tenfore, *a lady trucker*

Setting: Gravel Trailings, Gravel County, Oklahoma
Act: I: Mayor"s home office: late morning
Act II: EZ On EZ Off Motel: an hour later
Act III: Mayor"s home office: early afternoon
Act IV: Mayor"s home office: mid-afternoon
Act V: Mayor"s home office: immediately after

Time: Mid-1970s

ACT I: Scene 1:

THELMA, AMOS, LUBBY, MADGE, MAYOR

A front room in the Mayor's house that serves as his office. It is lavishly but tastelessly appointed. Up center right is the mayor's desk, down left a table with four chairs. Down center right a sofa and further down right sitting chairs. There is an outside door (center left) and an inside door (far stage right). Windows flank the outside door. The desk has a phone and is covered with scattered papers. Portraits of large-eyed children, little animals, and family members adorn the walls. Some of these pictures are obviously paint by number pictures, most unfinished. Several framed campaign posters of the Mayor are prominently displayed. There is a dartboard on one wall, featuring a picture of Castro. Along the up left back wall there is an Elvis shrine, before which burns an obviously fake candle.

*[**ONSTAGE** as the curtain opens: AMOS LYNCH, County Judge; THELMA GRASP, Director of Human Services, MADGE SNIPPERI, Superintendent of Schools, and LUBBY SNATCH, Director of Public Works. Throughout the play, MADGE is continually looking to AMOS for approval. THELMA is going through the mayor's papers. The others sit silently playing cards. Just before the MAYOR enters THELMA hears him and retreats to admire the Elvis shrine.*

***ENTER** MAYOR, J.R. DUMPSKER, through interior door: He is a powerful, cunning man. He notices that his papers have been disturbed, stares at THELMA who feigns ignorance. The MAYOR immediately takes charge]*

[Atmosphere: Anxious anticipation to mutual blame.]

MAYOR:
Friends, in case you're wondering why I've called you here, prepare yourselves for the worst! We can expect a little visit—perhaps he's already here — from a federal inspector—an Inspector General. And given the state of things, I'm worried sick.

AMOS:
An Inspector General! From Washington! Here?

THELMA:
No!?

MAYOR:
Yes, an Inspector General, and *incognito*, to boot.

AMOS:
A fine hello this!

LUBBY:
Sweet Jesus!

MADGE:
If we hadn't trouble enough!

AMOS:
Just when things were so going so well!

MAYOR:
Well maybe, Amos, that's why I was warned.

THELMA:
Warned, J.R.! Why didn't you tell us?

MAYOR:
It was a dream, Thelma—a nightmare to be exact. Two nights ago I had a dream about two rats. Huge black beasts! They scurried all about, sniffed everywhere, then—they vanished. They did it over and over. At first, I thought nothing of it, just a bad dream. Then this letter arrived from my nephew in Washington. *[He holds up a letter.]*

MADGE:
But the rats? *[Looking around nervously.]* Did you call the exterminator?

THELMA: They were only a dream, Madge.

MAYOR:
Hush! *[Reads.]* "My dear uncle, ... " *[He mumbles, glancing rapidly down the page.]* Ah, here it is: "Washington's all a buzz; word's out that the Administration is trying to divert attention from its own problems by cracking down on misuse of federal money going to municipal governments. Inspector Generals—*incognito*, they say—are being sent to root out corruption, no matter how small. Not that you have anything to fear, ha, ha..."

AMOS:
Humph!

MAYOR:
"...But seriously; they're going after the little fish first before attempting a bigger haul. Little towns ... *[Raises his finger significantly.]* I learned this from a 'highly placed source', so while I'm sure you'll say you got nothing to hide, best hide it all the better. . ."

AMOS:
A comedian!

MAYOR:
Heh, heh! Always likes his little joke. *[Reads.]* "Anyway, they say the Inspectors have all been trained to act like common

citizens, just to catch you off guard. By the way, what's the scoop on your daughter's driving up onto … "

[Abruptly stops and places letter on table.]

So there you have it.

AMOS:
Extraordinary, most extraordinary!

[Rises and crosses toward Mayor's desk.]

LUBBY:
Sweet Jesus! Why should he come here?

THELMA: *[Getting in a dig.]*
Fixing those beauty contests isn't going to help.

MADGE:
Or Mary Jane running over Bobby Joe Wump's beagle up on his porch.

AMOS: *[Confidently.]*
Inspector Generals aren't interested in such little fish.

THELMA: *[Getting in last word.]*
But that "mistake" of your wife down at the Beauty Parlor with the Baine's girl's hair wasn't "little fish," Amos.

MAYOR: *[Losing his temper.]*
What else was a father to do!? Let Mary Jane lose Miss Grain Elevator? Didn't I buy that Baine girl a wig out of public *† funds an' send her off to that scalp restorationist in Dallas?!

[All look at him incredulously. AMOS tries to sneak a peak at the letter, but the Mayor snatches it and stuffs it in his pocket and sighs.]

Anyway, the trap is about to snap—and on us, my friends. *[To himself.]* Who knows where he'll look?

***THELMA:** *[Loudly, under her breath.]*
Federal.

MADGE:
Why us? It's only *elected* officials he'll go after.

MAYOR: *[Dismissive laugh.]*
And don't forget family appointees? Where there's little fish, there's big ones nearby.

MADGE & LUBBY: *[With submissive nod/Anxious exclamation.]*
Oh!/sweet Jesus!

AMOS:
In my opinion, J.R., the cause of this investigation is deeper than a little helping of family and friends. It can mean only one thing — communist subversion is finally being rooted out of Gravel County! Washington's finally taking care of commie subversion once and for all, and, God bless America, it's starting right here.

MADGE:
I knew that!

MAYOR:
Ah! A regular Solomon! Commies, here in Gravel County, Oklahoma?! Why, you'd have to drive around for a month before you'd find someone whose brother-in-law doesn't want to be the Imperial Wizard of the Klu Klux Klan!

LUBBY:
The judge got a point there, J.R;

MAYOR:
A one man FBI!

MADGE:
Y'know, J.R., I heard some fur'ners talking Migrant behind the Dairy Queen last Wednesday.

AMOS:
Mexican, Madge.

---

† * Indicates overlapping dialogue.

MADGE:
I knew that.

THELMA:
It's called Spanish, Amos.

MADGE:
I knew that.

AMOS:
Look here, J.R.; Thelma here shouldn't be putting on airs just because she lived in Missouri some. It seems to me Lubby and Madge know what's going on a lot better than she do. How many times have I told you those migrants are part of a highly trained guerrilla vanguard just waiting for the Kremlin to give the word to swarm across Texas and destroy this country! Make us all talk Chinese! Until now none dared call it treason. *[Thoughtful pause.]* Why else would Washington send an Inspector General out here?

MAYOR: *[Irritated, frustrated, angry.]*
Because somebody squealed; didn't like his slice of the pie! That's why! Believe what you want; but this inspector won't get anything on me, regardless of what some sniveling whistle blower might say. I'm an old hand at this; last night I did some work on my records, and I advise all of you to do the same. Now Thelma, the first thing he'll go prying into is Human Services—the *public* welfare always seems to being doing a little too much *private* good. For starters, I'm sure he'll be very interested in that trailer park your brother-in-law built out by the land-fill with last year's welfare payments. First thing I recommend is repainting the sign; call it "Public Housing," like over in Tulsa. That'll make it look authentic.

THELMA:
Right, J.R. But what about all Lubby's wife's kin-folk you moved out there after their trailer burned down?

MAYOR:
Let'im be; Washington inspectors can't be expected to tell one type of trash from another.

[THELMA makes a sound intermediate between M and A.]

MAYOR:
Amos, you'd better look to the courthouse. The building stinks to high heaven from those *purebreds* your wife's *breeding* there—not that the building's ever used anymore since you lost the money for the new roof on that Vegas trip last year. Move them out, right away.

AMOS:
Well, I could move them over to the chicken processing plant for a while

MAYOR:
Brilliant idea! And that *county clerk* reeks of booze, and likes to talk. Send her over the state line until all this blows over. [THELMA *makes the same sound as before.]* Madge, send one of your teachers over and tell her to look busy—correcting tests or something.

MADGE:
I'll get right on it, JR.

MAYOR:
And make sure it's not that loony one who teaches English. I dropped in at the high school last month and she was completely out of control—waving some book and crying "Drink to me with twined eyes" or something crazy like that. That might impress them back in Arkansas or wherever she's from, but some federal inspector might think the woman's insane.

MADGE:
Right, J.R.

MAYOR:
He'd want to run a background check on a lunatic like that, and you know how one things leads to the next, especially if he starts talking to some of those football players she "socializes" with after the games.

AMOS:
Some sins are better hid.

MADGE:
Yes, they are.

MAYOR:
Why, of course, there isn't a soul alive who hasn't some sin to hide. That's the way God made the world; and in *his* due time he'll total the bill; it's just that these damn Washington types want it totaled on *their* time. Lubby!! *[*LUBBY *snaps nervously to attention.]* Now our industrious Director of Public Works, what will you have to say about the state of our town?

LUBBY:
Sweet Jesus, don't scare me like that. You know my budget's so small, J.R., I'd never get anything done with the little I get. Sure I accept gifts for services rendered, but you couldn't call them bribes; they're too small—a sack of doughnuts here or there.

THELMA: *[Mimicking Lubby.]*
They lubricate the wheels of government.

MAYOR:
I'm sure our Inspector General will see it that way.

AMOS:
Come now, J.R, why shouldn't a humble public servant be entitled to enjoy a family sized bucket down at Kentucky Fried now and then ... without charge? Let's be philosophical: it all depends on how you look at it. Why those bureaucrats in Washington get more pork for breakfast than we could get in hundred years!

MADGE: *[Starting to whine.]*
Who doesn't have to put a little aside, as a precaution against ... well, you know?

LUBBY:
Is it our fault; our budgets are so small, and our sense of duty so high?

AMOS: *[Arguing.]*
Surely a little precautionary budgeting won't cause him to raise an eyebrow.

MAYOR:
Precautionary budgeting! We'll be lucky to get off with fifty years! Lubby! *[Who jumps.]* What about that leaking barrel of pesticides your wife's brother got stored out at the water treatment plant? Don't you think that might raise an eyebrow?

LUBBY:
Sweet Jesus, you can't pin that on me! Is it my fault it was left in the kitchen over at the elementary school, and the state health inspector said it had to go? Where else were we going to put it? Tried to send it over to Swelter County, but they wouldn't have any of it. "Who'll ever know," you said, "after all, only bottom feeders and trailer trash drink tap water anyway."

MAYOR: *[Losing temper.]*
That was then, but this is now! Something's got to be done, and it's you, the *public servants* of Gravel County, who's got to do it, so get on it—all of you!—before we're all carted off to jail!

[They rise to leave.]

Scene 2:

THELMA, AMOS, LUBBY, MADGE, MAYOR, DOLLY

[Atmosphere: "On alert" to conspiracy.]

*[**ENTER** DOLLY, the Postmaster.]*

DOLLY:
Oh my God, an Inspector General?! Is it true?

MAYOR:
How did she know?

THELMA:
Dolly's postmaster; you know, she *handles* the mail?

DOLLY:
Now, don't go accusing people, Thelma; I sort it; that's all! Is it my fault the glue's so bad on the envelopes that letters are always slipping out? My! You'd be shocked at what some of those letters say. People think a sealed envelope is like a locked door. The stuff that goes on! Oh my! Remember Ruby Charles' daughter? Well, she ran off with some Tulsa Romeo and… *[Notices everyone is staring at her.]* Oh… But I do *have to* read them to see what letter belongs in what envelope. Remember, Mr. Mayor, I told you about this problem, and you said Amos said they wasn't no harm as long as I shared what I read "in the sanctity of this office."

[MAYOR coughs over the last phrase as AMOS looks down.]

MAYOR:
So, Dolly, you been reading my mail?

DOLLY:
No! Your letters are always taped shut. Staples even.

THELMA:
Then what makes you think an Inspector General's coming to town?

DOLLY:
Lola Mae Bobsie told me. She was in the post office just now. *[Worried.]* Oh, I hope you don't think I've done something wrong?

AMOS:
Tampering with the mail might be a federal offense.

MAYOR:
Best keep your *legal* opinions to yourself, Amos.

DOLLY:
Federal offense! Could that cost me my job?

THELMA:
Only if you're put in jail.

[THELMA motions MAYOR, and they consult.]

AMOS: *[Conspiratorially to* DOLLY.*]*
You ever see any letters written in Mexican, you know, with a Moscow postmark?

DOLLY:
We got a letter from Canada once, but it was stuck to another letter … had a Kansas address.

AMOS:
If we can bring those commies to their knees, there's a Presidential Medal of Freedom in it for you.

DOLLY:
I'll keep my eyes open. In fact, we just got a sack of mail this morning.

MAYOR: *[Returning from huddle w/ THELMA.]*
We're all good as family here, and I know

as well as anyone that sometimes families have their little spats, so I'm sure you all understand that it's not just my own skin I'm worried about. Together we've made this county what it is today. Who got the interstate exit put here instead of over in Swelter county? We did. And I mean *we*. And that big truck stop, and that new EZ On EZ Off Motel. That's all *our* doing. And don't forget the Wal-Mart that's coming out by the highway. True, the Wal-Mart'll put the merchants on Main Street out of business, but that's progress; adapt or die, but our present *unpopularity* with those bottom feeders will pass.

THELMA:
Good government has its price.

MAYOR:
Indeed, it does. True, my friends, mistakes have been made, but when all's said and done, who in this room would want to trade places with bottom feeders and trailer trash? *[No one answers.]* Just as I thought. So the important thing is to find the rat who squealed and see that he's ... temporarily of course, until the inspector's left town.

Scene 3:

THELMA, AMOS, LUBBY, MADGE, MAYOR, DOLLY, BOBSIE, DOBSIE

[Atmosphere: Impending catastrophe; alertness crescendos.]

***ENTER** LOLA MAE BOBSIE & LOLA MAE DOBSIE through front door, out of breath.]*

BOBSIE:
You'll never guess what we just learned!

DOBSIE:
Such juicy news!

BOBSIE: *[Interrupting.]*
Just as we were about to...

DOBSIE: *[Interrupting.]*
Please, Lola Mae, who's telling this story?

BOBSIE:
Let me; please; you'll get it all wrong.

DOBSIE:
As if you could remember a thing.

BOBSIE:
I will, I promise, I will.

DOBSIE:
As we were about to enter...

BOBSIE:
PLEASE don't interrupt! Do let me tell the news; don't interrupt! Pray, help me, Mr. Mayor, and tell Lola Mae not to interrupt.

MAYOR:
For Heaven's sake! What's going on? Lola Mae, a chair. And Lola Mae, a chair.

[All sit back down indifferently around BOBSIE and DOBSIE.]

Well, now, what is it?

BOBSIE:
Permit me, I'll tell...

DOBSIE:
Permit me, I'll tell...

MAYOR:
Ladies, enough!! *[Long pause.]* Lola Mae, start from the beginning.

BOBSIE/ DOBSIE:
Which one? / Which one?

MAYOR:
The beginning beginning.

BOBSIE:
Well, it was...

DOBSIE: *[Interrupting.]*
He didn't say which Lola Mae he wants to speak. I'm Lola Mae too, you know. He

could have meant me, as well as meaning you. It's not my fault your mother gave you my name just because she ...Which Lola Mae did you mean, Mr. Mayor?

MAYOR: *[Bursting.]*
It doesn't matter which, just as long as it's one at a time.

[Long uncomfortable, competitive pause.]

BOBSIE/ DOBSIE: *[Jumping in.]*
I'll tell it all. / I'll tell it all.
[Competitive pause.]

BOBSIE: *[Jumping in.]*
And I'll tell everything ...

DOBSIE: *[Jumping in.]*
... she leaves out.

BOBSIE: *[Interrupting.]*
I'll not leave anything out!

DOBSIE: *[Imitating* BOBSIE.*]*
I'll not leave anything out! Okay, go ahead, if that's the way you'll be.

BOBSIE:
When I heard about that letter you received ...

MAYOR:
What letter?

[Sudden attention. Everyone pulls up closer, leaning in, like an impending detonation.]

DOBSIE:
The one from your nephew ...

BOBSIE:
He didn't ask you—the one from your nephew in Washington. I know all about it, all! As soon as I heard I just had to find Dobsie...

DOBSIE: *[interjecting]*
I was going into the Piggley Wiggley.

BOBSIE:
No dear, you were coming ***out*** of the Piggley Wiggley—stop interrupting!—and I said, "Have you heard about the letter from Washington?" And she had...

MAYOR: *[Interrupting]*
Who told you about it?

BOBSIE: *[Interrupting]*
Stop interrupting! Oh, excuse me, Mr. Mayor.

DOBSIE
I was standing in line in front of Mary Jean Clumpster...

[BOBSIE begins to cut in.]

...Lola Mae! Please don't interrupt...

BOBSIE: *[Interrupting]*
She was behind Mary Jean. Then I said, "Let's go down to the new motel on the highway and you tell me all about it over some coffee and cobbler." No sooner had we pulled into the parking lot than we laid eyes on the cutest young thing...

DOBSIE: *[Interrupting]*
OOEEE! And dressed fancy like one of those hosts on ***Hee Haw!*** If I was twenty years younger, I ...

BOBSIE: *[Interrupting]*
Oh, shame on you Lola Mae. You can't tell a story; upon my word, you can't. You lisp and that one tooth of yours makes a god-awful whistling sound. *[To the rapt listeners.]* He was pacing back and forth in front of the office, and we could tell the second we laid eyes on him he was somebody special.

DOBSIE: *[Interrupting]*
OOEEE! I was tingling all over! Just like the time Elvis' tour bus stopped at the filling station back in 1958!

BOBSIE:
So we went into the cafe, ordered coffee

and cobbler, and asked Vera, you know, that new waitress from over in Swelter County.

DOBSIE: *[Interrupting]*
What's *up* with that stranger?

BOBSIE: *[Interrupting]*
Lola Mae! You promised to stop interrupting!

DOBSIE:
I never promised any such thing! So Vera said, "He's a big shot from Washington, DC, and he's gonna be my ticket out of here."

MAYOR: *[Alarmed.]*
What!?

THELMA: *[To* MAYOR.*]*
Didn't I warn you about hearing her whining about Bobby Joe Wump's dog.

MAYOR: *[Hushing her.]*
What's a father to do? Just leave it there whimpering?

BOBSIE:
So I said "Aha!"

DOBSIE: *[Interrupting]*
No you didn't! I said, "Aha!"

BOBSIE:
So you did, but I said, "He must be who she told us about!"

MAYOR:
Who? Who told who?

BOBSIE:
Why, Reba your housekeeper, she knows all about the Inspector General! The one your nephew wrote about, the one who's coming to town *incognito*, whatever that means.

MAYOR: *[Terrified.]*
Great God! He's already here! *[To* THELMA.*]* And at the EZ On EZ Off!

AMOS:
Didn't I say that place would be trouble, J.R. A magnet for fur'ners of all sorts.

MAYOR:
What's his name?

BOBSIE: *[Not hearing or ignoring the question.]*
Why then he came into the cafe and started pacing up and down.

DOBSIE:
Giving me the eye.

MAYOR:
Damnation; he's onto us!

AMOS:
Did he do anything else?

DOBSIE:
Why he looked at our cobblers so hard that I thought I would die.

MAYOR:
His name! For God's sake, what's his name.

BOBSIE:
Jimmy Dean or something.

DOBSIE:
Jimmy Dean? No, that's the sausage king. Johnny, Johnny Dream.

LUBBY:
Oh, sweet Jesus!

THELMA:
Sounds like a nightmare to me.

AMOS:
His last name; what's his last name?

BOBSIE:
Funny sort of name—a lot of letters to it…

DOBSIE:
…sounded sort of foreign to me.

AMOS:
What did I tell you!

MAYOR:
Damn! How long's he been here?

DOBSIE:
A couple of days, I think.

LUBBY:
Oh, sweet Jesus!

MAYOR:
Who knows what he's heard! Who knows what he's seen?

[Clutches his head with both hands, raises them to heaven.]

Oh God! A whole universe of sins to punish; couldn't you have overlooked a few of ours?

[Atmosphere: Panic.]

MADGE:
Can't the sheriff take him out for a little ride?

AMOS: *[Sagaciously.]*
No! No! That would hang us for sure! This is a federal official, not some nickel and dime insurance adjuster!

LUBBY:
Oh, sweet Jesus!

MAYOR:
Shut up, all of you! *[Conspiratorially.]* I've been in worse before and got out of'im okay, usually better off than I started.

[Turning to the LOLA MAEs.]

You say he's a young man?

BOBSIE:
Yes, about twenty-three...

DOBSIE:
No! twenty-four!

THELMA:
Although that might be part of his disguise.

MAYOR:
Not very likely; it's easier to hide a truck in your front yard than your age. A young man's all surface, nothing more. Inexperience is written all over them.

[Goes to the phone and starts to dial.]

Friends, I'd advise you to put your business in order as quickly as possible, then wait for my orders. I'll put together the usual police escort and pay this Inspector General an official visit. And as for you all; I hope ya'll understand that's what's good for me is good for us.

AMOS:
And America, J.R.

MAYOR:
Yes, and America, Amos. Now isn't it time you two made for home?

[LOLA MAEs nod and slow **EXIT** *front door. MAYOR waits a long time for phone to be answered while everyone else puts their heads together conspiratorially.]*

Hey, Charlie, why don't you pick up the phone? ... Well, I'll make you busy, now start by bringing that new patrol car around, the one with all the whirling lights ... Who's that? ... Oh, so that's what you're busy with, "settling out of court" again. Damn it, Charlie, I don't care how pretty a young thing you've pulled in, I want you here in two minutes flat ... I'll tell you in the car.

[Hangs up.]

Damn!

[To the room.]

Don't y'all have work to do?

Thelma, meet me there, hear?

*[**EXIT** LOLA MAEs & DOLLY quickly.]*

*[**EXIT** MAYOR, into back room.]*

THELMA:

If only that inspector hadn't swooped down on us so suddenly.

AMOS:

I thought you were the careful sort?

THELMA:

It's not what I've done that'll catch his eye; he'll have to dig deep for that. It's what ya'll've done that'll catch his eye. Especially those leaky barrels out at the water treatment plant, I only have to open a faucet down at the EZ On EZ Off to know something's wrong.

AMOS:

Hmm. *[The great tactical thinker.]* Not as bad as fluoride in the water.

MADGE:

But fixing those beauty contests; that's pretty bad.

LUBBY:

And shooting Bobby Joe's dog!

THELMA: *[Sarcastically.]*

Oh, Washington's pretty touchy about that sort of thing now a-days, Lubby.

*[**EXIT** THELMA, AMOS, MADGE and LUBBY front door.]*

[ENTER MAYOR from interior door, carrying a jacket decked with military medals and a hatbox. He dresses while speaking, unpacking a well worn western hat, which he brushes through his speech.]

MAYOR:

How can a mayor make a good impression with clothes like these? Where's the dignity of office? All the fault of that miserable B.B. Baines; if she'd donated that nice 10X Stetson like I hinted she wouldn't be in the hot water she now is. Look at this stain! Took it to her to get cleaned and she only made it worse. An Inspector General! Why now?! He can't help but find out about those beauty contests or that dog. Damn! If Mary Jane wouldn't drive up on people's porches when she's had a bit too much. Damn! What was I to do, let the beast whimper like that all night and wake the town? Somebody had to put it down. Damn bottom feeding merchants; probably got to that inspector already and given him an earful.

*[Honking horn outside; **EXIT** MAYOR through front door.]*

MAYOR: *[Voice off.]*

You took your sweet time! Button up and look sharp.

CHARLIE-SHERIFF: *[Voice off.]*

This here, Sugar, is the mayor; I got to take him for a little drive.

MAYOR: *[Voice off.]*

Not bad, Charlie, not bad for someone your age.

Scene 4:

ANNA, MARY JANE, REBA

[Atmosphere: Alarm.]

*[**ENTER** ANNA and MARY JANE, interior door, snapping gum.]*

ANNA:

Where are they? Where are they? Oh, my God! *[Opening outside door.]* Dear! J.R! He's gone!

[Exasperated, to MARY JANE]

It's all your fault. Dawdling! Always dawdling!—"How's my hair—I need some more spray."

[Runs to the window and calls.]

J.R, wait; where are you going? What! He's

here? A real Inspector General? What is he wearing? Wait! We're coming with you.

[Flashing lights and sound of car]

He's gone! *[Disgusted.]* You'll pay for this! It's all your fault—you, with your "Momma, dear, coming, coming, just a moment, how's my hair." Now we won't know what's going on, and all because of your primping. As if an Inspector General would ever bother with the likes of you.

MARY JANE:

Whatever, momma. But who's been Miss Grain Elevator six years in a row? And Daddy says he'll get me made Miss Access Road as soon as the political climate changes.

ANNA:

You think just because a bunch of red neck meatheads vote like your daddy tells them you're going to impress an Inspector General from Washington, D.C.?

MARY JANE:

Say what you like, but it is a long time since any of those meatheads bothered with you.

ANNA:

The nerve!

MARY JANE:

Anyway, we'll know everything in a little while.

ANNA:

A little while! Why don't you say, in a month? Or a year! We'll know even more by then!

MARY JANE: *[She leans out of the window.]*

Oh! Here comes Reba back from the Piggley Wiggley.

ANNA:

She took her sweet time!

*[**ENTER** REBA, with groceries.]*

ANNA:

And where have you been! Did the Mayor tell you where he's going?

REBA:

Beats me.

ANNA:

The nerve!

MARY JANE:

Don't let her talk like that momma; it shows a lack of respect.

ANNA:

You imbecile! Go back to the Piggley Wiggley and see what you can learn. I want a full description—how tall he is, what color's his eyes; how he wears his hair. Drop whatever you're doing and don't come back until you've got some news.

REBA: *[Dropping groceries.]*

Fine.

*[**EXIT** REBA. ANNA and MARY JANE exchange dagger looks as curtain closes.]*

ACT II: Scene 1:

JD, VERA

[Atmosphere: Trapped, desperation, despondency.]

*[A tacky motel room. A fuzzy TV is playing a game show. **ONSTAGE:** A young man, J.D. KHLESTAKOV, is lying on the bed watching. He is dressed in flashy western wear.]*

JD: *[Lying on bed.]*

Door number three! Three! You mo-ron! Not four! Buncha mo-rons!. *[Grabs phone and dials.]* Just get me on that show and I'd win every time. Vera, dear, how about a burger and fries and a nice cold coke? What do you mean I can't have anything until I pay. Come on, peaches, you can do it; haven't I said I'm taking you places? Look, just sneak into the kitchen and swipe me a little something, okay? I'm waiting; *ciaoi bella.*

[Hangs up. Notices watch and jumps up to change channel.]

Oh my god! I almost missed it!

[Sound of exercise program. Disco music playing. J.D. begins exercising and singing along, jumbling the lyrics as he dances over to the mirror and starts primping.]

Oh, you hunk! To die for, oh! baby! WooEEE! These trailer park honeys need a city boy to teach them some class. Shouldn't have gotten off that bus in the first place. And then those pool sharks cleaned me out good. Lucky for those guys I got that ride out of there when I did.

[Sitting on bed, depressed.]

Fifty-dollar shirt, hundred-dollar boots, and a thirty-five dollar hat. A lot of good this stuff's doing me here. That Vera's a peach. This sure is a dump of a town; all they want is cash, up front, except for this stupid motel, and now they're cramping my style ... Maybe I should pawn these clothes and buy a bus ticket home? Then what would I wear. Forget it. Not when there's momma.

[Punches the bed then picks up phone.]

Can you believe it, a dial tone! They're slipping, or am I just too slick? *[Dials.]* Damn, answering machine! ... Momma. Pick up the phone, momma; it's me, Jimmy Dee. *[Singing.]* Momma, momma, oh, momma, where are you momma? ... *[Changing to fake disguised gangster voice.]* Listen lady, you get my message? This is the last time I'm asking. *[Changing back to his own voice.]* I hope that new moron husband isn't erasing these; naughty, naughty. *[Gangster voice.]* You know how you'll feel when you see'im lying in the morgue. *[His own voice, screaming, beseeching.]* Please, MOMMA!!! Answer the phone, will you!! He's gonna ... Please, no, don't kill me! MOMMA!!! ... Just kidding. Send money, or *this* could be ***real***. *[Speaking slowly.]* EZ On EZ Off Motel, room number one, Gravel Trailings, Oklahoma. Love ya!

[Kisses phone, hangs up, pumps fist, looks at TV and starts exercise dancing again. A knock on the door. He stops suddenly, composes himself into his super cool look.]

Entree.

*[**ENTER** VERA, a homely girl in a waitress outfit. She's carrying a plate with a sandwich and a cup of coffee.]*

JD:

Vera! Baby! You're to die for.

VERA:

The cook says this is it.

[She puts the plate down. He ceremoniously prepares to eat, then stops and waits.]

JD: *[He holds up a towel.]*

S'il vous plait.

VERA:

Just like those fancy French waiters you was telling me about in New York, Jimmy Dee! *[She tucks the towel around his neck. JD flashes "Romeo" eyes, looks down, and cries out in horror.]*

JD:

What! You expect me to eat this? This, this, this isn't fit for a dog. *[Peels apart sandwich.]* It's peanut butter and jelly. *[Tastes a little.]* You call this jelly; it tastes like glue! They think they can get away with treating me like this. Any other place the people'd be lining up just to watch me pass. I'll report them to the Board of Health!

VERA: *[Terrified; wanting to please.]*
But the cook says if Mrs. Grind finds out I'm feeding you she'll fire me!

JD:
I spit on Mrs. Grind.

VERA:
You still can't have anymore.

JD:
The nerve! Let that cook say what he likes; I'll shut this place down and have that Grind woman thrown in jail! No! I'll give her the chair!

[Feigns electrocution.]

She can't treat someone with my connections like this.

[Sips coffee, blows it out, making horrible face.]

Where do they make this stuff? The toilet? They won't get away with this! What else did he say?

[Jumps up and grabs pencil and paper.]

I'll write it all down. I'll tell them in Washington!

VERA:
Well, first he said he'll go right to the owner, and she'll have the Mayor get the sheriff to take you for a little ride.

JD:
A little ride? I'll tell them in Washington, you hear!

VERA:
Well, that's what they do around here with anybody they want out of the way; take them for a little ride. And they never come back, kinda strange, don't you think? *[Stretching out on bed.]* Somebody never coming back. Sure wish somebody'd take me for that kinda ride.

[Sensing opportunity, JD sits beside her.]

JD: *[Putting the moves on her.]*
It could be arranged.

VERA: *[Jumping up.]*
Jimmy Dee, what do you take me for?

[She rushes to door, pulls it open, revealing Mayor and THELMA, listening.]

Mr. Mayor! Mrs. Grind!! I swear, this ain't how it looks! I ain't that kind of girl.

*[**ENTER** MAYOR. THELMA hangs back and disappears.]*

*[**EXIT** VERA. JD drops coffee, goes pale and shrinks back.*

Scene 2:

JD, MAYOR, THEN THELMA

[Atmosphere: Horror, fear, relaxation.]

[The MAYOR advances a few steps and stops. They stare at each other a few moments, wide-eyed and frightened.]

MAYOR: *[Recovering himself a little and putting out his hand, which is viewed cautiously but not taken.]*
R.P. Dumpsker, Mayor, at your service, sir, and my Director of Human Services, Mrs. Thelma Grind.

[He turns to introduce THELMA, but she's gone.]

JD: *[Withdrawing.]*
Hi. The mattress... I was showing her... where it ... it sags. I can't sleep on a saggy mattress... it's, it's my back. *[Pushes down on bed.]*

MAYOR:
Excuse my intruding.

[He looks for eavesdroppers.]

You alone?

JD: *[Attempting casual: sits on bed, crosses leg nonchalantly.]*
Something wrong?

MAYOR:
Wrong? No, no! Nothing wrong, nothing at all. Just…

[Looking around door then sits next to JD, pistol falls out of his belt onto floor.]

…seeing how things are going with you, …sir. As mayor, it's my duty to see that visitors suffer no inconveniences while in town.

JD: *[Halting at first, but then in a loud, firm voice]*
Well, … I don't know … what that cook told you, but, but you see; it's not… I'm a… I have the fullest intention of fulfilling my obligations here.

[Gaining courage and bravado as his explanation comes together.]

Yes, at any minute I… expect an important communication from Washington that will make everything clear.

*[**ENTER** THELMA, slipping into room, nods at JD and makes a thumbs-up to MAYOR. JD notices gesture and begins to speak conspiratorially.]*

He's trying to poison me! That cook.

[Extending cup to MAYOR & THELMA.]

Smell it! This coffee smells like it's brewed with insecticide! Who knows what's in it!

[THEMA and MAYOR exchange quick horrified glances. JD rises, enraged.]

But someone like me can't be disposed of with such amateur ploys! *[Pounds bed.]* You're not dealing with some mo-ron, you know! Washington will hear of this, yes sirree Bob! I've already put in a call, less than ten minutes ago. *[Finishes triumphantly.]*

MAYOR: *[Scared]*
I assure you our water has a reputation second to none. Must be the china—cheap stuff from Taiwan. May I suggest we go for a ride to more comfortable lodgings?

JD:
Ohh nooo! No sirree Bob. *[Puts on a bold front.]* I know what "more comfortable" means—a little ride, then … *[Eyes them knowingly.]* Comfortable for you, but not so comfy for me. No sirree!

MAYOR: *[Aside.]*
My God, he knows. Those damned bottom feeders were here.

JD: *[With bravado]*
I won't go. *[Bangs his fist.]* Of all the nerve! Barging in here and threatening me!

MAYOR:
Have pity, your honor, please; don't ruin me.

[Drawing himself up stiffly and formally but shaking as he steps, arms outstretched, towards JD, who misunderstands his imploring movement for an attack.]

Think of my child.

JD:
Just try! Did I ever say I wouldn't pay? Never! Yet you'd take me for a ride!

MAYOR: *[Trembling.]*
What man born is above temptation when his family's at risk. I tried to do my best; I swear. I only did what any good father and husband would do. Take my salary; it's barely enough for food. If I've taken a little gift here or there to supplement my

meager income, they were nothing—a bag of groceries, a toy for my little girl.

[Hands outstretched, palms up, beseechingly.]

It's that Chamber of Commerce! They're to blame, your honor; they've been after me for years, ever since I refused to go along with their selfish scheme to keep competition out of town. God is my witness! They're squeezing my family dry. And that dog; it was suffering; someone had to put it out of its misery.

JD:
[Realizing he's not in trouble.] So you're not going to ... ? Well. *[Looking at* MAYORS *open palms.]* If you're looking for a handout, you've picked the wrong man. I'm short on cash. You'll have to find other ways to feed your family; I can't help you there. As for the Chamber of Commerce, they're not my concern. I'm after bigger game. And let that lady feed her own miserable dog. I'm not a dog-catcher, you know.

THELMA: *[Aside to* MAYOR.*]*
J.R., he's dumber than dirt.

MAYOR: *[Aside to* THELMA.*]*
No, it's all part of his disguise. Oh, he's a shrewd one; he's setting up his sting. What a pro, and so good for his age. *[Turns to* JD *quickly.]* Your honor.

JD:
Don't try getting rough. I never would have even got off here if it hadn't been looking for a phone. No sooner had I turned around than the bus was heading down the road, and there I was, stranded in this God-forsaken place for God knows how long. Like you, I don't have a nickel to my name.

MAYOR: *[Aside to* THELMA.*]*
Ah! There's the bait, playing the sympathy card, but watch how I counter his hand. *[Aloud, to* JD.*]* Hmm, it's a pity you're so short on cash, but I don't see what I can do? Tomorrow we could go to the bank and I'd vouch for a loan.

JD:
A loan? *[Reflecting.]* That's it! All I really need is a loan. A couple of hundred dollars, and I'll be out of here today.

MAYOR:
Today? Did you say two hundred dollars and you're gone? *[Taking out his wallet.]* Well, if it's only a loan, I suppose I could front you the money myself, but I'd need a receipt. Everything up front and in the open, I always say. A man in my position has to be above suspicion, you know. "Up front and in the open," that's my motto. Write him a receipt, Thelma.

[THELMA takes out pen but has no paper. She picks up crumbled hotel bill and, repulsed by its filth, tears off corner.]

JD:
Well! That really would help.

THELMA: *[Aside.]*
A receipt! Brilliant, J.R. *[To* JD.*]* Received by whom?
JD: I see I have nothing to worry about with either of you. Oh, name. James Dean (like the sausage king) Khlestakov: K-H-L-E-S-T-A-K-O-V.

THELMA:
That's a foreign name; Russian?

JD:
White, not red. But, please, be seated; now that we're friends. I must admit that, at first, I was a bit worried about that ride...

[Laughing confidentially but somewhat idiotically.]

I'd offer you a drink, but, as you know, this county's dry. Let me get you a glass of water?

THELMA:

NO!

[The MAYOR throws her a reproving look and signals to sit.]

MAYOR:

Funny quirk of hers, only drinks distilled water since her husband drowned at an Italian restaurant over in Tulsa.

*[JD gives curious look then **EXIT JD** into the bathroom for a glass of water.]*

See how chummy he's acting now that I've outwitted his sting, he wants us to pretend that we don't see through his disguise. That will be useful for him later on, when he goes after the "big fish."

JD:

The water here tastes especially sweet in this town. Absolutely delicious!

*[**ENTER** from bathroom. THELMA winces as he drinks.]*

MAYOR:

Sad to say, there are some mayors who'd try to give a man like you the bum's rush if you showed up in their towns. We're different. Now, I don't want to appear to brag about it, but have you noticed our school mascot? The Good Samaritan. Not many towns can wear something like that on their sleeves.

JD:

Who knows how long I would've rotted away here if you hadn't come along. MAYOR: *[Aside.]*He's good; real good, trying to get us to drop our guard.

[Aloud.] May I ask JD—I can call you JD?—where you're headed?

JD:

Back home.

MAYOR:

And where might that be?

JD:

Amarillo.

MAYOR: *[With an ironical expression on his face.]*

Texas, you say; then you're sightseeing here in Oklahoma, I suppose?

JD:

I suppose.

MAYOR: *[With great interest.]*

Your parents are well I hope?

JD:

Could be better.

THELMA: *[With exquisite human interest.]*

What a shame.

JD:

Well, it's not momma; she's fine; gives me whatever I want. But that new husband, he's such a mo ... *[Checks himself.] Declassé*, like they say in Washington. Claims I didn't "advance fast enough," but momma understands. She says it's just because I'm from Texas that those Yankees stand in my way. She says those damn Yankees should kiss the ground I walk on, * but it's not that easy because you see Washington is technically in the South, ** so they're not really Yankees. ***

MAYOR: *[Aside. overlapping above.]*

* He's good! **What a performance! *[Aloud.]* *** I see. But still you must be pretty excited about getting home and seeing your momma.

JD: *[Assumes a "sophisticated" voice.]*
Don't think me a momma's boy, but to be perfectly honest, Amarillo's so *declassee.* I'd rather be in D.C, *[To* THELMA.*]* wouldn't you. Now there's a city for you. Power, high culture, senator's daughters just looking for a man like me to drape themselves across. A town like that needs a man like me.

MAYOR: *[Aside.]*
Amazing; what a disguise ...

THELMA:
... and such a puny looking, no account.

MAYOR: *[To* THELMA.*]*
Unbelievable! *[To* JD.*]* You're right about that; nothing good ever comes out of dead end towns. Take Gravel Trailings, for instance. You lie awake nights thinking up new ways to serve the public good and the moment you try to do something someone stabs you in the back.

[He looks round the room.]

I'm sure the rooms in Washington must be better than this.

JD: *[Momentarily forgets his sophisticated voice.]*
This dump, I don't see how the owner dares to charge money.

MAYOR:
An important person like you shouldn't be subjected to such indignities.

JD:
And the TV has none of my shows.

MAYOR:
If I might be so bold—I have a lovely guest room at my house, light and cozy.

JD:
Yeah?

MAYOR:
And you can't imagine how happy my wife will be to host someone from Washington, D.C. It's a fault of mine, excessive hospitality; it's the way I was raised. Honest to goodness American generosity, like we showed those little people over in Viet Nam.

JD: *[Reassumes faux voice.]*
Charmé! The pleasure's mine. If there's one thing I can't stand, it's selfish, two-faced people. *[*LUBBY *puts head through door and gives thumbs up.]*

MAYOR: *[Indicating to leave.]*
My car's out in the lot.

[AMOS puts head through door and gives thumbs up.]

Would you care to inspect a few of our local institutions?

JD:
I don't know; why?

MAYOR:
Well, you'll be able to see how we do things and speak favorably about us to your superiors back in D.C.

JD: *[Momentarily drops sophisticated voice.]*
Sure. What else is there to do in a place like this.

MAYOR:
So while you're gathering up your things I'll just write some instructions for my wife. I hate to impose, but have you any paper?

JD:
Paper, no. Only this bill. *[Picking up torn paper.]*

MAYOR:
That'll do just fine.

*[**EXIT** JD into bathroom. MAYOR writes, talking to himself all the time.]*

We'll let's hope lunch and that bottle of Gallo wine I got over in Tulsa does the trick. He's a clever one; we'll have to really be on our toes.

[He finishes writing ENTER JD w/tooth-brush. THELMA opens door & ENTER DOBSIE & BOBSIE, tumbling in. LUBBY & AMOS jump back.]

JD:

Oh!

MAYOR:

Oh, it's nothing. Happens to them all the time. Here, let me carry your bag.

[THELMA clears way for JD who climbs over human heap. MAYOR glares at DOBSIE.]

Couldn't you find some better place to fall? Here make yourself useful and take this note to my wife. And hurry!

EXEUNT

Curtain.

ACT III: Scene 1: *Mayor's home.*

ANNA, MARY JANE

[Atmosphere: Despair &recrimination, social ruination.]

[ANNA and MARY JANE standing at the window, same positions as at the end of Act I.]

ANNA:

It's all your fault. We've been waiting a whole hour, all because of your dilly-dallying. Not a car's gone by! Just to spite us.

MARY JANE:

Really, momma, you'll know what he's like soon enough

[Looks out of the window and exclaims.]

Oh look; someone's pulling into the yard!

ANNA:

Do you recognize the car? Why don't they get out?! The suspense is awful! Who can it be?

MARY JANE:

Dobsie, momma, with Reba.

ANNA:

Lola Mae Dobsie, with Reba?! What's she have to do with Reba? No way, that's Lola Mae Bobsie's car. *[Waves her handkerchief.]* Hello! Hello!

MARY JANE:

It is Lola Mae Dobsie, momma.

ANNA:

Of course, you've always got to contradict me, even when you're … There, didn't I say its Lola Mae Dobsie? Why must you always argue so? *[Calls through the window.]* Lola Mae, what's he like? What? What?

[Moves a little from window, exasperated.]

She's such a little idiot, talk on the street to any stranger about her dentures but won't say a word to me until she's asked inside.

Scene 2:

Anna, Mary Jane, Reba, Dobsie

[Atmosphere: Anticipation, curiosity.]

[ENTER REBA and DOBSIE, excited, with note in hand.]

ANNA:

Lola Mae, you ought to be ashamed of yourself, stampeding out with the rest of them. The least you could have done was told me where you were going. Who can one count on these days? And to think I… stood witness at your nephew's wedding to that little trailer park cheapie from Arkansas when not a soul on earth would have been caught dead within a hundred miles of…

DOBSIE:
Mary Jane, how are we today?

MARY JANE:
Fine. Auntie Lola Mae, and yourself?

DOBSIE:
Just fine.

ANNA: *[To REBA.]*
Stop lollygagging and find something to do.

[REBA retreats to edge of room and loiters.]

Tell me all about him; where's he from; how he's dressed; is he tall?

DOBSIE:
I have a note from J.R. *[Holds note until taken.]*

ANNA:
First things first; what's he like?

DOBSIE:
Oh! He's a looker! Dresses just like one of those hosts in those big Nashville shows. So refined! Knows how to treat a lady!

ANNA:
Ah! Here, in Gravel Trailings!

DOBSIE:
It was Lola Mae and me who first discovered him.

MARY JANE:
Tell me all about it.

DOBSIE:
Oh, at first he just shouted and pounded his fist about being treated so badly down at Thelma's motel. He said he was going to make a report to Washington and that we all would wish we were dead. But it's all right now. Once he found out it wasn't your husband's fault he became right friendly, and began telling us all about his people in Texas and the sorrows they've had to face just for living there. Then they went off to inspect the town. For a while there, I must confess things looked pretty worrisome. When a man like that begins to rant, you feel all squishy inside.

ANNA:
Why?

DOBSIE:
Well, you see, the Chamber of Commerce had already got to him and complained.

ANNA:
Chamber of Commerce! They've got nothing on us. What is he like? Young or old?

DOBSIE:
Young—about twenty-three. But he talks with such style. "I like," he said, "to compose, [*] but I am prevented because my room is *rather* dark." And he uses such fine words, like *dayclassey* when describing a town.

***MARY JANE:**
Compose?

ANNA:
See, no six-pack bubba like the redneck meatheads in this town. How does he look, dark or fair?

DOBSIE:
In between. And his eyes dart about like a little animal's. They make you right nervous.

ANNA:
What did my husband say? *[Snatches note and reads.]* "Take care, dear, things are looking good, but if we rely on two cheeseburgers with fries and a coke, $1.75 … " *[Stops.]* I don't understand. What have cheeseburgers have to do with this?

DOBSIE:
Oh, the only paper he could find was some kind of bill.

ANNA:
Oh, I see.[†] *[Goes on reading.]* "But if we rely on our wits, things will turn out just fine. Get the extra room ready and dig out that Gallo wine." Oh my! I must hurry. *[Throws down paper. Not seeing* REBA.*]* Reba! Reba! Where could she have gone?

MARY JANE:
There. *[Snaps chewing gum.]*

ANNA:
Oh, what do I pay you for? Don't stand there like an idiot; do as the Mayor says.

REBA:
Yeah, sure.

DOBSIE:
Tootaloo! I'll just be off to see how things are going.

*[**EXIT** REBA inside, DOBSIE outside.]*

Scene 3:

ANNA, MARY JANE

[Atmosphere: Competition, urgency.]

ANNA:
Now, Mary Jane, make yourself nice. He's not like that redneck deputy you like to show off for; he's sophisticated, so God forbid he don't laugh at how you're dressed. Put on your sky blue Sunday dress, the pretty one that comes down past your knees and has the high white collar and all that lace on the front. It suits you right fine.

MARY JANE:
No, momma! I'm not wearing that old thing; makes me look like I'm nine! I think my red skirt and black sequined blouse will do just fine.

ANNA:
Over my dead body you'll show yourself off in boy-bait like that. Your Sunday dress will go just fine next to my fancy cocktail dress. It gives me that sophisticated look.

MARY JANE:
Oh, momma, that thing makes your boobs stick out like two silos.

ANNA:
The nerve! You think so? Hmmm!

*[**EXIT** ANNA and MARY JANE, hurriedly, speaking as they leave.]*

If only your father had set some limits when you!

[As they exit, front door opens.]

Scene 4:

MAYOR, AMOS, THELMA, LUBBY, MADGE, DOBSIE, BOBSIE, CHARLIE-SHERIFF, JD

[Atmosphere: Tension, resentment.]

*[**ENTER** CHARLIE-SHERIFF, followed by the tipsy JD and the very sober MAYOR, then AMOS, THELMA, LUBBY, and finally MADGE, DOBSIE and BOBSIE with a bandage on her nose. The MAYOR points to a piece of paper lying on the floor, and DOLLY and LUBBY rush to pick it up, pushing each other in their haste. CHARLIE-SHERIFF snatches away paper and **EXITS**.]*

JD:
Excellent tour. Those other towns they didn't show me a thing.

MAYOR:
Other towns have something to hide.

JD:
I've positively overeaten. Do you eat like that everyday?

† Atmosphere #3: Social charade

MAYOR:
Only with guests of your high renown.

AMOS:
Never saw a human being pack so much away

THELMA:
Used his spoon like a shovel.

LUBBY:
My wife says that's how they do it in Texas.

JD:
I like to eat well. That's what a man lives for—to pluck the flowers of pleasure. Where did we dine? The trailer park, wasn't it?

THELMA:
Public Housing.

JD:
Yes, yes, yes; never saw anything like it. In Washington you wouldn't be caught dead in the public housing. It's amazing the way you treat that trash. Back east they'd be lucky to find an old car to sleep in.

MAYOR:
Not here; only the best for our less fortunate citizens. May I dare call your attention to how this is possible? Dedication to duty. Each one of us lays awake at nights praying for new ways to serve. "Dear, God, how can I manage this in a way that would make Washington proud?" Only then can we sleep with our consciences clear. Upon my word, I don't do this because I crave honors—they're tempting, of course, but compared to the joy of doing one's duty, honors are nothing.

THELMA: *[Aside to* AMOS.*]*
Oh, the scoundrel! Hear how he carries on! *[Trying to interest* JD.*]* I praise the Lord for blessing me with the opportunity to serve!

JD:
Yes. A wise man sometimes likes to philosophize. Sometimes it comes out prose, and sometimes it comes out poetry.

BOBSIE: *[To* Dobsie.*]*
He's so refined. Have you ever heard anything like that?!

JD:
Would you tell me, please, if you have any amusements here, say a pool table or a deck of cards?

MAYOR: *[Aside to* THELMA*]*
Ahem! I know where he's aiming; wants us to let down our guard. *[Righteously.]* God forbid! Thankfully, this county is free of those sorts of vices. I myself have never even touched a card, except of course to throw them in the trash when I catch some youngsters being led astray. I feel so disgusted I have to brush my teeth afterwards. How can decent people waste their precious God-given time on such worthless frivolities!

AMOS: *[Loudly.]*
Guffaw!

MAYOR:
And pool! Nothing but a waste of time!

JD:
Well, it's not such a waste when you win; *[Corrects himself.]* or so I've been told.

Scene 5:

MAYOR, AMOS, THELMA, LUBBY, MADGE, DOBSIE, BOBSIE, JD, ANNA, MARY JANE

[Atmosphere: Awe, envy, tension.]

*[**ENTER** ANNA in ravishing party dress and*

MARY JANE in Sunday dress w/high white collar and hideous, suffocating lace.]

MAYOR:
My wife Anna and little girl Mary Jane.

JD: *[Bowing]*
Charmé.

ANNA: *[Feigned surprise.]*
I do declare! The pleasure's ours.

JD: *[Showing off.]*
Excuse me, ma'am, but the pleasure's mine.

ANNA: *[Coquettishly.]*
Won't you sit down?

JD:
Just standing near you is more pleasure than a man deserves. But if you insist, I will sit down.

[JD sits; ANNA sits next to him. MARY JANE tries to sit on other side. ANNA sidles up to JD and squeezes MARY JANE off sofa. She quickly sits on the other side of her mother.]

I am just so thrilled to be at your side.

ANNA:
I do declare; you're too kind. I suppose you must have found Gravel Trailings very, how do you say? *dayclassey*! after living in a big town like Washington, DC.

JD:
Unpleasant's not the word. Being accustomed, *comprenez-vous*, to a life of fashion, then finding oneself on the road—dark, dirty rooms, rude people and cheap food.

[Giving ANNA a flirtatious look. MAYOR grows increasingly anxious as he tries to understand what is happening.]

But at this moment, it was worth all the pain.

ANNA:
I do declare! You're too kind; I don't deserve it.

JD:
But you do, ma'am; you do.

ANNA:
But I'm only the wife of a small town mayor.

JD:
Well, small towns, after all, *[Whispering to her.]* have their unique charms. *[Winking towards* MARY JANE.*]* Of course, they can't compare with Washington. Ah, D.C.! The monuments! The intrigue! What a life, to be sure! *[To MAYOR.]* Maybe you think I am only a data entry clerk.* But don't let that deceive you into thinking that I'm not on the friendliest terms with the highest people in the land. Department heads! I lunch with Congressional aids, have cocktails with Supreme Court clerks, and eat supper with the White House staff. I just drop into their offices several times a day to see what needs to be done. They are always offering me posts overseas—Europe, Southeast Asia, Latin America, Canada—but I have to say, "The real work is here at home." *[He notices that everybody is staring at him in awe. To the* MAYOR.*]* Why are you standing? Please sit down.

***THELMA:**
Data entry!?

MAYOR:
Our rank is such that we can…

ALL:
…stand.

MADGE:
We don't mind.

JD:
Please, please, sit down. *[All sit.]* I don't like such formality; it's embarrassing. I'm an American after all, not some foreign royal. On the contrary, I like to work unobserved. *[*MAYOR *nodds to* THELMA *knowingly.]* But it's impossible to conceal oneself, impossible. I no sooner show myself in a place than some admirer says, "There goes James Dean Khlestakov!"* Once I was even mistaken for the English Prime Minister. The White House guards rushed out onto Pennsylvania Avenue and stopped the traffic so I could cross.

***AMOS:** *[To* LUBBY.*]*
A Ruskie name?

ANNA:
I do declare!

JD:
Oh, at times, it's not bad … when the admirers are those pretty young things *[To* MARY JANE.*]* in those big Vegas shows. *[To* ANNA.*]* I did tell you I know Elvis, didn't I? *[*ALL *turn towards the Elvis shrine in reverent awe.]* He's opening his next show in Vegas with one of my new numbers.

ANNA:
I heard you compose. How exciting! You write for Broadway shows too, I suppose?

JD:
When they can afford my fees. I've penned a few—*Sound of Music, My Fair Lady, The Music Man, Man of La Mancha … Oklahoma!* I can hardly remember them all. I usually knock one out an evening—surprised everybody, even myself at first. I am extraordinarily light of thought.

MARY JANE:
And TV?

JD:
I'm a serious artist; I'd never touch their dirty cash, no matter how many millions they throw at my feet. I live for art. Someone in my position has to be careful. I keep a townhouse in the village—Greenwich, that is — and a house in Beverly Hills, *[To* ANNA.*]* a cabin at Tahoe, but my Georgetown mansion is dearest to me. *[Addressing the company in general.]* If you're ever in town, do call. I have plenty of room, and at least twice a week I hold little gatherings for the diplomatic corps. Last month I entertained Prince Charles—a regular bloke, like we use to say at school.

ANNA:
I can almost taste that meal.

JD:
Sushi flown in from Japan; caviar from the Caspian Sea; salads tossed by the finest Parisian chiefs. And, if you'll pardon the custom, the rounds of cards—D.C.'s a regular Babylon! The English Minister of Foreign Affairs, the French Ambassador, the Soviet Premier, and myself. (I speak several dozen languages at least; learn a new one every month or so, if I'm not too busy. It comes in handy you know.) We play so seriously you'd think we were negotiating a nuclear arms treaty. The tension! There's nothing like it. Then after it's over I'm so tired I take the subway home, grab some carry out Chinese and bolt up the stairs …

THELMA: *[Suspicious.]*
The subway? Carry out Chinese?

[JD hesitates in terror; he's ready to run. Flash of partial realization mixed with confusion flashes across the MAYOR'S face. Everyone stares at THELMA.]

ANNA:

Thelma, for shame, don't interrupt our guest.

AMOS:

You should know those commie types can't take a hint; need to be carried out when they won't leave. *[To* J.D.*]* Go on.

JD:

I really shouldn't say, but a private, state department subway connects my building to downtown, only stops at the Capitol, the White House, and at … but that's top secret, so shhh. The lobby of my building is an interesting place indeed—senators and ambassadors and CEOs, all jostling each other and humming like bees. All you hear is buzz, buzz, buzz, buzz, buzz. Sometimes the President—*[The* MAYOR *and* ALL *rise in awe.]* He's a regular guy. And once I even had charge of an intelligence agency—an absolutely to-die-for appointment. Thousands of letters flooded the President's desk, asking for that job. At first, he gave the position to a retired general who had organized supplies for D-Day, but he couldn't handle it. Things got completely out of hand, then the vice president called on me one morning—I was still in the shower. He said, "JD, this is hush-hush, but the president needs you, the fate of the free world hangs in the balance … " I turned off the water, stopped him right there and said, "Towel." *[He looks provocatively at* MARY JANE.*]* Within a week the Soviet Premier was begging me to let up. "Look, you red devil, I told him, one more word from you and you're a hydrogen cloud."

[The MAYOR and the rest tremble with fright. JD works himself up more and more as he speaks.]

Usually, I don't like being so rough, but that commie mo-ron needed to tow the line. The President called me in after that; gave me a commendation then said, "Next time, go a little softer; that Ruskie wet his pants."

[He makes a wildly dramatic gesture, slips and almost falls, but is affectionately caught by ANNA, who savors the moment.]

MAYOR: *[Approaches trembling, speaks with effort].*

Your hon-on-on-

JD: *[Curtly.]*

What is it?

MAYOR:

Your hon-on-on-

JD: *[As before.]*

Speak up. You trying to speak Chinese? *[Laughs loudly at his own humor.]*

MAYOR:

Your hon-on-on-or … Your Honor, wouldn't you like to rest a bit?

JD:

The rest? Hell! I didn't leave a bit! That lunch was fine. *[Declaiming.] Sautéed* Prairie Oysters and Gallo wine! How do they ever shell the things?

*[**EXIT** JD & MAYOR, stumbling, led into the back room by MAYOR.*

[AMOS, THELMA, LUBBY and MADGE huddle, deep in conspiratorial conversation.]

BOBSIE: *[To* DOBSIE.*]*

Never in my life have I been in the presence of someone so important. I thought I was going to die! Just wait until I tell Bobby Joe Wump.

DOBSIE:

That's what I call a man. Tootaloo!

*[**EXIT** DOBSIE and BOBSIE, front door.]*

THELMA:
It makes one's heart sink but I don't know why. *[Alarmed then cunningly conspiratorial.]* Suppose after his nap he sends a report about us to Washington. If you'll excuse me; I just remembered something I must do. Good day Anna; good day Mary Jane.

AMOS:
Why, yes, so did I; good day, ladies!

LUBBY:
Sweet Jesus; me too.

MADGE:
Tootaloo, Mary Jane, and don't forget your homework now!

*[**EXIT** THELMA, AMOS, LUBBY and MADGE, front door.]*

Scene 6:

ANNA, MARY JANE

[Atmosphere: Building Rivalry.]

ANNA:
Oh, what charm!

MARY JANE:
He's neat!

ANNA:
Such style. I'm tingling all over! You can always recognize the real thing once you see it. Did you notice how he kept looking at me.

MARY JANE:
Momma, he was looking at me.

ANNA:
Come on.

MARY JANE:
But really, momma, you were only in between.

ANNA:
What would he be looking at you for? Tell me, why would a sophisticated man like that be bothering with an immature girl like you?

MARY JANE:
You tell me, momma. He looked at me when he was talking about dropping the hydrogen bomb.

ANNA:
Well, maybe he looked at you once or twice to be polite.

MARY JANE:
Well momma, when he called for that towel it wasn't politeness I saw in his eyes!

[ANNA looks at MARY JANE with furious, jealous realization.]

Scene 7:

MARY JANE, ANNA, MAYOR

[Atmosphere: Exhaustion, worry, aggravation.]

[ENTER MAYOR from within.]

MAYOR:
Sh-sh! I wish you hadn't given him so much so to drink. Even if half of what he said is true—oh but could it be? *[Sunk in thought.]* When a man's tanked he always blurts out whatever's on his mind. Of course he fibbed a little, but all that talk about ambassadors and cabinet members; he couldn't have made that up. Oh! thinking about it makes my head spin. Just being around him leaves me unnerved.

ANNA:
If you ask me, it's a pleasant change to be around a man with some culture. Just being near him fills me with the most charitable feelings.

MAYOR:

Hmf! You haven't the sense to be afraid of a fellow like that even if he were the devil himself. A stranger winks at you and you start to carry on like you're seventeen years old and Miss Grain Elevator, 1954.

ANNA:

Don't worry none about that. *[Glancing at* MARY JANE.*]* We know a thing or two about men.

MAYOR: *[To himself.]*

A lot of good it does talking to you! Damn it! He doesn't even look the part; he's such a wimp. *[Silent pause.]* Everything's upside down. How in the world can I figure this out? He may talk in circles, but sooner or later he'll say something that…

[JD is heard to give a short cough in the next room.]

MAYOR:

… Hush! *[Tiptoes to inner door, trying to get his wife and daughter to speak in an undertone.]* Don't disturb him for heaven's sake!

ANNA:

[To MARY JANE *loudly.]* Come, dear, I'll tell you something I noticed about our *guest* that I wouldn't care to say with your father around.

*[**EXIT** ANNA and MARY JANE, arm in arm, through inner door.]*

[Deep in thought, looks at inner door, trying to decide.]

MAYOR:

Aghh! *[Goes to outer door, opens it, motions and whispers.]*
Charlie! Stand on the steps and don't let anyone near, especially that bottom feeding scum from the Chamber of Commerce. The instant you see anybody who even looks like he's got something to say, get Jim Boy to take'im for a ride. I'm going down to the courthouse and check up on some things. Now, no complaining, you can let those pretty young things speed through town for at least one afternoon. Stay right here, you might be needed.

*[**EXIT** MAYOR, quietly through front door.]*

CURTAIN/INTERMISSION

ACT IV: Scene 1: *Scene same as Act III*

AMOS, THELMA, MADGE, DOLLY, LUBBY, DOBSIE, BOBSIE

[Atmosphere: By character: terror transformed into relief.]

*[**ENTER** AMOS, THELMA, MADGE, DOLLY, LUBBY, DOBSIE and BOBSIE (with bandaged nose), cautiously, almost on tiptoe. They cross to the inner room door.]*

AMOS:

For God's sake, let's have some order here. This is a man who goes to the White House and raises hell. You have to show respect to a man like that.

THELMA:

How Amos? Grease his wheels?

MADGE: *[Eager to support AMOS.]*

Exactly, Thelma, grease his wheels.

THELMA:

That's a one-way ticket to jail.

AMOS:

True, Thelma, it's risky. * He might fly into a rage; he's an Inspector General, you know, not some insurance adjuster. Maybe it should be in the form of a gift?

* **LUBBY:**

Oh! Sweet Jesus!

DOLLY:
Or, maybe, we could tell him we want to return some money that fell out of unsealed envelopes, and we don't know what to do with it?

THELMA:
You ask me, there's too many of us here; we need to pay our *respects* individually, and do … what has to be done. The fewer eyes and ears the better. That's always best, right Amos? We'll just step outside, and you break the ice.

AMOS:
No, no, no. Ladies first.

THELMA:
If that's the case, then he's all yours, Madge.

MADGE:
I can't, I can't! In the presence of the high and mighty I might blather like an idiot. Who knows what I'd say.

THELMA:
Looks like it's you, Amos; your *eloquence* is your strongest suit.

AMOS:
Just because a man has a minor gift …

THELMA:
Now, don't be modest.

ALL: *[Pressing around him.]*
You're our only chance! / You've got to! / Don't let us down! / Oh! Sweet Jesus! / You have no choice!

[THELMA pushes AMOS toward door.]

AMOS:
Let go of me, please!

[Footsteps and coughing are heard from inner door. All rush to front door, squeezing and struggling to leave. Half-suppressed cries.]

BOBSIE:
Oh, Lola Mae, you stepped on my foot.

DOBSIE:
No, you mine!

LUBBY:
Sweet Jesus! Oh, sweet Jesus! You're squeezing me to death.

*[**EXIT** all, through the outer door, and the stage is left empty.*

Scene 2:

JD

[Atmosphere: Appreciative.]

*[**ENTER** JD, sleepy, carrying a glass of water that he puts on desk.]*

JD:
That was a fine snooze. Whatever they gave me at lunch sure knocked me flat. My head's pounding like a drum. But still, I could pass some time very nicely here. They're so generous and hospitable—plain, simple folk, real heartland types. And that mayor's daughter's a dish, and the mother too. Play your cards right, and one could make a killing off these morons. Yes, siree; this ***is*** the life!

Scene 3:

JD, AMOS

[Atmosphere: Terror & despair, then as each one leaves, relieved; JD become increasingly joyful.]

*[**ENTER** AMOS, stops anxiously, muttering to himself.]*

AMOS:
Oh, God, Please! *[Drawing himself up, aloud.]* I have the honor to present myself—Amos Lynch, Gravel County Judge.

JD:

Have a seat. So you are the Judge around here?

AMOS:

I was elected by a fair election in 1954 and served ever since.

JD:

Does it pay to be a judge?

AMOS:

Pay? Ah, … ah, … *[Aside.]* I'm burning up; I think I'm going to faint.

JD:

What's that in your hand?

AMOS:

Oh no, oh no, nothing at all! *[Dropping wad of bills on the floor, then looking at them in horror.]* I just cashed my welfare check. Oh God, why did I say that!

JD: *[Picking it up.]*

It looks like Uncle Sam gives you a lot. A generous country we have, don't you think?

AMOS:

Better than Russia. *[Shaking all over. Aside.]* Oh, Lord! I'm lost!

JD:

I tell you what *[Scooping up the money.]*—make me a loan.

AMOS: *[Eagerly.]*

Why, of course, of course—with the greatest pleasure. *[Aside.]* Sweet Jesus, stand by me!

JD:

I'm short on cash, what with one thing and another, you know. I'll send you a check as soon as I'm back in DC.

AMOS:

Don't mention it! It is a great honor to have you take it. I'll try to deserve it—by serving with renewed zeal and vigor.

[Rises from chair and draws himself up straight, hands hanging at his sides.]

I'll disturb you no longer. You don't care to give me any orders?

JD:

Orders?

AMOS:

For the County Court.

JD:

What? A man like me doesn't bother with the courts!

AMOS:

I understand. *[Bowing. Aside.]* Doesn't bother with the courts! Thank God!

*[**EXIT** AMOS front door.]*

JD:

Such a fine fellow.

Scene 4:

JD, DOLLY, MADGE

*[**ENTER** DOLLY and MADGE: front door, with mail bag.]*

DOLLY:

I have the honor to present myself—Postmaster, Dolly Crust.

MADGE:

Madge Snipper, Superintendent of Schools.

JD:

Glad to meet you both. I like the pleasant company of lovely ladies. Have a seat. *[They sit obediently.]* Do you live here?

DOLLY/ MADGE:

No, sir, next door. / Down the road.

JD:

I like small towns. Of course, there aren't many people; it's not very lively, but what of that? It isn't Washington, after all. Isn't that so—It isn't the capital?

DOLLY/MADGE:
No, no.

JD:
It's only in the capital that you find sophisticated people; while here it's mostly *hoi polloi.* Isn't that so?

MADGE:
Yeh.

DOLLY:
Quite so. *[To* MADGE.*]* He's so kind, talks to anyone.

JD:
And yet you'll admit that one can live happily in a small town.

DOLLY/MADGE:
Quite so. / Yeh.

JD:
In my opinion, one can live anywhere as long as you're treated with respect and sincerity. Isn't that so?

DOLLY/MADGE:
Quite so. / Yeh.

JD:
I'm glad you agree. And I hope you'll share my viewpoint on another matter as well. *[Looking* DOLLY *in the eye.]* Such as lending your fellow human being a helping hand.

DOLLY:
Quite so, quite so.

JD:
I've happened to have run out of cash. Can you lend me... say... three hundred? I hate like the devil to deny myself. And why should I? Isn't that so?

DOLLY/MADGE:
Quite so. / Yeh.

[Both pull bills from their purses, shove them forward and rise to go.]

DOLLY:
We'll not disturb you, Mr. General, anymore.

MADGE:
Would you care to make any suggestions about education in our town?

JD:
No... ignorance is bliss; that's all.

[EXIT DOLLY and MADGE, bowing.]

[JD counts the money.]

JD:
Such nice people, so obliging. Everyone should be like that.

Scene 5:

JD, LUBBY

*[**ENTER** LUBBY who is practically pushed onto stage. A voice offstage is heard whispering, "Don't be chickenhearted."]*

LUBBY: *[Drawing himself up, trembling.]*
Oh, sweet Jesus. I have the honor to present myself—Director of Public Works, Lubby Snatch, your honor; my wife's the... something... of the mayor.

JD:
I'm glad to see you. Have a seat. You look nervous. Here, have a glass of water?

[Stares at the glass in horror, hesitates, hands trembling; water spills. He jumps up and frantically brushes it off.]

LUBBY:
Oh, sweet Jesus!

JD:
You're right there, sweet as Jesus, best tasting water I've ever had. You should do something about your nerves. *[*JD *points to glass.]* There, drink it down. It'll put hair on your chest!

[JD sits and waits. LUBBY, twitches in place, barely controlling himself.]

Don't you ever talk?

LUBBY:

I'm... your Hon... I mean, Your General... *[Aside.]* I'm... done for!

JD:

You're scared? There *is* something awe-inspiring in my eyes, isn't there? Single women can't resist it, nor married ones for that matter. Have I met your wife?

LUBBY:

I... don't... know.

JD:

A strange thing happened to me on the road. I ran entirely out of cash. Can you lend me three hundred?

LUBBY: *[Clutching his chest, he takes out a wad of bills.]*

I ... *[Horribly long hesitation.]* ... can!

[Thrusts bills at JD.]

JD:

Thank you very much. *[*LUBBY *stands trembling before him.]* Toot-a-loo.

*[**EXIT** LUBBY, frantically twisting the doorknob.]*

Scene 6:

JD, THELMA

*[**ENTER** THELMA.]*

THELMA:

Mrs. Thelma Grind, Director of Human Services, your honor.

JD:

Howdeedo? Please sit down.

THELMA:

I had the honor of receiving you personally at the philanthropic institution committed to my care.

JD:

Oh, yes, I remember: that dandy lunch. Ah, prairie oyster! How ever do they shell those things?

THELMA:

I am honored to do all I can on your behalf.

JD:

I admit, my weakness is good cuisine. Tell me, please, won't you—it seems to me you were a little shorter this morning, weren't you?

THELMA:

Quite possibly *[After some consideration, she scrunches down.]* I spare myself no pains in the performance of my duties.

[Draws her chair closer and speaks in a lowered tone.]

There's the postmaster, on the one hand, she does absolutely nothing except open and read through the mail. Investigate for yourself, if you like. Then there's the Judge, the man who was just here. He does even less; his wife breeds dogs (or at least that's how she puts it, but she really just steals them off people's lawns) to sell to city folk. Even though he is a distant relative and *my friend*, his conduct is so reprehensible I'm forced to speak. If you were a woman and you were in a room alone with him, you'd know what I mean. And Madge Snipper, the Superintendent of Schools—the woman can barely write her own name; and there's ... something going on between her and the Judge; that's how she got the job, if you catch my meaning. And that Lubby Snatch, the Director of Public Works, a cowardly cheat if there ever was one, and a pinko to boot. He voted for Stevenson back in '52'.

JD:

You don't say. I would never have known.

THELMA:
I can document it all!

JD:
Very well, why not? It'll give me something amusing to read. What did you say is your name?

THELMA:
Mrs. Thelma Grind.

JD:
Oh, yes. Tell me, Mrs. Thelma, have you any children?

THELMA:
Two, already grown. Never did anything wrong!

JD:
You don't say! Grown up! And what are… their…

THELMA:
You mean that you deign to ask their names?

JD:
Sure, tell me their names?

THELMA:
John Boy (he's in Viet Nam), and Peggy Sue; she got married and moved to Texas.

JD:
Smart move. Viet Nam? *[Musing.]* I'll do something about that.

THELMA:
You don't mean… you could bring him home? Thank you your honor, oh thank you! What a great man! What a great man!

JD:
The least I can do.

THELMA:
I won't disturb you any longer; I'll bring you that evidence before you leave. *[Bows and makes for the door.]*

[She almost breaks down and rises to go.]

JD: *[Escorting her towards door.]*
Of course, of course. What you told me is all so very amusing. Call again, please. I like that sort of thing. I say! What is your … I keep forgetting … your name?

THELMA:
Grind, Mrs. Thelma Grind.

JD:
Do me a favor, Miss Rind. A curious accident befell me on the road. I ran entirely out of cash. Have you four hundred dollars you could loan me?

THELMA: *[Fingering her purse.]*
Well, I've got five.

JD:
Five hundred, well! How generous! That'll do just fine. *[She hands him a single bill.]* Oh. Well, times are hard. I'll send you a *receipt* as soon as I get home.

THELMA:
No, don't bother; no need.

*[**EXIT** THELMA.]*

Scene 7:

JD, BOBSIE, DOBSIE

*[**ENTER** DOBSIE and BOBSIE (with bandaged nose), eagerly, holding an autograph book.]*

BOBSIE/ DOBSIE:
Lola Mae Bobsie. / Lola Mae Dobsie.

JD:
Oh, yes, I've met you before. I believe you fell? How's your nose?

BOBSIE:
It's fine.

JD:
That's nice. I'm glad it's fine. *[Suddenly and abruptly.]* Have you any money?

DOBSIE:
Money? How's that? Money?

JD:
A thousand dollars to lend me.

BOBSIE:
Not me; how about you, Lola Mae? ?

DOBSIE: *[Clutching purse.]*
Maybe some loose change.

JD:
Well, if you haven't a thousand, then a few hundred would do.

BOBSIE: *[Fumbling with purse.]*
I might have a quarter.

DOBSIE:
I might have a dime.

BOBSIE:
No; remember Vera gave you change for a quarter, you ... *[Indicating her purse.]*

DOBSIE:
For shame, Lola Mae; mind your own business!

JD:
Well, never mind; whatever you have will do. *[Takes their coins.]*

DOBSIE:
May I ask a favor of you? It's a matter of greatest delicacy.

JD:
I love delicacies; go ahead.

DOBSIE: *[Very nervously and sincerely.]*
It's a delicate matter. My nephew; he was born before my sister was ... you see, my sister, sh... he... , she... , he... she wasn't, but Jimmy Ray he made her an honest woman... oh, never mind.

JD:
No skin off my nose.

BOBSIE:
I *have* a favor to ask.

JD:
Yes?

BOBSIE:
Your autograph, please? And could you write, "Love Me Tender" above your name.
[JD signs books.]

DOBSIE:
And? *[Nodding eagerly like a dog.]*

JD:
Yes.

DOBSIE:
When you get back to Washington and are hobnobbing with senators and ambassadors, could you drop my name? Lola Mae Dobsie. Just say I'm someone you know, especially if Jackie Kennedy's around.

JD:
I'll try.

BOBSIE:
Oh, thank you, your highness; all I've ever really wanted was a little recognition, you know.

*[**EXIT** BOBSIE & DOBSIE, bowing and nodding.]*

Scene 8:

JD

[Atmosphere: Satisfaction.]

JD: *[Alone; counting money.]*
My, oh my, must be almost a thousand. If only I could find a game now! What a place, this town; they think I'm some type of government big shot. What a bunch of mo-rons, generous though! *[Snaps his fingers with glee.]* I'll write a letter to

that Sunday feature, "There Ought To Be A Law." I bet the editor would find this bunch hilarious. *[Sits at desk.]* Ah, county letterhead; this'll give it the right touch.

[Proceeds to write letter, chortling.]

Scene 9:

JD, VERA

[Atmosphere: Fear of impending catastrophe.]

*[**ENTER** VERA, from inside door.]*

VERA:
Jimmy Dee? I had to sneak around back, the Sheriff's out front on guard. What's'ya doing there?

JD:
Writing a letter to a friend in D.C.

VERA:
The motel got a call, from your momma.

JD:
Not now, baby.

VERA:
Manager told me to tell you that she …

JD: *[Writing.]*
I'm busy!

VERA:
…wants me to tell you right away.

JD:
All right, what did she say?

VERA:
She paid your bill with a credit card, over the phone!—can you believe that?—and she told the manager to buy you a ticket on the first bus out of town. *[She holds up a ticket.]*

JD:
What do I care about bus tickets. I like it here.

[Stops writing and waves bills at her.]

VERA:
My god! Where did you get that?

JD: *[Writing.]*
From these hick officials. Look baby, they think I'm some kind of general or something! *[Continues to write.]* This letter will make me the talk of the town.

VERA: *[Sitting in despair.]*
My god, Jimmy Dee, don't you see how mad they'll be when they find out you're not a general. They're going to take you for that ride. Here, take this ticket; I got one for me too; like you said, "I'm taking you places." The bus leaves in less than an hour, at six, from the motel. If we go now we can make it in time.

JD: *[Sealing letter.]*
Done! All right, give it here.

[Takes ticket and gives her the letter.]

Be a peach; mail this for me.

VERA:
You'll take me with you? Won't you?

JD:
Sure, doll.

VERA:
I'll meet you at the EZ On EZ Off at quarter to six.

VOICES OFF: *[Arguing]*
Where are you going? Nobody's allowed in. / Let us in, Charlie. / You can't keep us out. / We're here on business. / Get out of here! Mayor says, leave him alone. / Here's ten! Does that change your mind? / Then take a twenty.

*[**EXIT** VERA through inner door.]*

Scene 10:

JD, MERCHANTS

[Atmosphere: Terror and Fury.]

[ENTER MERCHANTS, bursting in, waving petitions, carrying gifts, and crowding around. Patrol car heard driving away, siren blaring. What's going on?

B.J. WUMP:
Protect us, your honor!

B.B. BAINES:
Hear us out!

R. SNOOK:
We've been framed!

JD: *[Takes the petitions and reads.]*
"To his most honorable, Inspector General ... " What does this mean!?

MERCHANTS:
We beg you.

JD:
What do you want?

B.J. WUMP:
Don't ruin us, your honor. We're being ruined.

JD:
I don't understand?

MERCHANTS:
The Mayor!!

R. SNOOK:
He's destroying our lives!

B.B. BAINES:
He ruined my daughter's hair! She should have been Miss Grain Elevator!

B.J. WUMP:
And he uses the sheriff to cover up his crimes.

R. SNOOK:
They stole my dog!

B.B. BAINES:
Say anything and your lucky to get off with just your tires slashed.

B.J WUMP:
And if he really wants to give you trouble, the Sheriff takes you for a ride.

JD:
My, what a mean man!

B.B. BAINES:
So help us God! _

JD:
You make it sound like he should be in jail.

R. SNOOK:
The sooner the better, and throw away the key.

B.B. BAINES:
Here, we've brought you some gifts.

JD:
No, no! I don't take bribes. But, I am open to a loan; that's a quite different matter. Say, a hundred from each of you? _

B.J. WUMP:
If you like. *[They take out wallets.]* It seems I'm a little low on cash. Ruby, can you lend me a fifty?

R. SNOOK:
This is no time to be cheap, B.J.! Here, your honor, I'll make it two hundred, just throw him in jail.

JD:
Obliged. Would you like a receipt? _

B.B. BAINES: *[Shoving money at him.]*
No! It's yours, all yours.

JD:
My wallets awfully full; can anyone swap some fifties for a couple of hundreds?

R. SNOOK: *[Taking his hand.]*
You must help us now. Once he learns we've been here; he'll stop at nothing; he'd even burn down our stores.

JD:
But you've insurance for that?

B.J. WUMP:
Protect us, your honor, or we're as good as dead.

JD:
Of course, of course; I shall exert my best efforts on your behalf.

*[**EXIT** MERCHANTS, bowing gratefully.]*

WOMAN: *[Off.]*
Your honor! Your honor! Hear me, please! Before he comes back!

JD:
Come in.

Scene 11:

JD, TWO WOMEN

*[**ENTER** TWO WOMEN.]*

[Atmosphere: Mounting fury!]

WOMAN #1: *[Kneeling.]*
I beg you, your honor. He had the Sheriff take my husband for a ride.

WOMAN #2:
He stole my dog.

JD:
Your dog; how mean. Who?

WOMAN #1:
The Mayor!

JD:
The brute; imagine stealing a dog!

WOMAN #2 / WOMAN #1:
Give us justice, your honor. / No, revenge, your honor. Let him rot in hell!

JD: *[Ushering them to door.]*
I'll do what I can. I don't suppose you could … no.

WOMAN #2:
Give him the chair.

WOMAN #1:
I want to be there when he fries! .

*[**EXIT** TWO WOMEN, hurried out. JD closes door and shivers with repugnance. A clamor of voices outside.]*

JD:
All right, all right. Coming.

*[JD opens door and **ENTER** partially a figure appears in a shaggy cloak, with unshaven beard, swollen lip bandage over his head. Behind him **APPEARS** a whole MOB, shouting and clawing for attention. JD slams shut door.]*

Oh, god!

Scene 12:

JD, MARY JANE

[Atmosphere: Coy, tension, passionate.]

*[**ENTER** MARY JANE from inner door: in boy-bait: short red skirt, tight black sequined blouse.]*

MARY JANE:
Oh!

JD:
Did I scare you?

MARY JANE:
Who me?

JD: *[Showing off.]*
Charmé. Looking for someone?

MARY JANE:
No, not really. I was just wondering if momma was around.

JD:
No, only me.

MARY JANE:
I hope I'm *not* disturbing you; you must have so many important things to do.

JD: *[Showing off.]*
You couldn't possibly disturb me, unless you were to leave.

MARY JANE:
You're just being polite.

JD:
No, not at all. Please, have a seat. Ah, this mere sofa will have to serve as your throne.

MARY JANE: *[She sits down.]*
You probably think I've never sat on a throne before. But just last year, Daddy had me elected Miss Grain Elevator for the sixth time. And he says, I'll be Miss Exit Ramp once he takes care of those bottom feeders!

[He moves closer and tries looking into her eyes. She gets nervous.]

I really should go; momma's probably looking for me.

JD:
What a beautiful scarf.

MARY JANE:
You're teasing me because I'm from a small town.

JD:
Oh, how I long to be that scarf, so I might wrap myself around your alabaster throat.

MARY JANE:
I haven't the faintest idea what you are talking about! Awful humid today; think we're in for storm?

JD:
Yes, a thunderstorm of passion.

MARY JANE:
You're a poet too? I'd like a poem for my scrapbook.

JD:
Anything; just ask!

MARY JANE:
Whatever, as long as it's pretty, but not too long.

JD:
I've just the thing.
Drink to me only with thine eyes,
And I will pledge with mine;
Or leave a kiss within the cup
And I'll not ask for wine."

MARY JANE:
I know that! You wrote it? I hear it in English class all the time. When the English teacher gets loony she reads it and all the football players just go wild.

JD:
Yes, it's quite famous. And I've tons more where that comes from, but just now I can't remember a bit of it. My love for you is killing me; ever since your first glance…

[Moves nearer.]

MARY JANE: *[In a coy voice.]*
I'm afraid I don't understand.

[Moves away.]

JD: *[Moving nearer.]*
Why do you move away? If you were closer I could help you understand.

MARY JANE: *Moving away.]*
Daddy always tells Momma that distance makes the heart grow fonder.

JD: *[Moving nearer.]*
But Love's easier to grasp when it's close at hand.

MARY JANE: *[Moving away.]*
I can't see why.

JD: *[Moving nearer.]*
It's not something that you see, but feel. If

I held you in my arms, you'd know what I mean.

MARY JANE: *[Looking desperately towards window.]*

What was that? It looked like something flew by. Do you think it was a bird; they mean good luck?

JD:

Then it was. No doubt a lovebird. Oh, my dove. *[Kisses her shoulder.]*

MARY JANE: *[Leaps to feet, indignantly.]*

That's not fair! You didn't even look! *[Rushing for door.]*

JD: *[Blocking her way and embracing her.]*

Forgive me, *mon cherie*. It's love that makes me bold. Love and only love; it makes the world go round.

MARY JANE:

What kind of girl do you think I am?! *[Struggles to be free.]*

JD: *[Still holding her; falls to his knees.]*

Consent, or I'll die ...

MARY JANE:

I'm sure you will when my daddy finds out! *[JD clasps her knees.]*

Scene 13:

JD, MARY JANE, ANNA

[Atmosphere: Desperation; amazement.]

*[**ENTER** ANNA.]*

ANNA: *[Seeing JD on his knees.]*

Young lady! What's going on!

JD:

Oh, god! *[Dropping flat.]* Nobody move! My contact lens!

MARY JANE:

Momma! Don't you ever knock?

ANNA:

Go to your room. I'll deal with you when I'm done with him.

*[**EXIT** MARY JANE in tears. ANNA walks over to JD, looming above him; she puts her foot firmly down in front of him, as if smashing a 'lens'.]*

There it is.

JD: *[Looking up, then aside.]*

She's a dish. *[Flings himself at her knees.]* Indeed I have. *[Tries to pull her down to him.]*

ANNA:

What!? On the floor? Oh, what would people say?

JD:

Give me love or give me death! My heart's aflame.

ANNA:

Please—*[Changing to a coy voice, just as daughter had.]* I don't quite understand. You've heartburn? It's something you ate.

JD:

No, my heart's aflame ... with love! Consent, or I shall die!

ANNA:

Oh, now I understand; you're making a proposal for my daughter's hand.

JD:

If ***you*** don't satisfy my love, then I'll surely...

ANNA:

I'm stunned... haven't you noticed I'm already... married.

JD:

What does that have to do with love! *[Pounding his heart.]* Nothing; nothing at all. Love conquers all. Let us seize the day and fly to the shadows of murmuring delights!

Scene 14:

JD, ANNA, MARY JANE

[Atmosphere: Shock, horror.]

*[**ENTER** MARY JANE, running.]*

MARY JANE:
Momma, papa says you should… *[Seeing JD on his knees, exclaims.]* Oh, momma, how could you!? He's mine!

ANNA:
Could what? Whatever do you mean?

MARY JANE: *[Through tears.]*
Momma, I thought…

ANNA:
Thought?! Have you no shame!

JD:
Mrs. Dumpsker, forgive her. Don't let disappointment stand in the way of our happiness; give us your blessing.

[Scrambling across room and seizing MARY JANE'S hand.]

MARY JANE: *[Stunned surprise.]*
Me!

JD:
My life is in your hands.

ANNA:
What?! You want her? *[Aside.]* What did I do wrong?

[She apprehends the opportunities.]

You little idiot! Our guest gets down on his knees to ask me for the hand of a nitwit like you, and you come running in and almost ruin everything with your dirty-minded suspicions. If I had any sense I should refuse; a man like this doesn't deserve to be married to an imbecile like you.

MARY JANE:
Momma, I don't understand…

Scene 15:

JD, ANNA, MARY JANE, MAYOR

[Atmosphere: Desperation fighting against despair, turns to shocked disbelief, then jubilation.]

*[**ENTER** MAYOR, front door, with files.]*

MAYOR:
Your Honor, don't ruin me, don't ruin me. Everything they told you was lies …

JD:
[Leaping to his feet.] Ah, here it is! *[Pretends to stick lens back in his eye.]*

MAYOR:
…cheats and fakers of the worst kind. They wouldn't know how to sell water at a fire, so they blame me for they're businesses going bad. They're all insane, certified insane. I can show you the papers. We try to keep them locked up but one of them's the wife of the head of the Chamber of Commerce and he bribed the doctors into letting her go. What can one do when faced with corruption like that!? Her dog wandered out into the road and got hit by a car; if I hadn't put it out of its misery it would have howled for hours and woken the whole town.

JD:
What should you care about a crazy woman? There are more important things on hand.

MAYOR:
Don't believe them, don't believe them. They'll stop at nothing, no matter how vile the lie. They're crooks, maniacs, and liars and swindlers and…

ANNA:
…J.R., calm down before you have a stroke. Calm down! Mr. Khlestakov here has done us the great honor…

MAYOR:
Honor?

ANNA:
...of requesting our daughter's hand.

MAYOR:
Mary Jane? Have you gone insane. Please understand, your honor—she's a little batty; it runs in her family.

JD:
But it's true. I really am asking for your daughter's hand.

MAYOR:
No! You're putting me on?

JD:
I kid you not. I'm head over heels in love.

MAYOR:
Unbelievable!

ANNA:
How many times does he have to say it, you numbskull, before it sinks in?

MAYOR: *[Collapsing on sofa.]*
I'm overwhelmed.

JD:
If you deny your consent, who knows what I could do?

MAYOR:
Who would have thought this morning that today would have ended up like this.

ANNA:
JR!

MAYOR:
I can't believe it; am I going insane?

JD:
Give her to me, give her to me! I am a desperate man; I could do anything. If I shoot myself, they'd be an investigation.

MAYOR:
Oh, my God! No! Not that! I'm just a sentimental father not ready to lose his little girl. Pay me no mind; I've never been so confused.

ANNA:
Well, give them your blessing.
[MAYOR stands, grabs and joins their hands, then starts to weep.]

MAYOR:
May God bless you; I'm not going to jail?!

[JD takes MARY JANE in his arms. The MAYOR rubs his eyes in disbelief.]

Can you believe it? They're engaged. Thank heavens! Engaged! He's really going to be our son-in-law!

[Cries out, jumping with glee.]

Oh, J.R. Dumpsker; you've finally made it big! What an amazing turn of events! Top of the world, just when it seemed you were being smashed to smithereens!

Scene 16:

JD, ANNA, MARY JANE, MAYOR, VERA

[Atmosphere: Triumph, disappointment, glee.]

*[**ENTER** VERA.]*

MAYOR:
And what do you want? The Inspector General's occupied with important affairs.

VERA:
Your honor, an important message came for you down at the motel. The man said it was urgent.

JD:
Oh! All right. Let me see.

[VERA hands an envelope to JD; he tears it open.]

From Washington ...

[He pretends to read.]

Hm, important orders; I must leave at once.

MAYOR/ANNA/MARY JANE:
Leave?

JD:
Yes, I'm afraid it can't be helped. *[Thinking fast.]* Some Russian spies have been caught over in Amarillo, and they need me to interrogate them. I speak their lingo, you know.

ANNA:
But the wedding plans?

MAYOR:
Duty before pleasure; that's how I've always lived, and from my son-in-law I expect the same.

MARY JANE:
But when will you be back?

JD:
Oh, tomorrow or the next day. I usually make short order of these Ruskie spies.

VERA:
Sir, the bus leaves in five minutes. You can't afford to miss it.

JD:
Of course, of course. Good-by, my dear—oh, how can I ever express what's in my heart. Good-by, my heart.

[Kisses and handshakes all around.]

MAYOR:
You're taking a bus?

JD: *[After a moment's hesitation.]*
It preserves my cover, draws less attention than a government car.

MAYOR:
I've a better idea. *[Taking out keys.]* Here, take my county car—the red Caddy with the big rack of lights. Run the siren all the way. The sooner you're in Amarillo, the sooner you're back here.

JD:
You're too kind. *[Takes keys.]*

VERA:
Sir, we better leave.

ANNA:
She's going too?

JD:
Of course, didn't you know; she's an undercover agent, planted in this town, top secret, hush-hush stuff. It wouldn't be safe for her to stay now that her cover's blown.

MAYOR:
But you can trust us.

JD:
In times like these, only the dead can be trusted.

MAYOR:
You'll be needing to fill up the tank; it's a four hour drive. *[*MAYOR *takes out wallet.]* All I have is a hundred.

JD:
I'll bring you change. *[Snaps bill.]* They say new money means good luck.

MAYOR:
Quite right.

[Handshakes, kisses and tears all around.]

JD:
Good-by, JR. May I call you father? Mother? And my lovely little peach. *[JD enjoys a long kiss from* MARY JANE.*]*

*[**EXIT** JD and VERA.]*

MARY JANE: *[Romantically.]*
Just like James Bond.

MAYOR:
Strange that he'd travel by bus. If I was in his place I'd have a limousine.

ANNA: *[Seductively.]*
The way I see things, you'll be in your place and have more than a lim-o-zeen.

[The MAYOR gives ANNA a fully comprehending look, grabs her up and whirls her around. ANNA screams like a teenager as sound of screeching tires and a siren closes the scene.] &BLACKOUT (PAUSE)

ACT V: Scene 1:

MAYOR, ANNA

[Atmosphere: Triumph, self-congratulatory.]

A few minutes after Act IV.

MAYOR:
Well, Anna, I'll be hanged. Who would have thought Mary Jane would ever marry a big shot. Quite frankly, I always figured she'd have to settle for some good old boy.

ANNA:
Speak for yourself, JR; I always knew she was meant for something better than that, even if you couldn't see it yourself.

MAYOR:
Anyway, we're headed for the big time. Straight to the top! With my talents who knows where we'll end up. *[Crossing to window.]* But first, I'm settling some scores. *[Shouting through window.]* Charlie, round up the Chamber of Commerce. I'm going to put the fear of God in every last one of them. Rough them up good; any trouble, cuff'em. *[Embracing wife.]* Well dear, where should we live, here or D.C.?

ANNA:
What a question, you big lummox, how could we ever stay in a one light town like this?

MAYOR:
Then Washington, D.C.! You know, dear, I've always fancied a seat on the Supreme Court.

ANNA:
Just play your cards right.

MAYOR:
Ah, I can see us now—owner's box at the ball games, chauffeured limousines, fancy steak dinners, even a bowling alley in the basement, if we want!

ANNA:
Whatever you want. I'm going to get my own hairdresser, and someone to do my nails. I'll wake up in the morning and she'll be right there, "Ma'am, what will it be today, straight or curled." And a bathroom right off our bedroom—with a big color TV.

MAYOR:
Now, you're talking. And when this local trash— especially that blowhard Amos Lynch—comes looking for a favor, I'll make'em wait. Then after a week or two I'll tell'em, "Get lost."

ANNA:
You're always so coarse. You'll have to change once we move into high society; that joke about the blind bull and the two-legged cow won't go over like it does in this one-light town.

MAYOR:
Come on; a little salt makes the meat better.

Scene 2:

MAYOR, ANNA, CHARLIE (SHERIFF), MERCHANTS: BB BAINES, B.J. WUMP, R. SNOOK

[Atmosphere: Triumph, on top of the world.]

*[**ENTER** CHARLIE with MERCHANTS.]*

CHARLIE:
They was celebrating down at the Dairy Queen.

MAYOR:
You bottom feeders, so you thought you had me, but there was one thing you didn't count on.

MERCHANTS: *[Groveling.]*
Please, Mr. Mayor, it's all a misunderstanding; we can explain.

MAYOR:
Explain?! I'd love to hear you try, if I had the time. But you see, I'm going to be very busy the next few days inspecting certain businesses *[Losing temper.]* … so you complained about me, you bottom feeding, pieces of crap!

ANNA:
Good heavens, J.R., watch your language; in Washington you won't be able to talk like that.

MERCHANT #1:
Please, J.R., … Washington?

MAYOR: *[Delighting in his power.]*
Of course, my dear. *[To* MERCHANTS.*]* Haven't you heard? The Inspector General is marrying my daughter? Ah! Now, you'll change your tune! While you were up here denouncing me I was down at my office gathering up some files. *[Shaking papers.]* Got it all here! I'll send you all away for twenty years. *[Shaking papers.]*

B.B. BAINES: *[Taking out wallet.]*
Please J.R., let's be reasonable; we can work this out.

MAYOR:
Trying to bribe me, eh? You never learn. You're my witness, Charlie.

ANNA: *[Taking* MAYOR *aside.]*
J.R., we don't need trouble just before we leave. Who knows where an investigation could lead.

B.J. WUMP:
Forgive us, J.R. We'll do anything you want.

R. SNOOK:
I'm guilty, J.R.; I confess it before God. The devil tempted me, and I failed. But give me another chance, J.R., so help me God.

MAYOR:
Let God forgive you; I won't! Agh!

[Getting control of himself.]

To hell with the pack of you, but listen good—it's not some used tire salesman who's marrying my daughter but a mighty Inspector General with access to the most powerful men in the world. Remember that when I send a deputy around to collect wedding gifts. Now get out, all of you, before I change my mind.

*[**EXIT** MERCHANTS w/SHERIFF.]*

Scene 3:

MAYOR, ANNA, AMOS, THELMA, SCRATCHY & GERT WINSHELWYPA, ALIGAITA, DOBSIE & BOBSIE, LUBBY, MADGE, MARY JANE

[Atmosphere: Relief, envy.]

*[**ENTER** AMOS, THELMA]*

AMOS: *[From the doorway.]*
Is it true, JR? Has such extraordinary good fortune really befallen our town? Congratulations!

THELMA:
I'm amazed, J.R.; you did it again. *[Kisses* ANNA.*]* So where's the wedding going to be, here or D.C.? You must have it here; it will be the biggest thing this little town's seen since the pesticide plant burned down.

*[**ENTER** SCRATCHY & GERT WINSHELWYPA.]*

SCRATCHY:

Congratulations, Mr. Mayor. We always voted for you, J.R. We knew you were on your way up. Remember us in Washington, and if the government ever needs a taxidermist, I'm your man

GERT.

I got the perfect hairdo for you. Big and gorgeous, just like Loretta Lynn's! I can do it up for half what you'd pay in one of those fancy Washington saloons.

*[**ENTER** ALIGAITA TENFORE.]*

ALIGAITA:

J.R., you bandit, I hear you've hit a stretch of wide-open road. Well, don't forget us little people when you pick up your next load, and remember, if the federal government ever needs any hauling, I got a sixteen wheeler just ready to roll.

*[**ENTER** DOBSIE, BOBSIE, jostling. MARY JANE opposite]*

BOBSIE / DOBSIE:

It can't be true? *[Kissing around.]* Oh, Mary Jane! / It can't be true? *[Kissing around.]* Oh, Mary Jane!

[They go to kiss MARY JANE at the same time and bump heads.]

And may you have a dozen children who all grow up rich!

DOBSIE:

And let none of them cause you one bit of grief!

*[**ENTER** LUBBY, MADGE and more guests, kissing and hand shaking all around.]*

LUBBY:

It's a miracle! A regular rapture! Not since Sweet Jesus himself parted the waters has there been a more welcomed escape! I dropped my packing and came as soon as I heard. * And to think this morning …

[No one listening so his voice trails off.]

*** MADGE:**

Congratulations, Mr. Mayor, I knew the moment I saw him that good things were coming our way.

CHARLIE:

Congratulations boss, and don't forget me in the big city, okay. If they need any help down at the FBI, I'm your man.

MAYOR:

Ladies and gentlemen; please have a seat. Reba, Dr. Peppers and pork rinds all around!

*[**ENTER/EXIT/ENTER** REBA from inside.]*

And break out the Rotel and that spray can of processed cheese; we're going whole hog!

[EVERYONE sits, ready to party.]

AMOS:

Well, tell us, J.R., how did you ever pull this off? Seemed a little rough going an hour or so ago.

MAYOR:

It was unbelievable.

ANNA:

He proposed right in this room. *[Everyone turns to listen.]* It was the most respectful and delicate thing, just like the movies. And he spoke so beautifully; and his manners were so genteel! "Without her love, my life is worthless; give her to me or give me death!"

MARY JANE:

Oh, momma, he said that to me.

ANNA: *[Casting a look that could wither.]*

Of course he did, Mary Jane. Children

always want to be the center of attention. *[Continuing.]* "Ma'am, ... " he said ... He was down on his knees, and the suffering in his voice – I could feel his pain.... "Ma'am, my life is in your hands." I swear; it brought me to tears.

MARY JANE:
Really, momma, he said that to me.

ANNA:
Of course, of course. She acts like she's jealous of me, imagine! Her own mother! Teenagers!

MAYOR:
But he gave me a scare. When she hesitated he threatened to blow his brains out, in this very room.

[The crowd gasps various exclamations.]

AMOS:
Well, I'll be damned.

LUBBY:
Sweet Jesus, must have been ordained.

THELMA:
Yes, ordained. Years of faithful service, my friends, brings a reward like this. *[Aside.]* Luck like this always crawls into the mouth of swine.

GERT:
But where's the handsome groom? I heard he's gone.

MAYOR:
Yes, he was suddenly called off on important White House business.

ANNA:
To interrogate a Russian spy they caught over in Amarillo.

AMOS:
I knew it all along! God bless America!

[The MAYOR gulps his Dr. Pepper and almost chokes to death.]

CHARLIE:
Best of health.

BOBSIE / DOBSIE:
God bless you. / God bless you.

THELMA / GERTA:
Choke yourself! / Go to hell!

MAYOR:
Much obliged, and to y'all the same.

ANNA:
We intend to move to Washington; we'll plan the wedding there. There's so much that one can't find in such a backwash of a town. My husband will, of course, have to resign; our son-in-law is having him assigned to a high level position.

MAYOR:
Yes, I'm afraid so.

AMOS:
Great ships need deep waters.

THELMA:
Reward according to service.

AMOS: *[Aside.]*
Wonders never cease.

THELMA: *[Aside.]*
He's conceited enough to pull it off. *[Addressing the* MAYOR.*]* You won't forget those who got you where you are today when you're hobnobbing with all those big shots, will you, J.R.?

MAYOR:
No, no. Just give me a call; it'll be just like old times, just a longer trough. *[Laughs vulgarly.]*

ANNA: *[Squeezing his arm.]*
Starting right now.

MAYOR:
Come on! I can always find the time to help family and friends.

ANNA:
From time to time, but he can't listen to every dog that barks.

ALIGAITA:
Well, she's a good buddy!

GERT:
Set a pig at the table and up goes its feet.

[People in immediate vicinity snicker.]

Scene 4:

MAYOR, ANNA, AMOS, THELMA, SCRATCHY & GERT WINSHELWIPER, ALLIGATOR, DOBSIE & BOBSIE, LUBBY, MADGE, MARY JANE, DOLLY, STATE TROOPER

[Atmosphere: Disbelief, denial, horror, abject defeat.]

*[**ENTER** DOLLY, rushes in with unsealed letter.]*

DOLLY:
Ladies and gentlemen, your attention please. I have the most shocking news! The inspector we took for an inspector is not an inspector at all.

ALL:
What? How can that be? What do you mean? Not an inspector? Impossible! It can't be!

DOLLY: [*Holding up letter.]*
But it is. He's a nothing. It's all here.

MAYOR:
What are you talking about?

DOLLY:
This! Him! Your son-in-law! That waitress down at the EZ On EZ Off posted it just before they drove off in your red caddy. I cancelled it myself, then I noticed it was addressed to Central Post Office in Washington, D.C. Must be official business, I thought, then I flipped: "Suppose he discovered I was inspecting the mail and was reporting it to the Post Master General." I was beside myself with fear; I had to find out, so I …

MAYOR:
Opened it?

DOLLY:
It wasn't well sealed. I felt like I was possessed. I shook and shook until the seal split, then the letter just slid out. At first I was terrified to touch it; my whole body was on fire and my fingers froze.

MAYOR:
How dare you tamper with an Inspector General's mail?

DOLLY:
But he's not … he's nothing!

MAYOR: *[Caustically.]*
You idiot! If he's not an Inspector General then what is he?

DOLLY:
A fraud!

THELMA:
I knew it all along.

MAYOR: *[Furiously.]*
Outrageous! You're under arrest. *[Nobody moves; they stare at the* MAYOR *in disbelief.]* I'll have you know that your *nobody* is engaged to my daughter! *And* I'm about to receive a powerful federal position, and you're going to be a smudge on the floor!

DOLLY:
I don't think so, J.R. *[General consternation.]* Ladies and gentlemen, do you want to hear what it says.

ALL:
Read it. Yeah, right away, etc.

DOLLY: *[Reads.]*

"To: There Ought To Be A Law," (That syndicated column in the big Tulsa paper, you know.) "Have I got a hot one for you. The world's never short of mo-rons, but a town full of them is news. I got stranded in the most pathetic little town. The inhabitants all look like some evolutionary dead end."

[Gasps of religious horror.]

"And when it comes to brains they're really back of the line. At first I was holed up in some slimy dive of a motel, but then the most fantastic thing happened: the whole town thought I was some kind of federal inspector and before I could blink they put me up in the cheesiest looking house—a real dump, owned by the mayor. His wife and daughter are something else. One's more desperate for me than the other. I don't know which one I'll go for first but probably the mother since she thinks I'm pretty hot. The rest of the town just tripped over each other making me 'loans.' You'd just crack up watching them shower me with cash. The biggest loser is the mayor ..."

MAYOR:

Impossible! You're making this up.

DOLLY: *[Holding letter to his face.]*

There, read for yourself.

MAYOR: *[Reads.]*

"... your average bottom feeder has more brains." Impossible! You wrote that yourself.

THELMA:

Go on.

LUBBY:

Yeah, let's hear more.

DOLLY: *[Snatching it back and continuing.]*

"...the Mayor; your average bottom feeder... "

MAYOR:

That's right, just repeat it. Have your laugh.

DOLLY: *[Continuing with relish.]*

" ...has the brains of a pigeon. Then there's the Postmaster; she's so... " Well, we can skip that part.

MAYOR:

Oh, go on; don't stop now.

LUBBY: *[Grabbing letter.]*

"...she's so... " Sweet Jesus, this is good; *[Looking up.]* Any children around?

DOLLY: *[Grabbing letter in his moment of hesitation then evading LUBBY.]*

Here, here, it is! "The Director of Human Services..."

[DOLLY sneezes; THELMA grabs letter.]

SCATCHY:

Come on, don't stop now.

THELMA:

The handwriting's barely legible. Besides, it's evident this was written by a very vulgar man.

SCATCHY:

Give it here. My eyesight's really good.

THELMA: *[Refusing to give up the letter.]*

No. This part must be omitted. There's church-going people in the room.

SCATCHY:

Yeah; give it here.

THELMA:

I'm quite capable of reading it myself. Ah, here it starts to make sense.

DOLLY: *[Enthusiastically.]*

Every word! Every word!

ALL:
Leave nothing out. Give him the letter, Thelma. Let him read. *[To* SCATCHY.*]* You read it.

[Scratchy grabs letter.]

DOLLY:
Read it all; read it all!

SCATCHY: *[Reading.]*
"The Director of Human Services is a withered up prune. Whenever she sees a…" Whoa, this is bad.

THELMA: *[Shouting over this reading.]*
Nothing but the foulest lies.

SCATCHY: *[Continues.]*
"The Superintendent of Schools is a total loser; drools when she reads and thinks counting on her fingers is advanced math."

AMOS: *[Aside.]*
Thank God, there's nothing about me.

SCATCHY: *[Continues.]*
"The Judge … "

MADGE:
I have to hear this!

AMOS:
Now, now, fun is fun, but this is going too far. There's no legal precedence for reading evidence outside of court.

DOLLY:
No, go on.

GERT:
We're all ears.

SCATCHY:
"The Judge looks like Ronald McDonald…"

AMOS: *[Seizes letter, tears it to shreds.]*
Terrible, simply terrible. A commie through and through! I knew it the minute I laid eyes on him.

MAYOR:
He's slit our throats, slit them from ear to ear. I'm done for, completely done for. I can't see a thing. Nothing but pigs' snouts instead of faces. *[Waves his hand.]* Catch him, bring him back here and I'll skin him alive!

CHARLIE:
Catch him! How, boss? You gave him your new Cadillac car!

THELMA.
That was smart.

CHARLIE:
I could call all the surrounding counties and have them chase him down.

MAYOR:
No, we'd never live it down!

AMOS:
But you have to catch him; he borrowed three hundred dollars from me.

MADGE:
And me.

DOLLY *[sighing]*
And from me, too.

BOBSIE:
I gave him a quarter.

DOBSIE:
Oh, no you didn't, it was only a dime.

BOBSIE:
No, a quarter.

THELMA: *[Throwing up her hands in perplexity.]*
How's this possible? How could you have been so off guard?

MAYOR: *[Beating his forehead.]*
How could I, how could I? Thirty years of public service and I fall for a swindling impostor like any school boy. Thirty years! And not one merchant, not one

contractor; not one insurance adjuster has ever been able to put it over on me. I've got the best of them all—IRS inspectors, state police; I've beat them all, and now some puny no account …

ANNA:
This isn't possible, J.R.; he's engaged to Mary Jane.

MAYOR: *[In a rage.]*
Engaged! A fart for her engagement! We're lucky that's the least she is with him! *[In a frenzy.]* He's made idiots of us all.

[Shakes his fist at himself.]

Oh, you stupid idiot; you mistake that little turd for someone of importance!

[To audience.]

What are you laughing at? You think this is funny? You're laughing at yourselves!

[Stamps his feet.]

What I wouldn't give to have that bottom feeder and anyone who laughs at what he's done; I'd smash them to a pulp and …

[Shakes his fist and stamps his heel on the floor. After a brief silence.]

Get a hold of yourself, JR. How, how did this happen? All of a sudden everybody is calling him an Inspector General. Who? Who said it first? WHO!!!???

THELMA: *[Throwing up her hands.]*
You could torture me and I couldn't remember. We were so frightened and confused.

AMOS: *[Pointing to* DOBSIE *and* BOBSIE.*]*
I'll tell you who.

BOBSIE:
So help me God, it wasn't me!

DOBSIE:
I never said a thing, I swear to God!

THELMA:
Of course!

LUBBY:
Yes, you did; you came running in here chattering, "He's a big shot from Washington, DC."

AMOS:
I remember it all! You said "Aha!"

[All crowd around them.]

BOBSIE:
She said "Aha!"

DOBSIE:
But it was you who said he was an Inspector General.

BOBSIE:
Official, maybe, but not an Inspector General.

MAYOR:
I ought to take you for a ride.

*[**ENTER** STATE TROOPER with warrant in hand. MERCHANTS, WOMEN huddled behind.]*

CHARLIE:
Boss; there's someone here.

TROOPER:
Your attention, please.

[Presenting warrant.]

You all are summoned to appear immediately before the Inspector General; room #2 at the EZ On EZ Off Motel.

All are struck as by a thunderbolt. A cry of amazement bursts from ANNA and MARY JANE simultaneously. The whole group suddenly shifts positions and remains standing as if petrified.

FINAL TABLEAU:

The MAYOR stands in the center rigid as a post, with outstretched hands and head thrown backward. On his right are his wife and daughter straining toward him. Back of them the Postmaster, turned toward the audience, metamorphosed into a question mark. Next to him, at the edge of the group, three lady guests leaning on each other, with a most satirical expression on their faces directed straight at the MAYOR'S family. To the left of the MAYOR is THELMA, her head to one side as if listening. Behind her is AMOS with outspread hands almost crouching on the ground and pursing his lips as if to whistle or say: "A nice pickle we're in!" Next to him are MADGE and LUBBY, turned toward the audience, with eyes screwed up and making venomous gestures at the MAYOR. Next to them, at the edge of the group, are DOBSIE and BOBSIE, gesticulating at each other, open-mouthed and wide-eyed. The other guests remain standing stiff. The whole group retains the same position of rigidity for almost a half a minute before the curtain.

THE END

Appendix 1
List of Additional Plays

This book has presented only one representative play for each of the twelve years of Waldorf Education. The author has, however, many more plays that can be made available if desired. Here follows a short synopsis of plays, which can be purchased individually by writing: <pedtheater@gmail.com> for a price list.

Any teacher who has purchased this book and wishes an electronic version of any of its plays for production with his or her elementary or high school class may write the author at the email address above and receive one for free. In all other cases, performance rights must be attained in writing from the author.

Teachers wishing to perform *Der Rabe* or another German play can contact Ms. Coltman through this author at the address above.

The Wolf of Gubbio: This play for third grade presents the St. Francis legend about the Wolf of Gubbio. It is in verse and can accommodate a class of fifteen or more students. It runs approximately 20 minutes.

The Wisdom of Solomon: This set of short third grade prose skits were written by third graders. Three stories from the story of Solomon are told: *The Eggs and the Beans*, *The Three Merchants*, and the *Two Mothers*. Together, they run about ten minutes.

Noah's Ark: This short third grade verse play presents the story of its title. It can accommodate a small class of students, about ten minimum, and runs approximately twelve minutes. It has a small section suitable for eurythmy.

Baldur's Doom: This play for fourth grade is in poly-rhythmic verse and presents the story of the death of the Norse sun-god Baldur. It is in masque form, poly-rhythmic verse and can accommodate ten or more students. It runs about fifteen minutes and is suitable for eurythmy.

Ariadne at Naxos: This play for fifth grade is an original play telling the story of what happened when Theseus, Ariadne, and Phaedra are trapped on Naxos after their escape from Crete. It is pseudo-tragedy and written in classical Greek verse form. The choral pieces are written for a eurythmy chorus, boys (as the Athenian youths) and girls (as the Cretan youths). Except for Theseus, the leads are girl roles. It can accommodate a class of twenty or more, and runs for about thirty-five minutes. It also provides opportunities for original student musical compositions.

Joan of Arc: This historical prose play for sixth grade uses Mark Twain's novel about the life of Joan of Arc as its foundation. It has a wider variety of roles, major and minor, and allows for the students playing minor roles to play multiple parts. It has intrigue, pathos, a trial scene, battle scenes, and an inspiring ending. There are several opportunities for musical accompaniment. It requires a class of at least twenty-five students and runs for about forty-five minutes.

The Holy Blissful Martyr: This sixth grade prose play tells the story of conflict between Archbishop Thomas à Beckett and Henry the Second of England. In addition to the principal roles of Eleanor, Henry, and Beckett, it features a chorus of Canterbury women, Death and its assistants. It accommodates a class of twelve or more and runs for about twenty minutes.

Oliver Twist: This full-scale eighth grade prose play presents the Dickens novel. It is rich in roles and has everything adolescents love: pathos, adventure, violence, wretched workhouse urchins and sneaky child pick-pockets, the very nasty Fagin and Bill Sykes, the pathetic Nancy, the noble Mr. Brownlow and Rose, and a wealth of supporting roles. It accommodates a large class and runs about seventy-five to eighty minutes.

A Tale of Two Cities: This full-scale musical treatment of Dickens' novel can accommodate a full high school of over a hundred or more students; but it could be produced, including student orchestra and tech crew, with a minimum of fifty students. It has everything the French Revolution can offer the theater: supercilious aristocrats, a blood-thirsty, starving mob, the evil Madame Defarge and the Vengeance, all pitted against the noble Manette-Darnay family, a respectable English banker, Miss Pross and the grave-robber Jerry Cruncher, and the great anti-hero Sydney Carton. The libretto is in three acts and runs for two hours and forty minutes. The musical score by composer Peter Stopschinski is for full orchestra, and has more than twenty vocal, choral, and orchestral numbers. Carton, Lucy, and Madame Defarge have absolutely delicious musical numbers. The musical performance rights need to be attained separately, and anyone interested can contact Mr. Stopschinski through this author at the email address above.

Les Misérables: This prose play treatment of Hugo's novel is suitable for middle or high school and runs at about two hours.. It can accommodate a large cast and has plenty of boy and girl roles and allows for extensive multiple casting.

The Hairy Man Cycle: This series of three short Halloween skits, *The Hairy Man, The Hairy Man Returns, and The Hairy Mam* are suitable for middle, high school, or faculty performance at a Halloween party. Each skit runs about fifteen minutes, and some lucky people get to play Wiley's hound dogs and run around the audience barking. In *The Hairy Mam* the Hairy Man and his woo-man have become survivalists who come out of hiding to fight big developers who want to displace their furry forest friends.

Sophocles' *Antigone*: Two versions of this play are available, a shorter puppet theater version that runs about fifty-five minutes, and a longer eurythmy/actor version, the latter being in polyrhythmic verse that runs about seventy-five minutes. Each version can accommodate a class of fifteen or more, including tech crew and musicians.

Aristophanes' *The Birds*: This modern prose adaptation for high school is set in millennial Texas. The refugees to Cloud Cuckoo Land are the last 1970s hippie and the last 1980s slacker in Austin, and the Grand Hoopee is the mythical Elvis Bird. Chirpy lyrics that the students can set to music and show-dancing provide the choral parts of the play. The invaders consist of a cell-phone chattering mom, a major developer, an angry young man, obnoxious hipsters, the Clintons, refugees from academia, and whoever deserves a satirical sendup. It can accommodate a class of fifteen or more.

Playboy of the Western World: While Synge's masterpiece is freely available and in the public domain, this abridgment strictly retains the structure and dialogue of the original but shortens some of the speeches. It runs for about an hour and forty-five minutes. With tech crew, a senior class of twenty can handle this play nicely.

Appendix 2
Photographs and Diagrams

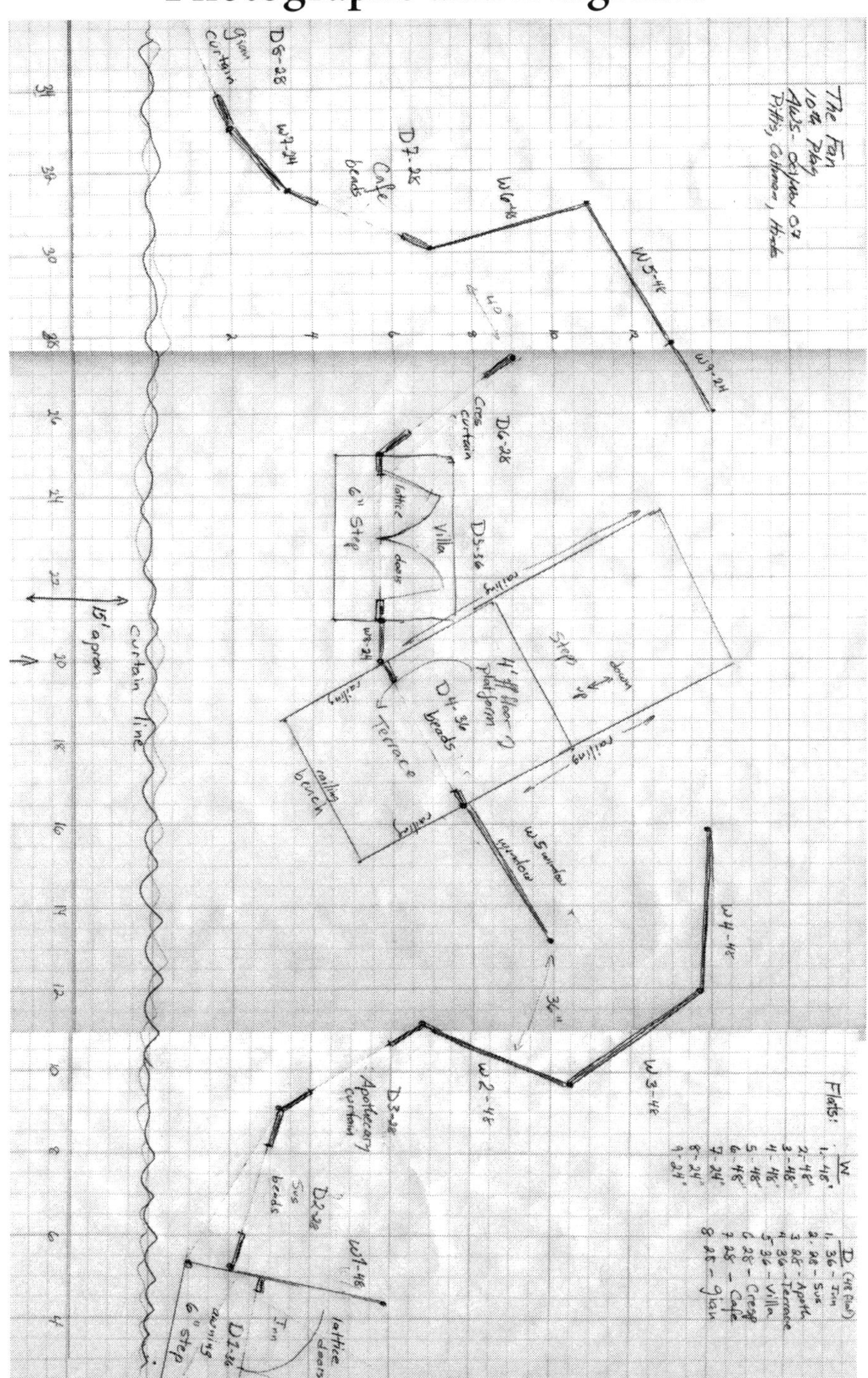

Full Set Plan for the 10th Grade Production, *The Fan*

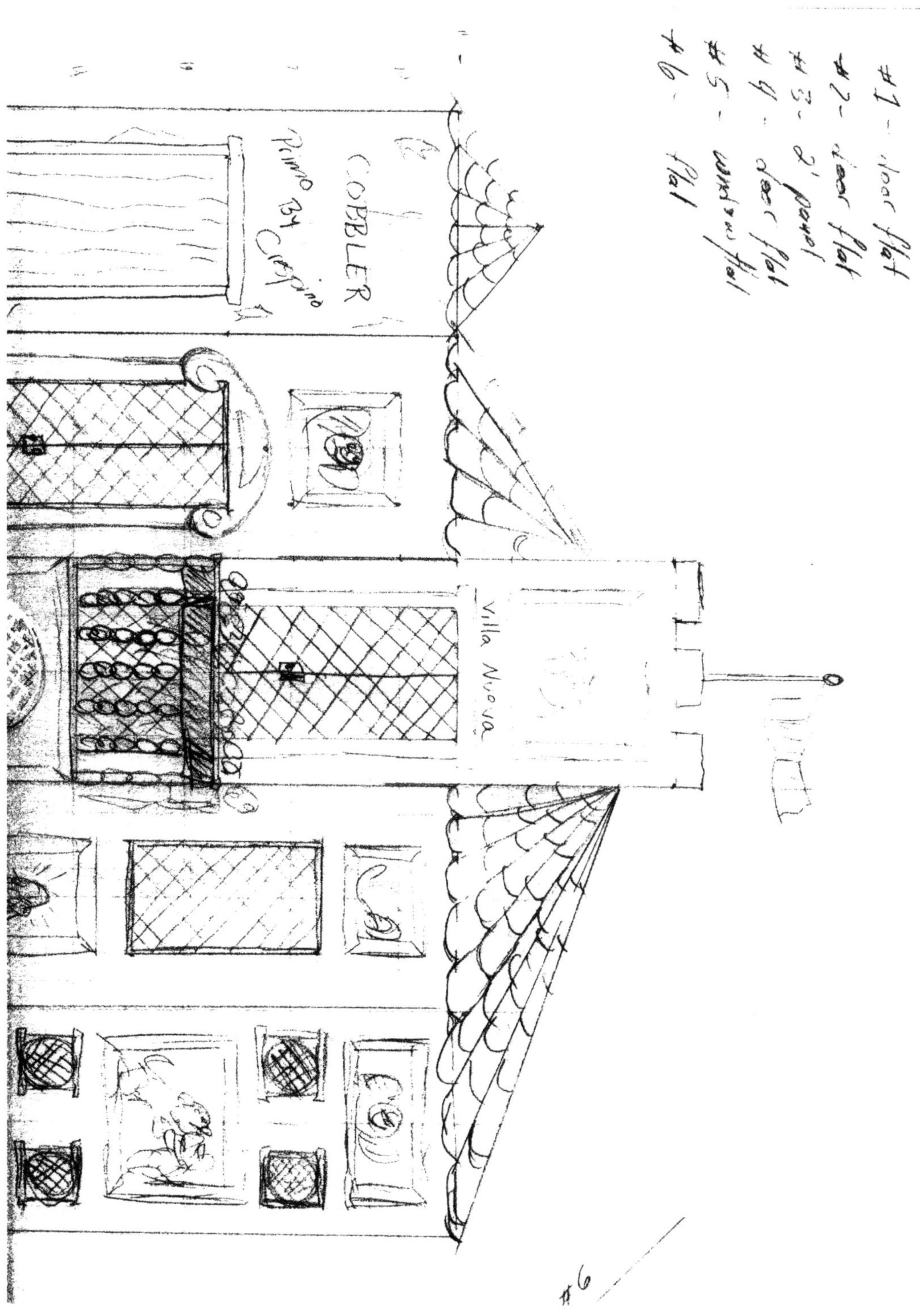

Set Plan for "The Villa," from the 10th Grade Production *The Fan*

Performance Set: 2007 Austin Waldorf School 10th Grade Production *The Fan*

Photos: Daniel Hindes

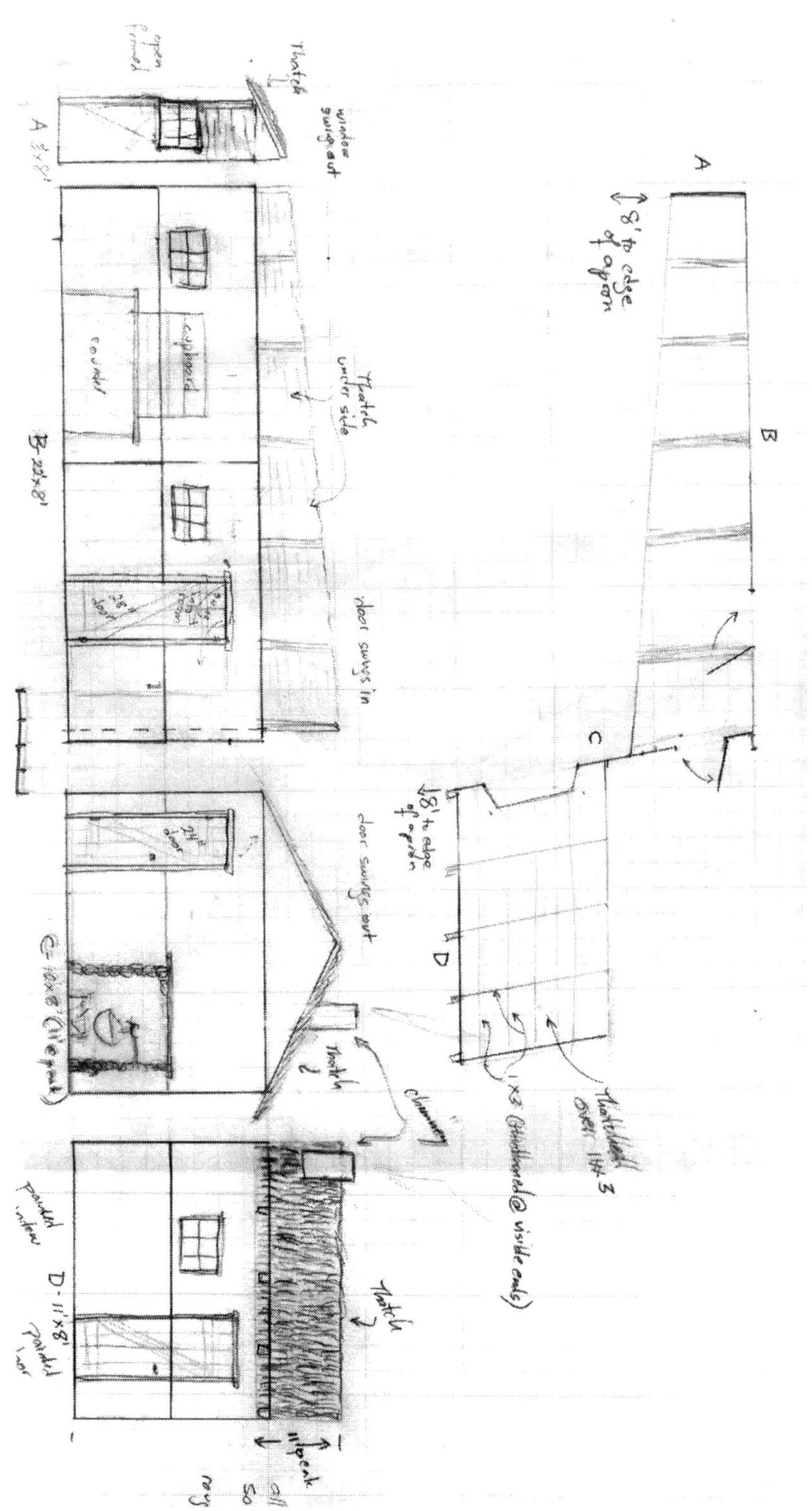

Set Plan for 2008 12th Grade Production *The Playboy of the Western World*

Performance Set: 2008 12th Grade Production *The Playboy of the Western World*
Photos: Daniel Hindes

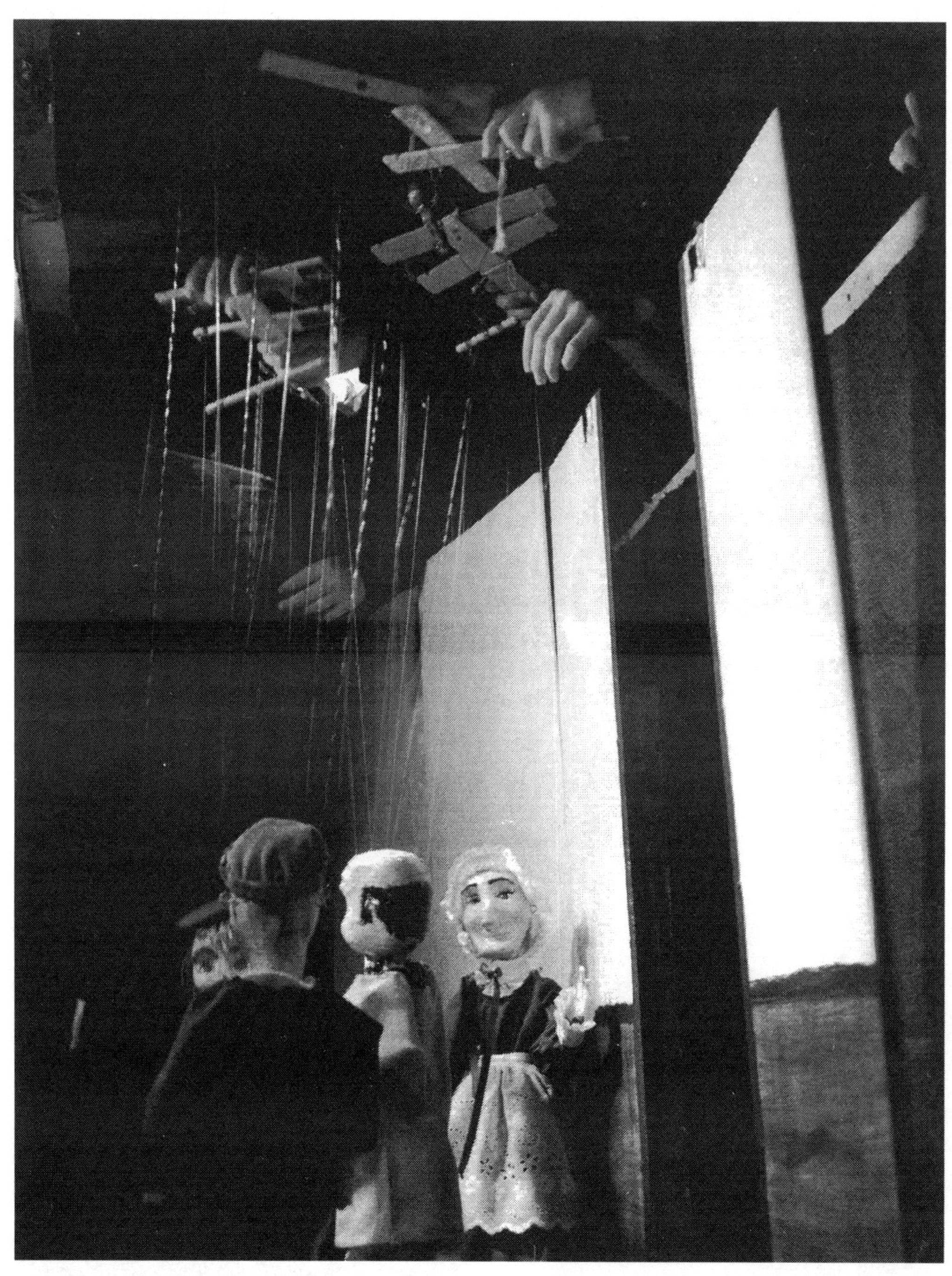

Performance Set: 1999 7th Grade Puppet Play Production *A Christmas Carol*
Photo: Mark Simmons

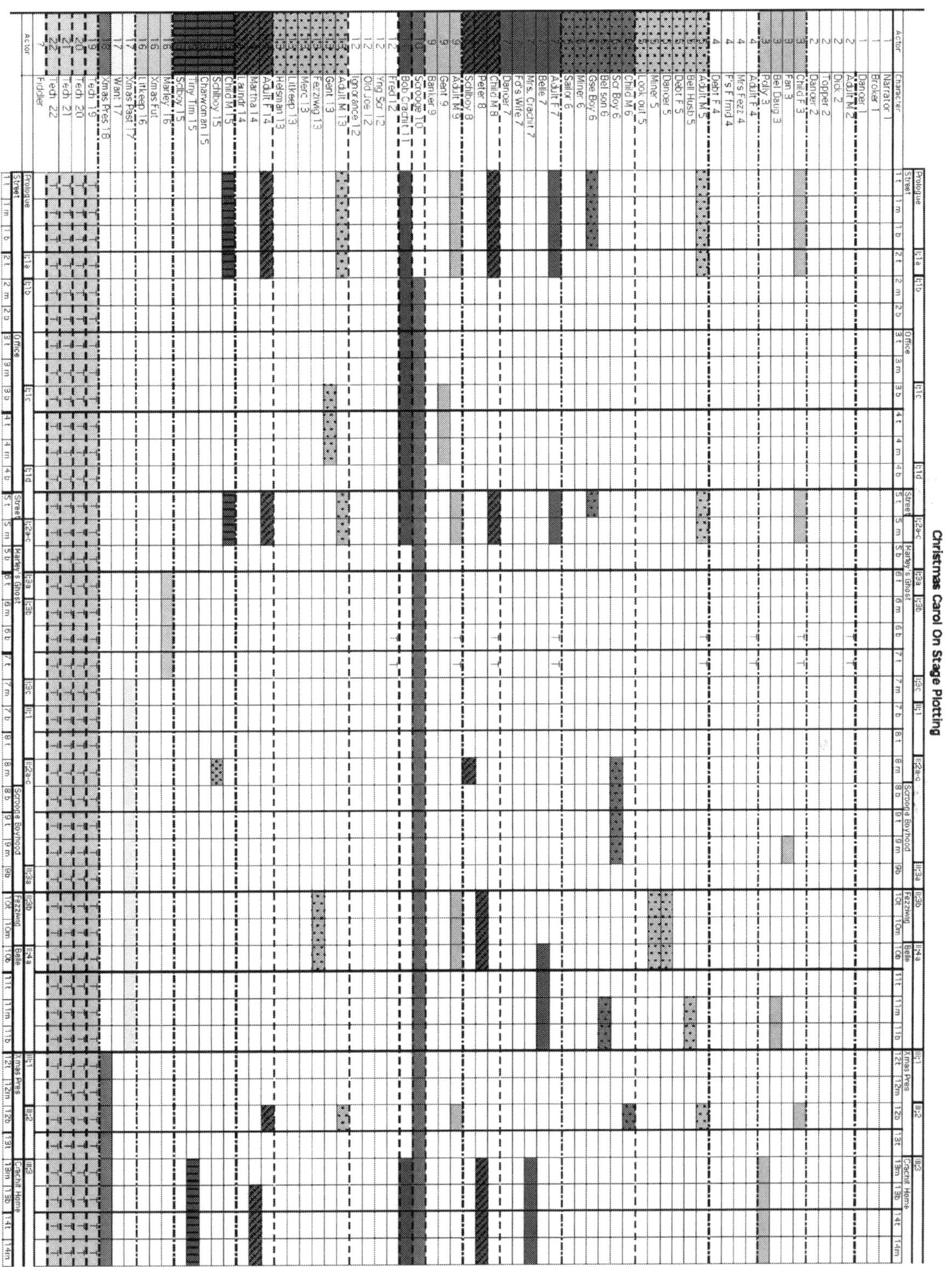

Onstage Plotting: *A Christmas Carol*

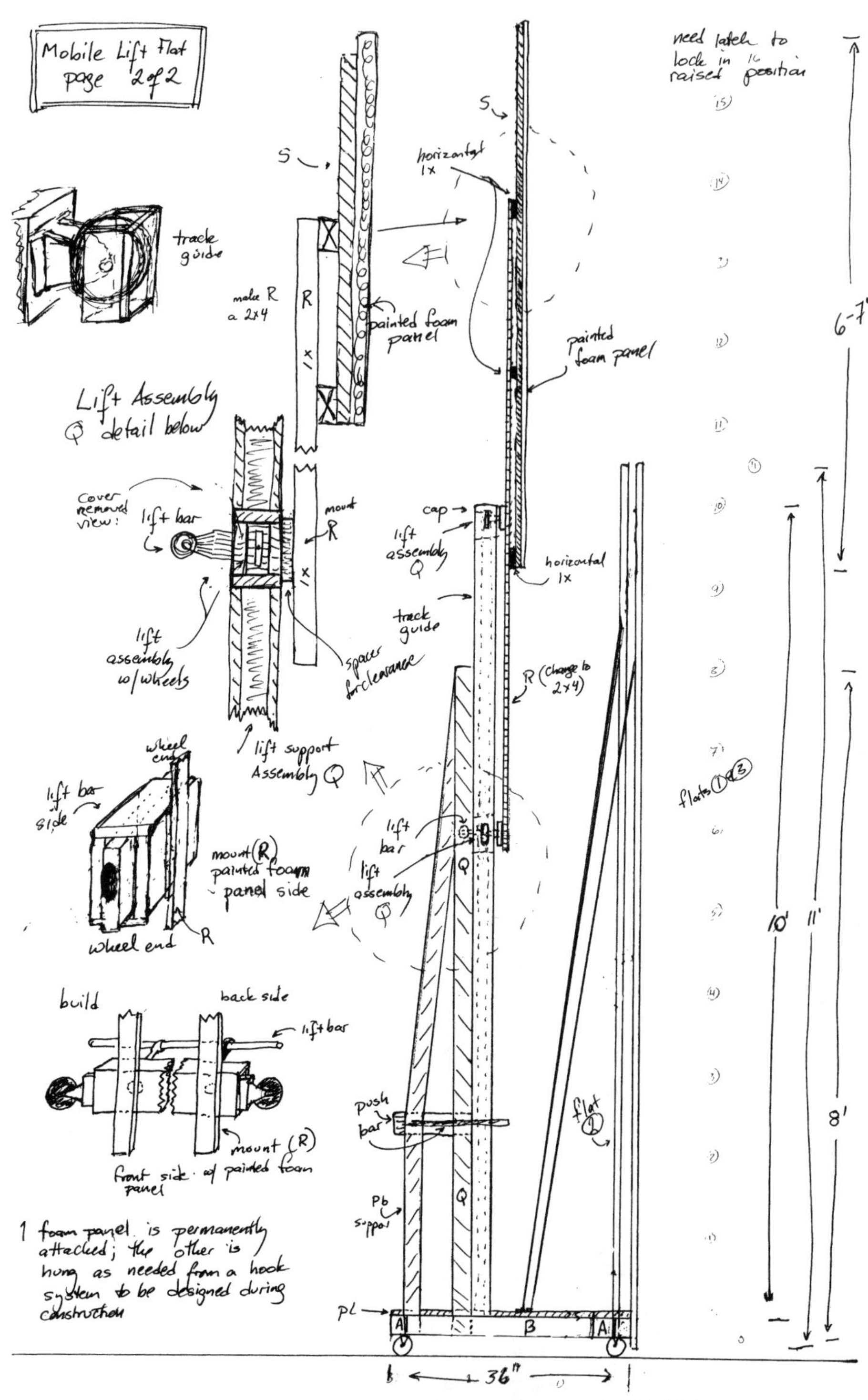

Shop Drawing: Telescoping moveable flat, *A Tale of Two Cities*

Endnotes

1 Strictly speaking, theater comes from the Greek *theatron*, which means "the witnessing place of the god's suffering," and drama from *dromena*, a term which comes from the Eleusinian Mysteries and means "the things done," the enacted story of Persephone's abduction that was shown to the neophytes during their initiation ceremony. In post-Renaissance usage the terms are used interchangeably; but academically, drama refers to the literature, specifically the text of plays, while popularly it follows the ancient usage. Theater, on the other hand, still refers to the physical performance space but its spiritual meaning has been diluted, or expanded, to encompass the whole art of enactment, including not just dramatic plays but dance and opera.

2 The word play has the double meaning of describing both the everyday, recreational activity of children and the text and performance of a piece of theatre. While I have deliberately chosen to use this interrelatedness of meaning, I do not want to confuse the reader. As a result, I have tried to be as contextually clear as possible, but have occasionally reverted to italics as a way of either coining a phrase or attempting to differentiate between the two meanings of the word.

3 Dramaturgy is a technical term for adapting or shaping a story for performance. It can (but does not necessarily) include the actual writing of the text for a play. The term originated in nineteenth century German dramatic theory, but the practice can be traced back to Aristotle's *Poetics*. In the modern American theater the dramaturg is the individual responsible for representing the creative intentions of the playwright; revising the text for performance; researching historical background of the play and its setting and educating the director, producer and actors about these; and writing whatever program notes a production will need. In this book I have used the term in its broadest meaning to include the writing and producing of plays.

4 The pedagogical work of Rudolf Steiner, which provides the inspiration for and direction to Waldorf education, uses this metamorphical process as one of the foundations for its developmental understanding of the evolving human being. The reader is encouraged to read further on Waldorf education and Rudolf Steiner's work.

5 There is no need for theatrical work with children before the change of teeth since the children's formative life forces have not yet finished sculpting their physical bodies, and energy diverted into such a self-conscious artistic activity as theater is not in the children's best interest. Self-initiated imaginative play and seasonal celebrations in which the children dress in simple, representative costumes are all the theater very young children need. Only with the entry into the elementary grades should the simplest work with pedagogical theater begin.

6 In Waldorf schools the core language arts, math, social studies, and the sciences are introduced in main lesson, or morning lesson, blocks. This lesson comprises the first two hours of the school day and is taught by the class teacher. A block lasts from three to four weeks and is a period of intensive focus on a particular subject. Over the course of a school year, a class has between ten and twelve such blocks. In Waldorf schools the specific choice of stories is dictated by the subject matter of the block and which story speaks best to a particular class.

7 It is important to note that the Eurocentric use of age-appropriate material is currently undergoing a transformation as Waldorf Education itself becomes much more culturally diverse, resulting in stories and historical topics from a wide variety of cultural traditions entering the curriculum. The students in any given class and their ethnic origin inform the diversification.

8 In Steiner's conceptualization of human development he described the birth of four "bodies"—the physical, etheric, astral, and ego. Each of these bodies has a gestation period, during which the body is prepared for its "birth," after which that body's forces are available for education and work in the world. The physical body is the same as what is conventionally meant by that term. It is prepared in the mother's body during gestation, and upon birth its substance and powers are available for the individual's work in the world. The etheric body consists of the formative life forces that sculpt the physical body; and as the carrier of memory, it is instrumental in the development of the individual's habit, or rhythmic life, especially healthy repetition of physical and beauty-imbued activities. During early childhood the etheric body is the primary vehicle for educating the child; thus the predominance of habit-building activities in a Waldorf early childhood or kindergarten program. It is born at the second dentition, at about the age of six or seven or approximately the time a child starts elementary school. Its birth marks the full individualization of a person's physical body. From its birth forward, the formative, rhythmic forces of habit and memory are freed and available for a more emotionally and then intellectually-based education. Through the use of artistic and feeling-based educational activities Waldorf Education uses the emancipated forces of the etheric body to educate the child in the foundational thinking skills that need to be habituated for later conceptual life. Drudgery cripples the etheric body. At the same time, this type of external pedagogical activity is sculpting the soon-to-be-born astral body. During puberty, the astral body, or soul body is born. It carries our life of emotion, especially wishes and desires. It is the vehicle of sentience and allows us to move forward in our life of striving. The immature or damaged astral body is given to powerful swings of emotional and mood changes. Teenagers' passionate attitudes of loving or hating something, as well as their fierce loyalty, are symptomatic of the immature astral body at work. Socially, the astral body needs taming. Educationally, its forces need tempering and training in rational, and morally purposeful activity. We communicate through our astral bodies, so an education that develops clear, positive and idealistic communication is a healthy one for adolescents. Meaningless work incites

cynicism and anger in the astral body. Connecting the powerful emotional forces of the emancipated astral body to the development of an ethical, purposeful thinking life is at the heart of Waldorf high school pedagogy. The full maturation of the astral body takes decades and metamorphoses from outer education to inner self-development. The last body born is the ego, which is the bearer of our full and unique individuality, our sense of "I-ness." The first inkling of this body's gestation occurs very early in life when the child first uses the word "I" to indicate his or her sense of personal uniqueness. The "I" is "born" at about the age of twenty-one. It is our most spiritual body and its gestation is the longest; its birth the most subtle; and its maturation, unlike the physical and etheric bodies, the slowest, taking not just decades, but multiple incarnations.

9 Historically, tragedy originated in early classical Greece as a public religious activity in which the whole community gathered to witness the enactment of a hero's fall within the context of the play competition held during the Greater Dionysia. Its origins were in the Eleusinian mysteries, into which the competing playwrights had been initiated. In its most primitive form, tragedy had represented the suffering of a god. As a public activity, the plays induced in their audience members profound feelings of pity and dread that culminated in a shared feeling of purification, or catharsis, with the close of the play. The tragic plays were not entertainment, even though they were great works of art.

10 Tragedy was reinvented in the Renaissance, and the preeminent examples are the plays of Shakespeare and Racine. Racine's work is largely derivative of classical models, while Shakespeare created a new, modern form. The protagonists of both writers are personages of noble character. With the Romantic and modern eras, tragedy took a new turn; whether the result can even be classified as tragedy is subject to intense debate. Nevertheless, the modern play that comes the closest to tragedy is the first part of Goethe's *Faust*. Arthur Miller's *Death of a Salesman*, in my opinion, is marginally a tragedy. If arousing feelings of pity and dread, alongside respect, even admiration for the protagonist, is a requirement of the genre, then Moisés Kaufman's 1997 play *Gross Indecency: The Three Trials of Oscar Wilde* is a true modern tragedy. This play would not be produced in a high school setting.

11 The general agreement is that comedy originated in extemporaneous rural skits in which the common people ridiculed their social betters. Eventually the writing of comedies in the form of political satires became part of the Greek play competitions. Naturally, they did not enjoy the same high regard as did the tragedies. Although presented at the play festivals, they closed the ceremonies and served as great public outbreaths of laughter. Since its inception as a theatrical genre in Greece and its perfection in Rome, comedy has remained largely the same. As to modern comedies, throw a soda can out the window of a car anywhere in America and you'll hit some form of comedy in the eye, at least on the second bounce. A beautiful example of comedy suitable for tenth grade performance is Goldoni's *The Fan*.

12 Melodrama is a modern form, originating in the eighteenth century. It derives its name from a deliberate French variation on the classical Greek *melos* (music) and Latin drama (to perform). A drama professor of mine in graduate school insisted, however, that its deepest origins was actually from the Greek *meli*, meaning honey. Given the sweet sentimentality expressed in melodramas that is an interesting perspective to take. Dickens' *A Tale of Two Cities* is a historical melodrama, as is Hugo's *Les Misérables*. The movie *Casablanca* is a perfect example of the genre. The most serious type of modern melodrama, one verging on the tragic, are the plays of Eugene O'Neill, especially *Mourning Becomes Electra*. Brecht's *Caucasian Chalk Circle, The Good Person of Sezuan*, and *Galileo* are melodramas.

13 The great majority of Sophocles's *Oedipus Rex* happens before the climax since the play is essentially a detective story. In *Hamlet*, however, Shakespeare gives almost equal time to the rising and falling action, all of acts 2 through 5, realizing that the first act is essentially all exposition. His thematic interest in that play is examining consequences.

14 The 1942 melodrama *Casablanca* plays with false climaxes and a surprise twist brilliantly, delaying the actual climax until Rick tells Ilsa at the airport that she is leaving with Laszlo not him, thereby resolving the central romantic conflict of the movie. Rick's shooting Major Strasser and then walking off into the rain with Captain Renault—the former rivals now partners—resolve all the plot's complications.

15 This moral ambivalence deeply troubled nineteenth century general audiences. Gounod's operatic treatment of the Gretchen story delights in all of Faust's nasty behaviors until the end; but in the end, instead of having Faust escape with Mephistopheles as the angels rescue Gretchen's soul, Gounod has Faust repent, and an archangelic sword bars Mephistopheles from grabbing his soul—as banal an ending as nineteenth century bourgeois taste could want.

16 The reader is referred to either Rudolf Steiner's short book *The Four Temperaments*; chapter XVI in A.C. Harwood's *The Recovery of Man in Childhood*; or Thomas Poplawski's *Completing the Circle* for a complete description of the modern concept of temperaments.

17 Tolstoy originated the concept of counterfeit art in his book *What is Art*. Counterfeit art is a form of aesthetic expression that is devoid of "contagious" ethical intentions, yet is so highly accomplished that it deceives its beholder into believing that it has value. Most of popular entertainment is counterfeit, according to Tolstoy.

18 The "nine-year change" is a nodal point in the soul development of the child, characterized by a feeling of wondering about and even doubting personal identity within the child's set of familial and social relationships.

19 Eurythmy is an art of movement, a new impulse for dance that was originated by Rudolf Steiner at the beginning of the twentieth century. It strives to make visible,

through an archetypal alphabet and language of gestures and movements, the archetypal, gestural nature of sound, whether speech or music. Eurythmy works by allowing the human figure, moving in three-dimensional space, to sculpt the surrounding space in the same way the human larynx or the pipes of an organ sculpt the column of air that manifests the tones of speech and music. There are two types of performance eurythmy—speech and tone.

20 One of the more aesthetically dumbfounding things I once saw in a class play: after Columbus had brought the spirit of exploration and Renaissance Europe to the Caribbean, everybody (Caribs and Spaniards alike) joined hands and sang the class' favorite song, which contained a nice sentiment but had nothing to do with the historical reality behind the play just performed.

21 Upstage and downstage describe the physical geography of a stage. In the Renaissance theater most stages were raked, higher in the back, to facilitate viewing from the flat floor where the audience stood or sat. In the modern theater the seating area is raked, giving everyone a view of the stage floor. Upstaging and downstaging refer to an actor's physical placement on the stage in relation to the audience. An actor is said to be upstaged if another actor forces that actor to turn away from the audience. This is usually done by the upstaging actor taking the more powerful downstage (nearer the audience) position, pushing the upstaged actor further away and thereby making him/her less important. An actor upstages him/herself when he turns from the audience when speaking or does something as simple as standing with the downstage leg forward, forcing the body to turn upstage. So an actor who upstages another actor can be upstaged by the upstaged actor if that actor moves closer to the upstaging actor, forcing him or her to turn away from the audience.

Much delightful self-referencing theater comedy has been devised by consciously using this forbidden practice of upstaging. The classic solution to the problem of upstaging is the acting triangle, in which a group of actors together form a triangle. In a two-actor situation, the apex of the triangle is an imaginary point between and just beyond, forcing the audience to continually direct their attention from one actor to the other. In a three-actor scene, the one actor at the apex is physically upstage from the other two but is actually in the most powerful position in relation to audience interest. The other two actors forming the base position themselves so the spread of legs allow their bodies to be open to the audience. In a multi-actor scene, the most effective, attention-grabbing triangle is to have the apex downstage, thereby giving the audience a feeling of being the focus of the action. In a well-blocked scene, the place where any particular actor or group of actors stands onstage has dynamic meaning from the perspective of spectacle, being a carrier of meaning.

22 Theatrical stage lighting did not become technologically possible beyond general stage and house illumination until the mid-nineteenth century when gas and limelight were developed. But it was not until the beginning of the twentieth century that

the type of electrical lighting characteristic of the modern stage became available for artistic purposes.

23 In the second lecture of his course published as *Curative Education* Steiner stated:

> Here we encounter a law, of the working of which we have abundant evidence throughout all education. It is as follows. Any one member of the being of man is influenced by the next higher member (from whatever quarter it approaches) and only under such influence can that member develop satisfactorily. Thus, whatever is to be effective for the development of the physical body must be living in the etheric body—in an etheric body. Whatever is to be effective for the development of an etheric body must be living in an astral body. Whatever is to be effective for the development of an astral body must be living in an ego; and an ego can be influenced only by what is living in a spirit-self. I could continue, and go beyond the spirit-self, but there we should be entering the field of esoteric instruction...

24 The etymology of rehearsal, which means "to repeat, to work over, again and again," derives through French from agriculture, "to harrow" or, in American farming terminology, "to fit; to prepare" the field for seeds. Just as in agriculture, where harrowing is the final step before planting, in theater rehearsing is the final step before the play's imaginative seed is planted in the audience's imagination.

25 The expressive power of the hands for the actor was profoundly understood by the early screen actors of the silent era; something one can immediately see when watching Lillian Gish or Mae Marsh in a silent era film or Karloff in the original *Frankenstein*.

26 It is important to remember how the classical Greeks understood the paradoxical situation of the actor. Actors were disciples of Apollo, the god of illuminated, sun-cleansed, rational consciousness; while the festival in which they performed was in honor of Dionysius, the god who reigned over the unbridled passionate aspects of our human existence.

Made in the USA
Charleston, SC
21 December 2015